Jane Doe 46
2nd Edition

by

Wanda Kuhl

To Kathy,
  For a very sweet
and dear friend. I
hope you enjoy this
second edition.
        Wanda Kuhl

To the memory of my loving father, who was there for me through difficult and tumultuous years.

It was the smell, finally, that never goes
away. Those old priests didn't bathe
often, and when they did, they didn't wash
well. It was the dense, cloying smell, of old
men.

The smell of excrement, semen, and
unwashed genitals rises from my nightmares
to haunt me, even now, six decades later.
The smell is of my childhood, betrayed.

ACKNOWLEDGEMENTS

I have so many people who have been part of this life journey whom I want to thank. I begin first with my dearly departed father, Willis Kroll. If it were not for his tenderness and love my chance for survival would be low. He always knew when to whisk his family off for a camping and fishing trip that took us children away from the danger and unhappiness of our daily life. He was smart enough to help me set up my own bank account, which helped me save money that I needed in bad times.

I give my thanks and gratitude for Lion's Summer Camp; Mrs. Grandy and her family; Mrs. Spaulding and spelling bees; Mr. Phillips, my 8th grade teacher who inspired me; Diane and Sharon (daughter/mother, legal guardian) who took me in and rescued me when I needed help; the judge who did not send me back to my parent's house and later emancipated me; Aunt Dolly, my mother's sister; The Azure family at Rocky Boy who took me in; my maternal grandmother and grandfather, Uncle Jim and Aunt Maxine; my cousin Karen; Mrs. Miller my landlady and employer; Mrs. Benson my surrogate mother; Mr. Voiles my high school Vice Principal; neighbors like Ruth and Mrs. Kirby; Gary, my first love; Dan, a trusted friend; my husband and life-long love, friend and father of my children Jim Kuhl who was there for me until his death in 2016; my sister Barbara, and my children, grandchildren and great grandchildren. I want to thank my dearest friends Wanda and Maryann who saw me through the horrors of losing everything in house fires and helping when Jim was ill.

I especially thank all those who worked to get my book printed and published: Talon who created the book covers; my son Michael for his long hours of printing; to my editor of the second edition of *Jane Doe 46*, Katherine Sterling M.A. in Religious Studies, writer, & friend.

Preface

My purpose for writing this book is two-fold. My hope is to heal myself and to help other victims who have experienced the heinous crimes of pedophilia by Roman Catholic priests. It took me over sixty years to write my story. After urging from my therapist, I began the process of disclosure in 2011, finishing and publishing my book in 2014.

What I have written in <u>Jane Doe 46</u> was as difficult as it was necessary. The writing aroused old terrible and familiar images, physical pain, abandonment, injustice, shame, solitariness and rejection, however, as limited as I felt in any literary experience I began writing down my life in earnest for my own sake and for the sake of others.

This book is not perfect. It is my story. Many others who have suffered from a similar past cannot expect that using their voice, the one that matters has anything to do with a classic work. It is a messy, unforgiving, hidden life that when given a voice emerges onto the page in whatever way that it can. Some parts of this book might seem too detailed about other life events or not detailed enough. It is written chronologically like a biography, but I feel in some way this is a memoir, or taken from life memories that have shaped me these past sixty-nine years.

I found empowerment in my quest to root out this evil that had stricken me as a child, a teenager, a young adult and an adult. Questions such as, why (a justice question) did I have such bad things happen to me, and why did I make the life choices and decisions that I did were answered because of the writing.

As you wander through these pages, please remember that I believe I was given great gifts when I was born that helped me to survive. There are those people that cross our paths or whom we are related to that reach out a helping hand as we struggle through our pain and suffering. I am incredibly thankful for their compassion, love, and sense of justice. I further believe that we were all born as our true selves, born with great gifts and that we must not be defined by the crimes against us as children or youth.

My final hope is that any who read Jane Doe 46, whether they have a shared story or are reading about these crimes for the first time, will gain a sense of knowledge, understanding, and urgency. The Church must accept accountability and move forward to reform for this unholy destructive indignation against the innocent.

Wanda Kuhl
Katherine Sterling - Editor

CHAPTER ONE

My father was stationed in France when he was in World War II. He was a frontline medic in World War II and fought on the beaches in Normandy at Omaha Beach. When he came home from the war in August of 1945, he had earned the purple heart for being shot on the top of his forehead, and the bronze star for continuing to carry soldiers out after being injured himself. He was truly a hero to his family and friends, for fighting and earning recognition for his bravery. He loved his country and would do it again he said. My father never spoke of the war again to anybody until his later years in life saying it was "a living hell on earth."

My mother moved to Montana to work at the smelter in East Helena since the war was still being fought in February of 1945. Her job was making nuts and bolts for planes for Boeing. My father met my mother three weeks after arriving home from Military Service. Dad said they spent every minute of the entire two weeks obsessed with each other and they were married within a month. I was floored when I heard this. I asked dad how he could marry someone he had just met and make a huge commitment without meeting her family and knowing her family history. He said he fell in love. I wonder if he mistook love for lust, but if both were involved, my sister Bonnie was born ten months later. My parents were married for fifty-nine years in spite of a whirlwind romance. Mom passed away before they celebrated their sixtieth anniversary.

Bonnie was born in Helena June 19th, 1946, and was eight months old when my parents decided to move to Redding, California because dad had a hard time finding work in Montana. It just so happened that my uncle, my mother's brother told dad they needed a lineman for a company right away in Redding. He needed to get there as soon as possible. Mom and dad packed up and moved to Redding with a baby in tow and another on the way. Dad really enjoyed the work, but it was awful to work in the heat in Redding. The summer months were pretty much in the nineties and hundred's.

My parents and sister lived on my grandparent's ranch that was a few miles out of Redding. My parents had a tough time finding a place to live. My sweet grandmother invited them to live with them since my mother was pregnant with her second child. My mother had previously had a baby girl that was given up for adoption to my mother's aunt before she met my father. We were told that my grandmother found out my mom had married a convict who had escaped from prison without my mother's knowledge. My grandmother put a halt to the marriage and had it annulled leaving my mother several weeks pregnant and unmarried.

I was born in Redding, California June 5th, 1947. My mother had suddenly gone into labor. My grandmother tried to reach my mother's pediatrician, turned out he was enjoying a baseball game in Sacramento. After I arrived, my grandmother told me I was a screamer who weighed in at 7 pounds 1ounce, 18 inches in length and had a head full of dark brown black hair. I started walking at nine months old. I was told that my mother had to put me in a harness and on a leash hooked to a clothesline to keep me from wandering off. I had wandered off and they always had to go looking for me. Bonnie had to play with a little sister on the clothesline leash. She was apparently a better listener than I was.

When dad got home from work, he would give a hand on the ranch to help pay for rent and food. He wasn't the type to take charity from anyone if he could help it. My grandma told me how she and my mother would have arguments about how my mother was taking care of her children. She told her how lazy she was about keeping the house clean. My mom would wait until dad left for work

9

then slip back into bed. She didn't feed us and left me in the harness and let Bonnie dig holes and play with grandma's dog. One day, mom failed to harness me; naturally, I wandered off. They had to get neighbors and law enforcement to help find me. I was found off the ranch property with scrapes and bruises several hours later.

Mom and dad had a huge argument this particular day. Dad threatened mom with taking the kids and leaving if she ever ignored us again. Dad demanded that she keep a watchful eye on her children, or lose them. Until this job was over, she could not be lazy and had to take care of us, like it or not.

One morning, my grandmother heard awful screaming and ran over to our house. Bonnie had been bitten by the family dog and needed medical help. They rushed her to the hospital where she received seven stitches above her mouth. My grandma and mom had quite an argument. Grandma told my mom if she'd been watching over her children and not in the house reading books or sleeping, it wouldn't have happened. Mom wanted dad to move back to Montana to get away from her mother's watchful eye, but dad told her he wasn't about to quit a job because she couldn't get along with her mother. Grandpa shot the dog that bit Bonnie. He said he wasn't keeping an animal that he feared would harm a child ever again, especially grandchildren.

Within a year, my mother was pregnant with her third child. Willard was born on the evening of August 25th 1948. We now had a boy in the family. He was thirteen months younger than me and was a happy baby. Dad's job was winding down and mom was more than happy because now she wouldn't be under grandma's watchful eyes. It was a sad situation for my grandma, grandpa and uncle to see us move back to Montana. My uncle said he couldn't save us from the horrible spankings we were getting when dad was at work. Grandma was sad about us leaving. She told my dad that he needed to watch out for his wife's anger issues. Dad of course thought Grandma was referring to mom hurting him, of all things. All I remember about moving back to Montana was being cramped up in the car with three kids in a corner and a lot of boxes on the other side tipping over as Bonnie and I protected Willard from any falling boxes.

Dad found us an apartment on West Main Street right after we arrived in Helena. The previous occupants that lived there before us left the place in a mess, which needed a deep cleaning before we could move in.

My Aunt Dolly was thrilled to have us back in Helena. She and my dad had been very close growing up. My father came from a family of seven brothers and two sisters, which didn't include the two who had died young from influenza. Dad was the oldest, Aunt Dolly the youngest. My aunt was here helping my mom get the house suitable for us to live in. Dad said he was thankful it was late spring because we surely would have frozen had it been winter. The apartment was in an old brick building that was built in the late 1880's.

Being a World War II veteran didn't help dad find work any faster than anyone else. He took what work was offered doing odd jobs just to get food on the table and to pay rent. We had to be careful to stay on the sidewalk in front of the house because traffic whizzed by on West Main, and a child wouldn't have a chance in heaven if they stepped off the sidewalk. We did not have a place to play because our house had no backyard. Work was hard to come by; food and necessities were made to last as long as possible. Many times we had very little to eat and sometimes would have to miss a meal or two. Dad would accept any job offer that came his way.

In October, my dad came home, carrying two large pumpkins for us to carve. Bonnie and I were so excited to carve pumpkins with our Dad. It was rare that he was home as he was always looking for work. I was at the table, working with a large butter knife carving out the large square teeth on my pumpkin. Bonnie sat across from me carving hers. Suddenly we heard what we thought was thunder. Then it grew in intensity to a shriek of cracking timbers, breaking stones, and shattering glass.

Dad grabbed us under his arms and yelled at mother to get Willard out of his crib, and hurry. All of us scurried out of the apartment, down the stairs, and out into the cool evening air. The thundering and crashing continued behind us. When we reached the sidewalk, my dad stood holding us as we looked up at the two-story brick apartment building. We were both crying, and then we saw the roof cave in. The timbers popped and cracked and fell into bedrooms; bricks fell to the ground with a thud. Dad thought the building was in bad shape from the 6.3 Magnitude Earthquake of October 19, 1935 which destroyed more than three hundred buildings in Helena including the City Hall, Kessler Brewery, St. Joseph's Orphanage, and many homes. We were lucky to make it out alive, but now we were homeless.

We stayed with my Aunt Dolly until dad found land for sale and decided to build a house. He had bought this little silver trailer that was ten feet by eight feet wide. This was what we lived in on the property while he was building our house. In the meantime if we had to use the bathroom, we had to use a temporary out-house that dad had installed. Mom got pregnant again. It was bad enough that five people lived in this tiny trailer as it was, but a sixth person was just about to show up, and soon!

Our mother was turned in to the authorities for child abuse while dad was at work. One morning, Bonnie and I sat at the table in the tiny trailer eating our breakfast when suddenly two policemen showed up at our home. The policeman told us that we would be going away for a while. In the meantime, my mother was asking the officers who the hell had turned her in for child abuse. The officers told mom that their hands were tied and the complaint had been made to Department of Family Services (DFS).

At the police station, a large woman took my hand and told me that we were going away for awhile. We were placed in an orphanage. We were three and four year old toddlers.

As I walked up the sidewalk holding my sister's hand very tightly, the Victorian building towered above me with its gothic brick edifice, pointed chimneys, and massive windows that looked like playing cards. I was terrified. I felt as though I was walking into a castle of darkness, much different than the ones in my storybooks.

We cried ourselves to sleep the first two nights. I snuck over to Bonnie's bed to seek comfort, but the nun found me and grabbed my hand pulling me back to my bed. She handled me very roughly and she should have understood considering why we were there in the first place, and how vulnerable we were since suddenly we had been removed from our family.

On the good side, I thought we were lucky to have clean beds and food in our empty tummies. We were also able to bathe daily and use a real toilet, which we didn't have in the little trailer.

I thought mom was cruel, but the nuns were no better. We had to sit and be quiet and if we made any noises we would be smacked with a wooden ruler or reprimanded by being sent to the priest for disciplinary measures.

The first time Bonnie and I were sent to the priest in his office, we were punished for something I had done. He made me get up on his lap and fondled me in a way I knew my parents didn't do and caressed my privates. I remember his finger hurting me, but nothing else. He made Bonnie get on his lap, also. He told us this was what happened to bad little girls who did not listen and do as they were told. He ended up hurting both of us that day.

Bonnie and I were thrilled to exit as quickly as possible from this orphanage. Our daddy came to pick us up. Mom was not with him. We hugged him and cried at the same time just happy to be away from that place that did strange things to us. We asked where Willard was. He remained at home as far as we knew since the subject was ignored. Who would take two girls to an orphanage and let the baby stay home with someone they said was unfit?

Believe it or not young children do remember memories

from time to time, especially very unpleasant memories.

CHAPTER TWO

We were thankful that we were home with our family again. We hoped the house would soon be finished, but that would take a long time because it was just framed in. The roof had plywood and there was plywood on the outside. It was not livable until the insulation and sheet rock were installed. Dad had found a job with a construction company so we only saw him a few hours a day, most of the time he was late for dinner or came home a few hours after we were off to bed. That summer dad built on the house after work until dark and then on the weekends. All three of us were told not to go near the house until it was ready for us to live in. Dad was worried about somebody getting hurt with tools and nails lying about.

Bonnie was the oldest and would have to watch out for Willard and me. I was four years old now. We never had birthday parties in my family since we couldn't afford to splurge on things that were "not necessary." I guessed it was because we were so poor. Bonnie's birthday was in two weeks. We would finally move into the house even though the inside wasn't completely finished.

We were happy to get out of that tiny trailer with the walls closing in. When it was bath time, we had to bathe in a round metal washtub because the bathtub was not installed. I was so thankful that we no longer bathed outside with all of us using the same bath water. The house now had running water. We still had to wash clothes outside with a wringer washer. Mom would roll the clothes through the wringer, into the tub of rinse water and roll them out of the rinse water to hang on the clothesline. It was the same tub my mother would give us baths in.

Mother went into labor in September. Once again it was time for dad to load us back up and off to the orphanage we would go. We could not stay with any aunts or uncles as they had large families to care for, and taking in three more children with mouths to feed in those days, was not an option. They knew the orphanage was available to poor families. We were crying when dad told us we had to go back. Our tears were not enough so we told him it was a bad place! He just thought that we did not want to be away from home.

We were taken to the dorms where Sister Mary Magdalene told us sternly that we knew the routine, and I expect you to follow the rules. If I should have to repeat myself," she said with one eye squeezed tighter than the other, "Well, you know the punishment. Is that clear?"

A couple of days went by with no incidents. Then, I made a mistake. I did not make my bed to the nun's expectations. I went to the cafeteria and sat down to have breakfast with Bonnie. The boys were on the other side and the toddlers under age two were in a different area towards the back of the dining hall. Bonnie and I were sitting still and waiting for grace when all of a sudden I felt my hair being jerked and pulled. I was told to come to the dormitory. The nun then pushed my face into the pillow on the bed and lifted me up by my hair and said to me, "What do we do first thing when we get up in the morning?"

I responded, "Get dressed?"

The next thing I knew she had slapped my face, "We do what first thing in the morning?"

I cowered, dropping my voice, "I forgot."

She told me to get my bed made neatly and then took me to Father Callan and told him I was being obstinate and very disrespectful of the rules. Father Callan told her to leave and join the other children in the dining room. He pulled me towards him as he opened his robe and motioned for me to put my face down. I just stood there as if frozen scared to death. He said, "Now! I am not asking you again." He pushed my face into his crotch and said, "Suck on this until I tell you to stop." I gagged. He held my face down, "Do not stop until I say stop." Moments later after he

16

groaned, I vomited on him and on myself. He pulled me across the hall to the bathroom and made me clean his robe with a wet towel. He then took me back to his office to clean the floor. I was crying, and felt sick. I just wanted to leave but he made me sit there in a corner with bits of vomit on my clothing.

I do not know how long I sat there but it seemed like a very long time. I just wanted to go to bed and lay down. Instead, I had to go to the chapel and kneel on the pew and say I was sorry to God for my sins. He then sent Sister Mary Magdalene to me. She took me to the dorms and told me to go to bed for the rest of the day after changing my clothes. When Bonnie came back from the cafeteria and catechism classes, she asked me what had happened. Sister Margaret grabbed her by her shoulder and told her I was not to speak and to get downstairs and stay away from me the rest of the day.

Night came and lights out. Bonnie waited until she knew she could whisper over to me. I told her what happened and that I never ate that day. I also told her I wanted to run away, but I knew a little four-year-old girl wasn't going anywhere. Bonnie also wished we could run away. We were assaulted every day from then out. Some days, father Callan had both of us in his office and made us watch. We were told this was our punishment for being obstinate and rebellious children, and not listening to Sister Mary Magdalene.

Our Mother had another baby boy named Wesley and he was born on September 12th. We would soon get to go home, we were told. We couldn't leave fast enough.

The day we heard the news we were going home soon, I was sent to Father Callan again for not flushing the toilet, which contained my feces. This time they made Bonnie wait out by the door, as she had nothing to do with my mistake. He laid me on the desk and made me perform oral sex. Then he raped me. When I stood up, I had blood on my panties and again, I vomited. He took me to the door, and handed me to Sister Mary Magdalene telling her to clean

17

me up. Then he took Bonnie into his office. I had to stand where Bonnie stood. I could hear her and knew she had heard my cries as I heard hers.

Father Callan said, "It was our punishment from God." It was his way of condoning what he had done to us. The nuns stood and listened to everything going on. One would have thought they would report him, but they didn't.

Finally after six weeks of our hideous torture, we finally were going home. Dad picked us up at the orphanage. We cried because we were so happy to be in his arms and away from the evil things that had happened to us. He carried me, while Bonnie held Willard's hand to the car.

Bonnie and I were thrilled to be home! We actually had a bedroom. The bathroom had the plumbing in but no fixtures like a tub or sink. The floors were cement until Dad could afford to put linoleum down, which would be awhile. Dad paid for things, as he got his checks. He would try to pick things up at sales and would frequent garage sales, too.

I thought mother would have been happy to see us. The first thing she told us was to stay away from the new baby. She told us, "We could look at him but do not touch." She was happy that he was another healthy boy. Bonnie and I noticed that mother was more attentive towards Wesley than she was to Willard.

Two weeks after we got home, there was a terrible accident. Mom was doing dishes and not paying attention to Willard. We were eating our lunch. "Mommy, Willard's standing up in his highchair," we screamed at her.

"Shut the hell up and eat," she screamed back at us without looking. "Mommy!" we screamed once again.

It was too late. The chair began to wobble as we were yelling. All of a sudden it toppled over and I heard Willard's head hit the floor with a horrific thud. It sounded like a watermelon had just been dropped. He had blood coming from the backside of his head. He was unconscious on the floor. We were screaming and frightened. Mom shouted, "Shut the hell up!"

Mom shouted at Bonnie to run to our neighbor Lucille

who was an LPN. When Lucille came in, Mom was sitting on the floor beside Willard with a towel. "Have you called for an ambulance?" she asked. Lucille had to return to her house to call the ambulance since we had no phone. It took forever for the ambulance to arrive.

The ambulance medics made Bonnie and I go to our bedroom and stay out of the way. They took Willard to the hospital. Dad was called at work to meet mom and Willard at the hospital. Mom told Lucille to call her son Carl to watch us, while she went in the ambulance with my mom. Dad came home and took us to my Aunt Dolly's until we could find out if Willard would be okay. It turned out that he had to have a steel plate put in his head after the swelling went down. The doctors didn't know if he would make it or not. He was not quite two years old and in a coma.

My aunt had five kids and was married to an alcoholic, so she couldn't keep Bonnie and me. Dad had no choice but to put us back in St. Joseph's again so he would be able to work and go to the hospital.

~~~

The sad thing was Bonnie was in Kindergarten. I would be at the orphanage alone until she came home from school. I was always happy to see the bus pull up to St. Joseph's. My sister would be back with me so then I would feel safe-- she couldn't protect me while she was in school.

Father Callan had a new priest that was working with him at the orphanage. I cannot remember his name because we were told to just call him Father. We were happy to have someone else at the orphanage besides Father Callan. We hoped the assaults would come to a halt, but that wasn't in the cards for us.

The new priest was also a pedophile who liked boys and girls. Who knows if that was why Father Callan had him there. Two religious authorities' word against kids would probably not be believed if the molestations came out to the public. Father was much rougher than Father Callan. He seemed to enjoy what he did to us. He was violent if a child did not do what he wanted, telling them to "perform" as he called his act of rape.

We had to spend that Christmas at the orphanage. We did not hear a word from our parents. We thought Willard had died and no one wanted to tell us. It was almost Christmas and nothing was worse than not knowing and not getting to see our brother in the hospital. It was heart-wrenching to children who were four and five to not know what was going on with their family. We felt so alone and unwanted.

It seemed weird that the priests chose certain children for their pleasures. I always felt like Bonnie and I were the only ones that were assaulted. We bonded with the girls who lived by my Aunt Donna as we had kids our age to play games with. They also were victims in the orphanage we later learned.

Now as an adult, I know another whom I was a friend with that was also assaulted. Some are still too ashamed to come forward.

CHAPTER THREE

Dad returned to get Bonnie and me when Willard was out of danger and would be coming home from the hospital soon. He told us that Willard was recovering and he would never be normal again which we didn't understand at that time. He was severely brain damaged and would be mentally disabled. At that time, my sister and I didn't care. We were thankful he was alive and told dad we would do anything to help him. Dad told us that we would have to help mom before Willard came home from the hospital. We were talking about Willard, not mom. We already knew we would have to help her.

When we got home, mom was sitting in a chair and feeding Wesley his bottle. She told us to go put the books up and help dad in the kitchen. Our mother never hugged or kissed or showed any kind of affection for Bonnie and me. We grew up always thinking she did not like girls and couldn't love us. Very seldom did she even take pictures with us.

After supper was over, Carl, our neighbor, came over to babysit us so mom and dad could go to the hospital and visit with our little brother. We were not allowed to see Willard and always wondered why they distanced him from us. Mom took the baby with her so it was nice when Carl came over to watch Bonnie and me. He played games and taught us to write. We never went to preschool, especially in those days. In time, Saint Helena's parochial would be our school through sixth grade.

Willard finally came home from the hospital. He couldn't talk yet so he did a lot of grunting. We began to understand what he wanted by his using motions and pointing to us. He was such a good and sweet boy. Mom had withdrawn from Willard and would have nothing to do with him. It was like she erased his existence from her mind. I think his grunting and odd noises were finally getting to her. We overheard mom telling our father that he would need to be institutionalized or she was going to lose her mind with the rest of us to care for. Mom persuaded dad that Bonnie and I should be learning to cook and clean as four and five year olds because she needed our help more than ever taking care of the other children.

It was now March, and mom was once again pregnant. We cringed every time she or dad told us another child was on the way. They never had time for Bonnie, Willard or me. We had begun to think that we were not even wanted. It seemed less time was spent with us and more was given to Wesley since he was the baby. It sounds selfish, but we grew up having so much happen that should not have happened to us from negligence on our mother's behalf. It was unsettling to realize that mom's work was now to be our work.

~~~

Dad took the family camping on weekends during the summer months, which we loved every minute of. Finally, we were getting attention from somebody in this family. I don't think mom was too thrilled with the cooking and picking up after four kids, even though Bonnie and I did most of the cleaning and the picking up. She would make us take naps to give her a break. Then tell us to change Wesley's diapers and start getting things ready for dinner. A few times, dad would pipe in and say he was taking Bonnie and me fishing with him while Willard and Wes could nap. As long as mother got to rest and read books it was fine with her that we went fishing. Mom loved to read and she read every free moment that we gave her.

Wes was nine months old when we found out another baby was on the way. Now, more would be expected out of

Bonnie and me. I had just turned five and Bonnie would be six in two weeks. I think the reason we didn't hear "I love you" or get hugs was because mom was tied down with kids and had mental illness to boot. She had horrible mood swings and swore a lot. She would get angry at anything and everything. She was beginning to hit us a lot. In public, she was unkind and would scream at us and yank us around.

Once we were in F.W. Woolworth's with mom while she picked up a few things. Like normal children will, unattended, we set out to investigate. I picked up a roll of lifesavers and opened them. I started eating one of them without asking permission for the candy. My mother had seen me open the package but did not attempt to stop me. She came over and grabbed my right hand and bit into my hand as hard as she could possibly bite. It bled so badly that the lady behind the counter gave me tissue to hold over it. She told my mother that it was "The cruelest thing she ever saw anyone ever do to a child."

"Mind your own Goddamn business, if you value your job," my mother yelled at the lady. She paid for what she had, including the lifesavers I opened. Then we left the store with her in a real huff. The second, I entered the car she continued her rampage. She kept hitting me in the face. She called me a little thief and said, "If you ever steal again, I will bite both hands." This was how I was treated in public.

I was indisputably excited about getting to go to kindergarten. I loved the idea that we would get away from mom as long as we could and maybe have some happiness in our lives each day. I remember my aunt bringing us a couple of dresses she had made for Bonnie and me for the new school year. We didn't get to wear them to school because we had to wear uniforms that were black pleated skirts, white blouses with a black tie, white tights and black shoes, and a vest.

It didn't matter to me because now I felt like I was getting older, and would be a schoolgirl now.

One night my parents had an argument about helping my dad's grandmother with getting firewood. Dad brought up the subject pointing out that summer will be winding down real soon so "I'm thinking of taking the girls to help me."

"What the hell am I supposed to do about it," mom yelled.

"There is no use talking to you," dad responded angrily. "I'm just saying…"

"Take the goddamn kids and run to your grandma!" mom interrupted crudely. She was speaking of my great grandmother on dad's side.

"Then we're gone," he said grabbing Bonnie and me as he stomped out the door.

Mom stayed home with the boys and we went to get firewood with dad and loved every minute of it. He made us stay close while he cut the wood. We carried it over to the truck for him. It was a game to us. We would see who could carry the bigger pieces and who would be the strongest. Dad called us "his little helpers." When we took the wood to great-grandma, he proudly announced, the girl's helped and worked hard giving us more than enough praise.

Our great-grandmother was starting to lose her eyesight. So we would grab her by the hand and walk her out to watch dad unload the wood. We would visit with him while he worked. When dad finished, she always had us stay for dinner. Then, we would go out by the creek while my great-aunts who lived with her would watch us.

The great-aunts never married and neither did two of our great-uncles who worked for the railroad while living with great-grandma. Great-grandma and great-grandpa migrated from Germany to Minnesota when the two of them were quite young. They eventually left Minnesota for Montana in 1885 by covered wagon. When they arrived in Montana, they built what was to become known as the Mitchell homestead in 1886. They chose to build by Priest Pass, which is just north at the bottom of McDonald Pass on the eastside toward Helena.

Great-grandma told us several stories while growing up about their travels to Montana. She told us how they hit blizzards and thunderstorms. She told us how great-grandpa had to fix broken wagon wheels and encountered Indians (trading goods) and robbers on the trail. The worst part was giving birth to babies. My great-grandma lost two children from influenza and fever on the trip to Montana. It must have been a terrible trip. To add to her grief, she lost another baby born stillborn after they settled in their new home. In time, they settled in Baxendale outside of Helena.

My great-grandma shared her stories, of going to the Broadwater Natatorium (built in 1889) and relaxing in the hot springs on special occasions. She said it was one of the most beautiful places to relax when she was a young mother. They rarely went because it took several hours to get there, and of course there was the expense. The family would take the horse drawn buggy to the Natatorium, resting along the way.

My great-grandmother's homestead and the original log house that she and great-grandpa built are still stand with the original corrals. My dad was born in the log house on September 9th, 1903. The schoolhouse my father attended was moved closer to Helena from its original place. It still looks the same and stands by an antique store off Highway 200 entering Helena.

~~~

Summer was over and the excitement of getting to go to school awed me. Mom had to drive us across town to go to St. Helena's, a private Catholic school. On the first day, we finally got to wear our uniforms. I was overwhelmed with excitement being a schoolgirl.

Tragically, my excitement was short lived. I found my new teacher, Sister Fidelis a confusing person. I couldn't figure her out. One minute she would be angry and then the next minute, a switch would turn on and she was happy.

She was very helpful to the children who were not good at penmanship. She taught us good penmanship. She spent extra time helping children who could not write as neatly as others. I could tell she was an organized person because everything was neat including our desks that had to be kept clean. I knew I had excellent penmanship because of Sister Fidelis. She always remarked how nice my penmanship had improved throughout the school year. Mother never took the time to teach us to read or write so it was to my advantage that I was a fast learner once in school.

Nobody in the class wanted Sister mad at them, except for some of the boys. They had to be sorry though when she hit their behinds with her hard wood ruler right in front of the class. If any of us talked or played around, out came the ruler. And she meant business!

Before I knew it, snow was on the playground and it was almost Christmas time. The happiness wore off when we had to go back to St. Joseph's because Mom went into labor. Bonnie and I were swooped back to the place of horror and evil. It was never a happy place. The second I walked in the door I knew what lay in store for us.

St. Joseph's had a new nun that worked with Sister Mary Magdalene. She seemed kinder. Her name was Sister Mary Francis. We enjoyed her as she was kind to us. When we were baptized before we started school, our Godparents names were Al and Francis Griffin. Maybe it was the name Francis that made her kind. I was hoping she could protect us from the priests. As it turned out she looked after the dorms and the children in the cafeteria.

The second day that Bonnie and I were there the rapes started again. The priests would inflict their sexual acts on us as they had before. People think that priests take an oath of celibacy, and keep their vow, but I for one would argue differently with that belief. Where we were concerned this was untrue, a lie that created agony for my sister and me. Some of them thrived on the pleasure of hurting and sexually assaulting little girls and boys who could not protect themselves or each other.

CHAPTER FOUR

My parents left us there for six weeks. The violent aggression of the priests was inflicted as soon as we arrived. They were brazen men to act the way they did. I would have thought the nuns would put a stop to all of the torture by these "men of the cloth." But, the priests were the ultimate authority. Maybe, the nuns were abused. Who was to know, certainly not me.

~~~

Bonnie and I were excited to be away from the evil of St. Joseph's and back home. We had a beautiful baby sister named Barbara. She had a head full of black hair that made me laugh. I felt like she was mine from the very beginning. Mom would not let us hold her. I spent a lot of time at her basinet wishing that I could. I kept hoping that dad would sit with me so I could hold her.

Hopefully, mom would not have any more babies, as she could not take care of the ones she had. She made Bonnie heat bottles and
I had to wash them. Dad built a little crate box for me to stand on when I helped do dishes or helped him in the kitchen. When we got home from school, she had us to do the laundry and clean the house. It seemed like every other day I was washing diapers. Mom taught us to use the washer. Dad was angry for fear that one of us would get our fingers or hand caught in the ringer.

Mom and Dad got in the first real fight we ever witnessed when Dad yelled at mom "Get off your lazy ass and take care of the kids!"

"I am sick of doing everything for these goddamn kids,"

she yelled back. "I am getting the hell out of here!"

"You see how far you get, with abusing my kids!" He warned her that none of us should get hurt because of her laziness. She slammed their bedroom door and the shouting ended.

Dad slept on the couch, and I helped him fix his sandwich for work. Mom slept with the basinet in their room so I didn't get to peek at my baby sister.

My mother never complimented us for the good things that we did or for cutting her workload. We were little girl's doing a grown woman's work. Our mother was never happy with us. We assumed it was because of something we had done to her and it was our fault she was unhappy. Mom had threatened us that if we told dad we did her work that we would have very red bottoms which would not be noticeable. She said, "We wouldn't be able to sit down for a week."

I loved playing with my little sister's tiny hands. She would laugh and coo at me. I bonded with this tiny little baby the moment I saw her and I think she did with me as well. She always smiled for me. When she was three months old, dad let me hold her. Mom told him I wasn't ready yet. He told her if I am able to clean house and change diapers, I could hold the baby. I was very careful with her so as soon as mom saw this I got to hold her quite often.

It was June. I was finally six years old. The school year had gone by extremely fast. My birthday fell on the last day of school. Between taking care of the baby and doing mom's housework with Bonnie, there wasn't a lot of time for play. Once in a while she would let us go over to the neighbor's to play hopscotch or jacks. I asked to play with the neighbors for my sixth birthday. It seemed quite trivial that we wouldn't get to play as much as the neighborhood kids did. They sometimes came over to the house to ask to play with us and mom would always tell them to go away because we were busy with our chores.

Dad decided that we needed to go camping more often.

We got to go to Park Lake and go fishing with Daddy again. He loved that we could put our own worms on the hooks, and was not sissy girls who were afraid to do so. Mom told dad that it was too hard to camp with two babies and three little ones. Dad shot back at her that those little ones do a heck of a lot of chores and they needed a break away from her work detail. She didn't find that amusing at all but he sure did. I only wish dad knew the truth of what she really was like with us.

At the end of August, Mom decided to have Willard institutionalized because she didn't want to deal with a child with special needs and listen to his babbling that he could not help. He was going to Warm Springs. We had to prepare ourselves to take him there and leave without him. We were crying and couldn't stop when we left him. None of us wanted to leave him except mom. I could tell my dad was upset but he would not say anything for fear of upsetting mom. My mother did not even hug Willard goodbye. I think she sent him to Warm Springs so she would not be reminded everyday about ignoring him in the highchair in the first place. That was what dad said when they had an argument about her not paying attention to our safety. This wouldn't have happened to Willard if you had paid attention and noticed he wasn't fastened in.

~~~

School started and I had to go to mass every morning. Kindergartners did not have to go, so it was a new experience for me. We were taught how to say the rosary by memorizing the Apostles' Creed, Glory Be, Our Father, Hail Mary's, and the seven mysteries, which was a lot for a child to memorize. We had our catechism books that we had to learn and memorize as best as we could for our first communion. The cathedral was overwhelmingly huge to me as a first grader and I had to study for my first communion.

I did not like my first grade teacher; Sister Mary Marie

was a very cranky nun. She was always wringing her hands together. She was loud, and overbearing. She walked the class to the Cathedral for mass and then lined us up in a ridiculous straight line for confession before school. She always seemed very impatient with those wringing hands while waiting for Father Gilmore to finish confessions.

We were taught what confession was in the first two weeks of school and it did not take long to learn how to confess. I was afraid of going to confession because Sister Mary Marie told us what God expected us to confess. She made it quite clear that he wanted us to confess every sin we remembered. "Oh dear God" I thought to myself at that time. How can I ever go through this ordeal?

If I did bad things then I needed to confess to Father Gilmore what those bad things were. I told Father Gilmore I was confessing about what had happened to me at the orphanage. I told him why I was at the orphanage in the first place. I told him Father Callan said I was an obstinate child. After I was done confessing, he told Sister Mary Marie that I had to remain to be spoken with and that he would return me to class when he was finished with me.

He told me that I should never tell lies in a confessional. I could tell he was angry with me. I told Father Gilmore, "You told me to tell you if I did something bad or if someone else did to confess my sins." He still accused me of lying. I told him it was not a lie and these were not untruths. Father Callan did do these things to me. Father Gilmore told me I was not to ever repeat my lies or I would receive the same punishment that Father Callan and the other priest had done to me.

He took me back to my classroom and took Sister Mary Marie in the hall and when she came back in, she gave me a horrible look. The next day when I went to mass and confession I was last in line for some reason. I always was in front with all the girls. When I went into confession I wouldn't say anything because I was scared. He asked me if I was going to tell more lies today and I told him they were not lies, and I was telling him the truth.

31

He came into the confessional and walked me up into the choir balcony. He said this was what was going to take place until you tell me the truth. "You are going to show me exactly what you claim took place at the orphanage. When I said exactly, I mean exactly." He opened his robe and pushed my face into his penis, "You know what to do don't you since you claim this happened. You have had plenty of practice so you claim," he said to me.

Now I was being assaulted at my school for telling the truth. Father Gilmore threatened to kick me out of school if I repeat my lies. He said this was God's punishment for being such a bad girl and doing bad things such as lying.

I was going to a school where I thought I was a bad child because I had Father Gilmore telling me I should be thankful for the love he shared with me by sexually abusing me in the galley and in the confessionals after the other children were dismissed. What was the reason that this was happening to me? I always wondered why I was last in line every day at school for confession. Why didn't it take the others as long to confess their sins? He wasn't doing this to anyone else in my class that I knew of.

It got to the point where Father Gilmore made me get in his side of the confessional as he lifted his robe and made me sit on his penis. The days he made me perform oral sex on his smelly parts was the worst stench I had ever smelt. He reeked of an odor that I couldn't to this day describe which was embedded in my mind forever. I had to suffer his abuse from first to fifth grade.

CHAPTER FIVE

Mom was becoming increasingly violent and angry with us. When we didn't hurry and get things done or if the kitchen floor wasn't swept to perfection, she would smack me on the back or butt and then pick something up to beat me with, if the smack didn't make me move quicker. To make matters worse, mom decided she was going to raise rabbits and chickens. With the prices of meat, food wouldn't be as expensive. Both of my parents were hunters and game was the only meat on our table growing up. We always had plenty of venison and elk. We did not know the taste of beef. Mom told dad that we would need to a plow a garden to grow our own vegetables when summer came. "You might as well get the girls prepared for that chore," she warned dad.

Dad told her that was a lot of work for us since we were already doing her house cleaning, dishes and laundry. He told her she was taking care of the chickens and rabbits and wanted no part of it. She agreed that she was taking care of the animals. He warned her that he didn't want to hear of us doing it. The animals were her job and hers alone. Little did he know, we were threatened within an inch of our lives if we said a word to him, so we ended up feeding and caring for her animal's.

I hated going to school. My teachers would always say I was daydreaming or sleeping in class. I was a first grader, who had been traumatized and hated her mom because of situations she could not handle. They did not realize all the work we did when we went home. Plus, I was being molested at school. Needless to say, I was petrified and afraid of what would happen to me next. I was a lost child.

Some days when dad would pull up in the driveway and I heard the car door close, I would go running out to my daddy. He would open the gate and pick me up and carry me in the house like a little girl should be treated. As soon as he put me down the other kids got their share of hugs. Those were rare days because he would only get to come home early if he had only one job at the time, which wasn't often. He would pick Barb up out of her crib and give her smooches, her share of love. Dad was very loving when we were little and made us feel very special.

He would always ask who did what chore and told us "Good job, girls!" He would ask mom what she had done that day. Sometimes, he seemed to be very upset with her. He let her know in his own way without starting an argument that he knew he would lose. Then he would give mom a kiss and listen to her complain about this or that.

I could think of few occasions when she was good to dad. Some days she was not a nice person at all and would call dad names. It is now that I look back and think that mother might have been bi-polar or suffered from depression. People were rarely diagnosed with bi-polar or depression in the fifties. I know because they certainly would have known my mother was not in her right mind for beating her kids so viciously. I was sure my mother would never tell a doctor what she was like for fear of losing control. She was always right and everyone was always wrong, including my poor father or anyone who would disagree with her. She always argued with anyone to prove she was right.

One day, one of us took some crackers out of the cupboard because we didn't have snacks to eat when we were hungry and of course we got caught. My mom ordered my dad to put locks on the cupboard doors to keep us from stealing food. When Aunt Dolly saw this, she asked him, "What the hell is with the locks on the cupboards?"

He told her that Helen (my mom) had ordered him to do so including putting a chain around the refrigerator with a padlock on it. Aunt Dolly told Dad, "It would be a cold day in hell before someone does that to my kids!"

My mom made it clear to Aunt Dolly, "To mind her

own goddamn business or go home. This matter does not pertain to you, period!"

Aunt Dolly asked Dad, "Why he would ever let a woman tell him what to do, especially when it pertained to the well-being of his children."

Then Mom replied to my Aunt Dolly, "I bet your kids don't steal things out of the freezer or cupboards, do they?"

My aunt replied back to mom, "They don't have to ask if they are hungry. I let them eat a snack when they want one."

"Not my kids," my mother replied back to her and added, "It wasn't your concern so butt the hell out before you and I mince words." Aunt Dolly unwittingly backed down.

Dad told my aunt that mom was the head honcho, and what she said went. I knew my aunt didn't want to get into it with my dad so she left well enough alone before all hell broke loose.

~~~

School was out for the Christmas holidays. For the first time since leaving California, we would be in our own home for Christmas. Dad took us up Priest Pass to get a tree and visit great-grandma who always made us stay for dinner. Great-grandma and grandma, dad's mother, did not approve or like our mother and it showed. Mom stayed home with the babies. Honestly, I think my dad was relieved because he was always in a good mood and happy when it was just us. I asked dad if Willard was coming home for Christmas. He said mom did not want to drive there to get him, and so he would not be home with us and maybe he could come home next year. We got our first Christmas tree and had dinner with great-grandma. She filled a paper sack with goodies and whispered in our ears to hide it in our room when we got home.

We got to help decorate the Christmas tree at our house and put the tinsel on because mom hated that part of decorating. Dad said Santa Claus would be coming to our house since we had been at the orphanage the other times and didn't receive anything for Christmas. Bonnie and I sat up waiting for Santa and fell asleep knowing we would finally get something for Christmas. We woke up very early Christmas morning and saw that Santa made it to our house after all. We saw presents under our tree for the first time ever. Mom put grandma's name on the present and not Santa Claus which upset our dad. She made it clear to dad the money belonged to her that her mother had sent it to her and not to us.

We had Christmas dinner since mom received the money from grandma to buy dinner and presents for us. Instead of buying presents, she signed grandma's name on the Salvation Army presents that were delivered to us. Mom made sure she did what grandma said to do with the money for Christmas dinner, but not the gifts. Grandma was coming for a visit after school was out. My mother made it clear to us that we had to tell grandma she bought us gifts for Christmas, or else. We knew what the "or else" stood for so we lied.

Grandma came from Palermo, Italy when she was nine years old. She was born in Catania and left from there to live in Palermo until her mother brought her to America. She lived in Los Angeles when my mother was born and stayed there until after my mother graduated from high school. They later moved to Northern California and then to Washington, and back to Northern California. My mom's dad passed away and grandma remarried a few years later to my Grandpa Dan who was an incredibly kind man.

Grandma kept up with mom and dad on what was happening with us. She was not pleased when she found out 00we were being shuffled to and from an orphanage. Grandma told her she had no business having so many children when she knew she couldn't care for them.

While visiting, my grandma taught me to spell my words and would treat me with candy for each right answer. My mother was furious with her for treating me with all of these goodies and bribing me to learn. "This little girl knows her math and spelling very well in spite of you not teaching her," grandma replied. "Wanda you keep up the good work and try hard," grandma would say hugging me tightly. "Obviously, you haven't done much of a job with these kids, Helen!" she told my mother without hesitation. "Look at their first report cards. Doesn't that tell you something is haywire here," she said.

It finally got so bad that I remember to this day my mom yelling at grandma to "Pack her bags and leave her the hell alone! Why do you think I ran away and got married, to get away from you!"

"This will bite you in the butt for the way you treat and talk to your children let alone your mother. I wouldn't be a bit surprised if they were taken away from you!" Grandma said to her without any hesitation.

All of us hated watching our grandmother leave and we cried uncontrollably, until we got smacked and told to shut the hell up or we would get an ass whooping once grandma wasn't there to protect us.

I was thankful grandma had been here to help me know my true potential, which I will always be grateful for. She would boost my self-esteem making me realize my self-worth. It was like she had placed a seed of hope for me to always remember, "Never let your mother or anybody take your self-worth from you," she would whisper softly in my ear.

I was dreading the thought about going back to school after Christmas vacation and praying that everything had changed. I kept telling myself maybe Father Gilmore would be gone and I wouldn't have him sexually assaulting me or hurting me anymore. How wrong I was to even think that. He didn't waste any time what-so-ever. It made we wonder if all priests were like this. They punished us for little things just so they could manipulate us back into their laps once again without thinking how we felt or how they hurt us.

At six years old, I did not know what these evil men

were thinking. The time seemed to drag for the school year to finish, and I was relieved when it finally came to an end. I wasn't the little girl who was so excited to start her first day of school anymore. Now, I was terrified of the thought of ever coming back to school.

Sister Mary Marie was a blessing in class and helped me make it through the school year with wonderful grades. I think she knew what I was going through because she was always kind to me. She tried to get me to get my work done in class. She seemed nervous at times when I was gone too long with Father Gilmore.

Sister Mary Marie would always catch me daydreaming and would come over and gently put her hand on my shoulder and say, "Wanda get your work finished so you don't fall behind." She wasn't as cranky as she had been at the beginning of the school year.

I was happy that I passed the first grade and had fairly good grades. I had just turned seven. My birthday was treated as if it was another day to mom. Dad took us to get ice cream cones at his cousin Margaret's restaurant. The thrill of eating ice cream was a pleasure I couldn't describe to other children. I was so thankful I had that moment, licking and tasting something so delicious! An ice-cream cone to me was a special birthday gift from our dad knowing we couldn't afford more. We looked up to dad for trying to make a special day, special. Dad knew how thrilled I was to go to Park Lake for my birthday as well. He took me fishing just to get away from doing the house chores mom made me do. I loved him dearly for that special thought.

CHAPTER SIX

Summer was halfway over and I was very excited that school was still almost two months away. I dreaded what would happen upon my return. I held on to the high hopes Father Gilmore would be long gone. If by some miracle he was gone I could breathe again. I would much rather be beaten by my mother than to go near him. Dad said we were going to do more camping up at Park Lake or Canyon Ferry if he could get the time off. He loved to fish and so did Bonnie and I.

I found out that Bonnie was going to the Lion's Sunshine Camp. I wasn't happy because I could not go. One had to be eight years old and Bonnie was eight June 19th and the camp started the next week. Dad told me to quit pouting; I would be going the following year. He said we would go camping the weekend that Bonnie was gone. Dad was a man of his word. In the meantime, mom had plenty for us to do before Bonnie would leave for camp. We planted her garden that she wanted so badly and had to be diligent about pulling weeds that sprung up with the newly planted vegetables.

We still did house chores every day. We would hurry to get them done so we could go play with the neighborhood kids. One day we were playing with our friends and didn't hear Mother calling, neither did Bonnie. It was close to dinnertime and we were not paying attention to the time on Clay's watch. Mom left Wesley and Barb home alone as she hurried to find us. It was a sneak attack! We didn't see her as she approached the ball field. When we did we saw that she had a wire hairbrush in her hand and by her expression, meant business.

Suddenly, my friend Carol yelled, "Your mom has a brush in her hand and looks mad!"

We quit playing and ran over to where she was coming. Our intent was to avoid her so we could run home before she got us. We almost ran right into her. She made us stop in our tracks and beat our bottoms with the wire part of the brush. When we got back to the house she continued beating us. She called us names while beating on our behinds embedding the sharp bristles into our flesh. She sent us into our rooms before dad arrived home and made us go to bed without our dinner.

I could feel blood on the backside of my panties and Bonnie said she also had blood. Our bedroom was right next to the bathroom, which was right off of the hall to the kitchen. We snuck in there very quietly, since she was in the living room watching the other two kids and reading as if nothing had happened. We hurriedly cleaned the blood off and saw little pinholes on each other's butt. We were crying softly because it hurt so bad and burned at the same time.

I told Bonnie when I was old enough I was going to run away from home. She had the same sentiment as we sympathized with one another. At this point, my mother was always freaking out on us and the beatings began to get worse. If I mopped the floor wrong, she would grab the mop and hit me with the handle, and tell me to do it over anddo it right or I would have to keep at it until it was clean.

When dad got home from work, she told him what we had done and lied about what actually took place. She did not tell him she had just beaten us. Daddy came in the bedroom; he asked us why we didn't listen for our mother calling. We told him we didn't hear her over the noise the kids made while we were playing baseball. He told us we could get up if we never did it again and have dinner with the rest of the family.

Mom had a fit and said, "Absolutely not! I told them no dinner and I meant what I said." He shrugged his shoulders and didn't want to argue with her so we went to sleep without dinner. When we woke up, our butts were so sore we could hardly move. We got dressed and had breakfast. Daddy bent down and kissed us good-bye. I knew he felt bad for us not having our dinner.

The next day, we had house chores and garden detail. There was no going outside to play, no fun with friends. The chickens were big now and the rabbits kept having more babies. It was overwhelming to take care of them on top of other chores. Even under those circumstances, Bonnie and I said we would gladly be doing the chores, instead of being at the orphanage or school. Father Hartman was molesting Bonnie, while Father Gilmore was molesting me. Neither of us was aware of the other's abuse. Right then though, all we could think about was to play with the other kids as we heard them all day while we were working. That was torture in its own right.

Our friends always asked us why we had such a cruel and mean mother that wouldn't let them come over to our house and play with us. Someone would pipe in and make a remark about who would want to be around their mother in the first place. We began to be known around the neighborhood as the kids with the mean mom. They actually felt sorry for us and wanted to sneak us over to their houses. Carol's playhouse was behind our alley. Sometimes, we snuck off to play when mom was napping. We had to take that chance and knew the consequences if we were caught.

Bonnie left for Sunshine Camp and would be gone for an entire week. After I finished the house chores, I would play with my baby sister Barb. I read stories to her and pretended she was my little girl and not mom's. She was a two-year old toddler. I loved pretending with her. I would tell her not to let mom hear her call me mom, or I would get a terrible spanking for permitting it. My brother Wesley played alone with his little trucks all day, since Willard was in Warm Springs and the neighbor boys were older than Wesley.

Dad said Willard was going to be transferred to the institution in Boulder so we were going to go visit him and take him to the Lewis and Clark Caverns before he was transferred. He would be closer to Helena now and maybe we would get to see more of him and spend some special time with our little brother.

Dad took us to Park Lake like he promised and we finally got to have some fun fishing together. I loved hiking far from the camp without mom harping at me to do her work. Dad loved the woods since he was born and raised in them. We loved to venture off and come back to camp a couple hours later.

Mom had to stay at the camp and take care of Wesley and Barb. So I had daddy all to myself for the first time ever. A little girl of seven alone with her daddy fishing was something to cherish in my family where there was no peace of mind for her. He made me know that I was a daddy's girl. He also loved our baby Barbara and picked her up and squeezed her and got her to laugh for him. Dad loved to talk about her pretty blonde hair; he said he had blonde hair as a child himself. He said she looked like him the most because of her blonde hair and her blue eyes. She was too young to take with us when we went fishing together.

This was the best camping trip ever that I remembered. I was very happy. My mom couldn't make me do all the chores because dad would take me with him fishing and hiking. He told her she had to stay and take care of the young ones since she was not the outdoors type to begin with. She hated our camping trips. She spent her time reading and not engaging in family fun.

When daddy and I returned, my mother would yell at us, "Where in the hell did we take off to without letting her know?" She would tell me "...to get my ass busy right now." She gripped openly, "I am left here to take care of the kids while you two were out there having a blast fishing and doing as you please!"

"Shut the hell up!" Dad yelled at her. "The entire camp could hear your rampage and screaming," he told her.

"I am ready to go home if this is what you call

relaxing," she yelled back at my father.

"Wanda works her butt off for you, and I for one am not in the mood to fight about taking her fishing."

Oh no, I thought to myself. When I get home and dad goes to work she is not going to forget this. The only thing I had to do in the morning was, straighten up the tent and bedding on the sleeping mats, and then dad would cook our breakfast and after eating tell me to grab my pole.

Mom angrily piped in and said "Not until these dishes are done!"

I told Dad I would do them if he would wait for me. "That's it," Dad said when I was done. "Let's go fishing," but then mom said I had to watch the kids.

"The hell she's going to watch the kids; she is going fishing with me as I promised."

Mom glared at me and I knew this wasn't over yet. Dad and I went fishing and came back a couple hours later and fried up our fish. He could tell Mom was angry as she glared at us without saying a word. She happily ate the fish and corn that we cooked but said nothing the entire time. After dinner she finally yelled at me "To get the goddamn dishes done and help get the kids to bed." Dad just shook his head and walked away angrily. I was not thrilled when we headed for home from Park Lake. I knew that dad had stepped on her toes and now I would be paying the price for our fun time together.

Bonnie came home from camp and right into having to help me weed the big garden and feed animals as soon as we picked her up from the bus. She told me that the camp was so much fun. There were eight bunk beds to a cabin and counselors that helped keep it clean. The only work was making her bed and picking up her own clothes. They made things in craft classes, went on hikes and got to swim every day in the pond made from a creek. The food was great compared to what we ate at home. The food is what she would miss the most. I told her I couldn't wait till I got to go with her next year. It gave me something to look forward to.

I told Bonnie what had happened at Park Lake and she told me to watch out and not get mom mad because she wouldn't forget what happened. I needed to watch my back. I told Bonnie that we were going to see Willard the next weekend and that he would be going to another facility in Boulder for mentally handicapped children where they actually got schooled.

Mom yelled at us to get our asses in the house right now! The dishes were in the sink and not done and the floors still needed cleaning and the animals needed to be fed. We told her she wanted us to go out and weed the garden first and feed her rabbits and that was what we were doing. She grabbed me by my very long hair and started beating on my back and all over me as I tried to tuck my body in. She finally gave me a bloody nose and quit beating me. She threatened if I ever mouthed off to her like that again I would get it worse the next time.

Bonnie asked mom a question about something she wanted finished and she slapped her face and told her that there would never be sassing in this house ever again. Bonnie did not talk back to mom, as mom accused. Mom looked over at me and in a chilling voice told me, "If I ever pulled the stunt I did at Park Lake again, that all hell will break loose in this f—king house and you will be the one to blame. Don't you ever forget that?"

We were finally going to see Willard. Dad made it clear to mom that we were going to spend the weekend, and take Willard to the caves like dad promised he would. Mom did not want to spend the entire weekend there, but dad won this argument and she was not pleased. He said it was ludicrous that she didn't want to spend time with a child she never saw and was severely injured by her neglect. So we listened to the argument most of the way there. When we arrived dad went in to get Willard while all of us were outside waiting for them.

Mom sat in the car with Barb because Barb had only seen Willard once and she was a baby. Willard came rushing out the door. He was so excited because he kept saying hello over and over to all of us. He was all cheery and bubbly and happy to be with us once again. The clarity of his speech impairment had improved too so that we could now understand him.

Dad got us back in the car and Willard kept saying, "Hi, Mommy!" until finally she acknowledged him. We headed to the Lewis and Clark Caverns, which were not far from Boulder. There was a campground close by and dad said we would get up in the morning and go to the Caverns. In the meantime, we had to help set up camp and were more than happy to help daddy. We were allowed to go to the creek and catch minnows and frogs as long as we kept an eye on the little ones. Barb was two at this time and would just hold onto me and stayed by my side. Bonnie kept Wes and Willard with her. Our brothers were catching little frogs while we would try to get minnows in a bucket. After showing our parents what we caught, we released them back in the water. Then we got cleaned up for dinner. Dad built a campfire so we could roast marshmallows. Morning came and we were all excited about getting to go inside the Caverns. We broke camp and headed for our adventure.

The tour guide took us down into the dark wet caves, and we saw the beautiful stalactites and stalagmites hanging from the caves, sparkling like crystals. The bats were huddled against the wet limestone. I was so glad we dressed warmly because the caves were deep underground; they were cool, and even cold in places. Willard was in awe and his eyes bulged and glowed with delight. We all were in awe from the beauty before us.

We were together as a family. It was a wonderful and glorious day. I did not want this day to ever end, but like other happy occasions it did. Then we had to take Willard to Boulder, we cried as we pulled up to the grey stone building before dad even stopped. Each of us, Bonnie, Wesley, Barb and I had hugged and told him goodbye and told him we would be together again soon. My mom just sat there and gave him a tiny hug with the car door open. Then my dad took him back inside with Willard waving and

45

crying all the way through the door.

Mom told us, "To shut the hell up, as she had had enough of the whining and crying in the back seat for the day."

It was a very sad day riding home knowing we wouldn't see each other again for a long time. We had shared a wonderful weekend. We hoped and prayed that we would not have to wait too long before we got to share another outing with Willard. I felt sorry for Willard over the coldness of my mother and the feelings she could not share with this very special child.

Daddy loved all of his children but back then they didn't say I love you and I missed you like we do today with our children. Mother was overwhelmed with children. She only knew anger. She appeared to have no concept of the pain she inflicted upon us. She never showed any kind of affection, emotion or playfulness. To this day, I cannot understand why she had so many children and was always so unhappy with us when we would do everything to try and please her. We could tell she favored Wesley. My uncle said he picked up on that vibe immediately. He sympathized with us watching us work while Wesley played. He felt that it was not in Wesley's best interest to be favored over the girls.

CHAPTER SEVEN

Summer came to an end and I was dreading the inevitable. Father Gilmore would still be at school, and I would be assaulted over and over again. I kept praying that a new priest would be at the school. I was dreadfully wrong, and I knew that it was wishful thinking on my part. I was in the second grade. I had a nice teacher, Sister Mary Michael, who seemed very kind and nice to us and told us if we needed any help just ask her for it. Time would tell because the nuns seem to have good days and bad days. Father Gilmore told my teacher that I would be the last child in line for confessions and she had asked why I was so special. She asked him for the reason and he took her aside for a few moments. He took me to the end of the line and told her not to ever question his authority again.

I knew what was coming and did not know how to stop it. One day in class after a month or so after school started, I raised my hand and asked for permission to go to the bathroom. Sister Mary Michael told me I had to wait until recess like the other children. I kept shaking because I had to go so bad. I raised my hand again and she told me to put my hand down and wait. After a few moments, I wet my uniform and made a puddle on the floor. I put my head down on the desk and shed a few tears then suddenly I was crying uncontrollably.

She came over and took me by the hand and told me to follow her to the office. She called my mom. She told my mom she needed to come and get me as I had an accident in class. I had to sit in the office in my wet clothing until mom arrived.

In the car, I listened to my mother tell me what was going to happen to me when I got home. "What second grader pisses her pants, right there in front of her classmates and thinks nothing about it," she ranted? What was she talking about? I was embarrassed beyond belief.

When we got home she took Wes and Barb out of the car and left them in the living room. She took me into the bedroom. She made me strip off my school uniform. Then she whipped me hard on my wet butt. It stung more than any plain spanking ever could.

She filled the sink with cool soapy water and ordered me to wash my uniform up and down in the sink for a long time. As I rinsed it in cold water, my mother watched with her hand on her hip. I cried. I told her how much I hated her. I told her I wish I had a different home and a different life. I hung up my uniform dripping wet on the back of the bathroom door.

The embarrassment of going back to school after my mishap that day was so degrading, but nothing was said by my classmates or Sister Mary Michael. She smiled at me and made everything seem okay. She was so kind and thoughtful with me that I appreciated her more than any nun that I could remember. She was very helpful with my schoolwork and keeping me caught up in class. She had witnessed my mother's cruelty in the office.

Sister Mary Michael made the horrible times fade somewhat when I came back to class after being trapped at the Cathedral with Father Gilmore. I cared for this woman in the strange habit she wore. She was the first nun who showed me kindness and affection. The other nuns treated me unfairly. I truly cared for this amazing woman.

In early November, I received a message at school that my dad had been in an awful accident at work. My Aunt Cecil picked us up from school. Mom had to go to the hospital to be with dad, so she asked Aunt Cecil if she wouldn't mind collecting us from school and taking us to St. Joseph's because dad had broken his back. She had Wes and Barb with her already. She collected us from school and told us where we were going. I could tell she felt sorry for us. She had two of her own at that time and couldn't watch us too.

When we arrived at the orphanage it was the same routine: We walked in the building where the nuns greet us. Bonnie, Barb and I were settled in the dormitory. A large room lined with two rows of single white iron beds. We placed our bags under our beds. Bonnie and I helped Barbara find a bed close to us. Bonnie took one farther out so Barb could be right next to me. By the second day, I was very relieved that I hadn't seen Father Callan yet. I thought that perhaps he was gone.

In the cafeteria that night for dinner, Bonnie and I sat next to one another. Barb sat with the toddlers. Before our food was dished up on our tray, I accidentally dropped the knife and fork on the floor. Sister Mary Magdalene came over and grabbed my shoulder, harshly pinching me at the same time. She took me out of the dining room fuming with anger. She went to Father Callan's office and pounded on his door. She told him I was already starting the same problems again and needed to be retrained and reprimanded.

He opened the door and said - something he would say again and again, "To what do we owe the pleasure of your company young lady?" Sister told him I was fooling around at the table before Grace was said. This was a lie. He excused her and told her to go back to her regular routine. He said to me, "This is getting very old young lady and you know better than this. You have misbehaved before and you were not here a day and started in again."

After she closed the door, he walked around to the desk and said to me, "Why was I so disruptive and disrespectful?" He just couldn't understand. I just stood there in shock not able to speak for fear of what might happen next. He pointed his finger downwards and said, "Now!" His voice was angry. I learned quickly what that word meant. He made noises I had not heard from him before pushing my head up and down harshly. I tried go somewhere else in my mind, but just couldn't. It seemed to get worse as I got older. I felt pain everywhere—in my mouth, my back, and in my heart.

It took Father Callan longer to get done with me. Right as he was done with me, Sister Mary Magdalene opened the door and drug Bonnie in. He made me stand there, watching him do the same thing to Bonnie, as I cried. I tried to tell him, I was the one who dropped the silverware, not Bonnie. He told me to be quiet or I would be punished again. As I cried out for help, I looked down at the floor. I felt so guilty, so lost right now so terrible because of me, he was raping my sister. It was my fault. He told me I was full of evil and the devil was in me making me do these bad things.

Father Callan told both of us that we should be used to the punishments since we were always the troublemakers whom he had to punish. He told us again and again that God would forgive us for our sins in due time, but only if we prayed enough, said our rosary and learned to be quiet like we were told to do. When he did these awful things to us, he sounded like Father Gilmore, except Father Gilmore called me a liar and did not believe Father Callan did this to me. Father Gilmore repeated what he accused me of lying about. I always thought who was this evil person? Surely not me, I thought to myself.

The next day at St. Helena School, I fell asleep in Catechism class. Sister Mary Michael asks me why I was so tired. I couldn't tell her what was happening at the orphanage and what was also happening at school since she was unaware of what was taking place. Sleep was my only escape. Sleep was my refuge—sometimes.

The weekend came. Bonnie and I hoped we would hear news about dad, but we did not. No one called. Or if they did call, no one told us anything. I cringed at the idea that we were stuck in this awful place.

When I got up in the morning, I heard these terrible screams in the bathroom. The voice sounded like my little sister Barb. I look over at her empty bed and realized it was she screaming. I threw back the cover, jumped out of my bed and ran as fast as I could to the bathroom. When I arrived, Sister Mary Magdalene was holding the back of

Barb's head so she was face down in the toilet. Sister was repeatedly flushing the toilet while holding Barb's face firmly in it and yelling at her for wetting the bed.

I pulled at Sister Mary Magdalene's habit while screaming at the top of my lungs, "You leave my little sister alone!"

Sister Mary Magdalene shoved me hard, thrusting me against the wall. I kicked her in the shins. I tried to land a kick through the dark heavy cloth of her dress, kicking as hard as I could while struggling with her at the same time. She turned to hit me. I was desperately trying to save my baby sister. I didn't care what happened or took place. I grabbed her rosary at the front of her robe and pulled it as hard as I could. Beads went flying everywhere across the tiled floor. The other girls in the dormitory were laughing hysterically at the commotion I had created. Some were egging the situation on hoping it would continue. Sister Mary Magdalene was yelling at Sister Marie to get over to her and help her get this demonic child away from her.

In the meanwhile, Sister Marie was in the room and had placed Barb into a bathtub full of ice water. She yelled back at Sister Mary Magdalene that she couldn't do both things at once. Then Bonnie joined in to help me pull Barb out of the water while the two of us were fighting off Sister Mary Magdalene. Both the nuns were fighting us off while we were trying to save our little sister from being dunked in the icy water of the bathtub repeatedly.

The laughter of the other girls continued until another nun appeared and made all the girls return to their beds. They needed to make their beds and get ready for breakfast. They mimicked us because they couldn't believe what had just happened.

The two nuns fought us off as we realized we had no chance to help Barb now. Sister Mary Magdalene grabbed me and held me in place against the wall. Bonnie stood with Sister Marie. Barb was screaming for her daddy and us. The other nun assisted the sisters to get things under control and help with Barbara. Once out of the icy water,

Barb was dried and clothed, then Bonnie and Barbara were marched off to Father Callan's office.

I was given a new punishment. I was taken to a different area in the building. It was a dark room that had a hole in the door. The hole was the size of a plate and had a screen covering it. I was told that I would not be fed while in confinement until further notice. Now I understood why the other kids in the orphanage call it "The Hole."

"The Hole" was the name given by the kids in the orphanage that had occupied it at one time or another. There was a cot on the floor and one blanket. The child was left there until the nuns decided the child had been sufficiently punished, usually a day or overnight. I was left in it overnight and the entire next day! While I was in "The Hole", I found out what it was like to have a visitor in the night on top of me. He was holding his hand over my mouth while I tried to scream. A priest was raping me. I lay there in blood and agonizing pain as he pushed up my legs up to my head. He made his moaning sounds and sweat fell in my face. The awful stench covered me like a suffocating blanket. He threw a robe on the floor and told me to cover up. When he was done he told me to get down on my knees and pray to God for forgiveness for being a bad child. I was to think about how disruptive and aggressive I was. I needed to heal my compulsive disruptive behavior and honor authority.

He called me an obstinate and rebellious seven year old who needed to pray for forgiveness and my mortality every day. Maybe, God would forgive me for being such a bad child and then maybe bad things wouldn't happen to me as often. I had to repent my sins for the bad things I had done to the sisters and apologize for the chaos I caused in the dorms. I did not plan on apologizing if I could help it, I told myself. His voice was harsh and stern. Until I quit sinning this would be my punishment from the Lord, our God. "Sister will bring you a change of clothing and a washcloth to wash your sins away, he said." I had to say the rosary until morning and go to mass when they let me out on Sunday morning. Then he shut the door to "The Hole" and I heard the sound of his footsteps fade away into the darkness.

I guess I was rebellious because I said the rosary once and cried myself to sleep. I knew they would not check on me or at least hoped they wouldn't. At that point, I did not care. Bonnie said she knew "The Hole" real well.

"Why didn't you tell me I asked her?"

"I didn't want you to know what was happening to me," she replied.

It seemed that anytime someone did something wrong or something the nuns disliked, we were punished in one form or another, but why like this. There were no good times in the orphanage. No playground equipment, games or fun things for children. We did see movies of animals or religious related movies. We did get to bring books from the library at school back to the orphanage to read and that was our entertainment, which I learned to enjoy. It helped my reading skills and made me enjoy reading books. The books allowed me to escape the madness of the orphanage and school. Reading created a fairytale life I dreamed of. I was a hopeless dreamer.

The daily sexual assaults continued and became more violent. I had a hard time believing that a priest or any man whatsoever could find enjoyment in sexually assaulting toddlers and little girls. What made them want to hurt us in this manner? What enjoyment could it possibly be?

I grew up as a child thinking I was a bad girl and was being punished by God.

"Be a good girl and bad things won't happen to you." But yet they took an oath to God, to teach people right from wrong, to be kind and celibate, and to live a simple and godly life. Our so-called teachers of the Catholic Church instead of thriving to live by the faith robbed us of our childhood.

We went home in February of 1955. Mom was the one who picked us up. Bonnie and I had decided we must tell mom what was happening to us so we would never have to go back to St. Joseph's Orphanage ever again. We had to get out of St. Helena's School by telling our mother. As we drove down the snowy streets, Bonnie told her first, talking as my mother maneuvered the steering wheel, listening. I chimed in, "Please believe us mom, please." She pulled the car over and began to slap Bonnie and then me. She slapped our faces again and again. "But mom," I said, "This was the God honest truth."

"You are little liars and whores, liars and whores!" she repeats over and over while continuing her rage, "Chippies! You are trash and liars. If you ever repeat those lies, you will go straight to hell, and I will beat the hell out of you!" she ranted on. "If you ever speak of this again, I will give you the belt and beat your ass until you cannot sit down for quite a while. Understood! Now both of you shut your f— king mouths and do not open them again until I say so." Our mother didn't even try to investigate like any normal parent would do. Or better yet, call the authorities and put a stop to the pedophile priests and abusive nuns.

It fell silent, except for the sounds of our whimpering. I think Wesley was in shock from all the commotion going on. Barbara finally realized she must be quiet or she would be struck and beaten as well.

Knowing what we had told her, she did not bother to check our privates to see if we were hurt or if we were being raped which could have been proven. "If you tell your lies to your father," she said, "I will take you back to that orphanage as fast as I can get you out that door. I've had enough of your girl's bullshit for the day. I do not ever want to hear a word about this again. Do you hear me loud and clear?" We shook our heads, yes.

I truly think my mother could have cared less what really was happening to us. We were alone in this ordeal and just had to let it continue regardless of what it did to us. Father Callan, Father Gilmore, Father Hartman and the other Father had won. We never again spoke of it for fear we would receive worse than we were getting. We knew we were doomed and alone in this abuse.

Dad came home the next day. Mom had us get everything clean and dishes that were stacked in the sink done before she arrived home with him. She didn't do any chores while we were in the orphanage. We had the house spotless and were very tired, but it was worth it because daddy knew we worked our butts off for him, not her. We really felt bad for the pain our dad was enduring. I could see it on his face as he climbed into bed. He was not the type to complain to anyone if he was in serious pain.

CHAPTER EIGHT

Dad had recuperated and school was out. I was now eight-years-old and Daddy took us for ice cream cones at the Zip-In-And-Out, which was a drive-thru restaurant in an A-frame type building. It was all we could afford. Daddy was getting Workers Compensation, which was barely enough to support our family. After dad had recovered from his injuries, he received a job offer from Bill Carson. Dad worked on the Carson Ranch and others in the surrounding area when he was growing up. He was given a job driving a cement truck for Helena Sand and Gravel. It was a little easier work until he was one hundred percent healed. He couldn't stand sitting around as he was a hard worker and he went to work a little sooner than he was supposed to.

That summer Bonnie and I went to the Lion's Sunshine Camp together hand in hand. I was excited and extremely happy. I had never been this excited to get away from everything and everybody. Bonnie and I sat next to each other on the bus trip.

The camp was fun from morning to night: a foreign experience for me. Camp routine was glorious: eating, playing, hiking, snacking and never a worry. We got up, made our beds, put our clothes away and off to breakfast. After we ate, we went to the recreation room and did crafts, beading or leatherwork that we could take home at the end of camp. We ate lunch. It was delicious food, far better than what we ate for lunch at home. We went on a small hike, then came back to our cabins, changed into our swimsuits, and went to swim in the creek. The beavers had built a dam in the Little Blackfoot Creek. It dammed the creek into a small swimming pool for all of us. Our adult counselors were always present for our safety. After we swam, we laid down for an hour to rest. In the late afternoon, we all trundled over to the recreation hall to learn a skit we would perform for the parents who came to watch the last day of camp on Sunday the day before campers headed home. Our parents, of course, would not be there, I was sure. Mom would not let dad waste gas to drive up the Little Blackfoot to see us perform when we would be coming back to Helena on the bus the following morning. But it was fun, anyway, learning to memorize our parts and putting on costumes.

Then came suppertime, I thought lunch was great but supper was delicious. We got to have a great big meal: fried Chicken, baked beans, and corn on the cob. We got to drink milk, fresh milk. The only time we had milk at home was powdered milk, which our mother mixed for us to have with cereal. We had desert: pie, cake, and ice cream with every dinner. It was the one time; we were not hungry during the day or night. We got to eat beef. We actually ate fish, pork and chicken. We had sandwiches with lunchmeat—not our usual peanut butter and jelly. Our sandwiches actually had real meat.

There were track days, with events such as the 50-yard dash with competitors sorted into different age groups, and if one won, there were different colored ribbons. Another night, we hiked with my group to a spot where we camped overnight. In the dark forest, under a canopy of pine trees, with tiny glowing twinkling stars, listening to the sound of the crickets and coyotes, and last but not least we put on a little play that the counselors helped us with. As we sat around the campfire, we roasted marshmallows and wieners, and sang campfire songs.

On the bus ride home, as I sat on the hard leather bench with Bonnie, I said to her, I don't want it to be over. Bonnie and I laughed and joked with the other kids and sang campfire songs once again on the way home. When dad picked the two of us up in Helena, I was relieved it was just dad and not mom. He picked each of us up, one in each arm, and hugged us tightly, kissing our cheeks, and asking if his little girls had fun and enjoyed ourselves.

Dad asked if we had a good time not having to do mom's chores, as we laughed knowing that remark could have gotten him into trouble. We told him about our new friends and the food, the hiking and the singing. He said, "I was glad you girls had fun because as soon as you get in the house, you will have house work to finish. Well, you know your mom," he sadly commented. "As soon as you walk in the door she is going to put you to work getting the laundry done."

Dad was wrong. It wasn't laundry. The first thing she said as we came in the door was, "The garden needs weeding and you need to get it done now, so go and change into your garden clothes." We went out to the garden and it was muddy from being overwatered, but she still made us do it.

Our shoes would stick and slide in the mud and sometimes one would come off. As we would search for the lost shoe we would begin to sink in the mud once again losing yet another shoe. I laughed back at Bonnie, as we were slipping and sliding in the mud like a slapstick routine. We began to laugh and make goofy sounds sliding in the mud without a care, knowing our clothes were soaked with mud, and if caught, the trouble we would be in. We made an absolute mess of our clothes and lost our shoes and socks. We laughed and said "Mom was going to be furious with us," but at least dad was home and we wouldn't get into as much trouble. First we hosed ourselves real good before going into the house unnoticed, shivering from the cold water and soaked clothes. We snuck in the back door just in case and changed clothes quickly. We washed up without being detected. Then we finished our chores so we could reminisce about the wonderful time we had at camp.

The rest of summer was nothing but work. Whenever one of the neighborhood kids would come over to ask us to come out and play, Mother would yell back at them and tell them we were not going to get to do much playing for the remaining part of summer; we had too many chores to do, and not to bother us for the rest of the summer.

While she napped, we would sneak away to play. Bonnie or I standing guard, but it was a chance we rarely took. We knew what would happen if we were caught. At this time, we really did not hesitate to think about the consequences of our actions. We really wanted to have fun with our friends. Even if it meant that we had to sneak off to have a little time out of the house and away from mom. She took long naps thank goodness and unknowingly gave us this opportunity to have friends.

CHAPTER NINE

Bonnie and I were in third and fourth grade. We cleaned house for mom, which meant sweeping and mopping. One day, I mopped up the floors, but when I finished, my mother yelled that I did not get the floor "good enough" and I had to do it again. When I poured the mop water into the sink, the bucket was too heavy for me, and the water spilt over the counter and down the cupboard. My mother almost pushed over her chair to get to me. She pushed me to the floor. She started kicking me in the stomach and the sides. When I turned over, she kicked my back. I was screaming and crying in pain.

Bonnie was yelling, "Mom! Stop! She has blood coming out of her! She is peeing blood! Mom!! STOP!" All the kids were screaming at her to quit hurting me. I suddenly lost consciousness. Finally, she stopped.

I couldn't get up or move. Bonnie ran out of the door to get help. Mom screams, "Get your ass back here right now! Do you want some of this too?" Bonnie ran out the door anyway, she did not listen and could have cared less about the consequences. She ran to Lucille our neighbor. Lucille was not home, but Bonnie told Lucille's daughter to call for an ambulance because my mother would not and Wanda was bleeding on the floor.

Mom kept trying to get me to stand up but I bled more and couldn't move. "Get the hell up and quit faking!" she was screaming at me. I was whimpering. I couldn't move or I bled more. I once again lost consciousness. As soon as the ambulance and paramedics arrived, they asked what had happened to me. As they were preparing to carry me on the gurney, Bonnie told them my mom hurt me.

They called the police on their car radio, and told them

they wouldn't let the mother ride in the ambulance. She was not allowed to leave her other children at home alone. They took me to Shodair Children's Hospital. Aunt Cecil arrived at the hospital as soon as she found out what had happened. They told her she had to wait for my father to get there before she could see me. She was beside herself that mom would do something this bad.

When my father arrived, they wanted to know what had happened to me. The doctor told them that my mother had kicked me so hard she had ruptured my kidney, which flooded my urine with blood. The doctor told my dad that it was bad and mother was to be questioned by the police.

"Your daughter will be hospitalized for a few weeks," the doctor said. "We have to turn this in to the authorities. This is an extreme case of child abuse," the doctor explained to my dad. Aunt Cecil warned dad to do something or else, asking him if he wanted to go to jail for something his wife did.

Mom made Bonnie and Barb go to the bedroom when she saw the police pull into the driveway. She told them not to say anything except that I fell off a chair getting into a cupboard if asked. If they told the truth they would get the belt. They lied to the police. The police left the house and came to the hospital to see if they could get to the truth. They could tell the girls were too frightened to tell the actual truth.

I told the doctor what happened and they called DFS and had the other kids removed from the house because of my mom's non-compliance and false statements to the police. I was in the hospital for over three weeks. I was in horrible pain from all the other bruises that had turned black and blue from her vicious attack.

I was very fortunate to have Sister Rose Marie bring my homework and when school was out she would come and help me with my work. She would stay real late worrying and praying for me to heal quickly. She truly cared for my well being as well as Sister Mary Michael, my favorite.

A lady from Social Services came and asked me what

really happened and what led up to me getting hurt and wanted to know if I had provoked my mother. She even asked me why I got my mom so upset. I told her I accidentally spilled the mop water and got the cupboard wet. I let her know that mom was having a lot of anger issues but she was never mad at our brother Wesley. I think she thought I was jealous of my brother, which I could honestly say I was because of the preferential treatment he got compared to the rest of us. This was not my brother's fault that mom cared for him more than us. We loved our brothers regardless how mom treated us. They were good kids.

As soon as dad came to the hospital, he learned what had happened from the doctor. I found out from Aunt Cecil that mom was staying at a neighbor's house. They had a big fight over her physically hurting us and making us do all of her work as she sat reading or sleeping. It ended with mom taking Wesley and going to stay at the neighbors. Dad was home alone, except when he was at work.

Mom was not allowed to come to the hospital. I was told that the kids were at the orphanage because we were taken away from mom, once again. Mom didn't get to keep Wesley after they found out that she hid him. One would think that the system would only give her so many chances. They didn't really care because they tried to keep families together whether it was safe or not. When I got out of the hospital several weeks later, I was taken to St. Joseph's Orphanage right away to be with my sisters and brothers.

The doctor told the nuns I would have to rest and heal for a few more days and was not ready for school either. This was, the first time, the evil priests ever left me alone, and for that I was thankful. They did make me go to the cafeteria to eat, and then I was sent back to the dorms to rest. "We don't do preferential treatment here" Sister informed me. "You will eat with the others and not in the dorms."

Bonnie and Barb, whose beds were near mine again, were very attentive. They tried to leave me be, but ended up asking me questions about how long we would be here? I didn't know. I told them that they did nothing wrong. I thanked Bonnie for running for help. I told them all I knew was that Aunt Cecil said mom and dad had a big fight. Aunt Cecil had visited me along with dad.

For a week, I let Barb lay on my bed next to me, while Sister Marie visited me. By the next week when I was back to normal, I went back to school. The nuns were back to their old ways of telling me I wasn't any better than the other kids there. There would be no more special treatment or sympathy since I was on the mend and almost fully recovered, regardless how I felt.

Sister Marie was kinder if Sister Mary Magdalene wasn't around. I knew she did not want to treat children badly, but when Sister Mary Magdalene was around, she had to follow her example or be in trouble herself.

Poor Barb was going through her own holy hell. I only pray that they were not touching or molesting her while I was away at school. I wanted to ask her but I did not want to tell her what was happening with us so I just kept it to myself.

I was by now used to the assaults that kept happening. It didn't take long for Father Callan to begin again with his sexual assaults. He kept telling me I provoked my mother with confrontations and I need to be punished for not being a good Catholic girl. I had better find a resolution to my bad behavior. "Why on earth would you be such a contentious and quarrelsome child involving yourself in strife and disharmony with your elders?" he would ask me.

He told me if I didn't change my ways things could go much worse for me. That scared the holy heck out of me because I did not know what he meant, but it sounded bad. Worse for me! I thought. I could not imagine what could be worse, the beating of my mother or some ill he would make up that was far more terrible than what he had already done.

Father Ferretti was another abuser; years later, the mention of his name called up the dread and darkness of his face looming before me. These "men of God" had absolutely no conscience at all or they wouldn't be doing this to the other children or to me. We could not escape what was going on.

CHAPTER TEN

As soon as we returned home, we found out that mom and dad were back together and mom had agreed not to abuse me any longer. That was it. I should have known she would connive her way back into abusing me. She told dad that Bonnie and I instigated all the trouble around the house. Deep down, I knew my father did not believe that, but I could not tell my own dad that my mom was lying to him.

Thank goodness school was out and we could have summer. Mom was less violent after talking with dad and the DFS. She wasn't beating us as severely as she did before. Now if she was unhappy, she just smacked us where the bruises wouldn't show.

When I turned nine, my dad took Bonnie and me to see *Cinderella* at the Marlowe Theatre. Watching *Cinderella* sweeping the fireplace at the behest of her awful stepsisters, watching her return to the attic each night where she visited with the mice, watching her wish for more happiness, more fun, I began to identify with her and was terribly moved. Mother, however was no stepmother, which made the truth more awful.

On Bonnie's birthday, two weeks later, we went camping. She received a fishing pole Dad made for her, and I could use it. The two of us caught rainbow trout at Park Lake. The fish arched and jumped and pulled at the line as we struggled to pull them onto shore. It was quite a commotion as we screamed with delight when we saw them glistening in the sun. Bonnie's was much bigger but she landed it. I caught two fish that day, which were smaller but I was proud of them. We had three fish between us. If a picture had been snapped you would see two small girls with big grins smiling in pure delight from ear to ear.

As we padded our way back to camp, we heard mother yelling at Barb for something. Dad asked her, "What the hell is all the yelling and commotion about? Tone it down." Barb had caught a couple of frogs and had turned them loose in the tent. Mom was fuming because she couldn't find them and oh how she hated frogs.

When the two of us walked up to the tent, she told us to drop the fish and help get the frogs out of the tent. We laughed hysterically because the boys and Barb had freaked mom out the entire time we had been fishing. Barb began to join in the laughter trying to catch the frogs and asking us what was so funny. If this isn't funny then why are you laughing we asked her while still trying to keep a straight face and couldn't. We finally admitted to her that we thought it would be funny to accidently leave one. We did not follow through with our plan. We knew we would get yelled at or worse and Barb would be in more trouble.

Mom yelled that Barb would be in trouble if the frogs were not found. Dad harped at mom that everyone in the camp could hear her screaming from here to kingdom come, and to turn it down a few notches. We laughed more at what he was saying to her. Life seemed to be more pleasant in our camp surroundings.

After camping, we were back to weeding the garden. Bonnie and I hated weeding the big garden because we did the work alone. We also ran the washing machine we did the rinsing ourselves without her yelling and telling us to do it right or else. Mom left us alone. We were very cautious with the washing machine. I was afraid of getting my fingers caught in the rollers as Bonnie pushed the clothes through to me to rinse and then I had to push them back to her.

Our grandma was coming for a visit again. She had not been feeling well, and the heat in California was getting to her and she knew it was much cooler in Montana. She enjoyed our cool evenings and sometimes had to wear a sweater to keep the chill off.

She helped Bonnie and I with our spelling and math.

She would give us treats if we were right. She told us we needed a little spoiling now and then. Mom said absolutely not which led to their last argument. "What she doesn't know won't hurt her," she giggled and gave us the candy. Grandma didn't listen to her and continued giving us little treats, which we were never used to having except when she was there, or the ones great-grandma gave us. Mom treated her own mother terribly but seemed happy when grandma first arrived. She apologized for not answering her letters as often as she should have. It didn't take long for her to begin to treat grandma in a bad way.

Grandma and mom were in a horrible argument after she was here a week. She asked mom to quit hitting and swearing at us with her F bombs. Mom told her to mind her own goddamn business. Grandma said she had enough of her rudeness. She quickly packed her bags and called a cab and kissed us goodbye. "Grandma you had only been here a week," I whined.

Grandma said, "I can't watch or listen to what is taking place any longer." She told us to write her and let her know if we were getting our birthday money. She told mom during the argument that she knew better about her spending our money. Mom would not be getting our birthday or Christmas money anymore. The checks would go directly to the children. Thank you Jesus, we knew better than to tell grandma thank you. After Grandma left, Mom went back to her yelling and screaming at us if she didn't like the way things were done.

Bonnie and I were off to camp again and we do not have to listen to mom or do all of her house chores. Dad said he was killing the chickens when we got back from camp since he knew who was taking care of them. As usual we had the time of our lives up there and the food was fabulous. Some kids complained about the food but not us. We enjoyed every bite. We participate in more activities now that we were older. We used the swimming pool and played volleyball at the YMCA camp down the road. We went to the YMCA camp for one day. They had a much nicer camp than ours. The kids in this camp were from wealthier families. The kids were nice except for a few who called us poor white kids. We had never heard that term before even when we knew we were poor.

When we get home if we got our chores done faster, we were allowed to play with the neighborhood kids more than ever before. Mom would always make us take Wesley and Barb, just so we would be able to do things for a change. We knew she was napping. We would go over to my friend's house and play hopscotch, jacks and baseball. Wes would just sit and watch since the older boys didn't want to play with him that much. My friend's sister Sandi was Barb's age so the two of them played in her house with dolls.

At the end of summer, we killed our chickens. When I saw the chicken with its head chopped off and the rest of it on the ground flopping around, I was disgusted. We had to help pluck the feathers off the beheaded chickens so they could be packaged and froze in freezer. When I saw the animals, the chickens, the rabbits, all of them waiting to be killed and then eaten, I suddenly lost my appetite for them. I could not eat them. I saw them as pets when we fed them. Nevertheless, I cringed when I was told to eat the meat or else I would just have to sit there looking at my plate, which happened a few times. We got to leave the table with food on our plate. Dad said to mom that he was not going to make us eat something we fed and took care of as children. They thought of the animals as pets he explained to mom. She said okay to this one argument. Dad knew she should not have raised the animals knowing we would get attached to them.

One morning before school, Barb could not get out of her bed. We tried to help her got up but she could not move. Mom did nothing. I sat by the bed reading to her, and tried to slide a plastic bowl under her to urinate in. I would hurry and scrub the bowl with a lot of soap before I got caught. I told mom Barb was not able to move and needed help because she had wet the bed. Mom made her lie in the wet bed. I slid a folded towel under her. Finally, mom had to get Lucille to come over again and see what was wrong with my baby sister. She told mom they would have to call an ambulance because she was paralyzed. Lucille did not know why. She asked my mom how long she had been lying there in the urine, as it smelled awful. Lucille told mom she was wrong for not getting her help much sooner than a week.

They took Barb to St. John's Hospital. She had a horrible virus that caused temporary paralysis. At the beginning, they thought it was polio, but we all had polio shots which led them to a different diagnosis. Barb was in the hospital for the first few weeks of school. Her teacher would help her get caught up when she got out of the hospital. It scared the daylights out of all of us. We thought she would be permanently paralyzed. This incident scared me enough to make me realize that I could have lost my little sister. It made me want to protect her even more from someone who would want to harm her in any way.

CHAPTER ELEVEN

When we went back to St. Helena's, Bonnie and I got new uniforms. Bonnie, for her fifth-grade year, mine for my fourth-grade year. Our new ones came with a different vest.

Father Gilmore was happy to see me. I saw his welcome smile and a wrench of dread formed in the pit of my stomach. I was again held back to being last in the confession line. He continued to molest me in the confessional that he knew he had to himself. Father Gilmore was a bold and evil man unknowingly. No one suspected him of having this lurid secret life, except for me or any other child who was going through what I was. Children were molested at the orphanage, so why not in the Confessional? No one ever caught him. Some days, he took me up to the galley. On those days, he took longer because nobody could see us. Sometimes, if he hurt me, he would cover my mouth so the sound could not be heard. I had to go back to class, with my vagina aching, feeling this wet stickiness in my underwear, and sometimes blood.

"Why, I wonder, hasn't anyone caught Father Hartman or Father Gilmore?" I didn't know any other priests at the school or at the church who behave like these men did. The exception was our other dreaded priests at the orphanage. He must have been seen since he was in charge of the nuns at the school.

I daydreamed or fell asleep a great deal in class. Sister Agnes my fourth-grade teacher asks me why I was not getting my work done. Each night, when we got home from school, I ran into the house, changed underwear and wash the soiled pair in the sink before anyone saw me.

Each night, before my dad got home, Bonnie and I swept and tidied up the house knowing how dad would praise us for our hard work, and mom wouldn't yell at us.

One time, Bonnie forgot to sweep under the counters and my mom grabbed the broom and hit her. Then she hit me with the broom handle because the floor still had crumbs on it. I had such a lump on my head that she sent me to bed before I could make a big issue of the lump. I had a terrible headache and could not eat my dinner. Bonnie had to sweep again before my father went to bed to satisfy mom.

Later Bonnie told me she asked my mother for a drink of water because she was thirsty. Mom got angry about being interrupted because she was doing something else. She picked up a hammer and hit Bonnie in the face breaking one of her teeth out and chipping another tooth in half. When I heard Bonnie scream, I ran out to the kitchen. There was a hole in Bonnie's mouth where her tooth should be, and a broken tooth next to it. Her lips were already bruised and bleeding, and blood was pouring from her gums down her chin and onto her clothes. I screamed at my mother, telling her how much Bonnie and I hated living in this house. Mom told me, "To get my goddamn ass to bed now, and mind your own goddamn business!"

I always wondered why Bonnie was alone at the table in our bedroom so much and stayed away from our mom as much as possible. Whenever she had time, Bonnie would draw beautiful pictures of deer, elk and bears. I guess that was her outlet of what was going on in this house. Mom had been swearing so much at us that we had learned to ignore the insults. She had even resorted to calling our dad names. I found it humiliating just to hear my Father called some of the names she used. I knew something was terribly wrong with my Mother for her to be so abusive to all of us. I could not say or do anything to change the circumstances; it was the same for my father. He just ignored her behavior as we did.

Mom started her beatings once again. They were uninterrupted and traumatic. The beatings became so bad that a neighbor turned her in to the Department of Family Services. Once again, they took us to St. Joseph's Orphanage. Dad wasn't home, when we were removed from home. He wasn't aware of why we were back in the orphanage.

Our sexual abusers began to do more damage. When Father Callan made me bend over for him in his office, I tried to think of something good, but when he held me down and hurt me with his penetration I couldn't think of anything good, only evil and thinking was I so bad that I deserved this kind of behavior? I apologized to Father Callan for being bad, knowing I did nothing but wanting it to end.

We had a new nun, Sister Ilna, who was there instead of Sister Marie. Sister Mary Magdalene was still there even though we wished she wasn't. Sister Mary Magdalene told us, "You know the rules by now and I shouldn't have to tell you anything." She looked straight at me as if I was the troublemaker who had caused all of the problems. Bonnie and I both felt horrible, because she did make us feel guilty. I asked if I could please be excused to go the bathroom and Sister Ilna came over and slapped me in the face, saying to me, "You do not ever interrupt someone when you are spoken to."

I cried when she struck me." I began to wet myself, as she grabbed my arm and pulled me behind her saying, I was going to be a problem around here and that Sister Mary Magdalene was right about us. After cleaning and changing my panties, she pulled me behind her and banged on Father Callan's door. After he answered the door, he excused her. Father Callan had a bed in the room with a cross over the bed. This was the place we were taken to. The sexual assaults continued on Bonnie and me. I was not sure if they had gotten to my little sister in my absence. We were left in the orphanage this time for several months then DFS returned us to our parents hoping the problem of abuse in the home was fixed.

Once we returned home a social worker would check in with our mother and make sure everything was running smoothly. For a while, there were no more incidents at our house. My mom would not have anything to do with any of the neighbors because she didn't know who had turned her in. Mom was determined to find out who the caller was. "I'll find the son-of-a-bitch and they can count on it!" she ranted in anger. "You kids keep your goddamn mouths shut..." she yelled at us "...or you won't be playing with anyone!"

We would hear her talking to herself saying that the person would pay just like she did and believe me she could be vindictive enough to start trouble. My mom did a lot of rambling and we had no idea what she meant. She talked to herself quite frequently when angered.

CHAPTER TWELVE

Poor Willard would always draw pictures and write letters to mom and they would always end up in the trash. She didn't show any feelings to any of us except to tell us that we were nothing but trouble to her. She wished she didn't have girls to deal with. Wesley was the exception. She told him, what a good boy he was. She bragged about things that he did and took him places. She left Bonnie, Barb and me with Carl, the babysitter. By the time I was ten, Mom did not even acknowledge my birthday.

Dad was working so much there was no celebrating with ice cream. The fault was my mom's, not my brother Wesley's. Wesley was a very quiet boy who meant no harm, except when he was horsing around and hitting and teasing Barbara. Mom had made comments to us that birthdays were just another day and nothing special to celebrate. I pretty much gave up on it being a special day since we never did anything special, except ice cream.

I really wanted and hoped that we would get to do some camping this summer but now that dad was working longer hours, we had to find something to entertain us for the summer without getting Mom upset so she gave us more work. Mercy arrived in the form of our neighbor, Mr. Minugh. He came knocking on our door one day, asking my father if Bonnie and I would like to help him with haying and cleaning his house. Mrs. Minugh had become too ill to do any housework. It was just a matter of time before she died. He told my father that he would put our wages to earning two horses, one for each of us. Dad told Mr. Minugh that right now we could not afford hay for horses, and that he would need help, putting up a corral and a barn for the horses. Mr. Minugh told dad that he was getting rid of his old barn. He added that he was keeping just one horse to ride. A huge black stallion that was glossy, tall, and beautiful. The two horses Bonnie and I were going to work for were a stallion that had to be gelded and a lovely Appaloosa that I had my eye on.

Dad told Mr. Minugh that we had to go to camp one week, but we could do it for the rest of the summer. He told Bonnie and me that as long as we got up early and did our chores at home, he was okay with the arrangement. Mom was furious with dad because he did not consult her. Dad told her we deserved a reward and nothing was going to get in the way of our taking advantage of it.

"What the hell do you think you're doing?" Mom screamed at dad. Mom was so angry that she was red faced and absolutely furious that dad was allowing us to have the horses without even discussing it with her further.

"I am the man of the house and what I say goes," Dad said in a harsh but firm voice to mom.

Mr. Minugh taught Bonnie and me to ride on his big stallion. He told us if we could not handle his big horse, we would not be able to handle our own. We worked hard. We stayed as late as we could at the barn. We received good meals at his house. He told us we were the hardest working kids he had ever seen. He told us how lucky our parents were to have such good girls.

It was the first time an adult had told me I was a good girl, and that I was a hard worker. "Here we have little Miss Independent," he said. I did my work without being told.

"Thank you for telling me that." I said with a big smile. "We don't get many compliments our way except from Daddy."

"Well, we will have to change that, won't we," Mr. Minugh said with a big grin on his big burly round face. He was a very tall man of six foot, three inches and well built.

We had been working for six weeks and would be leaving for camp on Monday. Mr. Minugh gave Bonnie and me extra pay. We put the money in my hiding place. I counted mine so I would know how much I had just in case mom found where we hid it. When Bonnie and I returned from our week at Lion's Sunshine Camp, Dad and Mr. Minugh surprised us with everything they had done for us. They had put the barn on a flatbed and had it trucked over to our place. Dad and two neighbors skinned lodge poles for crossbars and built a corral for the horses.

Mom told dad that the horses were not to be brought over until we had weeded the garden and finished the chores that had been left undone since we had been at camp. We had to do our laundry from camp, and theirs. The house was a mess. When we came in from weeding, Mom was watching the black and white television my parents bought while Bonnie and I were at camp. She had it on when we came in from weeding the garden. She told us, we could only watch it on weekends when the chores were done. Mr. Minugh brought our horses over the following weekend. Then he brought us two used saddles so that we did not have to ride bareback. One was Mr. Minugh's and the other belonged to his son who had a large ranch in Big Sandy.

Bonnie and I were ecstatic. We kept hugging this wonderful man who was so good to us. I told him thank you, again and again. So did Bonnie. He showed us how to put the blanket on the back of our horses and how to cinch up real tight on the saddle. He showed us how to get on the left side of the horse. He told my Dad that we had to practice cinching our horses up nice and tight so that our saddles did not come undone. We already knew how to get on a horse and to take the bridle. We were fast learners. The only time I could ride my horse was on weekends after chores, but at least for a few hours, I could get away with my sister on my Appaloosa. We rode the low, sage covered hills around Helena. My thoughts settled around the slow clip-clop of the horse's hooves. As the weather turned colder, Bonnie and I ask our dad if the barn was going to be warm enough for the horses. He told us they would be just fine. Mr. Minugh brought us a truckload of hay and wouldn't take any money from our father for it. He told dad that next year we could help him again during the summer for more hay if it was all right with our mom.

"I want you to know that the girls have been a blessing and helped me get my hay in on time. Your eldest daughter Bonnie works very hard keeping the house clean and neat," said Mr. Minugh. Dad told him that we could work for him next summer as long as we didn't let it interfere with our work at home. Our mother is the one who would be angry.

In fifth grade, dad told us that he was pulling us out of Saint Helena's after the school year was over because the school wanted a percentage of his income and we could not afford the tuition. I was ecstatic! Dad took a job with John Johnson, a house builder, and was making more money as a carpenter.

I was having what I thought of as a "normal" year. Father Gilmore's assaults were put in the back of my head. Each time I was violated, I just wanted him to finish so I could get back to class. When he assaulted me, he never talked or said anything except to shush me or place his hand tightly over my mouth in case someone came in. He pointed his finger to what he wanted done. It was usually fellatio. After I performed for him, I would go off to class, I always felt sick. My privates ached terribly. I could not tell anyone. Who would believe me if my own mother would not believe me. I did not want to be called terrible names. I felt dirty enough.

When I got home, I tried to wipe the memory of the day out. I fed my horse Patches and rode him trying to free me from the memory of the atrocities Father Gilmore performed on me. I prayed it would come to an end. I was grateful to hear my father no longer wanted us to go to St Helena's.

After I got my housework done, I would go play with the neighbor kids. Bonnie and I loved baseball and enjoyed playing it. The girls, there were six or seven of us, did pretty well against the boys.

While we were batting balls, pitching, running bases, the boys and girls ask Bonnie and me why our mother was so mean to us. We told them we had no idea. She was just an angry woman, so please, no more questions. My friend Carol piped in, "Yeah, we couldn't even have a friend come to our house because their mom didn't want anyone to know how horrible she was to them. Why do you think she chases them down over here and beats them within an inch of their lives, and then they are taken away from her?"

Carol was two years older than me and was my good friend"Her Mother doesn't let neighbor kids in the house either, she added. Their family, were Crow from Browning, Montana. Both parents were full blood and were very nice people. They had a very nice house compared to ours. They also had new furniture, whereas, Mom purchased ours at garage sales. Many times kids had made fun of us for being poor and not dressing as nice as they did. I think the whole neighborhood knew how poor our family was. It didn't bother us because we were good kids that did not get into trouble and liked everyone.

We had been asked by some of our friends if we could spend the night, but Mom would always make an excuse so we couldn't. The next time it happened, I was just going to push my luck and ask dad if I could. All she could do was spank me or hit me, and I had to take a chance regardless.

It was the weekend, dad told mom that we were going to go on a picnic and practice shooting Dad's twenty-two rifle. Bonnie was taking hunters safety and if she passed she was going to go hunting with my parents. Dad said, "If Bonnie hunts with us, it makes more meat for the table." Mom was grumbling under her breath because she had to pack a lunch. Dad was home so she couldn't make us do it. She wouldn't let dad in the kitchen. He offered to help her get things ready, but she told him to get everything in the car that we would need.

The drive up through Rimini was beautiful with leaves falling from the trees with gorgeous colors of red, orange, sienna and yellow mixed with greens. Mom and dad were both looking for a great spot for our picnic. Finally up Minnehaha Bear Gulch, Dad found what looked like a nice area with the mountain as a backdrop for target practicing.

I asked Daddy if I could please shoot the gun too. He said if it was okay with Mom, it was okay with him. She said I needed to put all the articles onto the picnic cloth for lunch and then I could. Bonnie and I were both excellent shots. Dad brought the targets in so we could see how well we did.

Mom said that lunch was ready and for all of us to sit down so she could dish up. It was a fun and enjoyable day. We were just finishing our lunch when dad asked us all to be very quiet. Dad pointed to the bushes. He heard noises in the far brush. He carefully grabbed the twenty-two and put bullets in the chamber and set it down on the picnic blanket with us. It was quiet, very, very quiet. Then suddenly as quick as I could blink, a black bear came charging out of the brush. Dad grabbed the gun and started shooting the bear as she charged straight at us. Dad was yelling to Mom "Get the kids in the car right now! He continued shooting anyway. All of the action took place in just a matter of seconds. The bear fell just before it got to the car. I was trembling so badly I couldn't stop shaking and tears were welling up in my eyes from fear. My brother and sisters were also shaking and crying.

Dad told mom not to let us out of the car for any reason, and to keep the doors and windows closed. He had to check if there was another bear or if she had cubs. He needed to find out. Mom was screaming for him to reload the gun. Dad went over to the bear he shot and made sure it was dead. Then he proceeded very slowly to the brush and found nothing. He looked further and found two cubs. He told mom he needed to drive into Rimini and call Fish and Game and tell them what had happened and that two cubs needed help.

"You are not leaving us here in the damn woods," my mom said. "What is wrong with you woman," my dad laughed? "Do you really think I would do that, use your head for heaven's sake?" We stayed in the car while Dad tied the dead bear to our front bumper. Mom had to help him get it on, pulling it up with the rope. It took forever. In the meantime we kids sat in the car crying about the bear that almost got us.

We pulled our car into Rimini and Dad used someone's phone to warn the Fish and Game about the cubs that were without a mother. Dad also told them about killing a bear out of season. We were up Minnehaha Gulch and the bear began to attack my family he explained to the officer. They told Dad to take the bear with him to our house and they would talk to us there. They sent an officer to go and find the cubs. Dad left a torn red flag tied to a tree by the road, to mark the place where the cubs could be found.

Upon our arrival home there was a Fish and Game truck in the alley where dad parked the car by the garage. They talked to Mom and Dad and then they talked to us. Dad was told to hang the bear in the garage until the wardens got back to him. The next day when Dad came home from work, the Fish and Game were back at our house. They had ticketed my dad fifty dollars for shooting a bear out of season. That was a lot of money in the fifties. Money we didn't have.

The Independent Record wrote an article about a man defending his family and the town was outraged that my father was ticketed for defending his family from a charging bear. The Fish and Game revoked the ticket and returned the money back to my father. Dad got an apology from them plus his money back. He also got to keep the bear rug. To this day I am scared to death of bears from this one incident.

It didn't take long for the fall months to get cold. It would soon be snowing and I loved the snow.

CHAPTER THIRTEEN

One winter day, Father Gilmore was particularly angry. He was brutal, pushing me down, telling me to lie still and not move at all. I was crushed underneath his weight, as he lay on top of me. He almost smothered me. When he finished, I hurt so badly that I ran to class, crying, trying to wipe the tears away so no one would see my face. When class began, Sister Bernadine asked why I had been crying after confession with Father Gilmore. I told her I had to go back after lunchtime and that he had never made me do that before.

When I walked into the cathedral, it was so quiet. I looked at the rows of benches that were polished and empty. They seemed to march up to the gold altar. I looked for him everywhere, hoping I would not find him. Turning around, I saw him standing at the back of the church. He told me to come up to him. He then took me to the choir balcony. And there, in this room washed in red and blue light from the stained glass window, he made me pull my panties down. He pulled me over and turned me around. Then he turned me around spread my legs, and made me sit on his penis. He was brutal. His sexual pleasure hurt me. He did not care about the harm he inflicted upon me. "This," he told me, was for being a rebellious, obstinate child from the previous time and not paying attention to what I asked of you. You are being punished for all your sins. This is what will happen to you. I was only teaching you what God wants you to learn how to prepare yourself as an adult." As he was jerking inside me, I was crying. He told me I brought everything, all of this, on myself. He placed his hand over my mouth and told me, "I needed to learn when and where to be quiet. Quit crying like a baby and acting so innocent when you know you are enjoying this. I am making sure you don't." I lay there quietly crying. "Enough of your nonsense and lay still, he said, "and there will be no pain." This time the pain was excruciating. When he was finished, I pulled up my panties, straightened up my skirt. I was still crying.

We walked down from the narrow stairs from the choir loft. He made me walk with him to the first row of pews. "Kneel!" he says sharply. He told me to say the Apostle's Creed three times until I understood what Jesus has done for me and to repent my sins. Then I had to say the Seven Sacraments before I was allowed to go back to class. Why was I being punished so severely I ask the Lord in prayer? What have I done to dishonor you and the Church? Why was I such an evil girl that I had to be punished so?

Father Gilmore sat in the pew behind me. As I knelt at the altar, saying the rosary: "Hail Mary, full of grace. The Lord was with thee. Blessed art thou amongst women, and blessed was the fruit of thy womb Jesus. Holy Mary, Mother of God, pray for us sinners, now and at the hour of our death, AMEN"

Sister Bernadine walked in; she asked Father Gilmore why I was away from her class so long. His face was angry. He told her, "This child's behavior does not concern you and do not interrupt my disciplining of a child again in the church. You have no business ever leaving your class. Do not let it happen again, EVER!"

As I prayed at the altar, I thought, if only she had come over sooner and looked for Father Gilmore she might have discovered what he was actually doing. Then again, I suppose nothing would have happened to him. He was the one in charge around here.

When I finished with the rosary, he let me go back to class. On my way back, I thought about the words rebellious and obstinate. I had no clue as to their meaning, but I was sure I was going to look them up. They were the same words Father Callan used to describe me. I had no idea what they meant, but both priests used the words a lot. I couldn't help but wonder if that was what I was to them.

I hate Father Gilmore with every fiber of my heart. I knew that I was a good child and had not done anything to hurt anyone. I had never hated like this. But, if anyone knew the hell I was living in they would understand why I hated these men. They were supposed to be like God, loving and forgiving and kind. I felt filthy, like I had let God down in some way. He was all I had in life besides my family right now. I was never sure of my mother's love. She wouldn't beat us making us feel bad if she loved us.

When my mother picked us up from school that day she was going on and on about all of the chores we had to do when we got home. All I could think about was what just happened to me. I broke down and cried. I could not understand why Sister Bernadine was being yelled at for trying to find a missing student. I was crying because none of this was coming to an end and I just wanted to be a little girl. I knew that Sister had an idea of what was taking place and that was why she came looking for me.

Barb was hugging me in the back seat, trying to console and make me feel better, but no one could at that moment. I didn't want to live anymore like this. My Mom screamed at the top of her lungs, "What the hell are you bawling about? You know you have work after school. If you don't turn it off, I will give you something to cry about." I couldn't tell her what happened because she would beat me and call me a liar and a whore again. I stopped crying before she could pull over.

When school was out for Christmas vacation, I was feeling a little bit better about not attending school. But, little Barb started clinging to me as if she knew what I was going through. I let her hang around with me when I went out to feed my horse, Patches, and Bonnie was feeding her horse. I asked Barb what she wanted from Santa for Christmas. She told me "We never get anything for Christmas from Santa. There was no Santa because he doesn't come to see us and bring us presents. I am not dumb; I know that the Salvation Army truck brings us food and gifts."

"Last year we got a gift from him," I replied. "You just don't remember." I knew this was a lie. "He is coming to our house this year," I told her. I stopped what I was doing and hugged her so she would feel better. I knew she was upset because of what Mom did to me in the car.

CHAPTER FOURTEEN

It was time to cut down the Christmas tree. This time, the entire family piled in the car with Daddy and we went up to Great-Grandma's house at Priest Pass out of Baxendale to get the tree and have supper with her. Mom stayed at the house with Great-Grandma while Dad and the rest of us went looking for the perfect tree. We walked in the forest thrashing through the thick pines behind her home. We heard all kinds of animal sounds among the small and large pine and Douglas fir. Finally, we found the perfect tree. Barb wanted to know if we might run into a bear out here. Dad knew she was thinking about the black bear incident. He told her they were in hibernation and she had nothing to fear.

Grandma cooked chicken and dumplings for us and gave us homemade pie with cherries she had brought from Flathead Lake. She topped the pie off with vanilla ice cream. Bonnie, Barb and I helped her clean up the kitchen. She slipped us our goody bags that she had made up for us ahead of time. As soon as the dishes were done, she softly whispered in our ears, "Hide your little goodies." Then she gave us a little pat on our behinds saying she loved us. We had to leave quickly as the roads were becoming very icy.

When we got home, we put up our tree. Mom and Dad strung up the lights and then Bonnie and I put on the decorations. Dad placed the star at the top. Bonnie and I put the tinsel on, one strip at a time. We showed Barb how to hang the tinsel on the lower branches.

Dad had the television on and we got to watch *A Christmas Carol* for the first time. Mom told him it was our bedtime, but Dad said we could stay up and watch the show and then go to bed, since we didn't have school during vacation. He told her we never stayed up late and tonight we could. On Christmas day, Bonnie and I got books to read. Barb received a little desk that lit up. Wesley opened his toy cars. We were disappointed that Willard didn't get to come home. My sisters, brother, and I knew Mom would not drive on the bad roads to Boulder to get him for a few days. We felt she did not want him here.

After New Year's Day, all of us helped to take the tree down. Mom had a conniption fit when Dad threw the tree out with the tinsel on it. She wanted us to save all the tinsel so we didn't have to replace it next year. "Are you going to force the girls to do that job?" He laughed and said, "I already know the answer to that one."

"Then why the hell did you have to ask me?" she responded. He continued laughing and saying how ludicrous it was.

Once I was back in school, all I could think about was getting out of St. Helena's and the Church. I daydreamed about being in another home with someone who loved me as they would their own child. I dreamed of being adopted into another family. Then all of a sudden I would come back to reality, and think how very much I would miss my daddy if that were to happen. At this point in my childhood, I hated my life because of what had been done to me.

I would pray that the Lord would make me strong and keep the nightmares away and let good thoughts run into my head as I tried to get a much needed good night's sleep. I tried so hard to think good thoughts and of pleasant things. I fell asleep quickly and my wishful thoughts soon became lost to nightmares.

I was being chased through halls and trying to run as fast as I could. I tripped and fell on the priest's robes as he caught up with me. Other priests had followed behind him grabbing at my clothes and calling me a sinner. They grabbed at my clothes undressing me while smothering me with their hands over my face. I was trying to breathe as someone was on top of me. I woke up in a cold sweat and crying. I lay awake praying to God to stop these awful nightmares. I was telling myself, that this was my punishment from God repeating over and over again, "I am sorry dear God. Please forgive me, please…"

CHAPTER FIFTEEN

In May, Mr. Minugh told my father; he could use his horse trailer, to go up to Big Sandy to fetch two more horses for us. Dad had done odd jobs and we helped clean his house over the winter to earn both horses. We would be staying overnight with his son and his son's family. We returned with horses that were, in theory, broken. Bonnie and I were excited to have the horses and be able to teach Barb to ride when mom allowed it. Wesley did not like the horses. He was allergic to them and had to stay clear or his face would swell and his eyes would close shut.

After a long drive we arrived in Big Sandy. Mr. Minugh's son was very nice. His wife fed us and made us comfortable for the night. They had a beautiful ranch. Bonnie and I got to ride horses with his two sons. Then, dad said we had to load up the horses and get on the road before it was too late in the day. Dad and Mr. Minugh's son had an easy time loading the filly in the trailer but the black stallion was another story. He wanted nothing to do with the trailer and kept backing out and kicking at it. Finally, they backed him in with his behind, and then he moved into the trailer while they quickly locked the door. On our way home, you could hear the black horse kicking and moving about while Dad fought to keep the truck on the road. When we got home, the two men couldn't unload the black horse fast enough. The filly backed peacefully out of the trailer.

The stallion immediately started stirring up trouble with the other horses. After haltering him, Dad made him settle down and behave. Bonnie wanted the black one, and I told her okay after watching his behavior. Her other horse, Lightning, was not too happy that Bonnie was giving all of her attention to the new horse. Dad told her to go over and worry about Lighting while he tried to get the black settled down. Then he added, "And Bonnie, he needs to be broken and gelded before you can ride him." I was so relieved!

I wanted the sandy colored filly that was three years old, and sweet as could be. She got along with the other horses and they got along with her. As soon as we fed and watered the horses and gave them a bucket of oats, mom was yelling at us, to get our ass's in the goddamn house right now before she beat us.

Dad told us we had better get in the house and get on with our housework and laundry before the shit hits the fan. "I do not want to listen to your mom bitch anymore today. I had enough all the way home, hearing about two more horses to care for," he said. Patches, my other horse ambled over for some love and attention. I hurriedly gave Patches a hug and ran off with Bonnie. Poor dad went off to take a nap because he had to work early in the morning.

The next morning when we got up for school, we were exhausted from the busy weekend, but we were excited about our new horses. Bonnie named her horse Dynamite. I named my filly, Sandy, the color of her hair. We knew we would share the horses with our little sister Barb when she was older, but for now they were ours.

By the end of May, I was finished with Saint Helena's Catholic School. I did not have to ever again see the faces of those evil men who call themselves priests and Apostles of Christ. I celebrated my eleventh birthday without a party, as mom never allowed us the privilege of one, or let us at least have friends come over to play. But, I knew those priests would never again abuse me. We were over wanting birthday parties. That was the least of our problems. Now, I was celebrating having my life back and trying not to look back at my childhood abuse.

~~~

My Aunt Dolly started to come around more to visit us once she and my uncle divorced. He was an alcoholic who was horrible to her when he was drunk. He would beat her and yell and kick at the kids. That was why dad did not go visit them much. He loved his sister but not her husband.

Growing up, my Aunt Dolly was raised around horses and was known as a top-notch horsewoman. They broke and gelded their horses on great-grandma's ranch. Aunt Dolly was the one who always brought the cattle in. She arranged to help us train our horses to take our commands whenever she had free time on her hands.

She was a good mother to her children and objected to what our mother was putting us through. At times, I wished she had been my mother and she likewise wished I had been her daughter. She always hugged and kissed me when she came over and told me how much she loved Barb and me. I was happy when she started coming around more after she and mother had the disagreement over the abuse we were receiving and the locks that were still on the cupboards.

I would be going to Central School for the sixth grade, and Bonnie would be in the seventh at Helena Junior High in the fall. Barb and Wes would be at Broadwater for the new school year. I was happy it was summer and really happy since I was finally away from the ugliness of the past. I even forgot about mom's temper when she was upset with us, but at this point I didn't care anymore.

Mom and Dad joined a new organization in Helena, *Search and Rescue*. They were both excited about it. Dad enjoyed helping others. We were dropped off at Memorial Park while our parents went to the meeting. At first, we enjoyed having all the time in the world to swing on the swings, spin on the merry-go-round, and slide up and down the slide. But after a while without anything to eat or drink, we began to get restless and hungry. When they finally arrived to pick us up we were hungry because we had missed lunch. We wanted to go home and have supper.

Once the swimming pool opened, we got to swim one of the two days on the weekend, but the rest of the time the park was our home. Mom dropped us off at the park while she went shopping and frequented garage sales. She left us there most of the day with nothing to eat. Bonnie and I were babysitting Wes and Barb, who were now six and seven. We had to watch them in the park at all times. Barb was easy to take care of because she would cling to me and would not let me out of her sight. Wesley, however, loved to wander off. I had to tell him to stay close. Sometimes I lost him and had to look all over for him. I would often find him watching the kids in the pool.

Bonnie and I searched for pop bottles and beer bottles. We put them in a wagon and took them to Moore's Grocery Store to get the three cents a bottle refund. We saved the money so we could buy food and candy when mom left us at the park with nothing to eat for the day. Sometimes I saved change for emergencies. One of us would run to the diner across the street from the park and order a burger or fries and then we would share the food among us. The people who owned the restaurant noticed that we were dumped off daily at the park and would give us an extra burger and fries. They could see the four of us in the park, day after day, without food or anything to drink except for the water in the drinking fountain. We thanked them profusely. They told us just to keep it quiet and not tell other children about it.

At home, Bonnie, Barb, and I were cleaning, washing, ironing and feeding the horses as quickly as we could. We wanted to get outside to play baseball with the neighbor kids as we could hear their laughter and the chattering as they played. We loved playing baseball since it was one thing we truly enjoyed, besides riding our horses. During the summer months, someone was always outside playing ball. Everyone enjoyed the game.

I loved playing baseball. I loved swinging the bat, the crack of the wood on the ball, the race to first base hoping I would make it before being tagged out, and the excitement of running base to base ahead of the ball, and finally, the slide to home. When I played baseball, I gave myself up to the game. We had regular neighborhood pickup games, each kid in the neighborhood had a place and we played hard. We played for our lives, which was why, the day my mother who had been calling us, was not heard. No one saw her coming towards us holding a board as someone was running from second to third.

"Get your ass's over here right now before I get the belt," she yelled at us. "Right now or I will use this board," she continued shouting!

I looked at Bonnie and she looked at me. We knew we were in big trouble. She grabbed Bonnie by her hair and held her tight. The kids in the field stood motionless. No one made a sound. Then Mom turned to me, took the board, and hit me. She missed my bottom and hit my back. I fell to the ground trying to escape her swings. She kept hitting and hitting. Finally, our neighbor Ruth ran out of her house and yelled at Mom to stop or she would call the authorities. "I am not kidding Helen. I will run in and call them right now!"

"Mind your own goddamn p's and q's and get your ass in your own house!" Mom screamed. "I'll take care of my own business and you take care of yours." Ruth didn't move. "I told you to get your goddamn ass in your own house and I mean it, unless you want some of this too!" my mother yelled at her.

Ruth ran into her house and called the police. This was the woman who took mother in when she beat me and damaged my kidneys.

"Now you have the goddamn neighbors involved in our business. Just wait until I get your asses home!" she was yelling at us. She was still swinging her board at whatever she could hit. I lay on the ground and tried to catch my breath. Bonnie and I were crying.

"Now get your ass moving, she said for a second time as I laid there. "Your damn horses are gone. Your dad has nothing to say about them, now get the f—k moving."

"I can't wait till dad hears what you did," I muttered under my breath. As soon as she pulled Bonnie and me into the house, she grabbed me by the hair. "I heard that," she said. She pulled my long brown hair and hit me again and again. Barb was screaming now. I fell to the floor, crying, and trying to cover up the welts and bruises from the board. My sisters were crying too.

My mother told me if I said one word to my dad about this incident that I would be shipped off to the Good Shepherd Home for wayward girls and your sister will go with you. I had my share of Catholic Schools for "good" girls. I could not imagine what happened in a Catholic home for bad girls.

Barb said to mom, "Daddy is going to hear what you did from the neighbors and not from us. The police were going to come, and I am going to tell them what you did to us." Barb was fearless.

"You shut your trap and get your ass to bed if you don't want any of this," mom responded.

I went into the bedroom and told Barb I would check on her later and told her "Thanks!"

My mom sent Bonnie and me to take care of the horses so we would be outside and not in the house when my dad got home or if the police came. The two of us were hurting pretty badly. Some of my hair was pulled out in patches as well as Bonnie's. Bonnie and I stayed out in the barn, brushing our horses. It hurt me to move the brush over the horses wide back. My horse was my only comfort right at this moment. I hugged Patches, seeking comfort in the warm, dusty smell of his bristly hide. When Dad called us to dinner and saw the red marks on our faces, arms, and on my legs, he asked, "What on earth happened to you girls?"

Mom told him, "Wanda pulled Bonnie off the fence and they both were hurt."

I knew deep down he couldn't have believed that story, or could he? I would never know. Bonnie wanted to tell dad what really had happened. I was so sorry she didn't, but I wouldn't have had the guts to either. She would have paid dearly if she had told Daddy what truly had taken place. So, we BOTH fell from the same fence. "What are the odds on that one?"

93

That was the beginning of the new threats towards Bonnie and me. Once again, she was beating us. We became her punching bags, her outlet for her insidious anger.

That summer, Bonnie and I couldn't get away to camp fast enough. As Bonnie and I were packing, mom asked Dad, "Who the hell was going to feed those horses with those girls gone?"

Dad said, "They do enough of your housework and you can feed their horses—quit complaining and trying to make a big deal out of them having horses. Besides, Wesley could help you too. Quit trying to take things away from those girls. You know what, you aren't happy unless you were complaining about the girls doing something wrong because in your eyes they don't do anything right as far as your concerned."

When we got to camp, we still had our bruises. Some hurt, but we didn't care because we were away from home, or the place the two of us called "The Hell Hole".

One morning I woke up with a terrible headache and I start vomiting. "What's wrong with you today," my worried counselor asked. The counselor took me to the infirmary. I had my headache all day, but I was released to go back to my cabin. The nurse came to check on me, by that time, my headache was letting up a little. In the morning it had dissipated, and I felt better. She told me I needed to give my parents a note that I'd had a migraine.

The rest of my time at camp I was fine. I participated in track and did well, as I loved to run. My parents did not attend any of the skits that we put on. I was sure my mother said it cost too much to drive up to see a skit, but we had fun doing it anyway. We made birdhouses out of Popsicle sticks. We sat up and told ghost stories around the campfire while we roasted marshmallows and stayed up late without anyone telling us we had to go to bed. At night, I could hear the crickets and the owls hoot. I could hear the coyotes and wolves howling. When I woke up in the morning, the first sounds were the meadowlarks and other birdcalls. I could watch the hum of hummingbirds around the feeders that were set up around the camp.

As an adult, I look back at that camp and I know now that it saved my life in so many ways. This was an outlet where I could eat well and sleep peacefully. It was one of the few happy times in my early life. I had some stability that was free of abuse. The kids at camp would be in school with me in the fall.

I wasn't looking forward to Mom picking us up. As soon as I saw our car, my stomach knotted. We got off the bus, picked up our suitcases, and walked over. My mother didn't get out of the car, didn't help us with our things or ask if we needed help. All she said was "The minute that we get home, I want that goddamn house spotless before your father comes home. You better not open your traps and say anything to your dad!" She emphasized louder, "Do you hear me clearly?"

When we arrived home, she told us to get our dirty laundry out while she gathered the other laundry from the bathroom and told us to get the washing done first. Bonnie and I told her we had to feed our horses. "Those goddamn horses can wait!" she replied angrily. "You were not going out to the horses until every single chore is done."

As we were washing the clothes, Barb told Bonnie and me that our mom and dad had a fight while we were gone. We asked her what it was about and she said that Dad told Mom to get off her lazy butt and get the house clean. Barb reports that Mom said that Bonnie and Wanda had to clean the house when they got back. He said, "Like hell they will." And the fight was on. We laughed when she told us the story. I could picture it as clear as day.

Her eyes grew large and she brought her finger to her mouth. "Shhhh," she said. "I don't want to get hit for telling you about it as Bonnie and I were laughing our butts off. We rolled in laughter over our parents arguing. We knew Mom completely deserved our father's wrath for her laziness.

I asked Barb if Mom ever hit her when we were not

95

around. Her answer was "Yes," but, she paused, "She doesn't hit me as bad as she hits you guys."

When Dad came home that night, he hugged Bonnie and me and told us we could ride our horses after supper. Mom said,we had to wait until the dinner dishes were done.

Dad responded, "The damn dishes can wait, the girls haven't been on the horses for over a week."

At the barn, Dad helped us saddle up Patches and Lightning and we rode all the way over to the road to Mr. Minugh's house, a pretty good distance from our house. Patches loved to lope so Lightning loped alongside. It felt good to ride again. Dad let us ride warning us we had until eight o'clock since it didn't get dark till ten o'clock at night. Dad complimented us on our riding, keeping the corral clean, and the horses brushed like they should be. We just once wanted one compliment like this from our mother. We knew that was not going to happen.

When we returned home, the sink was full of frothy and bubbly dishwater. Dad must have had mom run it. She was in the living room watching her television programs, *Grand Ole Opry* and *The Lawrence Welk Show*. When Barb came in the kitchen to help Bonnie and me, mom yelled at her to go to her room and leave the dishes for us. When we were done, we asked if we could watch TV. Mom said no. She said we had to get up early for chores so she could go to town to get groceries; it was clear we were going to the park to watch the kids.

The next day at the park, Barb was excited because she didn't get to do anything while we were gone. I asked Mom if we could swim at Memorial Pool. She said, "Hell no, hell no, do you think we were made out of money." This was now one of her favorite sayings. I told Barb, we could ask Daddy this weekend.

Around two o'clock, I was on the big bar, pumping the swing high enough so that I could hang by my knees. Barb loved to watch me. She laughed and clapped her hands. "More, more," she cried. As I was pumping very high, then suddenly my shoe slipped off the bar. I fell about eight or ten feet to the ground and was knocked unconscious. Bonnie ran to get help.

By the time the ambulance arrived, a crowd of people had gathered around me. My mom pulled up in the car and saw I was lying on the ground. She came running over and asked the other kids what the hell happened to me. The paramedics told her she had to follow them to the hospital in her own vehicle. Mom told them to take me to Dr. Marcellus's office instead, because she could not afford the emergency room.

The ambulance took me to St. Peter's Hospital. We went to St. Peter's since it was the closest. I had broken my shoulder in three places and had broken myHumerus bone. They had to make a special cast that was attached around my body. I also had a severe concussion and had to be watched for seventy-two hours. I was in a great deal of pain so the doctors administered small doses of codeine to ease my pain.

When I was released, my family was due to go over to the Montana School for the Mentally Retarded (now the Montana Developmental Center) to pick up Willard. My dad arranged to have Bonnie stay home with me and to have Carl come babysit me. Carl felt terrible for me. He pampered me and asked if I needed anything. Carl had his younger sister Sandi bring me a Popsicle from their house. His mom who was an LPN and a friend of our family also came over to check on me. Carl let Sandi stay to visit with me while our parents were gone that afternoon. It was an unusual event because my mom never let my friends come into our house.

Mom and Dad arrived home with Willard at dinnertime. Dad was cooking dinner and asked me what I felt like eating. I asked Willard what he wanted to eat, he said, "Cheeseburgers!"

"Cheeseburgers it is," Dad replied with a big grin. Willard's eyes lit up. It was clear he had not eaten a cheeseburger in a long time.

Willard stood by my chair. He wanted to hug me but

dad told him in the car that I was hurt. He kept asking me, "What is wrong sister? What's wrong?" He was a little kid of four, even though he was ten, but his brain did not work right.

Bonnie took Willard out to see the horses and reminded him not to go out there unless one of us was with him. Dad told Bonnie, she had to watch him close because the other kids wouldn't and he could get seriously hurt if he crawled through the fence.

Mother and Wesley were annoyed with Willard's repetition. It gave me a lot of satisfaction that he annoyed them so much. While he was home, my mother would have nothing to do with him. She told him to go away because she was too busy or to leave her alone because she couldn't read with his jabbering. My little brother was just a child who desperately wanted to be loved by his mommy and she didn't love him back. So very sad, the sadness in his eyes was very apparent.

My injury put the workload on Bonnie and Barb. Barb had to do the chores with us now. I reminded them that dad said we were going camping while Willard was home, if I was up to it. I told them not to worry I would be fine whether it was the truth or not, even if I wasn't up to camping, I would never turn down the offer! It would be unfair, especially for Willard, who never got to go out on camping trips with the family.

It was a lot of work when Willard was home but it was worth it so we could be with him. I was saddened that mother could not show affection or that she cared. She repeatedly would tell him to go away.

We were packing up for camping. Dad had taken a few days off from work so we could camp for five days. I felt bad for Bonnie because I couldn't help pack, I couldn't make beds with one hand, and I had to be careful because I was top heavy with all the casting. Dad said it would be better if I took Willard on a walk and just stayed out of the way so they could get things done.

Willard and I went for a walk and I helped him look for

the leaves and moss he wanted to collect for a project he was working on for my father's birthday. He wanted to finish it before he went back to the Home because they would not mail it for him. I told him I would help him the best I could. I asked what he was making for daddy. He told me he had some tiny rubber animals to place on a piece of bark. He wanted to find tiny leaves with stems for trees and little pebbles to look like boulders with moss to represent the forest floor. Then he began to go off in his own private language, which I never could understand.

Willard was one of the sweetest children, and I was patient with him as he faded in and out of his thoughts and speech. I knew what he wanted to do. He said "Daddy could put it in the garage where he worked a lot when he was home. It will remind Daddy of me and he won't forget me."

"Willard that was very sweet of you to want to make this for daddy," I replied. I told him "How sweet it was and that his daddy was never going to forget him and to always remember that." I realized it made him happy. I told him we would find everything and put it in a bag and finish it at home since we had no glue to put it together.

We found a cool piece of driftwood that Willard was so thrilled with that he jumped up and down with excitement, his eyes bulging out. It was L-shaped, with knots and crevices and little holes in different areas. I reminded him not to say anything to Dad because it was a surprise. We continued looking for materials. I found some great spindly-looking tree moss. I told him we would look over the next few days for rocks from Park Lake and tiny leaves with long stems. I told him we would watch for other things to add to the bag as we walked along. I loved watching him enjoy his walk. He was sharp, in his own way. He could repair televisions and most electrical equipment when he was deep in thought with nobody disturbing him.

When we got back to Park Lake and settled into the campsite, I asked Dad if I could fish one-handed, if someone would cast and help me unhook the fish, if I were to catch one. He told me he would cast my line for me, and I would just have to sit back and wait for a fish to bite my bait, and then he would reel it in for me. Better than nothing I thought. I did not want to be at the campsite listening to my mom grumble about how much she had to do. Dad told Willard he would come back for him when the fish were biting and that he had to wait at camp for a while because he was being too loud. I asked Dad why he could not fish with us. Dad said his loud voice would scare the fish away. We let him come over for a little while after we caught several fish for dinner.

Bonnie, Barb, Dad and I sat a while. We had to be patient to get the big ones. Bonnie caught a fish right away, and then Barb did. Dad and I waited then he moved upstream a bit and caught quite a few. I had nothing so he recast my line because the worm was gone. Daddy went to get Willard. He made him stand next to him so my dad could help him cast. Willard was so excited with his pole bouncing up and down. Daddy helped him, telling him he must be quiet to catch his fish. Finally, the pole bent and Willard felt the weight of the beautiful fish he caught. He was overjoyed, catching his first big fish. Wesley also caught a couple more fish. He was fishing upstream from us. I wasn't as lucky—I didn't catch anything—but my prize was seeing the joy and surprise on Willard's face that day. His laughter and joy in those big brown eyes was enough to create the memory forever.

Dad cleaned the fish so mom could fix dinner. It was a late dinner, and I was tired from the pain medication I was taking. After eating, I ran out of the tent and into the woods throwing up. I was sick all night. I fell asleep and do not remember anyone going to bed. Dad told Mom he thought it was the pain medicine and to see if I could go without it.

I just wanted to have fun and fish. I enjoyed camping and fishing. This trip was fun because our brother, Willardwas with us. Even Wesley had fun trying to catch frogs, tadpoles, and tree lizards with us. We all had a great day together with no arguments or squabbling amongst us. Daddycooked the fish that night and Mom made herself a sandwich because she hated fish. Dad told her to pick the bones out of Willard and Barb's fish so they wouldn't get any caught in their throats. The rest of us knew how to remove our own bones. Nothing was as delicious as fresh caught rainbow trout cooked over a campfire. Dad wrapped the fish in foil and let them cook in a little butter with salt and pepper. We loved the trout with baked potatoes and corn on the cob. I thought this was our best camping trip. I wished we could have stayed longer.

When we got home Willard wanted to work on his project. I told him I had to do chores. Dad went out to take care of the horses. He unloaded the camping gear and put it away. Fortunately, the house was cleaned before we left so all we had to do was get the kids to take their baths so we could wash the family's camping clothes. I hated the smell of the old campfire on the clothes. We had to use rose water to get rid of the smell. I hated the old washing machine and wished it would break down so we could get a new one. We were too poor to buy a new washer. We hung our clothes on the clothesline. The next day I did the ironing.

I helped Willard with his project. Mom made us work on the project outside on a wooden crate. She did not want us to make a mess in the house or make any noise while she watched television. Willard was excited gluing on the leaves that had dried a little. He was just happy to see it take shape and to do most of the work. He was happy with the finished product. I told him I would sneak in and get some Christmas wrap because I knew mom would say "no" if I asked her. She kept it in the closet in the hallway.

We put Willard's gift on dad's workbench to surprise him. I told Willard to put it right next to the tools our dad always used so he would see it right away. Then Willard and I went out to see the horses. He didn't get to be around the horses very much because dad was afraid he could be hurt again. Willard did not understand how he frightened the horses.

The next day Willard would have to go back to Boulder, I went to Dad that evening and whispered in his ear that Willard had made a gift for him; it was in the garage. Dad went outside and Willard followed him, hoping he would go to the garage. Willard peeked in the garage as his dad opened the gift. Willard raised his arms and yelled with joy and excitement.

Dad examined Willard's beautiful present, he paused and said, "Thank you, son, this gift was very thoughtful of you to make it. I will keep it right here to remind me of you, Willard."

"Do you like it Dad?" Willard repeated over and over. "Settle down son," my Father said, "I love it!" Dad knew Mom would not allow the gift of wood and leaves in the house, so he would keep it in the garage where he could see it when he worked.

The entire family traveled to Boulder to take Willard back. Seven of us were cramped in the car and it was hot and muggy. In the 1950s, there were no seat belts or air conditioning. Thank goodness Dad was a good driver. Mom didn't want to pay for a babysitter so I had to ride in front with her and Dad so no one would bump my shoulder or arm. My mother had bad body odor because she seldom bathed or took care of herself. It was not pleasant riding next to my mother. I asked Daddy if he would roll his window down because it was hot. He told everyone to roll his or her windows down as well so we could cool off the inside of the car. He must have smelled it too. I wondered how he did it with Mom.

At Boulder, we all said goodbye to Willard. We were hugging him, while Wes hovered in the corner. Before he was out of the car, Willard started sobbing and then it became a tantrum. We were sobbing, until mom told us to "shut the hell up," or she would shut us up herself. "I've had enough of your racket." I am not taking it anymore," she threatened.

That summer, Bonnie rode our horses. We did our chores and were dropped off at the park when my parents went shopping or went to meetings with *Search & Rescue*. I was still in my cast, so I couldn't do much but watch everyone else. At least we were not left as long as before. I think it was because the doctors told them that I needed to rest, and my father knew with the August heat it could make me ill. Once in a while my father would lift me onto Patches. It was hard for him to get me on and off Patches with my cast. He did not want me to ride my horse, but it was the only bit of fun I could have for what was left of summer. He finally told me I could not ride until my cast came off. He was worried that I could get hurt in another accident.

When Aunt Dolly came to visit, she saddled Patches so Barb could ride with her. She said horses needed to be ridden and Barb loved riding with her. She felt very safe with our aunt.

CHAPTER SIXTEEN

At the end of the summer I started school at Central School. I had a nice teacher, Mrs. Spaulding, who let us have a free morning so we could get to know each other. This was so different from Catholic school. I was thrilled. My grades improved immensely. I loved my teacher. I was happy. All through the sixth grade I did very well. I actually won some school spelling bees.

At home, however, my mom's abuse was spiraling out of control. I was afraid we would be taken away again and sent to the orphanage. I did not want that to happen. I never want to go back to that orphanage or the school again. It was a nightmare from all of those years being violated without anyone protecting me, a nightmare that continued in my dreams for years.

My teacher sent a note home to my parents asking if I could participate in the city spelling bee. I was a top speller at Central School. Dad said yes and Mom reluctantly allowed me to participate. I won the spelling bee and was chosen to go to Great Falls for the State Bee. Mom refused to drive to Great Falls. I told Mrs. Spaulding that my mom would not let me go, because she would not drive me there. Mrs. Spaulding called my house and talked to my father and told him she would take me. If I won the State Bee, the school would raise the money for me to go to the National Bee in Washington, D.C. Dad told Mom the problem was solved. I wanted to win so badly, but I took third instead. My teacher said to try again next year. But that wasn't going to happen. My mother threw a fit when I came home. She told me she was tired of my manipulating my father. I had better watch myself before asking my father first about anything before asking her.

I told myself I was going to run away. I didn't care

anymore. As soon as I was happy, Mom took away all the joy, or what little I had, and ruined it. Why she had so many kids but never wanted to be bothered with us I would never understand. It was a horrible feeling growing up and knowing that your mother could not tell you she loved you and that you could not tell her the same. I could not feel love for someone who hurt me like my mother did.

Sixth grade was a breeze. I was still in a cast at the beginning of the school year because my upper long bone in my arm had not yet healed. Of course, my mother made a point of telling Mrs. Spaulding that I didn't need help with my work, as I was ambidextrous and would be able to use my left hand even though I usually used my right.

My cast was finally removed in January with my arm and body looking thin and very scaly from wearing the cast so long. I was thrilled to finally have it off! Mrs. Spaulding was firm but attentive to her students and did not allow horseplay in the classroom. We went on field trips, which I never did at Saint Helena's School. Our field trips included the Coke Bottling Plant and a trip to the fairgrounds where we had a picnic and gunnysack and other racing games. This was the first school year I enjoyed. It was the first one I actually had homework that took up a lot of time and was fun to do.

Dad worked long hours and he wasn't home until late. He was doing extra work for his boss Harold who was very generous. At Christmas, he sent a ham and a turkey, as he knew Dad had a large family. When Bonnie and I saw the Salvation Army truck pull up with our gifts, we knew where one gift per child came from. Christmas for us had a different meaning, but we were thankful for the gift we received knowing that some children didn't even get presents.

When Dad bought something special for his lunch and put it in the refrigerator and it disappeared, my mother would say the kids must have eaten it. "How could they eat the food when there is a chain on the refrigerator?" He would ask her.

"They could have taken it when I was preparing dinner and I didn't close it up," she would respond.

He asked us if we got into his lunch food knowing perfectly well we didn't. He always held his temper, but this one time, he was mad. Often, my mom had my dad over a barrel with her lies, but this time he knew all four of us would not tell him that we didn't know about the food unless it was true. Food, in our household was not a joking matter. This time I did not take the blame. Mom actually took his food and tried to lay blame on us.

After Dad left for work and the washing was done Mom came flying out of the house with a belt. She swung it at Bonnie and me. We tried to dodge her. She yelled, "Get your ass in the house right now! You will never," she screams, "defy me in front of your father ever again." She was screaming and carrying on. Bonnie and I were crying and screaming as she cornered us in the living room. She whipped us until welts rose on Bonnie's arm and then mine. Barb was behind her screaming, "I hate you! I hate you!"

My mom turned to Barb. "Do you want some of this?" Barb fell to the floor crying. Mom told us "Get your asses back out in the yard and hang the laundry up. And when you are done," she added, coiling up the belt, "You get in here for the rest of the day. You both are not going anywhere soon."

Bonnie, Barb, and I finished the laundry and went to our bedroom; I looked at the welts bleeding on my arm. We hurt so bad that we couldn't stop holding our arms. Barb snuggled with me as I thought out a plan. "Bonnie," I said, "I am running away tonight. I am never coming back to this house ever again. Can't you see that Dad is turning his head to the abuse? He couldn't believe the lies she was telling him? Who had this many accidents and didn't question it?"

Bonnie looked me in the face, "Not me," she replied, "Not me. I am old enough to be sent to the Good Shepherd Home(a home for delinquent Catholic girls).

I told her we could go to Aunt Dolly's and she would

turn Mom in. Then maybe, Barb and I could live with her and help her with housework. Deep down, I knew this wasn't feasible. My aunt had seven children to support by herself.

We would have to leave when it was dark and be very quiet so the kitchen door didn't squeak. Thank God their bedroom was in the back of the house and the kitchen was close to our bedroom.

"You cannot make one sound," I whispered to Barb. "Remember, not one sound, and even though it is warm out we need to take a coat."

I didn't think about food because I just wanted out and away. I didn't care what happened to me. I worried about Barbara. If anything happened to her, I would never forgive myself. I told her I was scared to take her with me. But, she said she would leave by herself if I didn't take her. I had to follow through. I knew I could do it. The alternative was to be attacked by a maniac who really wanted to hurt me, and hurt me badly. I prayed to God, asking Him why I was being punished so badly. I was going through with my plan.

"How early do you think it will be before we are discovered missing?" Barb asked me.

I told her that I was going to be in so much trouble if we got caught, but I assured her that I could take her back so she wouldn't get in trouble. She wanted no part of going back home pleading for me to take her.

She was adamant. "No way am I going back to her beatings. I just want to go to Aunt Dolly's, or Ginger's house...whoever will take us!" There was fire in her eyes.

We hurried down the street. I was terrified of the dark. I told Barb if we could make it to my tutor's house by the Civic Center, we could sleep in the hallway by his apartment without being detected, and before anyone woke up. His apartment was across the street from the Police Station. He had two roommates who were students at Carroll College. We took all the side streets that would get us up to Benton Avenue so that we wouldn't get caught.

107

We hid when cars passed us. We went up to Cannon Street where our Uncle Melvin and Aunt Cecil lived; their lights were out. I knew Aunt Cecil would have helped us since she knew what Mom was doing to us. I asked Barb if maybe we should ask them and she said no let's go to my friend Ginger's house because she lived up by Aunt Dolly, who lived across town.

It was late and we were tired from walking when we finally made it to my tutor's apartment. It was about one in the morning. There were no cars running in the streets. Everyone's lights were out. He lived up a flight of stairs. There was no noise in the apartment so Barb and I huddled up together in the hallway not far from his door. It was very warm in the corner, so we used our coats bunched up as pillows; Barb rested her head in my lap while I leaned against the wall. We quickly fell asleep. We were awakened suddenly, by the sound of a door opening, and a loud clinking, clanking downstairs. It was the milkman delivering milk.

Barb and I stared at the cold creamy bottles of milk. We were starving, and thirsty. The milk looked very tempting. I told her I would go down and get one of the bottles. Barb suggested we leave because it was early and she did not want to get caught. We decided to both take a bottle and leave. We could go across town before anyone saw us. We had now resorted to stealing and we could go to jail for it. I felt very guilty stealing the milk from someone we did not even know. They would call the dairy asking for the missing bottles.

It was very chilly so as soon as we got up the street away from the police station and the Civic Center we put our coats on and hid the bottles of milk. We stopped in an alley behind a garage to sit and guzzle it down. We were in a hurry to be on our way before daylight. We left the bottles there, not wanting to be caught with them.

We knew our mom and dad were up and had discovered that we were missing. They would probably call the police. We hid as much as we could, but a lot of cars were on the streets now as people were heading to work. We hadn't been noticed, but we still had to pick up our pace if we did not want to get caught. Barb's friend lives on Broadway so we headed up the hill on Broadway to Ginger's house. I kept turning back to watch for a police car. Halfway up the hill, we spotted a police car and tried to hide our faces. The policeman stopped and told us to stay put. We obeyed him, fearing what would happen to us if we didn't. He put us in the patrol car and talked to us. "Your parents are really worried about you two girls. What were you girls doing running away at your age and where were you headed?"

I showed him all the belt welts on my arm and told him my mom's history of beating us. He told me I would have to go back home and so would my sister because we couldn't just decide whom we wanted to go and live with. The legal system would not allow us to do that. "Bad things happen to girls that run away from home," he explained to us. "Sometimes they disappear and are never found."

I really thought the police officer was trying to scare us.

He took us back home; the two of us were sitting in the back of this black and white patrol car when we pulled. When I saw my father he had this look of disappointment on his face. I broke down immediately and told him I hated Mom, and I was sick of being her punching bag. Dad talked to the officer for a while. The officer told him your children could be taken away if your wife doesn't quit beating them. He had seen the bloody welts on my arms. Furthermore, he had to report it to the authorities.

When my dad reported the policeman's conversation to my mom, she was furious. She said she'd had enough and left for the neighbor's house. She was disgusted with Dad and me. The neighbor took her in until Dad could decide what to do. We wondered why Mrs. Kirby let Mom stay, but she was a Christian woman who kept asking Mom to take us to church and for her to find peace with God. She thought if Mom found Jesus, maybe she'd change her ways.

A strange quiet descended on our house. My father was very upset. He asked me to tell Bonnie to take care of everything at the house, as she knew what had to be done while he was at work. Bonnie and Wesley had already left for school. I had to tell Bonnie what Daddy expected from us when she got home from school. He chewed Barbara and me out for making him late to work. When he arrived home that night, Bonnie and I showed him how clean the house was and how we had everything done, including feeding the horses. We shoveled up the manure and cleaned the barn. Upon finishing the chores, we brushed down the horses, which helped Barb and me relax. Barb asked me if I thought Mom would be back. Bonnie and I told her we couldn't answer because we didn't know. It all depended on how much Dad would take from Mom hurting us and believing her lies.

After a few days, he went over and talked to Mom at Mrs. Kirby's. Of course, they patched things up and she came home without apologizing to us. She had nothing to say to any of us upon her arrival home. We went out to feed the horses and stayed out there for a while wondering and pondering why Dad let Mom come back home after what had taken place. We were very upset that she was back and we knew then nothing was ever going to change in our lives. It was a sick feeling to know that you don't have a mother who loves you and doesn't want you, and furthermore, wants to hurt you. We found out later that the police had warned her that they didn't want to come back to our house due to a child abuse call. If it happened again, we would be placed in foster care or taken to the orphanage.

I thought maybe things would change because Daddy talked to her for some time. Bonnie, Barb and I went back into the house to do our work. The beds were all made and we cleaned house without her saying one word to us. We didn't say one word to her. When we finished our work, we went into our bedroom to read. Our house had never been so silent.

Bonnie finally went out to the living room and asked

her if we could go to the neighbors and play. Our mother said we could go over to the Kirby's and play with the girls but stay outside so we could hear her call us. We could not play baseball because we never heard her when she called. We left and played with the neighbor kids until we knew it was close to time to go home. Then we went into our bedroom and played jacks. We were afraid to do anything. Dad came home from work and asked if there were any problems and we told him no. We walked on eggshells at our house for some time.

CHAPTER SEVENTEEN

Our life seemed to be quieting down and becoming normal. On Thursday nights, our parents had their *Search and Rescue* meetings, so we were taken to the park. At the park, Bonnie teased Barb and me about running away, saying she was glad she didn't go with us. She asked if we were scared at all and we told her we were just hungry and laughed about it. I told her if I did it again, I would be older because the policeman scared us saying it wasn't fun sitting in a jail cell. We always got picked up from the park after 9:30 p.m. when Mom and Dad's meeting was over.

One time at the park, Bonnie found out that Dad and Mom were at the Central Bar and had a few beers before they came and picked us up. We had been at the park all day without anything to eat except for food the restaurant owner gave us. After Dad worked things out with Mom, he wasn't as affectionate as he used to be with us. We were left at the park more and more. We could tell that they had been drinking because we could smell it. Between garage sales, their meetings and wanting to go to the bars, we were spending a lot of time at Memorial Park. During the winter, the four of us were left at the ice skating rink until eight o'clock at night on weekdays and nine o'clock on weekends, when the skating rink closed.

I was attending Helena Junior High. I took French so I could get my work finished on time during school. It was an easy course. I worked hard in school and got my homework done so I could have more time with the horses. Bonnie had to take a Special Education class as she had trouble focusing on work and trouble with some classes because she could not pay attention. I was caught daydreaming and not focusing during class time myself, off and on. I tried to think of all the good things that happened to us during the school year and not the bad.

After school, we hurried to finish our chores so we could ride the horses before we were yelled at to do this or that for our mom. She told us chores came first and not to count on getting them done before dark. Mom did the laundry with the ringer washer; she hung out the clothes and left the folding for me. Bonnie swept the floors. I ironed and folded the other clothes. She made Barb mop the floors. Barb was the same age Bonnie and I were when we had to do it. She didn't seem to mind it except for squeezing the dirty water out of the mop.

Dad finally bought a used washer and dryer, which retired the awful ringer. He put the new ones in the hallway. Now we could do the laundry much faster. We got to watch television as well, but we had to watch what mom wanted to watch and not see the shows the neighbor kids told us about. The whole family watched *The Lawrence Welk Show, Hee Haw,* and the *Grand Ole Opry.* Once in a while, my mom actually laughed at some of the jokes and showed that she did have a humorous side to her otherwise nasty disposition. She spent a lot of her days watching television while we were in school.

When Dad asked us who wanted to get a Christmas tree, Barb and I were the only volunteers. Bonnie wanted to stay home to work on her art project and drawings.

Barb and I trudged up to Rimini Gulch with Dad to see if we could find a full bushy tree this year. On our way back, we got stuck in a snow bank and waited to see if someone would come and pull us out. Finally, a man with a truck pulled us out with a chain. I knew that Dad was freezing from the cold. There would be no trip to Great-Grandmas after this. We were all starving, including our Dad. We hurried home. We tracked snow into the house and Mom was mad as a wet hen. Dad yelled back, "It was only water for heaven's sake. Sit down, be quiet, and watch your television show."

After the usual Christmas of Salvation Army gifts and a dinner bought by Grandma, we had two weeks off with no school and lots of time to go outdoors and build snowmen and igloos with all the snow we had. We tried to roll them into balls and chop off the sides and have a square for the blocks. We had a hard time putting the tops in so Daddy would come out and help us with the top piece. Several times it caved in on him. We laughed as he was covered in snow. He didn't give up though and showed us how to make our igloo.

Wesley had destroyed our first one and Dad warned him if he touched this one, he would go in the house and remain there for a couple of days. After that, Wesley left our igloo alone. Bonnie, Barb and I would go into the igloo and pretend it was our house. Bonnie was the mother and we were the daughters. We had to entertain ourselves a lot as we did not have games, skis, or snowmobiles as richer people did.

I was in seventh grade and spring had arrived. I wanted to go out for track. I waited until Dad came home to ask. I was in a bind. I knew Mom would say no and yet, at the same time, she would be very angry if I asked him first. But I really wanted to run track. We had dinner, and I asked him before we got up from the table, if I could please go out for track. He knew I was a good runner and wanted to compete in the track meets. The coach said she would bring me home. However, she told me that on weekends when they had the big meets, my Dad or Mom would have to take me to the event. The coach would bring me home.

Dad said, "That's fine with me." as he looked at my mother.

"I guess so, but why did you not have the courtesy to ask me first before you asked your dad?"

I told her, "I was scared you would say no, because you were always mad at me for some reason. That was why I asked the two of you together."

She said, "From now on, you ask me first and not your Dad. I run things around here. Not, your dad. Get that straight from now on young lady."

She looked at Bonnie and said, "I suppose you want to

114

too."

Bonnie told her, "No way!" "I don't like track or any sport except for baseball."

My Mom said, "That's a good thing, because someone has to take up Wanda's slack and that means you do some of her work until she gets home."

Of course, I felt awful and told Bonnie I would make it up to her by helping her with her horse. She told me not to worry because we had to stick together when it came to Mom. I was so thankful that Bonnie, Barb, and I stuck together.

I went out for my first track practice. There were five events: the shot put, discus, long jump and standing jump, and the races. I had the best time on the track. I was third in the standing and long jumps. The coach bragged about how well I was doing in track to my parents. My record running long jump was twelve feet, two inches, which was excellent. When she took me home she could see from the look of our house that we were very poor. I told her there was no way my mother could afford track clothes for me. I knew that was what she was going to talk to them about. She said she would figure something out for me.

When we had our big track meets, I came home with blue and red ribbons for first and second places. With my wins, I was eligible to go to the state track meet, but Mom would not let me go because we did not have the money, just as we didn't have money for me to go to the state spelling bee in the sixth grade.

After that, dad told Mom that we could start babysitting for money. Bonnie and I had been asked several times by numerous families, if we would like to care for their children. We could save up our own money for events like this. I told him Mom was just going to take it from us and we wouldn't have any money saved. He told her that he was buying us piggy banks to put our money in and no one was to touch them. In the past, when I babysat, she took my four dollars and fifty cents leaving me with nothing. Bonnie shoveled sidewalks, and her money was taken as well.

Mom always had her hand out the second we walked in the door.

When the Grandy family found out that I could babysit, Mrs. Grandy told me she needed me in the summer. I told her I had to have camp week off. She asked if Bonnie could take over for me. I had a job and school wasn't even out yet. Mom made it clear that I had to feed and water the horses before I left for babysitting and the laundry would be waiting for me when I got home, and it had to be done before dinner.

Dad said, "That's enough, they work hard around here."

She retorted back, "I know, I wanted her to know what needs to be finished."

"You could take the slack up and do some of the housework," Dad replied. She was fuming and didn't utter a word to him as she could see he was done talking to her.

I started my babysitting job for the Grandy family. I watched the two boys and a girl from seven in the morning until four in the afternoon. I took them on walks and played games with them. They had lots of games and toys. I did the breakfast dishes while the kids napped. After I fixed their lunch, I cleaned the house for their mother. I would fill the pool up so the kids could swim after naps. I filled their squirt guns so they could have a water fight while I was squirted them with the hose. When Mrs. Grandy got home and saw that everything in her house was done, she paid me a couple of extra dollars. She said she would add it to my pay since she paid once a week, on Fridays. I made three dollars a day plus any extras.

Her husband told dad that I was the best babysitter they ever had. The others would just sit and watch television and never do anything around the house including cleaning up after their selves.

In the last year, I had learned some nice things about myself. I had learned that I was a decent person. It made me realize I was a good worker and person which was the complete opposite of what I was told and punished for by the priests. As often as I told my self that they were wrong,

I still couldn't shake that terrible place that had taken root in me.

For my thirteenth birthday, the Grandy's gave me a jewelry box with a tiny ballerina that twirled; in the box was a necklace. It was the nicest thing anyone had given me besides my horses. I told Mrs. Grandy this was the first time I had ever received a birthday gift, and thanked her for making me feel so special

When I showed Mom, she told me to put it away and get the laundry done. She did not even tell me Happy Birthday. When Daddy came home and saw it was my birthday, he said, "Oh my God, another teenager in the house." I laughed with him.

After dinner, Dad said, "What no cake?" I couldn't believe my ears. My mother had never baked a cake for our birthday. We only went out for ice cream if Dad took us. That evening, he took us for ice cream. He told everyone, "Get in the car whoever wants ice cream for Wanda's birthday. We'll buy double scoops so we can celebrate Bonnie's too." My mom pouted like a little child the entire way.

He said to Mom, "You need to start baking cakes for their birthdays."

She said, "They don't need to have sweets."

"Well they could have cakes on their birthdays, even if I have to buy the damn things," Dad responded without hesitation.

Bonnie began to tease Wesley and she knew that he was off limits with Mom sitting across from us. Dad quickly intervened and told Bonnie that she knew better than to tease her brother. We laughed because she was teasing him.

Mom told Bonnie and me to knock it off and to leave our brother alone. She never wished me Happy Birthday.

When I babysat the next day, I asked Mrs. Grandy if she would mind if Barb came to play with Arlene. Barb and Arlene were the same age, so we made a little baseball field with bases in their backyard and played baseball and the

117

kids loved it. Thank goodness there were no windows in the way. I didn't want to pay for windows with money I earned.

When the children went down for naps, Barb had to go home because Mom called and said her work wasn't finished when she left the house. Barb wanted to know why we didn't have a house like the Grandy's. I told her Mom didn't work like Mrs. Grandy did. They both have to work to have a decent home and nice things. I told her Mom would never work, because she had it easy with us doing all the housework, taking care of the horses, and weeding her garden. All she had to do was watch television and go to meetings.

My first paycheck from Mrs. Grandy was two ten-dollar bills. When I walked in the door at home, Mom wanted half of my money. I told her dad said I could keep all my babysitting money, and I was keeping it or I was quitting. I was not working for nothing. I would not give it to her. At the dinner table, I told dad that mom wanted half of my money.

Dad turned to my mother, "It is her money, and for the things we cannot afford to do for her. I made it clear that you were not taking their money. You just spend it at garage sales. It is their money not yours. If you want spending money, get a job just like the kids do to earn money."

She pushed herself away from the table, and screamed, "I am tired of this shit!! Since when do these kids run our house? And, since we are on the topic, they can buy their own clothes."

Dad told her that was not the point, and to quit being pissed about Bonnie or Wanda's money. He told me to put the money in the piggy bank.

The next morning, when I left to go babysitting, my mom told me to stop. She came over to me and stood close, looking me straight into my face and said, "If you ever pull that stunt again like you did last night, you will get an ass whooping you will never forget." Her face was red and flushed with anger and her eyes were bulging, "Remember no one sees your ass!"

"What stunt?" I ask. "What stunt did I pull?" She slapped my face.

"Don't talk back to me! Don't you ever talk back to me again," she glared at me "You are treading on very thin ice."

"Okay, I have to go or I will be late." I was furious and ashamed that she smacked my face. I was holding the side of my face to see if it would stop hurting and not look red and puffy like I had just been hit. Mrs. Grandy was ready to go when I arrived. I apologized for being a few minutes late. I put a cold washcloth on my cheek. The inflammation must have gone down because no one asked about it when they got up.

Bonnie was hired to work for Mr. Minugh for the summer. She was paid fifteen dollars a week to help with housework and cooking. She also helped with the haying season so our horses could have hay for the winter.

Barb and I went to the Lion's Sunshine Camp. Bonnie did not return because at fourteen was too old to go. Barb was excited about her first time at camp. She kept grabbing my arm on the bus and saying she couldn't wait to see the camp she had always heard us talk about. She was impatient asking every few minutes how far now?

When we arrived at the camp, Barb was awestruck by the number of cabins and the recreation center where we put on our skits. She was in cabin three with the younger campers, and I was in cabin ten where the oldest girls camped. This was my last year so I wanted to enjoy it as much as I could. We were just in time for lunch. They served bacon, lettuce, and tomato sandwiches with potato salad and cake for desert. Barb and I always remembered that lunch. We had never eaten a BLT until we came to camp. Then we hiked around the campground. They did this every year for the new kids to get acquainted with the camp. When we finished, everyone went to their cabins, made their beds and got situated. After, we went to the recreation room to meet our counselors and the camp personnel. This was our time to learn the camp rules and functions. Barb couldn't wait until it was dark so she could sit by the campfire and listen to stories and roast marshmallows. We got to sit by whomever we wanted to sit by at the campfire, and Barb hung onto me like a Rottweiler. When it was bedtime, I told her to tell her counselor she was afraid of the dark, and she would put a little light next to her until she fell asleep.

In the morning, we did the polar plunge. Barb wanted no part of it. She had hated cold water ever since the incident at St. Joseph's. After the polar plunge, we took showers and headed to breakfast. Barb was amazed at all that was offered to begin our day. There were a variety of cereals for a cold breakfast if we wanted or we could have eggs, hash browns and breakfast meats. At home, it was always oatmeal or Cream of Wheat. Barb couldn't believe the meals we got to eat at camp.

We went on a campout where they taught us about nature and showed us how we should respect the forest. Barb worried that it might rain. I told her campout would be canceled and they would bus the campers back to the main camp if it rained. She would be very disappointed so I promised her it wasn't going to rain. She slept next to me and felt very cozy and safe. In the morning, I told her how fast she fell asleep. We ate breakfast and packed up everything and headed back to camp a mile down the road. We sang all the camp songs we knew as we hiked to the main camp. The week went by so fast. Before we knew it, we were headed home and Mom was waiting for us when the bus pulled into the parking lot.

I returned to my babysitting job. Bonnie told us she got to go to the Great Falls Fair on the weekend with Mr. Minugh and his family from Big Sandy. They were there just for the day, but she said it was fun riding on the rides with his grandsons. I teased her about liking them, and she knew I was joshing her, but it was so fun to do. She would be going into regular classes in the eighth grade with me.

I cleaned and caught up on the housework for Mrs. Grandy because Bonnie did not clean the house for her as well as I did when she covered my job. I caught up on chores at home because it was only fair that I do them because Bonnie had to do my chores as well as hers as well as taking care of the Grandy kids. She told me Dad chastised Mom, while we were gone, about getting off her butt and helping Bonnie since Wesley did nothing.

"Did she actually do it?" I asked. "Give me a break," Bonnie laughed, as she rolled her eyes. "Did you really think she would do that when Daddy wasn't around?" We laughed like two cackling hens.

Mrs. Grandy was so pleased that everything was clean when she arrived home, that she gave me an extra five dollars. That was a lot of money in those days. The going rate for babysitters was fifty cents an hour for three kids and twenty-five cents an hour for one. "There was no mistake," Mrs. Grandy said. "You did such a nice job cleaning and getting our house back in order after picking up after the children. It's a full time job," she added.

I saved two hundred and eighty dollars, but I was afraid to keep it in my piggy bank. I asked Dad if he would take me to the bank so I could open a savings account. He felt I should ask Mom. I told him she would say no. So he told me we could go Friday when he went to cash his check. On Friday, I grabbed my piggy bank and waited patiently in the yard. I was worried that Mom would come out and ask what was going on. I told Bonnie that if she asked where I was, to tell her she did not know. I knew my dad would cover for me.

We arrived at the bank with ten minutes to spare. There was no cost to open a savings account, but since I did not have a social security number, I would have to use Dad's. She told me that I would get withdrawal slips in the mail in about two weeks. The slips had to bear my signature for anyone to withdraw my money. I was relieved because I did not want to lose my hard-earned money. I was so excited. I told Dad I was going to save all my money I earned and put it in my savings account.

Dad and I hurried home. Dad went in first and told me to stay in the yard. Mom asked him what the hell took so long at the bank, and he told her he had to wait in line to cash his check.

Bonnie asked where we went, and I told her we went to the bank and opened my own savings account with Dad.

Bonnie said, "Were you crazy? Mom will snatch that right up. At least with a piggy bank, there's a little key to lock it up with, and I hide that!"

I told her I would put more in because Dad said several people asked him if I could babysit their kids on weekends when they were away on search and rescue missions and mock trials. He assured them that I would be available.

Bonnie was sticking to cleaning Mr. Minugh's house on weekends and did not want any other work on top of what she had already. He tipped her well for a good job at his house so she made pretty good money, as well. I knew mom resented us for having money. So, we needed to watch out.

Mom told me I was going to have to give her some of my money, and Bonnie would have to also give her money for our school clothes. Dad informed her he had given her money for material to make the girl's skirts and blouses. She told him it was for other clothing: bras, slips, hair bands, coats, and school supplies. He informed her that he had money put aside for those items.

Several days later, we were in our bedroom, getting dressed to go shopping for school supplies. Mom came in and ordered us to get money out of our banks for school supplies. Bonnie and I refused. Mom backed us into a corner and started slapping us. Barb yelled she was going to tell Daddy that Mom was still hitting her sisters. She turned around and smacked Barb so hard she knocked her to the floor.

We're telling Dad if you don't leave our room. I stood, staring at her. I was shaking, and trembling. My voice was splitting in two as I looked into her wild, red face. She left the house, slamming the door behind her. Bonnie, Barb, and I thought she was leaving for good because that was one of the few times we had stood up to her. She was gone for hours. Quiet settled over the house. Then, just before my father came home, she slipped into the kitchen. She was just in time to fix his dinner. She didn't say a word as she was cooking. She knew we were there because she could hear us in our room talking.

When Dad arrived, everything was just like normal except she yelled at us to fill the horse trough. When we came back for dinner and sat down at the table, Dad's face was clouded. He was upset with us. Dad looked from Bonnie to me, and back again. He said to us, if you ever talk back to your mother again you are going to get in trouble from me. He had never raised his voice to us before. I tried to explain. He told me not to interrupt him. He was unhappy about us talking back to
Mom.

We sat in silence and listened to him. I had never seen Dad frustrated to the point where he wouldn't listen to us. After dinner, we were told to do the dishes and then go to our bedroom. We rushed through the dishes. Then we asked Barb what Mom had said to Dad. She said she didn't hear because they went into the bedroom and closed the door.

After Daddy left for work, I wrote a note to him and apologized.

> *Daddy,*
> *The only thing I could say was "no" to her because I did not want to get you in trouble for taking me to the bank and opening an account for me. I am sorry for making you angry with Bonnie and me. Barb didn't do anything but tried to help us.*
> *I love you Daddy.*

When my father came home from work my sisters and I were in our bedroom. Mommade us stay there for the entire day except to come out and do chores. Dad came into our room and asked us why we were in our room for the day?

Mom followed him in, "They will stay in their room until they do what they were told to do yesterday!"

"Well, I guess that is your punishment until you girls change your ways," he said. "It was your choice you know?"

We ate a second, silent dinner and after we cleaned up, we went back to our bedroom, took baths, and went to bed. The next day was the Friday before Labor Day. It was my chance to put my note into his lunchbox. Dad's lunch was always made the night before except for the refrigerated items. I knew, for him to get the note, I had to sneak it in his lunchbox after he went to bed.

I waited until the house was quiet and everyone sleeping. I knew it would be safe. I hid it under his apple, cookies and chips, and prayed that he would find it. I prayed hard that night and all day long hoping that dad would find the note. Sometimes he did not eat all of his lunch.

When he came home that night, we were in our room, huddled at the small table, drawing and painting. We waited for him to come in, to acknowledge that he had received the note, to say something. We heard Mom telling him dinner would be ready.

He asked Mom, "Where were the girls?"

"Where do you think?" She said.

He still didn't come in. I knew now that he didn't find the note. Otherwise, he would have said something. Mom called Wes in from outside to come in and wash his hands for dinner. They called us to come to the table. Bonnie, Barb and I trooped into the dining room and sat down. Dad said, "What, no hellos for Dad today?"

"We are scared to talk you." I said.

We started to eat.All that was heard was the sounds of forks and knives scraping plates. Then Dad asked Mom, "What did you say the girls had done the other day to get into trouble? Did you tell the girls they had to give you money for school supplies after I already told you we were getting the supplies?" Dad asked angrily.

"I did buy their school supplies and put them away in the bedroom closet,"she said matter of fact.

"I didn't ask you that Helen. I asked you if you asked the girls for their money."

"Hell no, why would I do that?" was her answer.

Bonnie, Barb and I couldn't believe our ears. She was lying to Dad, again.

"Yes, yes, you did," Barb piped in, not thinking of the consequences for talking back to our mom. "When you asked them for their money, they said no. Then you started hitting them. And you knocked me to the floor, too."

"You quit your goddamn lying or you are going back to bed," Mom snapped at Barb.

"Well someone is lying and I am going to get to the bottom of this," Dad intervened. He slowly folded his napkin and set it on the table. "You girls can leave your room because I am sick of what is going on. Let your mom and I talk about this while you are outside taking care of the animals. Tomorrow, I will saddle up your horses, and you can ride them since you have had more punishment then necessary from your mother."

The next morning after chores, he went out and saddled up the horses. I knew he believed the letter I had written him. He didn't say anything to me because I realized he couldn't. He was at the point of no return with our mother. He was beginning to realize she wasn't going to change. He could only hope that her anger didn't boil over enough to get us taken away. He had to think about the damage she had already done to us. I would never understand why he put up with her.

CHAPTER EIGHTEEN

Bonnie and I started eighth grade together at a new school called C. R. Anderson. Our favorite teacher was Mr. Phillips, who was a riot and an inspiration to his students in his homeroom and math class. He would egg us along until we got to the right answer he wanted. We rode our bikes to school on days when mom had appointments or garage sales. I would rather ride my bike than walk, as school was some distance from our house.

On Saturday mornings, Bonnie and I shoveled manure. If we didn't, Mom threatened that she would get rid of our horses. She made us pile it up and mix it with the garden soil. I thought it was disgusting. Dad said it broke down and made good soil and the smell dissipated. Dad would come out and help us, as we had to get the other chores caught up too. Barb washed dishes while we were shoveling manure.

I was always glad when school started on Monday. I would rather do school work than yard and house work any day. One day, I had to stay after school to finish my Spanish quiz. I was running a bit late. I grabbed my bike and pedaled quickly to catch up with Bonnie. While I was madly pedaling, I did not see a parked car along the road. Several things happened at once: the car behind me honked, I turned to look at what was wrong, and I hit the parked car and fell. The man who honked his car stopped. He brushed me off, and helped me get up and asked me if I was okay. Actually, I was very dizzy, and the pit of my stomach hurt. I had cuts and bruises up and down my legs, and my knee was bleeding. I am okay. I just need to get home. Seeing that I was determined to ride home, the man drove off.

I slowly walked my wrecked bike home; its front wheel wobbled and was hard to control. I was wobbling as well. I hurt everywhere. Relief flooded through me when I saw my dad's car coming toward me. He pulled over and asked what happened.

I repeated my story as I my eyes watered. He put the bike in the trunk and said he would fix it on the weekend. He asked if I was okay as he looked at my cuts and bruises. When we got home, dad told me to get cleaned up. He told Mom to put Mercurochrome on my wounds and bandage them.

"I'll look at the bike later. I'm just glad you're okay," he said as he kissed my forehead.

When Mom saw me and heard about my wrecked bike she said, "You will be walking to school now. You know we can't afford another bike."

I couldn't tell her about the money in the bank or Dad would get in trouble. The next day, I walked to school while the other kids rode. I was hurting so badly from the bike wreck that I was tardy. That was the first time I was late for all my years in school. The office lady gave me a tardy slip, although she was very sympathetic about my accident. Mr. Phillips also asked after me because Bonnie told him about my accident. As we walked out of the school and started to walk home, Mom was sitting in her car honking. Mom said she was picking me up because dad told her to. On the car ride home, she told me, "You better hope your dad gets your bike fixed because I am not doing this every day. From now on you need to pay better attention to where you are riding your bike instead of day dreaming." Mom always had the last word and rubbed salt in my wounds.

I sure hoped Dad would be able to fix my bike. I did not want Mom to make the accident a Capital offence. I was very fortunate that Daddy sympathized with me and repaired my bike immediately. He knew Mom would make me walk. It didn't matter to her if I was in pain or not.

I met Diane who became my best friend in 1961. She lived across the street from the school. Her mom had a beautiful house with a brick fireplace in the living room and a family room. Sometimes she asked me to come home with her for lunch instead of eating the free meals at school. Her mom always had lunch fixings ready for her to make sandwiches. It was fun hanging out with her in a warm house instead of on the freezing cold school grounds after lunch. Diane's mom, Sharon was fun and caring. Her dad was killed in a car accident when she was young; her father's life insurance paid the house off so her mother didn't have to worry about a mortgage payment. Sharon worked hard as a telephone operator and part-time waitress. Her mom always bought Diane and her brother nice things and beautiful clothing. Kathy was my friend from sixth grade. Her father was the Bishop of the Episcopal Church in Montana.

Diane, I and the other girls in my class would talk and giggle about the boys. The conversation often would cross the boundary into dangerous territory. The girls would discuss who they wanted to go out with, who was dating, and who was having sex. I didn't even think about these things. As the girls laughed and talked about boys, I felt frozen and dirty inside. I thought to myself, why do they want that? Of course, no one talked about anything similar to what had happened to me. None of the girls had any idea about my past at the orphanage and at St. Helena's. When the girls talked about sex, heavy petting, and about kissing their boyfriends, it set off a chain reaction for me. I felt dirty, naked, and ashamed. It made me feel guilty for what the priests did to me. I knew, of course, that all men and boys were not like the ones that assaulted me, but I never wanted that to happen again. The sexual acts were so brutal, and these girls were talking about wanting to have sex with a boy? That old feeling of sickness came up.

I did enjoy looking at handsome boys with my friends and wondering what it would be like to have a boyfriend, but that was it. Christian, the Carroll College student who was my tutor, must have been brought up in a good home because he never looked at me like that. I was only twelve, still a child. I was very leery around any boy or man. I did

128

not trust any of them. But I knew there were a couple of boys in my class at school who liked me. They sat by me and asked if I had a boyfriend. I just talked and laughed with them. I was not ready to think of having a boyfriend.

I started having nightmares, horrible nightmares, about the abuses that had happened to us in the orphanage. I woke up in a cold sweat, seeing the faces of the priests and nuns of the past. I would find myself shaking. Often, I was too frightened to go back to sleep. Sometimes I wish that I would not wake up at all. But then I realize how selfish that was, because I could not bear the idea of abandoning Barb. Then the thoughts of dying would evaporate. I kept my sanity by reassuring myself that I was getting older and to just hold on; things would change.

It was the Christmas Season and my father had just taken a new job at Sharbano Construction building homes. To celebrate, we went to my great-grandmother's house because she wanted to visit with the entire family. When we arrived, our great-aunts were there as well as our great-uncles, Charlie and Art. We loved it at her house. The log house was old but neat and tidy. Grandma had doilies everywhere on her furniture and her china cabinet. It felt very homey. This was a place where I found peace and tranquility.

I was so amazed at what my great-grandmother could do as she was completely blind. We had a cake that she had made. She gave us winter hats that she had crocheted. She could cook and bake and would feel for the things she needed. The one thing she couldn't do was go outside alone at her age, although she felt her way along the front of her cabin to water the flowers.

Dad cut down a Christmas tree left it in the snow outside while we ate dinner. Dad would always tell grandma we would do the dishes and sweep up the floor for her so our great-aunts did not have that chore to do when we left for home. She always remarked to Daddy that he had good girls that volunteered to do the chores when others shied away from that responsibility. Dad was proud of us and let us know in his own way that he appreciated us helping to take care of his grandma. She was like a mother to him since she did help raise him as a boy.

As the grown-ups sat and talked, Bonnie, Barb, Wesley and I went out to play in the snow. We had an enormous snowball that the four of us rolled from the heavy, wet snow. We could not make the ball any larger since we could not move the darn thing. Then we went out to the Prickly Pear Creek, which was skimmed over with ice and skated around in our slippery boots. Wesley almost fell in the creek by sliding on ice that wasn't completely frozen over. Thank goodness, Bonnie and I grabbed him by the arms. Dad called us to come back to the house as we were leaving soon. When we returned, my great-grandma had her typical goodie bags for each of us.

Bonnie, Barb and I were learning to hide our money from Mom. At Christmas, Grandma sent each of us ten dollars in letters addressed separately to each of us. Our Granny was a very wise lady and knew what had happened with all the money she had sent us previously through Helen. She did this because she found out in my last letter to her that we had never received the birthday or Christmas money she sent Mom to give us. Now, she sent it directly to us. I asked Daddy to put mine in my bank account and he did. We never got to go shopping for Christmas gifts. We never had the money to buy gifts. I was not touching mine and Bonnie felt the same way. She had a lot in her piggy bank, and I told her she needed to get it in the bank. I think she was spending some of hers. Barb finally had a piggy bank given to her. She wanted to buy something and Mom wouldn't let her so she would hide some of her money since she knew we did it as well. I had a lot of babysitting jobs. Dad said I had to keep some out for some things I wanted and to put the rest in the piggy bank to keep mom off-track. So, some of my money was still in my piggy bank.

Barb's birthday was December fifteenth. Mom never acknowledged her birthday. It came and went, just like ours had over the years. Bonnie and I both gave her five dollars each from our piggy banks. Barb hid it with her other money because she didn't trust Mom to stay out of her piggy bank.

At that time, I heard about the other girl's birthdays, about having parties with decorated cakes and invitations to friends. I just knew it would never happen in our house. If we got invited to a friend's party, my mother would just tell us, "You're not going. We do not have the money to buy you a present, let alone your friends." Bonnie, Barb and I were never able to attend a friend's birthday party.

I spent most of the winter doing homework. I received B's and C's and couldn't seem to get an A in Social Studies no matter how hard I tried. But I did have A's in spelling and math. We spent a lot of time with our horses, shoveling manure away in the barn, filling water in the trough and feeding them. Horses were a lot of work but they came up to us whenever we came out to see them. We loved taking care of them since they were ours. We talked to them as if they knew what we were saying to them.

Summer came, we were too old for camp and Barb would not go alone. Bonnie and I told her we would take her horseback riding. Dad let Bonnie and I ride alone so we could go where we pleased. We knew how to bridle and saddle our own horses. We cinched them up nice and tight. Dad and Aunt Dolly taught us well since they were raised with horses.

One Saturday afternoon, Aunt Dolly came to visit while I was riding Sandy out on the dirt road. I galloped to catch up with her before she got to the house. When Aunt Dolly got out of the car, I was still galloping down the alley to our house to reach her when, all of a sudden, Sandy came to a complete halt. I, of course, was not expecting that. I flew over her head with the reins in hand and hit the ground, scraping myself on the rocks and pebbles in the driveway. Everyone was laughing but it hurt like heck. I did not want to ride anymore but my Aunt said to me, "Get back on that horse and you let her know who is boss." I respected my

Aunt so I knew I had to do just that. With apprehension, I mounted my horse. Sandy was as gentle as a lamb. She had been startled when my Aunt suddenly opened her car door and slammed it shut. She had never thrown me off before.

I asked Aunt Dolly if she would like to ride Patches. She told me that Dad was going to help her fix something on her car. When he was done, she would come to the barn and saddle Sandy up. Because Aunt Dolly was with us, Dad let Bonnie and me ride all the way to the fairgrounds, a distance of a couple of miles. Aunt Dolly knew Jack, the grounds man who worked there.

Jack let us run our horses on the racetrack when we arrived at the fairgrounds. It was great fun, the three of us racing around the track, our hair flying, hooves thumping, to a stadium of empty bleachers. He told us later to come there anytime, that the track was only used for horse racing during the Last Chance Stampede in July. He told us, however, that we always had to check to make sure an adult was always there. We had a wonderful time riding with our Aunt. It was the only time we were ever able to.

By the time we got back to our house, dad was done with her car. The horses were thirsty and sweaty. Aunt Dolly helped us unsaddle them and cool them down. Dad told us Mom had gone garage sale shopping and by the time she got back, we had to have the laundry done. After Aunt Dolly left, Dad told us he and Mom were meeting up with Aunt Dolly and Larry, so Bonnie and I needed to get everything done and watch the kids.

Barb and I loved our Aunt Dolly and were very close to her. She always meant what she said. She was fun and straightforward with us. She told Bonnie, Barb and me she didn't approve of how our mother handled her behavior, and especially the anger she inflicted on us. She thought our mother was clinically depressed and had extreme anger issues and was taking it out on us

One family I babysat for had a three-year-old who threw the worst tantrums ever. Boy could that child scream. His mother told me if he had a tantrum to just let him scream it out in his bedroom. Boy, I thought that would never fly by in my house, not with my mother. My mom would have gotten the belt out or we would be smacked one way or another. I felt I earned my money at their house. He always threw a tantrum when his parents left and I did not force him to stay in his room; I regretted that decision real soon. They always paid me an extra few dollars for watching their children.

Dad let Bonnie and I return to the fairgrounds with the horses because Jack said we could bring them back down and run them around the track. We rode them to the fairgrounds and ran fiercely around the track.They were heating up and we realized we'd best cool them down. We had to get them to the barn to get out of the heat to where the hose was. Jack told us to water them down and let them drink after we hosed them down.

While we were standing there watching them drink, I felt a bite on my wrist. Bonnie saw a big black spider on the ground and stepped on it. She said it looked like a black widow spider. I started getting dizzy. I was pale and then I fainted. My arm was swelling.

"Jack, Jack, come quickly," Bonnie yelled.

Jack came running and saw me lying on the ground. He turned the spider over with his boot and saw the signature red hourglass. He then turned over my hand to see where I was bitten. He took out his pocketknife, and made a little slit in my wrist. As it bled, he sucked on my wrist hard and spit out the blood and venom. Then he rinsed his mouth out with water. My arm was very swollen.

Jack told me that we were going to the hospital. He told Bonnie, to "Lope your horse as fast as you can home, to notify your dad." "One of the workers can put Wanda's horse in a little corral, but you have to hurry home fast. Tell your parents what happened. "Get moving quickly, Bonnie!"

By the time Jack had rushed me to the hospital, I was convulsing. The doctors started me on anti-venom medication. I stayed in the hospital for two days. As I recovered, I had to listen to my mother go on about the hospital bill. There were no words of thanks to Jack for making it to the hospital in time, or relief that I was okay.

The next day, the doctor told them I could go home. "She is going to have to rest for a couple more days."

"She still doesn't look that good," my dad said.

"She was a lucky girl. "There was someone there who knew what to do," replied the doctor.

"That she was," my dad said. He thanked Jack for saving his little girl.

When I was fully recovered, my friend Diane called to ask my mom if I could spend the night. Mother told her I had a babysitting job and could not do it during the week. She gave false hope when she said that perhaps I might be able to on some weekend. I did not hold my breath because my mother was unhappy about my latest hospital ordeal. But two weeks before school started, Mom let me go because Diane's mother was coming to pick me up on Saturday morning after my chores were done and my mother did not have to drive me there. I had to be home by noon the next day.

I had so much fun at Diane's house. When I was in their house, Diane's mother treated me like I was her own. We went to Howard's Pizza for lunch with three other girls from school. We chatted and hung out for the day until the girls left at six. They were going to a school dance that Diane and I could not go to because my mom told Diane's mother I could not go. Diane's mother did not want to go against my mother's wishes.

Diane's brother, Eddie and his girlfriend took Diane and me in his car to the RB Drive-Inn for dinner. The RB Diner was where the high school kids hung out on Friday nights and weekends. This was the first time I had ever eaten the RB's locally famous halibut fish and chips. The older kids, teased Eddie, asking if he was babysitting his little sister and her friend. He told them they were along because we invited them.

I would be a ninth grader at Helena Junior High. I asked Mom if Bonnie and I could buy new shoes with the money we earned. Mom said it was okay. Bonnie and I bought Barb a new pair because Mom said she had to wear our Cousin Rita's hand-me-down shoes. Of course, Mother paid for Wesley's clothes and shoes.

I ask my mom if I could play basketball. Daddy asked how late I would have to stay, and I told him practice at four o'clock and the games usually last an hour and a half. He told me he would pick me up after work, which would be at the end of practice. He said that he would come in and watch the game while waiting for me to finish practice. The school furnished our shirts and I had to buy a pair of shorts and socks that the school sold to us. My gym tennis shoes were in my locker so I didn't need to buy new shoes.

Mom was not happy about Daddy coming to the games and taking up her time with him. "We are not doing this through high school. Just so you know. Let's clear that matter up right now before you decide on any more sports."

Dad came to my first game at five o'clock. He sat in the bleachers with other parents and watched me play for a half-hour or forty-five minutes. I was a forward and one of the shortest girls on the team. I moved quickly away from their guards and made good shots. On our drive home, my dad was proud of me as I scored quite a few of our points and we won the first game. I cannot remember how many games we played but we lost a few and didn't make the cut for citywide basketball game.

When winter arrived, my mom told us, "No activities until spring." What she failed to tell was that we had to join Civil Air Patrol; a youth group similar to the U.S. Air Force. She found out about the organization from a police officer and fellow Search and Rescue member, who told my Mom that her daughters would love it. She never even consulted or asked us if we wanted to join. She just went ahead and signed us up. Bonnie and I had to wear straight blue-pencil skirts, and white blouses with short sleeves and blue ties. We attended meetings once a week until school

135

was out. On top of the meetings, in order to go, we had to buckle down, scour the house and clean the horse barn before things froze.

In spring, she allowed me to join the track team. My father told her it was okay, if I got my work done and if I kept on top of the chores so we didn't have to do cleaning every day. My coach said she would drive me home after practice. The only thing that bothered me was when I participated in track meets on the weekends and all of the parents showed up to watch and cheer on their kids except mine. Mom and Dad had Search and Rescue meetings on Thursday nights and did mock searches on the weekends. I was positive that Mom wanted no part in watching me participate in school sports. She would rather that I didn't participate at all. She always gave me the evil eye if I asked Daddy to please come and watch. I had to realize Dad loved being a member of the Search and Rescue Organization.

CHAPTER NINETEEN

In May, there was a school dance at the Civic Center and I hoped we could go. I hated asking Mom so I told Bonnie, "It was her turn, I was the one who always asked, and you're the one who likes a guy who was going to the dance." I told her to do it at the dinner table so Mom couldn't get too mad. The dance was on Friday from seven to ten o'clock. On Wednesday evening at dinner, Mom and Dad were laughing about something and I poked Bonnie and whispered, "Now!"She asked in a soft sweet voice, "Mom and Dad, can we please go to the school dance at the Civic Center this Friday night? It is our end of the school year dance." Mom was very negative about the dance. But Dad said, "Hey, it is only for three hours and when the girls get home, we could go uptown for a while, and they could babysit, so why not."

Bonnie and I were so excited to go to our first dance. We asked if we could buy new skirts and shoes because we didn't have nice clothes to wear.

Mom shook her head, "Absolutely not, you already have clothes I made for the school year and you're not wasting money on clothes to go to a three-hour dance."

She had made us one skirt for the school year and I certainly did not want to wear it. Bonnie and I asked if we could buy our own skirt or dress and she told us, "I gave you my final answer, no means no."

At school the next day I told Diane and some friends that our parents were taking us and dropping us off, but my mom was not going to let us buy any new clothes for the dance. I was thinking that I didn't want to go after all. Diane told me she would bring something I could change into right away in the girl's room and would help me fix myself up. We could put my clothes in a bag. She told me to wear my longer coat so Mom wouldn't notice in the dark, because they would always sit and wait for us just out front to come out. I thought what a great idea, but I was very scared knowing that I was doing something behind my mother's back.

Diane asked Bonnie if she wanted a skirt too, but Bonnie was taller than us by three inches and the skirt would be super short. The skirts had to come to our knees at school functions and the dance. "I have a longer one and will bring it just in case it will work," Diane told Bonnie. Diane would bring mascara and lipstick for us. We had never worn makeup and we had to be sure and wipe it off after the dance.

Friday arrived and we were on pins and needles. Mom told us to get right out to the parking lot so we could get our chores done and ready to go by six-thirty. The dance started at seven. We asked Dad if we could go early. He agreed and took us to the Civic Center. He told us where he would be picking us up at the main door a few minutes before ten. He told us to be sure and be prompt because he didn't want to wait while an auditorium full of kids came rushing out. We promised to be out at five to ten, prompt.

After he dropped us off, we rushed to the girl's bathroom to wait for Diane and our party clothes. She had arrived early and had the bag of clothes with her. While I was changing into a pretty pink skirt, she was showing Bonnie how to put mascara on very carefully. I hurried so no one would see or hear me changing. Bonnie also had a cute white blouse for me to try on. This was the best. The skirt and blouse combo gave me total satisfaction!

Diane put lipstick and mascara on me and fixed my hair real cute and tied a ribbon to hold it. She fixed Bonnie's too. The band started playing but no one was dancing; kids were still showing up. The boys, of course, were checking out all the girls. This one boy that I liked at school came over and asked me if I wanted to get a coke. I said sure if my friends could come, referring to Bonnie and Diane. He bought all of us cokes. By this time, the kids were dancing.

I was scared to death to dance. Rick asks me to dance and Diane of course said she would watch my coke. She whispered, "Just follow his steps?" Dancing was easier than I thought.

"You look different than in school," Rick commented.

"Is that good or bad?" I asked him wondering what he meant exactly. "Good, he commented, really good."

We had a blast. We were dancing and visiting with friends. Our table was three away from the door and not far from the restroom. I kept looking at the clock. Bonnie told me to quit worrying and have fun. So I did.

We were sitting at the table, when suddenly I felt someone grab the back of my neck, squeezing it, painfully, the eyes of my friends growing dark with fright. "Get your ass up right now," my mother hissed at me. She yelled at Bonnie, "Grab your coats and get your ass to the car out front, now! I am taking your sister! Move it! NOW!"

Diane and our other friends were watching in horror. My mother was walking me out the back of the door by my neck. I couldn't get away because she was holding me so tightly it hurt and with the other hand, she was pulling my hair. She walked me to the car, shoved me in the backseat, and started pounding the daylights out of me with her fists. She kept hitting me and pulling my hair, screaming, "You tramp! You f—king little whore! Who do you think you are?" She punched my face and grabbed wads of my hair pulling as hard as possible. "You f—king whore!"

She screamed at Bonnie to get in the front seat and close the damn door. After severely beating me, she got in the front seat and grabbed Bonnie's hair and punched her in the face over and over again, calling her a whore and a prostitute. While still punching the two of us, she told us as soon as we got home that we would be getting the belt. We were sobbing.

When she asked me where in the hell my clothes were? I did not answer. Bonnie quickly said, "Right here."

"You f—king little whores," she screamed, as she began to punch me harder and harder. She tried to take a

139

swing at me again in the back seat while she was driving. She was crazy with hate. I was bleeding all over Diane's skirt and blouse, which were ruined, and holding my nose up to stop the bleeding. Dad was nowhere around.

I wanted to jump out of the car at that very moment to escape my mother's fury. I wished I were dead. My mom screamed at us "I will take care of you tomorrow when we get up. This is not over by a long shot!" When we got home, she continued her assault hitting Bonnie and me again and again and screaming her profanities. "Get your f—king asses in the back door right now," she screamed. "Go straight to your room so Carl doesn't see your faces."

We did exactly what she told us to do. We were terrified that we would be beaten worse than we were. I was a bloody mess. So was Bonnie. We heard her tell Carl, we were not to come out of our room and to make sure we stayed put. We knew then that she and my dad were out at the bar with my Aunt and Larry, and she was returning to continue drinking.

"I am leaving tonight," I told Bonnie. She looked horrified. "I don't care where they take me as long as it was away from here."

"No," Bonnie said looking at my face. "Your eyes are swelling shut."

I told her to look at hers. "I'm too old for them to take me to St. Joseph's so I am taking my chances," I continued my ranting. Bonnie snuck into the kitchen and called her friend Jerry.

Carl saw her face when he came into the kitchen. In shock, he asked, "What happened?"

"You think this was bad, wait until you see Wanda," she answered. "She is still sobbing and bleeding all over in our bedroom." She led him back to our bedroom. He turned on the light and looked at me in horror.

"What happened?" he asked me once again, "What on earth happened to make her beat you this bad? You need to go to the hospital and see a doctor."

I was still crying. We told him what happened as he

was trying to help me. "Your mom could go to jail for this," he said, his voice very quiet, but angry.

"I just want to get away from here! I am leaving tonight," I spoke stifling a sob. "Please don't say anything Carl or my mother will beat me worse during the night because she is drinking."

"I want to call the police," Carl said.

"No, please do not do that. I do not want to be taken away."

"Hey, you girls clean up now, lay down and you will feel better in the morning," his voice was soft and kind. "But listen to me, if you run, make sure you don't get caught or heaven knows what she will do."

"Can I call a friend, real quick?" Bonnie asked Carl.

Carl left the living room so Bonnie could use the phone. When Bonnie returned, she told us that her friend, Jerry, was coming to pick us up at one in the morning. "We will sneak down the alley from our house where he'll be parked waiting for us. We need to put a few things together if we were going to do this."

"How did you meet this guy?" I asked her.

"He's a junior," she answered, avoiding my question.

The phone rang again. Bonnie answered it thinking it was Jerry. It was Diane. Relief flooded through me.

Carl told us he was leaving, now that we were home safely, and the younger kids were asleep. "If I am asked any questions tomorrow, I won't know the answers if I leave," he figured as he went to go out the door.

Diane wanted to know if I was okay. "Are you kidding?" I continued crying, "I have scratches and a bloody nose, and I ruined your beautiful clothes."

"I don't care about my clothes," Diane said. "I care what happens to you."

"I am leaving this house tonight and so is Bonnie. She was beaten up too. Her friend is picking us up in his car at one o'clock. I am having Bonnie and him drop me off at my cousin's house across town. I will never live in this house again!"

"Hang on," Diane said, "I want to talk to my Mom."

While I waited, Bonnie packed me a pair of pants, a bra and blouse. I put my hair in a ponytail. I noticed that chunks of hair were missing. It was close to eleven. I panicked about Mom and Daddy returning home so I told Bonnie to turn off the light.

Finally, Diane came back to the phone and said, "Are you there?"

"Yes," I answered.

"Sorry," she said, "but, my mom and I were talking, and she knows how bad your mom beats you. She's seen your bruises. You could have your sister drop you off here and you could stay in my room with me until we can find you a place to stay."

I told her I didn't want to get them in trouble. She said her mother wasn't worried about that at the moment. Her mother was worried my mother might hurt me more severely when she returned home drunk.

"We can't leave until they come home. It will be very late when we sneak out of the kitchen door. Jerry is picking Bonnie up at one." I told her.

"Come knock on my window, and I will wait up to let you in," Diane said.

I got a bag and put my panties, bras, pants, shirts, and a toothbrush, toothpaste and a hairbrush in it. My face was swollen, my eyes were swelling shut and I had knots all over my head from my mother's fist. Bonnie thought I had a broken nose, as well.

"Go look in the mirror," she said.

"Go look at you, your face is as bad as mine."

Our bags were packed and ready. We got in bed with our clothes on before our parents came home. I was thankful that Barb slept through all of the commotion. She would lose it if she saw our faces. She would beg us to let her come along. I felt guilty leaving her behind.

"What about our horses?" I whispered to Bonnie. "Really, Wanda," She was shocked that I was worried about horses. "We can't worry about horses right now."

"We have other things to worry about, like our sanity, saving ourselves, and getting out of this nightmare."

I got out of bed, unlocked my piggy bank and shoved my money into my coat pocket that hung behind the door with Bonnie's. Thank God I remembered that.

"You mean you haven't done that yet," she worried, knowing our parents could come home at any time.

We lay in bed talking, so we didn't fall asleep. An hour later, we heard our parents pull into the driveway, which was right outside the wall of our bedroom on the other side of the sidewalk and fence. We pulled the covers up to our necks and rolled over so they would think we were sound asleep.

"Where were you going to go?" I asked Bonnie just as we heard the car doors open. "You know, Diane will let you come to her house. She asked me if you wanted."

Bonnie turned and said, "You know Mom knows, you two were best friends and they will send the cops to Diane's house."

"They will hide us," I said determinedly.

"I am taking my chances Wanda, and I don't care anymore, I am meeting other people and I am going to have fun and get away from here," she angrily answered.

The front door opened. We heard the sound of our parent's footsteps in the front room. We laid in bed, our hearts pounding heavily, listening and waiting for the moment of our escape to freedom. I knew I could get a job since I would be fifteen in a couple of days and Bonnie would be sixteen in two weeks. We had to take care of ourselves. We were strong and capable girls.

I heard Dad go from room to room, checking on all of us, turning off the kitchen light and then padding off to the bedroom. Mom must have gone straight to their bedroom.

Bonnie and I lay still, listening to the fan running in the living room. For a good half hour, there wasn't a peep in the house. Soon, Mom and Dad were in a deep sleep because Bonnie could hear them snoring loudly.

We rose out of bed and crept like two thieves in the

night out the kitchen door. We quietly walked down the alley, flinching at each scrape of gravel. We were hoping to keep the neighbor dogs from barking. Jerry and his car had not arrived. I was very frightened. "What are we going to do if he doesn't come?"

Then, we saw him. We jumped into his nice car. I felt my knee's knocking, my heart racing, and pounding about being frightened of what could happen to us. He looked at us and remarked about how we looked like we had been used for punching bags.

Bonnie told him where Diane lived. She introduced me to Jerry, and he said, "Hello kiddo. Sorry about your rough night, girls. "Remember, if you get caught tonight, young lady, I didn't give you a ride." He drove off into the dark night.

When we arrived at Diane's, I slipped out of the car, walked up the steps, and knocked softly on the door. The door cracked open and there was Diane. She gasped in horror when she saw my face, "Oh my God!"

"You haven't seen the rest of me yet."

Diane yelled for her mother to hurry into the living room. I told her I felt awful for what she did to us in front of everyone at the dance. I told them, "When we got into the car she wouldn't stop. She wouldn't stop pounding and beating us! It was awful," I began to cry again.

You need to see your face with all the swelling and scratches on it," Diane said. "I saw my face before we hid in bed," I said solemnly.

We were in the shadowy living room, talking, when Sharon, her mother came out of her bedroom. She saw me and stopped, gasped, and said, "Oh my God, what kind of mother do you have, honey? Only a monster would do that to her child!" She held my arms while studying my face. "We must get ice on you right away! You need immediate attention!"

"I don't know, I don't know. It hurts too much, I was afraid to put anything on it because of the pain." I began crying once again.

"We need to take you to the hospital and make sure nothing is broken,"

I was terrified knowing that I could be sent away to the Good Shepard Home or the Girl's Vocational School (reform school). "No Please, don't, I sob. If the police know I am here, they will show up at your house. Then you would be in trouble for harboring a runaway."

"We won't take you to the hospital or call anyone, now get into bed." Sharon went to the refrigerator, and got an icepack out of the freezer, and applied it to my face. She took me into the bedroom, and settled me into bed, "Put the icepack near your face and sleep, we will get you cleaned up in the morning." She bent over and kissed my forehead softly telling me I was safe now.

Diane crawled onto the other side of the bed, said, "Sleep in late."

The next morning, I was so sore I could hardly function. One eye was swollen shut and my face felt pulverized.

Sharon took pictures so there was a record after the swelling subsided. "The pictures would be my ticket to freedom," she said."No one in his right mind would make you go back to that kind of abuse. We have to document what you looked like when you arrived at our house."

"Look at the back of her neck," Diane said. "It looks like her mom choked her."

I took a mirror and looked at the back of my neck in the bathroom mirror. It was bruised and purple. This was how tight my mother squeezed my neck and pulled the hair out of my head while taking me to the car. I started to cry again remembering the awful details and pain.

I told Diane's mom that I ruined Diane's skirt and her beautiful blouse with blood.

Sharon said, "It doesn't matter about the clothes. Let's worry about getting you healthy again and not concerning ourselves over ruined clothes. Both your eyes are going to swell up more, honey, if you don't quit crying." This was the first time I heard someone other than my dad call me honey.

Sharon fixed us a nice breakfast after we got up so late. She told me to lie on the couch as I had a terrible headache after eating. I began to vomit. I told her I knew by now that my mom and dad had the police out looking for Bonnie and me. She told me to quit worrying about it because she doubted they would come to her house.

Sharon was right. My mom did not know that Diane and I were still best friends since I did not tell her about my friends at school. Sharon turned on the television so I could relax. I had never seen color television before and it kept me occupied. Diane grabbed blankets and pillows and we curled up on the couch to watch TV, until I fell asleep.

I did not wake up until almost dinnertime. Sharon thought I had a concussion because of the headache and vomiting. She was very concerned. Diane said I slept right through lunch and that I had nightmares and was talking in my sleep. They couldn't understand the nightmares, as I garbled my words in my sleep. I told her I usually had horrible nightmares. I did not say what the nightmares were about. They were not about the beatings.

The next day, Diane went to school to pick up our report cards. I asked her to tell them I was sick. She told them I was ill and they gave her my card. While she was gone, I tried to figure out what I was going to do and where I was going to live.

Diane and her mom told me not to worry. I could stay at their house until I got well. "We will lock the door behind you in the morning and just stay away from the windows," they told me.

When Diane's brother came up from the basement bedroom, he asked, "What truck hit you?"

"That's not funny, sweetie," his mom said. "She just went through a horrible ordeal."

Diane told him it was a long story but he said he had already heard about it since he was a junior at the school. "Word gets around about beatings like that. Don't worry, everyone is sorry about what happened at the dance to you and your sister."

"Nonetheless," Sharon told him "let her have her own space, Eddie, and leave it at that until she is healed."

I was so glad she said that, because I did not want to go through the explanation of what had happened to me at the school dance.

"How did the high school kids hear about it?" I asked Diane.

Some high school sophomores came as dates with some freshman," she answered.

All day long, I was frantic about what was going on at my house. I worried about involving Diane and her mother Sharon in this mess. Poor Barb never knew what happened last night and she must wonder why we abandoned her and ran away without talking to her. If only she knew what our mother had done to us at the dance. I was humiliated and in shock over my mother beating me in front of all my classmates and friends at a school dance. I wondered where Bonnie was and how she was doing. I wondered if she was safe.

I knew I couldn't go to school in the fall until I had a job and could support myself. I did not want to get behind in school. I had plans for my future. I had $428.00 in my savings account and money in my coat pocket from my piggy bank. Sharon told me that the bank would probably notify the authorities if I withdrew my money. I asked Diane to grab my coat so I could count how much money I had from my piggy bank. I had $286.75, enough for rent, food and necessities for a while. I offered Diane's mother money from my piggy bank for helping me.

"Hang onto that money! I have a friend, who manages The Monticello Apartments on the corner of Broadway and Warren who might have a studio apartment for rent." "Wait until things cool down and don't go out of the house unless you are in my car with us. Things will settle down and then you can apply for a job at St. John's Hospital as a nurse's aide." The hospital was close by the apartments Sharon added, "Just stay a few more weeks with us until you are one hundred percent healed."

147

Each night, I thanked God for finally giving me some peace in my life. I hoped it stayed that way. I did not want to return to my parent's home. I was starting to heal and the bruises were subsiding and the swelling was less. Diane and I would sit in the back yard, where no one could see me.We talked in the fresh air discussing some perspective on what I needed to do in order. I still had a black eye and swollen face from the brutal attack.

Sharon had developed the pictures for me to show proof of the beating. Diane bought me a wallet for my money and the photos in case no one believed what happened. I had told them my mother lied her way out of everything and had probably lied to the police about why we ran away.

Sharon took pictures the day after the incident, because I looked much worse. "These photos will be your protection of never returning home. Never let them out of your sight! They are your ticket to freedom. You must have a job and stay in school and work hard so the judge knows you are capable of taking care of yourself. It will be hard from the beginning," she said.

"Nothing could be harder than what work we had to do as kids for my mother," I replied back to her. "I'm not afraid of work and never will be. If they ever catch me and ask who took the pictures, I will never tell them who took the photos. I don't care what they threaten me with." Sharon could go to jail for harboring a runaway. I was so blessed to have these wonderful people helping me and getting me on my feet. I looked so much better, and felt like a better person because of them.

Diane taught me how to wear a little mascara and blush, and how to apply lipstick. She told me how pretty it made me look. She taught me how to curl my hair with rollers instead of those awful pink foam curlers our mom made us use. My hair was shiny and bouncy now that I was allowed to wash it every day.

Sharon kept me for six weeks. In time, she had Eddie take me to St. John's to place an application for a job. Within two days, the Director of Nursing told me I could take their Nurse's Aide Program that started on the following Monday. The program would last two weeks and if I passed they would hire me right away as a nurse's aide.

Sharon talked to her friend about a furnished studio apartment. He had a one bedroom to offer me for the same price as the studio. She shared my circumstances with Ed and said that I went to school with his daughter Donna. When we went to inspect the apartment, I loved it and paid him sixty dollars for the rent and utilities. Thank God I had Diane, Sharon, and now Ed to help me on my way!

Diane and her Mom took me to the store and bought me pillows and bedding for the full-size bed, a set of dishes, pots and pans and silverware. Sharon spent ninety dollars. I told her I would pay her back as soon as I could touch my bank account. She told me to consider this a birthday present since I was sick and couldn't celebrate my birthday. I told her we didn't celebrate our birthdays at my home. "Well you do now and remember that," she said.

They brought me back to the apartment and helped me fix it up. It was beautiful for a small apartment. "You will want to buy a television," she said smiling, "It will keep your mind occupied."

I would think of purchasing one with my paycheck. We got paid for going to classes in the Aide Program, which couldn't have helped me more.

The third day after I moved into my apartment there was a knock at my door. It was a man from the phone company. "I am here to install your phone service."

"You have the wrong address. I didn't order a phone," I said.

"No, this is the address the company gave me. Are you Wanda?"

"Yes," I replied.

"Well, a lady named Sharon has paid for a phone hook-up." He continued.

After he installed the phone and left, I called Sharon and thanked her for thinking of me. I told her the money for the phone was coming out of my paycheck or I could pay her with some of the cash I had.

"Hide that money in a safe place so no one will know you have it Wanda."

I kept telling Sharon how special she was in my life, and I could never thank her enough for all she had done for me. She would always say to me, "Love you, doll face."

My Nurse's Aide class started and I whizzed through it. The nun who taught the class said I would be a good nurse one day and she encouraged me to pursue nursing when I finished school. I told her my grandmother worked as a LPN. We worked with patients the first day as the nun followed us, making sure we did things correctly. She always rechecked each patient's blood pressure to make sure it was taken correctly. I was learning new things every day. Soon, I was on my own.

When school started, I let the hospital know I could only work from three in the afternoon to eleven at night. I settled into a routine, working weekdays three to eleven, doing my studies at six in the morning, and working weekends, which didn't matter to me at the time, because it gave me time to get my studies done. I always looked around for police when I walked home because I was still worried about them catching me.

One night as I was getting ready for bed, I heard a knock on the door. I had been living alone for six weeks. I thought it might be Donna. So, I opened the door. There was a police officer standing there before me. "May I help you?" was all I could think to say at that moment.

"May I come in, please?" he was very cordial. He came in and sat at my table. He seemed large in my small apartment. "Now we know where you are young lady. Your parents gave up and thought you had run away from town and that something horrible had happened to you."

"Something horrible did happen," I told the officer. "My mother beat me so badly I was laid up for almost six weeks. My own friends didn't recognize me."

"Do you have anything to back that story up?" The officer asked me.

"Of course," I reached into my purse and pulled out my wallet. I was thinking he was fishing for answers to find out who had helped me. The room was silent.

"This was you!" He asked me while looking at me. "Are you sure this was you?"

When he told me he had to ticket me, I asked him, "Why isn't my mother the one receiving the ticket for child abuse? She was the one who did this to me at the dance at the Civic Center."

"Do you want to charge your mother with felony assault?" The policeman asked. "Just to let you know, what she did was a felony and she will be arrested. The only reason I am not arresting you was because of what you have told and shown me. You can't run anymore, Wanda. You can't keep running and not expect consequences for your actions. You have to have a legal guardian until you are eighteen years of age. This is something you will have to discuss with the judge."

"I could never do that to my father," I told him. He would never forgive me if I charged my mother with felony abuse. My dad is everything to me and that would kill him."

"The court could order her to get help," the policeman said.

I told him that my siblings and I had been removed from the home more times than I could count. I told him I was going to school and had a job at St. John's Hospital.

"Bring your pictures when you go to see the judge," he said. "It will help your cause and he will be very sympathetic towards you." He looked at my hands, which were shaking. "Settle down now and go to sleep. You will have to appear with someone who will be your legal guardian. You're getting a ticket as a runway, but the judge will let you stay where you are because we checked out how long you've been here. Your work and school records indicate you haven't missed any days," he said. "Do you want a patrol car to pick you up?" He kindly asked me.

"Can I have a friend take me to court or call someone to

make sure that I am not late to see the judge?" I asked him.

"As long as you are there before eight in the morning, otherwise someone will be here to get you if you do not show." He replied as he wrote out a ticket and handed it to me. "Give this to the judge. Just don't be late," he warned me for the last time.

I thanked the officer and told him I would be there on time.

Early in the morning I walked to Donna's apartment and told them what happened. Her dad offered to drop me off at the police station, where the judge's chambers were located. He also volunteered to serve as a legal guardian if I needed one but he said he would rather Sharon assumes that responsibility. It was decided that Sharon should take me to court and go with me to see the judge.

I was terrified when I walked into the high ceiling, echoing building. Sharon was beside me. The officer walked me up to the judge's chambers with Sharon. She waited for me by the door since the judge wanted to speak to me alone. I gave the judge the policeman's ticket.

He told the officer to close the door. Then he turned to me. "Do you realize what your parents have been through?"

"Yes, your honor, but if you let me tell you why I ran away, maybe you won't make a judgment against me so quickly and make me go back there." I told him, "I had worked as a babysitter since I was eleven years old and put all of my money in the bank under my name and my dad's name. I showed him where I had not touched that money and had been depositing my recent earnings. I told him I had saved more than $280.00 in cash from the babysitting money without spending any of it except for rent and groceries. "I do not go out, and I do not run the streets. When I am not working, I stay home and do my homework."

The judge looked at me, then down at the ticket. He slowly ripped the ticket in half, the sound of the paper tearing ratcheted up a sense of hope in my heart. He had the ticket pulled from my file after reviewing the photos I provided for proof of abuse. I had shown him the pictures Sharon took and told him about DFS taking us away from my mother before, and putting us in St. Joseph's Orphanage several times. As I sat there, he called DFS. They confirmed to him that what I had said was truthful and that, in fact, I was hospitalized from one incident. He thanked them and hung up the phone.

He turned to me again, and asked me how I was able to survive on my own, for all this time. There was a knock on his door. The officer said there was a woman waiting in the outer office. The judge told the officer that he would call her in when he was ready.

Blood drained from my face. I was certain it was my mother.

While I sat on a chair in front of him, the judge called the school to ask about my attendance and grades. The attendance clerk told him I had not missed a day—except for today. He said she would be in shortly and told the clerk where I was. Then he called St. John's and asked if I was employed there and if I had missed any work. The nun on the other end gave him good reports of my work and conduct. He hung up and told me I could stay where I was but that I had to have a legal guardian because I was underage. "I do not understand how a mother could abuse someone who does as well as you do." He told me.

Suddenly the Judge asked me a question that cracked my life wide open. "Do you want to apply for emancipation from your parents?"

"My dad has never hurt me," I said "He is married to an abusive person and she even calls him names and belittles him at home."

"I could emancipate you from your mom, and keep your dad's name out of it. I could let your parents know that you do not have to come back to their residence because you have one of your own."

"Yes! Yes! But please don't let them know what my address is!" I pleaded with him, "I am so afraid my mom will show up at my front door."

153

She will not be at your door again. This is in the emancipation letter she will receive." He called Sharon into his office and asked if she wanted the responsibility of serving as my legal guardian.

"Absolutely, this girl needs peace in her life." She hugged me there in his chambers. The judge handed Sharon a form to fill out and file at the courthouse.

Then he called the First National Bank and told them to release my funds into my own name, giving them my address. The bank said I had to come in with my Social Security card and open a different account and take dad's name off of my account. I felt bad doing this to my dad but it was my money.

I felt lighter knowing I was free. I was my own keeper. I was relaxed without having to look over my shoulder. Friends who love me supported me. When I was back in my routine of work and school, Sharon called me to see if I needed anything. I asked if Eddie could take me to the bank on my day off. I took my money and put it in another account. I asked if I could please pay her back.

Sharon told me, "No, I will not take your money."

When Eddie took me to the bank with Diane tagging along, I was shocked to find I had more than I realized. I actually had five hundred and thirty plus dollars in the account, not counting the two hundred and twenty I still had in cash. I put it all in the account except for fifteen dollars. I hadn't received a slip before so I had lost track. I told Eddie since I was off work we should go to the RB Drive-Inn, and I would treat him like he did Diane and me. We sat eating hamburgers and drinking milkshakes, talking and laughing about things, and visiting with other kids who came after school.

I found out what I had been missing. This was easygoing friendship, with fun doing things with friends. I had a curfew of nine-thirty during weekdays except the nights I worked until eleven. When I was sixteen it would be midnight on weekends and nine-thirty on weekdays. I wasn't going to abuse the privilege of being on my own because I loved having the responsibility, and I was going to prove to myself I could survive. Later on, I found out from a friend of a friend that the policemen knew I was doing well because the judge emancipated me the day after seeing me.

On Thanksgiving, I worked for a lady who wanted to be with her family. Her shift started at seven in the morning. While I was working, I ran into my cousin Charlotte, the daughter of one of my dad's brothers, who had also been working at the hospital. We didn't get to see much of each other growing up because we lived on the other side of town and mom didn't go around Dad's family that much. She was able to give me some of the first news I had heard about my family. She heard from Aunt Dolly that I had run away from home.

I was still experiencing a lot of dark moments. Nightmares plagued me, and living alone made enduring them difficult. I didn't know what had happened to Bonnie. I was worried to death about what was going on with Barb. On my day off, I finally went over to my Aunt Dolly's house. She was glad to see me. She asked why I hadn't called her when my mother beat me, and I ran away. I told her I was afraid and didn't have her phone number with me when I left the house. I told her how I stayed with a girl and that her mother helped me.

The she told me some disturbing news. My sister Bonnie and Jerry, who had helped us the night we ran away, had met up with some other kids. They broke into the back of an Eddy's Bakery truck. They had been drinking and when they got into the open truck they just sat there, eating cakes and donuts and making a mess. They were caught and taken to the police station. Mom and Dad had to go and get her. Mom had her put in the State Girl's Vocational School, located seven miles north of Helena, which was a school for girls who were in trouble. She had to stay thereuntil she was eighteen. Aunt Dolly spoke vehemently about my mother being unfit to have children and how it was just painful to watch her make you girls

155

work like slaves. She couldn't stop herself, "Why I didn't throw myself in front of you, well there's just no excuse…your dad was my big brother so I felt I couldn't interfere! Damn all us adults! I'm so sorry. You kids are the ones who paid the ultimate price…I hope you can forgive your dad and me one day."

I hadn't seen Auntie so emotional before and felt sorry for her so I changed the subject. I asked her if she would give my sister Barb a note for me, but she told me that she had a falling out with Mom when Bonnie and I left. I told your mom, "One day you will destroy your family with your anger—treating your children like prisoners and war hounds, and you did just that." "We had a terrible fight," she told me.

"What did my dad do?"

"He just stood there dumbfounded, looking dazed and stupid."

Your mom told me "To get my ass out of there and to learn to mind my own goddamn business. Your mom started calling me an alcoholic because I had a few drinks once in a while. She also called me a few choice names of her own like the ones she used on you I was sure."

Aunt Dolly told my mom, "At least, I didn't hide it from my kids. I never lied to your cousins!"

She said she told my father to come and see her anytime he wanted, but Helen was NOT welcome in my home ever again!

"What do you mean?" I blinked my eyes in disbelief.

"I've said too much," Aunt Dolly said. She realized she had best stop there before she really got into it about the family's dislike of Helen over the years.

My dad's parents never approved of my mother's relationship with Dad. They knew she hung out with other women at the Blue Moon Bar in Helena before dad returned from World War II. After she met him, they figured she slept with him right away so she didn't have to work out at the smelter anymore. She would have a roof over her head and not have to live at the Y.W.C.A. When they married after two weeks of dating my grandparents were upset. Now, Helen had him where she wanted him. One thing they didn't like about her was her lack of moral fiber. Sexually, she just had no boundaries. With each oncoming baby she never considered our futures as we were so close in age, especially Bonnie and I as we were the same age for a few weeks.

I began to piece together their story. It seemed Mom couldn't get enough sex. How many times were we sent out in the yard after Dad got home from working late, then, a little later, we were allowed to come back in the house.

Dolly told me before her brother had come into the picture, my mother had dated a number of men at the Blue Moon Bar. "That is the truth, but your mom needs to tell you, and she isn't going to. That was why she called you girls those awful names when you were toddlers and didn't know the meaning of the words. Her guilt was her shame and she was inflicting it on her children. After you children were born, none of the family members told you anything."

Aunt Dolly told me that she had found out through police friends about the awful beatings we had received. She could not believe my mother wasn't put in jail for the beatings. She also told me my mother had the choice to bail out Bonnie, but she chose, instead, to have her put in the Montana State Vocational School for Girls. Aunt Dolly said that Barbara was at the house and looked like a lost soul.

That news made my heart ache. I shouldn't have left my little sister to fend alone in that house, but if I had taken her with me, I would probably be in the reform school with Bonnie. I had to get my phone number to her some way. But it was nearly impossible, as my mother didn't let her out of her sight except for school.

I tried calling the State Vocational School for Bonnie, but when I did, the operator told me the only person who was allowed to speak with her were her parents and my name was not on the list of contacts. When I told her, I was her sister, she said, that does not matter whatsoever. Your name was not on the list of visitors or callers.

When I told Aunt Dolly that they wouldn't let me speak to her, she said my mom and dad hadn't been out to visit her. They said, "She made her bed now she could lie in it."

I felt isolated from my siblings because of Mom and furious at my parents for doing this to us. They prevented me from speaking to my sisters because of the emancipation. Doubts swirled through me, about leaving my little sister, the one person I deeply cared for, and about not being there for Bonnie when she had to go with Jerry. I was furious about why we were allowed to go back to my mother over and over again. My mother, who just started hitting us again and again, who didn't believe what we told her happened to us at the orphanage, or she just didn't care.

I was trying, at fifteen, to understand my mother and her actions, the dark river of secrets, and the ongoing nightmares that haunted me. I told a friend I did not know what to believe. I could not confide in anyone about what happened to me. In my sex education part of my health class, I was finding out about sex. I realized the full extent of what had happened to me, and I was too embarrassed and humiliated to consider confiding in anyone. I was a teenager and the language of sex was everywhere. The girls laughed about their weekend of partying in the lockers. They talked freely about their sexual encounters. I was appalled that it didn't bother them to discuss it in front of others so freely. The boys were always wide-eyed with hunger for sex. It bothered me.

I was afraid, ashamed, and, lonely. I told myself the quiet in the apartment was temporary, and I would meet new friends soon and start feeling better about my decision to cut ties with Mom. I was thankful for friends at school but the judge told me I had a curfew to keep and I could not expect my friends to drop everything to make sure I got home on time.

Christmas came and went, and I didn't bother anyone. I left Grandma's address at Mom's house so I could not even contact her. I worked a lot to keep up with living expenses, and bills. It was overwhelming. I had doctor bills, a phone bill, and groceries to buy.

The worst time for me was in the middle of the night, when I would startle out of a deep sleep, heart pounding, waking from my awful nightmares. My nightmares, that would plague me for the rest of my life, were always the same. The priests were chasing me, trying to catch me. I was running as fast as I could to escape them, but they were big and I was small. They always caught me in the end. They would catch me and pin me down, covering my mouth as I struggled to breathe. I fought to no avail as they smothered me. One of them was holding me down, and the others laughed as they took turns, the entire time stifling my screams while they raped me over and over. I awoke panicked with tears streaming down my face. Eventually, my body was forced to breathe. I gulped the precious air of my wakingand found the dream broken for the moment. When I did fall back to sleep, sometimes the dream continued, and I would go through the whole process again. I cannot get the screams out of my mouth. I continued to struggle in the dark sleep reliving the horror of my sexual predators as they had their way with me every day in their care when I was a little girl. When I would finally awake, my forehead was drenched in sweat, and I was crying actual tears. I became so sleep-deprived from fear that I could not go back to sleep. My health was compromised through lack of sleep, and I lost weight among other symptoms brought on by extreme stress. I ached to sleep peacefully and prayed the nightmares would end.

I kept thinking something was going to harm Barb. I wondered if she was going to ever go through what Bonnie and I did at the hands of the nuns. I could not stop worrying that the priests had raped and hurt her too. I just wanted the nightmares to vanish, because now I saw Barb running in them too. I was having them nightly. I knew I was safe, but I was frantic about my sisters.

I worried about how Barb was doing at home with my mother. I worried about what Bonnie was enduring at the Montana Vocational School. My state of mind was

159

dangling like a noose over my head.

I had not seen or heard from Diane or her mother, Sharon, for several months. Then one day at school, I heard they had moved out of Montana. I was shocked! Shocked and hurt that they did not even let me know. I decided that something must have happened that I wasn't aware of and they didn't want to bother me. That was the kind of people they were. Always ready to help others but not letting anyone know, when they needed help, if they did need help. I missed them dearly.

CHAPTER TWENTY

I made friends with Georgia and her sister Dina. I started having fun again, and my self-esteem blossomed and seemed to be on the mend. After I got off of work, I would go with the girls to parties and we would drink, even though I knew we shouldn't. Drinking made the bad memories fade into the abyss until I would wake up the next day with a monster hangover. I told Georgia if I got caught I would get in trouble. I no longer had a guardian with Sharon gone, and the judge did not know that. She assured me that we would not get caught since we partied out at Canyon Ferry most of the time on private property. She says that the law cannot trespass on private property.

By my sixteenth birthday, I was working as a carhop at Eileen's Drive Inn across from the Helena High School. I was making the same wages I made as a Nurse's Aide, but I was also making tips. Eileen also fed me when she found out I was supporting myself and living alone and paying for all of my expenses.

Near to the end of July, my mom drove by Eileen's and found out from someone that I had another job at St. John's Hospital. She began to cause problems for me at the hospital and at Eileen's. The hospital said they would give me a good recommendation, but they could not keep me. They had issues with my mother threatening them. She was calling the hospital causing problems about hiring me in the first place. She said I was a run away. I sat in my supervisor's office where she told me how terrible she felt about losing me. She knew I wanted to be a nurse and told me not to give my dream up. She also told me I needed to find work where my mother could not cause trouble for me.

Without my job, I could no longer afford to keep my apartment. My mother was trying to make my life miserable. She was calling and threatening Ed, my landlord. I knew she wanted me to fail completely, and run back to her, but it would be a cold day in hell before that happened.

Georgia and Dina talked to their mom and dad about letting me stay with them after my rent was up. They had a large family. Five of the children were no longer at home. Georgia and Dina were the only ones left. They were a loving family with big hearts that made me feel good to be around. I told Mary I would pay rent for staying there and she refused to let me. We had a lot of good times at their house.

In the summer, they headed to the Rocky Boy Reservation, the Chippewa Creek Reservation in Northeastern Montana for a Powwow. Mary and George had a stand where they sold corn on the cob and fry bread along with chili. Mary made the best fry bread I had ever eaten. We helped her sell during the day and at night we watched male fancy-dancers in their outrageous colorful costumes as they stomped and whirled and propelled across the floor in competition.

Of course, I did more partying and drinking. It helped me forget everything: the terror of the priests, my lost sisters, my awful fights with my mother and most of all missing my daddy and Barb. I even missed my brothers for that matter. The drinking really helped my lonely nights and the awful nightmares that seemed to alter my existence. When I drank I passed out and didn't remember nightmares taking place.

The family had relatives at Rocky Boy that I became friends with. They asked me to stay with them after Mary told them the problems my mother was causing in Helena. If I stayed with them my mother would not know where I was. I would be going to school and not working. Mom would only be able to find me through my Social Security number.

I had to think about it. I had to stay in school. The Powwow was over and George and Mary were getting

162

ready to return to Helena. We discussed my being bussed to Box Elder where they would enroll me in school before the year started. It was agreed the best thing for me, so I caught the bus and began my school year with the Azure family.

The Azures were an incredible family. The girls were teenagers as well; Lois was seventeen, and Terry and I were sixteen and juniors in high school. The three of us had a large bedroom with three twin beds. The girls adjusted the room to make room for a desk. Lois and Terry showed me how to wear make-up so that it looked natural. Their Mom had taken me to buy school supplies, which I covered with my own money. I started feeling pretty. Especially when the boys at school told me I was pretty.

The bus ride was an hour and a half. Box Elder was a small school compared to Helena High. The teachers were very good and helped all of their students succeed.

I had my first real crush ever. His name was Pete Thomas and he was a senior. I sat with him on the school bus. Pete was a football player at Box Elder and a good quarterback. He was quarterback all four years.

I went on dates with Pete. We kissed, my first real kiss, which I could honestly say I enjoyed very much. I really fell for him. Pete helped me with my schoolwork at his parent's house. His mother, Mary was very nice and made us snacks as we did our homework. She always visited with me when we were done studying. After, Pete ran me home for dinner at the Azures. I was thankful for his help because my grades improved, and I had always been a studious person.

In Box Elder, I felt people liked me for who I was. My friends made me feel like I was someone who deserved some happiness. I never felt pretty growing up. I would never wish the ugliness I felt about myself on anybody. I always felt the ugliness would never go away, but now I felt better about myself, thanks to the people who had shown me they cared for me.

Nevertheless, even with everything going great with the

Azure family I couldn't stop thinking about Barb. Terry tried calling my house and asking for Barb for me as I was scared to be discovered.

"She can't talk on the phone," my mom rudely told Terry. "Who is calling?"

Terry told me your mom was very rude to me. I explained that was how she talked if someone called for us. I knew Barb was still at home.

My life was turning around.

And then my grandmother found out where I was. She was extremely upset and shocked when she found out where I was and what had happened.

A girl from Rocky Boy was sent to Montana Vocational School in Helena, for getting into trouble in Box Elder. The girl met Bonnie at the School and asked her if she was related to a girl named Wanda who had the same last name. She also mentioned that Bonnie and I looked a lot alike. The girl then told Bonnie she knew who I was and where I was living. Bonnie wrote Grandma. Grandma had been worried sick for months because she did not know if I was dead or alive. She was mortified that I was so far from home. She asked Bonnie to please get my address or at least the name of the school I was attending. She would take it from there.

Grandma notified the school officials to let them know she was my grandmother. She also told them a plane ticket had been purchased for me to fly to California. She sent it to the school to make sure I got on the plane once the ticket had arrived. She informed the school that I had no legal guardian and she would become mine. She told the school that no one in the family knew where I was until the girl at the Vocational School told my sister.

At school the next day, my teacher called me into the hall. He told me that my grandmother had spoken to the principal. I was told that I needed to pack to catch a plane in Havre where a ticket was waiting for me. I had two days to say goodbye to all my friends. Before I left, the school made sure I called my grandma to confirm I would be on

164

the plane when they picked me up in Sacramento.

When Granny answered the phone, she cried with joy. "We were so worried," she cried, her voice thick and quivery. "We thought you had been kidnapped. We thought you were dead."

"I am sorry Grandma. I will explain everything once I get there. What Mom had done was awful. She sounded so different from when I was a little girl, more vulnerable, shakier.

It was so hard saying goodbye to everyone. I thanked my principal and the counselor for all their help. I let them know how much I loved everyone's kindness—the Azure's who took me in without really knowing me, and the teachers who were so kind to me. The counselor hugged me told me to always be safe.

The day I found out about my grandmother's plans, Pete Thomas and I went out. I began to cry when I had to say goodbye. He promised that he would write to me and stay in touch.

I told the Azure family that night that they had been a true blessing in disguise sent to me from God. They were lifesavers for me in a time when I needed help.

"You need to be with family, a family that will love you like your grandparents," they responded.

At the airport, I walked up the metal stairs to the waiting plane, to what I thought was a future where I would live with people who loved me, where I would learn to be on my own, where I would be reunited with my sister. I was looking forward to a future of where I would become a nurse and marry. Now, I knew as the plane rose up over Havre, over the yellow and green checks of farmland and the spine of the Rocky Mountains, I knew my emancipation had truly begun.

CHAPTER TWENTY-ONE

When I disembarked from the plane in Sacramento, I saw my Grandmother, Uncle Jim, and Aunt Maxine. They lived in Yuba City, and Grandma lived just out of Marysville in a little town called Loma Rica, which was ten miles out of Marysville. Uncle Jim had driven Grandma to get me. We then drove to my uncle's house to have dinner and to meet my cousins for the first time.

My cousin Karen was a year younger than me. We hit it right off as for once I was not shy. Jimmy and Marsha were great kids too, and I loved and adored my Aunt Maxine who mothered me immediately. I remembered her from their visit to Montana when I was little, and I remember her caring about us. She realized about the treatment I received as a child growing up with a mentally disturbed and manic-depressive mother.

My aunt cooked us a fabulous meal. I visited with everyone, answering questions about what happened and why I was living so far from home when Grandma discovered my whereabouts.

"Why on earth were you living alone to begin with?" My Uncle Jim asked waiting for an explanation. I told my Uncle, who was Mom's brother that I would explain but not in front of the younger kids. Later, I explained the explosion that took place at the dance. I proceeded to tell him mom beat Bonnie and me terribly at the dance in front of school friends. Then I went to my suitcase and brought out the pictures and showed him, my aunt, and Grandma. He asked who took the pictures, and I told him a friend's mother who told me to keep these in case I got caught when I ran away.

Aunt Maxine was horrified at the photos and told my uncle that she knew something like this would eventually happen, because no one stepped up to the plate to tell Mom she was unfit. We should've tried to get custody of the children. She couldn't get over the fact that my face was pulverized. She remembered how my mother was slapping us around when they had visited us and couldn't believe that she would continue, as we got older.

Grandma piped in and said, "That was why I never went back for a visit and never will again."

"She was sick Grandma and no one would help her understand that she needed help."

Grandma continued, "Your mother does not want help honey. We begged her to stop having children after she was neglecting you and Bonnie on the ranch as toddlers. No one could get Helen to listen to what she was becoming and what she was doing to her children. I was wrong to leave you children with her when she kicked me out of your house my last visit. I am not forgiving her for what she did to you in these photos and her recklessness, and "Shame on her for putting Bonnie in a reform school!"

She and Uncle Jim told me how bad it was when we were babies and toddlers when dad was working long hours as a lineman in Redding. That was how I found out what happened to us as little toddlers.

I told them about being taken away and put in the orphanage, but I was too embarrassed to tell them about the molestations that took place and the shame I carried. I felt so dirty, the kind of dirt that can't be washed away. I was afraid if they knew how priests raped me throughout my childhood, they would judge me, even if they didn't want to, so I continued hiding the shame. I certainly didn't want the shame to follow me here.

Uncle Jim told me, I would be spending weekends with them and school days with Grandma and Grandpa. He would have me walk two blocks to where he worked at The Bay Ford Co. and I would go home with him from there. I had to wait for half an hour and they always gave me a pop to drink while I worked on homework.

Uncle Jim's house was absolutely stunning with a

beautiful kidney shaped swimming pool with a slide and bricking all around it. The pool had a diving board and a beautiful white gazebo adorned the lawn off to the left of the pool. My uncle owned acres and acres of orchards. They had a peach orchard across the road from where he'd planted almonds, walnuts and plums in an orchard out behind the house while lemon and limetrees grew in the back yard. There were far more varieties not mentioned; they always had fresh fruit on hand at any time.

Grandma's house was in a beautiful countryside setting with several pomegranate trees lining the back acreage. We pulled into Grandma's driveway and Grandpa came out to greet me. He hugged me and was amazed at how much I had grown since he had last seen me. You definitely have your Grandma's looks he said with a huge smile. He asked Uncle Jim if he needed a hand with luggage and he said there wasn't much here. I only had a little old carry on.

Aunt Maxine promised me we would go shopping for clothes on the weekend. After all, I couldn't start in a new school with old clothes. Grandma thought Maxine should take me shopping because she didn't know the first thing about teenager's styles.

Grandpa took me to get registered and then showed me the way to walk from the school to Uncle Jim's work. Grandpa had retired from Bay Ford Company years ago. The Bay Ford was close to my school. Grandma gave gramps a list of things we were to go pick up at the store. He also bought me soda and snacks for after school, which I never would have dreamed of getting at home.

I thought about Pete Thomas and my friends. I missed them and I missed having a guy I liked very much. Nonetheless, I was here and happy to be with family. My first day of school was scary. The school was so big and had several buildings on campus. We didn't have a school campus at Helena High School that was anything like this. The school was an entire city block. School started at seven fifteen in the morning. I chose the same classes I had in Box Elder except I had to take print shop instead of Typing

2. Print shop was something new to me, as I had never heard of a print shop for a class and frankly wasn't sure what it was. When my teachers introduced me they would say, "We have a new student today. Her name is Wanda." It made it easier for kids to introduce themselves.

The new school was friendly and I felt like I would be comfortable here. I met a lot of new friends in just the two days before the weekend. I was very anxious on Friday though because my aunt was going to take me shopping on Saturday and I had no idea what kind of clothes she was buying and really didn't care because I knew they would be new clothes, which was something I could never afford or was ever allowed to have. Instead of buying new clothes with the money I earned, I bought uniforms for work.

My uncle drove us across the bridge from Marysville to Yuba City. It surprised me that the towns were so close together. In 1955, my aunt and uncle lost their home in the big flood of Sutter County. They lost all of their belongings and to top that it was on or around Christmas time. The kids were very small when this had happened. I could just imagine what my poor aunt had gone through. I remember because they sent pictures of the flood to my parents, which I still had in my possession. I was trying to memorize the way to their house. It wasn't that hard to find as my uncle stayed on the main road until he came to Oswald Road.

Aunt Maxine had a great dinner ready. She made her famous peach cobbler, which everyone talked about, including my grandparents. I told her she had to teach me how to make it, as it was so incredible I wanted more and couldn't stop eating it.

Karen and I went swimming a little while after dinner. Jimmy and Marsha swam with us. It was a blast especially on the slide, which I had never done. Jimmy was quite a little jokester. I really enjoyed being around them even if they were a few years younger than me. My brother was nothing like him, since Wes was too serious all the time.

The next day we went shopping. My aunt took me to the beauty shop first. Karen and I both get our hair trimmed

169

and styled along with my aunt. Then we went to a department store and Karen helped me pick out clothes that were the style and very beautiful. I could never have nice things like these. She bought me three pairs of shoes, socks and under-garments. I did not have a good coat. She remarked mine needed to go in the trash bin, so she bought me a car coat and a dress coat. She bought me expensive make-up that Karen picked out. I actually told her I didn't need this much stuff and didn't deserve to be spoiled this way. I had never in my life been treated so exquisitely. I couldn't believe how much she spent. I adored this woman and my uncle, and my three cousins.

Karen and I became very close friends and always looked forward to weekends. We were not just cousins, but best friends. When it was time for Uncle Jim to take me back to my Grandma's house, Karen always came along. Aunt Maxine said she would see me the next weekend and then hugged me as she said goodbye.

I was excited to get back to Grandma and Grandpa's house too. Grandma asked how I liked the new school and if I made any friends, and I told her yes to all the questions above. I told her how happy I was to be here with everyone. We embraced in a tight hug. Grandpa looked at all the bags and said "It looked like someone got a little spoiled while she was gone Ma," his eyes twinkling. Grandma said, I think we will have to put a lot of my new clothes in the hall closet mine was way too small. It was so good I had a room of my own.

I always had to share a room except in my little apartment. That was really a dark time being alone and frightened while I listened to every noise in the halls when people got off the old elevator. I walked into my new bedroom. Grandma had bought a purple bedspread and carpet for my room, and a corkboard for me to pin school memorabilia onto. I was so lucky I could not believe it. She asked if I got my homework done.

The first time I came back from Uncle Jim's and Aunt Maxine's, Grandma asked me to sit down and talk with her.

I thought she was going to ask questions I wasn't ready to answer. I knew she was going to ask about quite a few things and she had every right to. Grandpa made himself scarce when Grandma and I talked at the table.

I told Grandma all about what my mom had done to make me run away and things that happened way before then. I also told her how we never once had Christmas or birthday gifts. That upset my grandmother because she had sent money all along for the gifts. She said, "Your mother will never get a dime from us again for being so bold to lie to her own mother."

I told her I hadn't heard a word about Barb or Wes. She never brought Willard home except when dad pushed his way to get him home. We took trips to see him most of the time because Mom hated being around him and didn't want him in the way at home. "He only came home three times in all the time he had been in Boulder. She treats him like he doesn't exist." I bit my lip.

Grandma said she would send a letter to Barb and let her know where I was and that I miss her terribly. At least she will know you are safe with your Grandpa and me.

Grandma continued on, "I was so ashamed of your mom's behavior. I never dreamed it would get this bad for you kids. She was cruel when you were babies and we thought she would change once she went back to Montana with your dad. When I came there to visit and she treated me so badly for telling her to leave you kids alone, I had enough. I should have gone back to check on the situation and deal with your mom's hostilities." She told me my mom had a severe mental condition obviously and should have had help.

"It wouldn't have made a difference Grandma when Dad couldn't do anything with her anger issues. He would just go about his own business," I said trying to assuage her guilt. I tried to comfort her for her feeling terrible about inquiring about the bad things that happened to us.

She sent me off to bed, and I quickly fell asleep. During the night Grandma came into my room and shook me. She

171

told me I was having a nightmare and crying in my sleep. She had me take a drink of warm milk; it helped and I fell right back to sleep.

The next morning, Grandpa took me to the school bus stop, which was at the end of their road. I told Grandpa I had walked much further than this when I was at home, so I could walk by myself from now on. He said, "Not on chilly mornings in the winter months."

I laughed and said, "Quit spoiling me Grandpa."

CHAPTER TWENTY-TWO

I met two girls while waiting for the bus. Carol lived across from us, and Karen who lived at the end of the street past Grandma's house. We struck up a friendship that would last between all three of us. Karen and I enjoyed doing our homework together each night since we had classes in common. We were the first kids picked up on the route and the last to be dropped off, as the bus driver always took a different route coming home.

I enjoyed Marysville High School. The kids were great and so were the teachers. I met a Yolanda and Tara in one of my classes. They asked me to go to lunch with them. This was an open campus so we had our choice to eat in the lunchroom or go to a lunch spot close to school. There was only one. It was a taco place, so we walked the two blocks from school. We ate and hurried back before the bell rang. My days went by very fast.

Life was very simple living with my grandparents. Grandma would ask me to make my bed each morning before and do the dishes. When I was done with my homework and dinner was over Grandma and Grandpa taught me to play their favorite game, Pinochle.Grandpa made the remark to Grandma, now we could have a threesome instead of a twosome (ha-ha) He thought it was pretty funny with his dry sense of humor. I learned to play the game even though it was hard to figure out at first. I enjoyed sitting with them and talking about how my day was at school and how many friends I had made and how I liked my classes. They would ask questions as we played our card game. Finally after a couple of hours, gramps would say, "Wanda, you can watch a television program and then it will be time to turn in young lady."

I told him no thanks I would rather take my shower

before bed, as I liked to curl my hair and sleep with rollers in. It always took some getting used to sleeping with those darn things, but I did it. It made me feel good to look great. I would put on a little make up in the morning and hurry out the door to wait for Karen and Carol. Carol always came out when I did then we would see Karen's head coming over the hilly road.

At least it was a paved road and not frozen dirt like in Montana. I loved living here the winter months. It was just foggy and a chill in the air in the early morning. Then it would get nice and warm for the day and again, no snow. I was settled in here and loved my surroundings and my weekends at my uncle's house.

My Aunt loved how well I styled her hair and she informed me she wasn't wasting money at the hairdresser's on weekends anymore. I learned to style French rolls with French curls from Jackie and Clara when I lived with them in Montana. They always styled their hair beautifully. Now I was doing it for my aunt who truly loved what I did with her hair.

Thanksgiving arrived and we were at Uncle Jim's house. We had five days off from school for Thanksgiving. Grandma would bring my clothes on Thursday. Wednesday, I was going to my uncle's work to ride home with him. I had no homework to do so we took off early. Before we organized to cook, I went with my aunt and Karen to do the grocery shopping for our Thanksgiving dinner.

My aunt wanted to stop at this cute dress shop to get new autumn colored dresses for all of us. Karen and I loved our new dresses. "No need for the beauty shop," my aunt said, "Wanda can do our hair for us." We laughed about my aunt's new beautician, me.

We got up early on Thanksgiving morning. My aunt had already put the turkey in the oven while we slept in. A little later in the day Grandma and Gramps arrived.

At times I felt like I was living this fairy tale life. This was not normal for me, and I was afraid it would end.

Everyone was happy and excited to sit down to a fabulous meal. There was none of the confusion or anger that I grew up with. I was observing what a normal family was like. I couldn't be any happier than I was at this moment.

I was full in no time at all. Then my aunt brought her peach cobbler and put it down on the table since it was everyone's favorite. "No pie here today," Grandpa said pointing at his full stomach and looking at his favorite cobbler. I too was exceedingly full but I ate a piece of the cobbler so I wouldn't hurt my Aunt's feelings. I was stunned at this beautiful ritual as we sat at the table and visited with each other. I was asked to say the blessing. I thanked God and all of them for giving me what I never had, love. I choked back tears.

My aunt said to me that one thing I didn't lack at all was manners. She also told me I looked like I was getting my confidence back. When I arrived I seemed to lack what my cousins grew up with and I knew it. Karen was a straight A student, and president of the student body at school. She had finesse and confidence that I lacked. I would love to be confident and stand before people and speak like she did. I was still afraid to get in front of the class and speak at all. Maybe one of these days that would happen but not right now.

Then Karen told me I should try out for cheerleading. She and I practiced out in the back yard at her house on the weekends when I was there. Karen had been a cheerleader in the eighth, ninth and tenth grades. I was a good gymnast and had no problem at all with Karen, but I needed to work on cheering in front of a crowd, which I knew was going to be terrifying. We did very well during the tryouts for cheerleaders. Only ten of us would be picked and Grandma said she would buy me the uniforms if I made it.

I asked if any mail came for me and she told me one came over the weekend. Pete Thomas had finally written. He was busy with school and had decided that when school was out what college he would be going to. Pete was going to Northern in Havre so he could be close to home. He told me he was dating another girl but he still wanted us to be friends. He missed me.

Now that I no longer had a boyfriend, I started paying attention to the ones who liked me here. There were two, Richard and Chuck. Chuck always walked me to the bus stop. He tried to be more than a friend. Richard walked me to the classes we shared. We had a school dance and Chuck asked me to go with him.

The dance was everything I thought it would be. I finally found out what fun was without anything bad happening to me. We had a twelve o'clock curfew and we made it home ten minutes before our curfew which impressed my uncle. He told Chuck he was a gentleman for getting me home safe, and before curfew.

I loved my life with everything being so calm and no yelling and no beatings. Both Uncle Jim and Aunt Maxine talked very softly compared to my mom's screaming.

When I got back to Grandma's she told me some disturbing news when we walked in. She said she found out that my mom and dad had sold the house on Waukesha and moved up to a place called Unionville. She asked if I knew where it was. I told her my aunt and uncle lived up there before they divorced, and we used to go up and see them. It was a crude house with an outhouse. Well apparently your mom loves living that way because that was the house they bought and moved into. Poor Barb, I thought to myself. Suddenly I wanted to call her and check on her status even though I knew Mom wouldn't let me talk.

My grandmother told me they still had the same phone number. She also said that my mother knew I was with my grandparents and that they were now my legal guardians. She told my mother that she corresponded with Bonnie in the girl's school. Your mom hung up on me. She was a handful when I was raising her. She was very defiant and only cared about Helen. Uncle Jim confirmed with a nod.

Christmas was coming and Grandpa asked me if I would like to go shopping for gifts. I did not have a lot of allowance left but Grandpa said he would help me. I had never gone on a Christmas shopping trip. I told Grandpa we never got to buy presents for anyone in the family before, because Mom never bought for us, let alone let us buy for others. I told him about not ever having birthday parties or getting to go to a friend's birthday and buy them a gift. "Well now you can," he smiled happily at me.

Get what you like for each person and if you need more money let me know. He handed me a hundred dollars and I started shopping in the store while he waited for me in the truck, reading the newspaper. I was overwhelmed to be in such a big the store. I bought Uncle Jim and Grandpa each a sweater. Grandma received a stationary set, as she loved to write letters. Aunt Maxine collected bells, so I found her a clear crystal bell that was etched; Karen received a new album for school memorabilia. I told Grandpa we had to go to a toy store with the money I had left.

At the toy store, I bought Jimmy a dragon kite. Marsha loved Barbie dolls, and I got her a fancy one. I was done shopping and gave Grandpa the change. He couldn't believe I had eleven dollars and some odd cents left. Most things were on sale except for the kid's things. He asked me, if I had picked up wrapping paper. I ran back in after he gave me the money back and bought a roll of bright paper.

He told me to keep the change for school. He knew I liked the taco place where we hung for lunch. I always wished that Karen and I went to the same school and could be together all the time. I loved hanging out with my cousin and now that she was dating Larry, he was constantly asking me how she felt about him. He was a really cool guy, and I was glad Karen was dating him. He was a great basketball player, but I couldn't say what position he played.

It was Christmas Eve and we went to my Uncle's house for Christmas. I had so much fun wrapping my gifts, and packing to go on a weeklong trip with my aunt and uncle after Christmas was over. We were going to Fort Bragg and park their new camper trailer by the ocean cliffs.

Myuncle had a new red 1964 Thunderbird convertible. He intended to pull the camper behind. That would be quite the sight! Grandma told me first I needed to focus on what Christmas was all about.

My cousins came running when we arrived getting right to work giving Grandpa a hand with the gifts. Karen helped me with my gifts. She asked me if I was excited about our trip. Granny and Aunt Maxine laughed and said, "That is all we've heard about this week." She told me this would be a nice time for you to be away from older people for a while and had time with your cousins. I loved living with my grandparents, but I would love to live closer to town and not so far away. Ten miles was a long way for a teenager. We only had a church, community center and grocery store in Loma Rica. It was pretty small, but I lived in a safe place and that was all that mattered.

We opened Christmas presents on Christmas morning, so the night of Christmas Eve we played games while the adults visited and watched television listening to Bob Hope's Christmas with the troops. We loved the music and sang along with them as we played the games.

Karen and I went into the bedroom, which had beautiful twin beds for when I came to stay. My aunt loved frilly things at that time so the beds had canopy tops. Karen told her Mom we were too old for them. My aunt told her that when she left to go to college it would be Marsha's room, and she liked the frills. I just laughed, because I was lucky just to have blankets on thebed that Bonnie and I had to share. It was time for all of us to get to bed. Jimmy and Marsha were the most excited, and deep down so was I. I just didn't let on.

Christmas morning when everyone was ready, Uncle Jim played Santa and handed out gifts. There were so many it was unreal. They were even on the fireplace hearth by the tree. The only thing missing for Christmas in California was the snow. Honestly I didn't care, as I did not have to walk in snow to school or shovel sidewalks anymore. I was looking at all the happy faces and seeing a whole different holiday than I was used too.

I had tears of joy in my eyes when I opened my first package, which was a little heavy. Inside the box was a white typewriter for me to type my compositions instead of going to the library. I thanked Grandpa and Grandma and told them how much I loved them and how much they meant to me. I had to catch my breath before I could continue to open gifts. The next one was from my Aunt and Uncle. It was a huge box and inside was a beautiful purple suitcase for me to put my clothes in for our trip. Grandma had old suitcases I could use, but this was my very own.

Another present from Aunt Maxine was a plastic bag that held lots of feminine essentials, makeup, and girlie items. "I kissed her and thanked her and whispered in her ear, "You knew I needed these, didn't you."

Jimmy kept saying "Open mine next please." He got me a beautiful cardigan of light lilac, which was my favorite color at that time. Marsha's gift was new pajamas and a nightgown. Karen gave me a camera in a little black bag with six rolls of film. I told her how much this meant to me. I would be able to take pictures of our trip. I was so thankful and felt I didn't deserve so much from everyone. To receive gifts like this made me feel guilty about Barb going without gifts this Christmas.

The entire family including Gram and Gramps enjoyed the gifts I had bought from Grandpa's money. It was such a Merry Christmas. Karen loved the scrapbook I got her. Inside on the cover I wrote a note to her telling her how I thanked God every day for giving me this time with her. Under my name I taped a friendship ring that Grandma had helped me purchase for her. Karen put it on and wore it for a long time after.

We had a feast of feasts that day. My aunt outdid herself for Christmas dinner with Grandma helping her. She was such an amazing cook. After Grandma and Grandpa left we started packing for our trip and I had clothes from Christmas, plus the clothes we brought for me to take, and I wanted to take all the goodies in the bag Aunt Maxine got me. I could get everything but my coat in the suitcase. I was ready to go.

The next day we headed to Fort Bragg but before we left town, Aunt Maxine requested we make one stop before we left. Uncle Jim pulled into Sear's and my aunt had my uncle and the kids wait in the car. She took Karen and me with her. Karen wondered why we were stopping and my Aunt told her I needed a bathing suit and a cover-up. She also had bought me some shorts. Karen told her mom that we better get me some sandals too.

It was so different to be treated this way. I knew Mom was brought up in a good home so what the heck happened to her. Uncle Jim said she did not like rules and was very rebellious as a kid. I thought to myself what the priests had said, and I hoped I wasn't like that. I asked him what happened to make her change. "When your Mother married the ex-con we felt it was out of spite to your Grandmother. When she was a teenager she never listened to Mother," he added.

We were finally on our way to Fort Bragg. It was a long drive but was well worth it. When we arrived I couldn't believe how far out on the ocean I could see and nothing beyond it but the horizon. I was fascinated with the ocean. I couldn't take my eyes off of the waves smashing into the rocks and throwing water everywhere.

Uncle Jim had unhooked the trailer from the car. He made it very stable with blocks and then put the awning up to shield us from the sun. We were all starving after the long drive even though Uncle Jim had stopped for lunch along the way and bought soft drinks. Aunt Maxine asked us to look after Jimmy and Marsha while she and Uncle Jim set up the portable barbecue and prepared dinner.

We set up the campsite table with a tablecloth, plates and salt and pepper. Aunt Maxine told us that dinner wouldn't be ready for a little while and we could take the dog for a walk. I don't remember the dog's name. He was an Airedale and had very wiry hair. He rode in the camper with a window open so he didn't get too hot. Actually he took us for a walk. When we returned, everything was set up for dinner including iced lemonade. My aunt always made the best fresh squeezed lemonade. When we were back at the house, Karen actually squeezed us fresh orange juice. They were teaching me a lot of things I could make.

In the morning it was so foggy I couldn't see anything for as far as the eye could see. We couldn't even see the ocean. Uncle Jim said it was always like this when they came here and then it would clear up by ten or eleven o'clock. We ate our breakfast in the fog and put sweaters on which made me laugh. It really wasn't cold, maybe because I was used to ice cold fog that sent chills down my whole body. This was a warm fog.

After the fog lifted, Karen and I changed into our bathing suits so we could get a nice suntan. My aunt told us to make sure we take the Coppertone. Jimmy wanted me to play checkers with him when Karen said she was going to close her eyes. It was getting pretty warm, but they were all used to it. It seemed crazy that just the day before yesterday was Christmas and here we were lying in the sun. Aunt Maxine was reading a book and my uncle was doing something with the front of the trailer. I actually saw him washing bugs off the windows too, bugs in December was unheard of!

On the third day, Karen and I put our suits on after breakfast and patiently waited for the sun to come out. Uncle Jim walked us down further to the beach to get seashells. We would chase the waves back and forth running in and out as fast as we could, getting soaked at the same time. We couldn't go in because the waves were really high. We dug for clams. I had never done that before. Aunt Maxine made delicious clam chowder so we were going to see if we could fill the bucket. My aunt made sandwiches and potato salad for our picnic lunch. We had ice water to drink, which we really needed since we were dehydrated. We helped crack the clam's open and they were so slimy. After we were done, my uncle took all

181

of us to the showers. It was so nice to get clean and get the sand out of my hair. My aunt told Karen and me that we were turning a little pink and to put shirts on. People could sunburn in the fog and not realize it until it was too late.

On our last night, Uncle Jim let us roast marshmallows over the barbecue. We were not allowed to have big campfires like we had in Montana. The trip home was very long.

Uncle Jim called Granny to let her know we made it back and said he would be bringing me home in the morning. Uncle Jim pulled in the driveway; Granny was asleep in her chair watching television when we walked in the door. She got up when she heard us come in and the first thing she did was look at my sunburned face. She chewed my uncle out a little. Granny told me we had to take care of my sunburn. She got vinegar water for the sting. It was worse than I thought. She told me I was going to peel after the burn went away, and it will itch like crazy. "Grandpa just giggled and said that was how these young ones had to learn Ma." I laughed at Gramps as he made his smart observation."

Grandma noticed, as she put my dirty clothes in the washing machine, that Aunt Maxine had bought me some more clothes. Grandma asked me if I liked it here. I hugged her and told her, "More than you will ever know Grandma." I also hugged Grandpa who I absolutely adored. He always smelled so good because he wore Old Spice cologne.

I told Grandma I would fold my own clothes; that it was my responsibility. I caught her getting ready to put them in the dryer and beat her to it. She loved to take care of me like I was a little girl half the time.

On Sunday, my grandparents let me sleep in to get caught up on rest. I spent the rest of the day hanging out with them. Grandpa asked me if after lunch I would want to play some pinochle with them. I could tell they missed their threesome at pinochle.I told Grandpa that Uncle Jim taught me how to play cribbage, but he always beat me. Uncle Jim said you and he played it all the time and you would clean his clock. Grandpa said "Darn right I did."

CHAPTER TWENTY-THREE

I was up early for school and asked Grandma if any mail had come at all. She said, honey I would have told you when you came home. I was walking out the door when Grandma told me not to worry about anything in Montana and to just focus on my schoolwork.

Chuck was waiting for me at the bus. He wanted to know how my Christmas vacation was. He was really a nice guy. At this point I did not know if I even wanted a boyfriend. I also liked Richard, but he was the one to always break the ice first. When I was at my locker after lunch, Richard was walking by and asked if I wanted to walk to class with him. He asked if I had a good vacation. I told him it was fabulous.

He asked where we went because of my sunburn and I told him to Fort Bragg for almost a week. I kept wondering why he had been waiting at my locker for me. One of my friends told me she saw him waiting by my locker a couple of times before I showed up. When I got to my locker once again, Richard was there and asked if he could walk me to the bus. I agreed without thinking that Chuck might show up. Richard said see you tomorrow and I left it at that. He was a really nice guy, tall, dark and handsome all in one package. I could not be rude to Chuck who also was a great guy and nice looking, plus he was a gentleman.

When I arrived home I told Grandma I was worried about Barb. Grandma told me write the poor girl a letter and see if your mom will give it to her. I asked her to please write, as I was worried about her and couldn't stop thinking about what she was going through. I needed to know if she was okay. I told Barb how much I loved her and that I was living with Grandma and Grandpa. Please write me as soon as you get this. Grandma gave me, a self-addressed envelope with a stamp for the letter.

I was busy with school all that week and did not want to worry about things while I was in class, but sometimes I would catch myself daydreaming, like the old days. I was not happy with myself thinking that I needed to stop this nonsense. If I didn't hear from my sister I figured Mom wasn't going to let her know what was going on with me. Friday came. I knew I could settle down once I told my Cousin Karen what was going on with me. "I don't want Grandma to worry about me. She knows that I was disturbed about not hearing back from Barb." Karen reminded me that I had just mailed the letter this week.

We went for a walk to one of Karen's friend's house. His name was Pat. He was a sophomore. He was over six feet tall and a year younger than us. He had an older brother that Karen knew. We visited with them for a couple of hours and his brother gave us a ride back to the house. The boys waited in the car and before we went in the house, Karen asked if I would go to the movies with Pat and she was going to go with his brother who was a year older than us. She told me I should ask Aunt Maxine since she always said yes to me. I told Karen I had just met Pat and was scared to ask. So Karen asked Uncle Jim instead. He told us since we were going to the late movie we had to be home by 11:30. Uncle Jim invited the boys in and they waited in the family room visiting with my aunt and uncle while we got ready. They knew the boy's parents real well.

I could have strangled Karen. Pat seemed like a nice guy but the only reason for the date was so Karen could go out with his brother. I asked her what about Larry, her boyfriend. She responded, "I like Larry a lot and this is just for fun," Karen felt I should be okay with the arrangement.

I told Karen, "Okay, but I don't want to call this a date." I did not need to have mixed feelings about what was going on. We had time for a soda at the soda shop and then we hurried to get to the movie. Pat was really a nice guy and I enjoyed his company, but he looked older then a sophomore; he acted older too. When we got home we were right on time, and Uncle Jim was sitting in the living room.

The weekends went by too fast, I was looking forward to spring break and had no idea what was planned for that. I had to get through the next couple of months with track activities and Chuck chasing after me. I think Richard gave up because he saw me with Chuck all of the time. Pat liked me too. On Friday, an hour after dinner, guess who shows up on my uncle's doorstep. We were always out by the pool because it was warm. My uncle kidded Pat and asked if he liked the girl or the pool.

Uncle Jim got a kick out of teasing us with the boys. I could tell Pat really was crazy for me. He asked if I felt the same way and I told him, I honestly didn't want to go steady with anyone right now. I really did like this guy but I told him please wait and give me a little more time to think things through. I reminded him that I also was dating Chuck.

Larry was going to bring Chuck over to my uncle's house. I told Karen it was okay because I was honest and straight forth with Pat. Uncle Jim kept teasing me when Chuck got there without letting him hear, and asked, "What was a girl to do with all these boys chasing her?"

Larry and Chuck spent the afternoon at our house. In the evening we went to the Drive Inn Diner.Chuck laughed and put his arm around me and softly squeezed my shoulder. He said, "You know how I feel about you. I want to ask you to prom before anyone else does because I know Richard likes you too. I don't want to take any chances," he grinned.

I told him prom was still two months away, then added that Richard and I were just friends.

Suddenly Karen turned around, and said, "We could double date because Larry asked me to go to your school prom."

We made it back by curfew and both my aunt and uncle were still up. We told them we were asked to prom. My aunt was so excited she said she would make our dresses.

While I was fixing Aunt Maxine's hair, she asked me if

something was troubling me because I wasn't my usual bubbly self. I told her I had some demons in my head that would not leave. I told her I had nightmares a lot. Aunt Maxine asked what the nightmares were about, but I couldn't let her know. I didn't want her to think bad things about me. I told her when I woke up I could not remember them. I couldn't tell her the horrible things done to me by men who were supposed to be good. I couldn't get the smell of an old man's penis to go away. I told my aunt it was all the bad things that happened while I was growing up. She would remind me I was safe and to try to think that way when I went to bed at night.

Karen and I were so excited about prom. We went shopping one weekend with Aunt Maxine and she bought us heels. I had never worn heels before like these. When we were in Civil Air Patrol, we wore a black pump heel. These heels were much higher, and I had to practice walking in them. Uncle Jim laughed at my wobbling and trying to walk gracefully in them. I practiced and practiced and finally got it down to where I walked pretty well. Karen wore them a lot to the Rainbow Girls balls and other fancy doings.

My days at school were always pleasant. My grades were A's and B's except for a C in Algebra and I was trying to bring that grade up. My Grandparents were very proud of me. My aunt and uncle wanted to know if things were good living at Grandma's house and if my grades were on par. I told them I had a C to get up and that was all and that I loved Grandma's house and how well they treated me. I wish I was a straight A student like Karen, but I was lucky to have the grades I did because I studied hard at Granny's.

Chuck had to come up and meet my grandparents because they wanted to meet the guy I was dating and goingto the prom with. Grandma and Grandpa made it very clear they would be coming in on prom day to see all of us leave the house in the limousine.

Chuck came out early Friday to take me to school.

Grandpa helped him to carry my things out and Grandma said they would see me tomorrow before the prom. Grandpa made a point of thanking Chuck for coming so early in the morning to give me a ride when Chuck lived in Marysville. "You must really like our girl," Grandpa said proudly.

"Yes sir," Chuck responded with a grin.

They told us to drive safely and get to school before the bell rings. On our way to school, Chuck was kind of acting funny. He asked if I would wear his class ring. I was silent for a moment. I asked why he wanted to give me the ring.

"Because I am crazy about you and want to go steady with you."

I told him I cared for him too, but could we take it slowly. Now, we were going steady like everyone else in our group. He then gave me a long kiss. When it was lunchtime, of course everyone noticed the chain with the ring, and Chuck showed up and sat down nonchalantly with a big fat grin on his face.

Karen showed me the class ring that Larry had given her. I asked when she got hers, and she told me Wednesday when he took her home from school. I asked if we were going to get in trouble for going steady and wearing their rings. Karen said her mom and dad already knew about Larry. She told me to tell them about Chuck. Sure enough, they noticed the ring around my neck at the dinner table and laughed about having double trouble.

Aunt Maxine commented that I seemed to have the jitters about going to the prom. I explained to her that I never had it this good ever in my life. I was remembering what happened at the dance in Helena. I told her, "Mom would never permit me to go steady or go to a prom. A dance was the cause of my leaving and running away."

My aunt replied to me, "No, your mother was the reason you left home, not a dance. We are all sorry for what happened to you. I want you to know, when you showed your Uncle and me the pictures of you, we thought no one should ever go through what you girls did. "You will have your special day tomorrow."

On Saturday, we went to the beauty shop with my aunt; she had her haircut a bit while we had our hair all styled and splurged for a manicure. I never had a manicure in my life. It was nice except the filing part, as that just felt weird. The manicure made my nails look nice and the polish was a soft peach color to go with my dress.

Grandma and Grandpa were there when we pulled in the driveway. Grandma loved our hairdos and was excited to see us get dressed. We had to take off the rings for the pearl necklaces Aunt Maxine had bought for us. Then she proudly marched us out to the living room for all to admire. Granny was teary eyed and Grandpa thought we looked very grown up. They took pictures of us in Aunt Maxine's parlor room, which they seldom use.

The limousine had shown up with the boys. They told us how gorgeous we were and then placed corsages on our wrists. Chuck shook my Uncle's hand and then Grandpa's. Grandpa told them "Take good care of our girls tonight."

Larry responded to my Grandpa, "They would make sure of that and that we will be home by curfew at one o'clock."

They took us to the best restaurant and the food was amazing. I let Chuck order for me as I did not know what to pick. The prom was just getting started when we arrived. The band was playing rock and roll music and we danced like crazy. Several times we had to leave and go outside for fresh air. We were not allowed to leave until we were ready to go home. We let the chaperone, which was outside know we were just cooling off. The dance was over at midnight, and when we left the school, Larry wanted to go park for awhile and we did which I wasn't too crazy about. But while he and Karen made out, Chuck just put his arm around me and kissed me as we talked softly. It felt awkward. I did not want to get grounded.

I told Karen we had better be getting home soon and she said we still had a little while. Chuck and I got out of the car and walked for a few minutes before I asked him what time it was. We got back into the car, and Chuck told Larry we had to leave or we would be late. Larry sounded put out, but was willing to leave. We barely made it on time. When we got in the bedroom I asked Karen why Larry was so persistent to stay parked, when he knew what time we had to be in. If I hadn't asked Chuck to say something we would have been late. She said she was glad I did, because he was getting fresh with her. She snapped and said sternly "He wasn't going to take any liberties with me!" When she talked to him the next day she told him and evidently they worked things out.

We were getting ready for final week at school, and I was studying like crazy. Karen called and said she was hitting it hard too. She asked if I was going to live with her for the summer after finals were over. Grandma said I could spend the summer with them once school was out the end of May. Karen, my friend, not my cousin, who lived down the street studied with me for finals. She was an excellent student. When school ended, I had a 3.4 overall average compared to Karen's 4.0. I think studying with her made such a difference for me; she was great in school and was on the debate team.

It was my 17th birthday on June fifth and my Aunt gave me the biggest 17th birthday party I could have ever wanted. I told her I had never had a birthday party in my life so she gave me a grand one. My Grandparents were there, my cousins, my friends from school, even Pat and his brother were invited since they were good friends of ours through the school year and of course, Larry and Chuck. We had a pool party and I was surprised at all the gifts. But the best part was sharing it with people who were now part of my life that I enjoyed. I couldn't have had a better birthday. I hugged my Aunt and thanked her profusely telling her that I had never known life could be so wonderful. I was forever grateful to my aunt and uncle and my wonderful grandparents who truly showed me how to love and receive love. They welcomed me with opened arms, a sixteen year old who had only known rejection, anguish, abandonment and abuse.

CHAPTER TWENTY-FOUR

It was the middle of June, Karen and I were enjoying the summer swimming and lying in the sun. Grandma called the house and told me to pack up that she and Grandpa were coming to pick me up. She said she would explain what was going on when they arrived. I was supposed to stay with Uncle Jim and Aunt Maxine for the summer. Karen called my aunt and told her there was a problem and she needed to come home quickly.

After my Grandparents arrived we went and sat at the kitchen table. They told me there was a horrible accident. Bonnie had to live at home for her remainder of her probation period after getting out of the girl's school. She was riding my horse Sandy on a paved road when a car came along and honked. It spooked Sandy, and she reared up and tripped on the edge of the pavement falling over. She fell on top of my sister.

Bonnie was in the ICU at the hospital and had a ruptured spleen and broken ribs. She was in critical condition. Dad wanted me to come home because she kept calling for me. Grandpa said, "Your sister needs you. She is asking for only you and no one else. They didn't know if she was going to walk again. Her spine was injured when the horse rolled on her. You must go home Wanda."

Grandma made me realize we could only call the hospital and ask about her condition. While Grandma called St. Peter's in Helena, I packed my bags. Grandma said if everything worked out I could come back and live with them. The hospital would only tell us she was critical since we were family members. I explained to my cousin that I loved my sister and wanted to be there for her, but I was terrified of seeing my mother knowing what she was capable of.

We waited for Uncle Jim to come home. He took off from work because it was a family emergency. He would drive me to the airport in Sacramento. Grandma told me, she was a phone call away, and said they would see me soon. My Grandfather handed me an envelope and said, "Don't open this until you are on the plane, as this will help you get situated."

On the way to Sacramento Karen asked if they could come to Montana this summer if things go well. My Aunt said they had to wait until Uncle Jim's vacation, which was in September. Aunt Maxine said that they would make sure I was okay and take a trip to Montana since they wanted to go to Glacier Park, which would be on the way to our house. Karen and I promised we would always keep in touch. I said goodbye to all of them crying and saying we would be back together again soon. Uncle Jim told me to call them with the details of Bonnie's condition. We have to know what you are doing after you see your sister. Tell Bonnie that everyone sends his or her love.

I told Aunt Maxine I would get an apartment. I could not bear to live in the same house with my mother. Barb told Grandma how bad the conditions were in the house they lived in now. They had to use the outdoor toilet and had no running water.

Uncle Jim called Dad to meet me at the airport. He told him that I wanted him to meet me alone because I wasn't ready to see my mom. Dad agreed he would pick me up. All the way on the plane my stomach was sick with fear for my sister and the thought of seeing my mother after a year awakened all my terrible memories. We flew into Helena and I was anxious to see my dad who I loved, but couldn't understand why he lived with someone like my mom. That was their problem I thought to myself, as I opened the envelope Grandpa gave to me while we were getting ready to land in Helena. I couldn't believe it, it was a money order for three hundred and fifty dollars along with a letter from him and Grandma. I put the envelope in a new purse I received for my birthday.

The plane landed. My dad welcomed me with tears. I hugged him and he held onto me. I apologized for putting him through all of the worry. I told him I would be getting an apartment because I could not live with Mom. Dad understood and said he was sorry for everything that had happened." I let him know I was happy to be with him and would see more of him after I found my own place. I hoped he would stop to visit with me when he could. I needed his help since I did not have a car or driver's license. I told him I would call for apartments after I saw Bonnie and then I needed him to take me to see them. I also told him I needed to get a job and he had to sign for a driver's license for me.

He told me how good I looked and that my grandparents and Uncle Jim took good care of me, and he was glad I was in a safe place with family. "At one point when you left Helena and we didn't know where you were, we thought you were dumped somewhere and left for dead." he told me. I apologized to him to make him understand it wasn't done deliberately. I had no choice if I wanted to survive. "I don't know why you didn't do more to protect us Dad?". I couldn't understand the hold my mother had over this wonderful man. I will never understand how she could lie to him so brazenly and get away with it.

Being in Helena once again was weird. Once again I revisited the awful memories of the priests and nuns, the orphanage and school, and my mother's constant abuse. I asked Dad if Bonnie was doing any better, and he just shook his head. I could tell he was worried about Bonnie. I was shocked when I got to St. Peter's. She was so bruised, black and blue, swollen, and cut all over. She was sleeping from the morphine. Dad said when they first brought her in they put her in an induced coma to keep her completely still. Her brain had dangerously swollen from her head hitting the pavement. She was immediately taken to surgery in critical condition.

Mom was sitting there by her bed being very

attentive,for a change. She said, "Hello." I think she was glad I had come home for Bonnie, but of course never asked about me.

At that moment, I didn't care because I was worried about my sister. I pulled up a chair and kept looking at Bonnie lying in the bed lifeless and not able to talk. Dad said she kept saying my name before they took her to surgery, but now she lay mute not even knowing I was there. Bonnie developed bleeding internally as they found that her ruptured spleen was hemorrhaging and filling her stomach with blood. Her blood pressure dropped dangerously low so they once again rushed her into surgery.

Grandma asked me to call her collect from the hospital if there were any changes so I called while she was in surgery to let them know what was taking place. I told Grandma I was terrified that she wasn't going to make it. They even did a code blue on her with everyone rushing in and rushing her out. "Sit and pray, Honey," she calmly told me.

We waited for hours and finally they brought her back from surgery. We just had to wait but she was stabilized. I just sat there crying once in a while. I did not want anyone to hear me so I would leave and cry in the hall. Then I would come back and sit by her and hold her limp hand in mine telling her I was here hoping she could hear me.

Late that evening, Bonnie stirred somewhat and barely opened her eyes. I stood up. I let her know I was there holding and squeezing her hand. "I am here with you now my sister," and I squeezed harder.

That night the nurse told us we should go home and get rest. I volunteered to stay so they could go home. They said they would be back in the morning. I told the nurse that I was staying with my sister and wasn't leaving her side. She nodded and said that I could use Bonnie's bathroom. Eventually, a maintenance man brought in a recliner chair if I needed to rest.

Dad said to call if anything came up, but Bonnie slept stirring only a little during the night. The next morning the nurses came in and asked me to wait while they went about taking care of her morning needs. I laid my head on Bonnie's bed shortly after the nurse's left. A little later, I felt her hand on my hair. I lifted my head up and her glazed eyes were fixed on me. She couldn't speak but offered a smile. I held her hand and she squeezed it very softly, and went back into her deep sleep.

Shortly after that my parents came into the room and I told them she was going to be okay, I hoped. She continued sleeping while Dad brought me a toasted egg sandwich he made with sausage on it. He reminded me that I needed to eat. Bless my dad. He must have known I hadn't eaten since yesterday.

Late that afternoon Bonnie woke up, but was still very weak and they couldn't get her to eat or drink anything yet. She looked over at me and softly said, "You are here."

I told her, "I would stay and help her get better." I knew she would be okay.

They moved her out of ICU after a week, and she was finally on the road to recovery. I called Grandma and Grandpa and told them the news about Bonnie's improvement. The doctors were hoping to get her up and walking if she continued to recuperate on track. She still couldn't walk as her ribs and spine had to heal.

I also told Grandmother, after mom and dad left, that I had to talk to a Mrs. Miller who owned a greenhouse out in Broadwater. She needed help since the man who worked for her had not shown up for work. A nurse at the hospital told me about the job when she was visiting with me while I was caring for Bonnie that day.

Mrs. Miller lived in a cute little Victorian house with furniture to match and had three bedrooms. The one she showed me was off the living room; it would be mine if I took the job. The kitchen was very large with a huge table for the people who worked there to eat. She asked if I knew how to cook. I said proudly,"Yes ma'am, I learned at a very young age. I helped my Grandmother cook when I was living with her."

"I love Italian food. I hope you can cook us several meals if you take the job." She showed me the greenhouse and how the plants were all priced. After we were all done I told her I had a sister in the hospital that I would need to go see after work.

Mrs. Miller offered the use of her car when I told her I had driven Grandpa's truck. He taught me to drive, and I was pretty darn good on the country roads. I asked her how much for the room rent and she said the room came with the job. I was thrilled because I would be done by 5:00 each day. I called Dad from her house and asked if he could bring my things. He said they were still in the trunk of his car and he would bring me back to her house.

I told Mrs. Miller I would love the job. She paid her help well for cleaning her house and taking care of the greenhouse plus occasionally cooking for the three men who she fed at lunchtime. The men did all the greenhouse work. I would just have to go out there when the buzzer went off that was connected to the house which meant there was a customer.

I had my own private door from the main house. The room I had was darling with French doors to the living room and a heavy lace curtain over each door for privacy. I couldn't ask for a sweeter person to work for. I knew her family and her grandchildren who were my age and younger. I wentto school with two of her grandsons who were younger than me.

Mrs. Miller insisted that I not call a cab to take me to the hospital. I could take her car instead. I asked her if she was sure because she had just met me and didn't know me at all. "I know you will be back and that is all that matters," she told me. I received the key to my door entrance and brought my things in when I got back. I thanked her and told her I would try not to wake her when I returned. I drove her little Ford to the hospital. Mrs. Miller gave me the phone number for her house. She told me to take a day to get settled and visit with my sister. She said, "Monday was a slow day anyway."

Bonnie was by herself when I arrived. She looked a little better. She still couldn't sit up but was able to talk and finally sip through a straw as they blended fruits for her. I told her I found the cutest place to live and that I would be working at Miller's Greenhouse. I was excited when I told Bonnie that Mrs. Miller let me drive her car, not even asking if I had a driver's license. Bonnie hoped I was staying so I assured her, "Why do you think I got a job and a place to live? I'm staying for a while," then changing the subject I asked, "Why won't Mom let me call and talk to Barb?"

Bonnie shrugged. "I don't know exactly why," then she switched the subject to herself. She told me her probation was over the end of August or the first part of September and she was going to Los Angeles to get as far away from Mom as she possibly could. She had a friend, Jerry O, who had promised to drive her there when she was off probation. She also had a friend who wrote and said getting a job was easy. I told her let's worry about getting her well before she makes any plans.

Bonnie hated living up in Unionville and told me Mom sold the other horses and only kept Sandy and Coaly. I told her I just didn't care anymore. I let her know Granny had me call collect to keep her updated on your progress. She and Grandpa want you to know they love you and are thinking of you.

I suggested to Bonnie, "You could stay with me if Mom would let you, but she most likely will say no. Mom's excuse would be that you are on probation and she needs to control what you do, but it might be worth a try."

I hadn't seen Barb at all, but when I called the house both our parents were there. I knew they must have been outside and didn't hear the phone ring. Barb answered. She told me she was spending a lot of time with people by the name of Roddy. They took her out to their cabin at Canyon Ferry.

When my parents showed up, I asked Dad if I could have him help me put the suitcases in Mrs. Miller's car. I could tell Mom wasn't too happy. I also told Dad I needed help to get my driver's license. He had to sign or I would have to ask someone else to sign as a legal guardian. He wanted to know if I knew how to parallel park. I told him I did. So when we went out to get my suitcases, I showed him where I parked. Dad commented that it looked good, and that I should do well on my test. He warned me about the written test, and told me to use common sense and study the driving manual while we waited. I passed the written test and took the driving test next and passed it!

When we returned, Mom was mad and asked Daddy where the hell he disappeared to for so long. He said we had visited and talked for a while outside. We needed to get some fresh air. He held back the whole truth, which I was thankful, but once again he got snapped at. No way would she have gone for him taking me and signing for me to drive.

I never told Dad how awful our mom treated us, and how badly she would beat us with whatever she could use at the moment for a weapon. I think he knew when they picked Bonnie up drunk in the bakery truck that Mom was responsible the damage to her face which was a bloody mess just like mine had been. I wanted to tell him how bad it was but I let sleeping dogs lie. One day my mother would go too far. I prayed my little sister wasn't her target for that explosion.

I told Bonnie I had an official Montana driver's license so was no longer afraid of getting pulled over. I was going nowhere, for now. I gave her the phone number to Mrs. Miller's house and asked she call only if it was an emergency. I also let her know I could only visit after I get off work.

Mrs. Miller was in her late seventies or early eighties but certainly didn't show it. My work was so light and easy I couldn't believe it. I kept the house spotless and she cleaned her own room, as she loved her privacy. I told her that if I was still here when school started that I had to find a place closer to the high school. She said she had an older granddaughter she could call to give her a helping hand when the greenhouse closed the end of August. With the money order Grandpa gave me, I opened a checking account of my own.

I ate my meals at Mrs. Miller's. I had to save for an apartment close to the school if I had to stay in Montana. Bonnie wasn't sure of her probation period. I wanted to save money for a car to get around; otherwise I would stay and get an apartment since I only needed two credits to graduate early from high school. Mrs. Miller wouldn't let me put gas in the tank.

I was making sixty to seventy dollars a week and sometimes more, getting tips from people, mostly guys, whose plants I carried out to the car for them. Some of them asked if I was married. I would tell them I was still in high school, and I wouldn't be here if I was married. Not many women tipped, but a few. I loved working at the greenhouse, and the work was the easiest I had ever done. Bonnie would be getting out of the hospital soon. I was worried for her living conditions in that house. When Mom and Dad were at the hospital visiting, I thought I would leave quickly so I could see Barb and not worry if Mom was there. It was really that I had to sneak just to visit my own little sister but it was my only way to know she was safe. I wanted her to know I had missed her. I was sorry I abandoned her that night I was beaten so severely. I have never forgotten looking at her sleeping in bed the night Bonnie and I ran away from home.

I drove to Unionville, I knocked on the door and Barb answered. We embraced crying like babies. I asked her where Wesley was for fear he would say I had been there. She said he was off at some "boy's house." I told her I was working for a nice lady. I was back and tried to call her. Barb told me she gets awayfrom the house a lot with the Roddy's. We drove to the Roddy's where Barb introduced me to Bill and Rachel. They were the nicest people. They invited me to go to Canyon Ferry with them in a couple of weeks so I could spend the weekend with Barb. No one would know anything about it. Barb apparently told them what had happened to Bonnie and me. They tried to keep Barb close to them as much as possible. They would tell my mom that Barb helped Rachel out a lot. Bill was a retired carpenter. Rachel fixed us sandwiches and asked how I liked California and what things I did while I was there. She asked if I had seen the ocean and was it as beautiful as people said. Obviously they never had been out of Montana and had no desire to leave.

She begged me to go with them to the lake. I told her I would, since Bonnie would be getting out in a couple of weeks. I asked Barb how she could stand to live in a house that one had to use the outside toilet. She told me not anymore since Dad put one in, but we have to flush it with a bucket of water that sat by the toilet. I thought, how disgusting! I would never understand why they bought this place knowing the plumbing was bad.

Barb walked me out to the car and I told her I needed to get back to the hospital before I went to Mrs. Miller's. I didn't want to misuse my privileges with the car. I gave her my work number and said Mrs. Miller won't care if you call after five, but no later than nine unless it was an emergency.

Barb told me, "I feel safe with you home again."

I could not believe my parents had not shared the news of my homecoming. Barb did not know that I had been at the hospital this whole time with Bonnie. I didn't have the heart to tell her I was planning on going back to California when all was well here. My plan was to get an apartment by the school if need be, have a job in the evening and graduate in December. Then I would head back to California to attend Cal State for the new semester in January. Everything depended on how things went here.

I was bound and determined to save every penny I earned. I stayed with Mrs. Miller on weekends watching TV and putting puzzles together with her. I was not interested in dating or going out. I received letters from everyone asking how things were going and asking about my sister. I talked to Grandma and Aunt Maxine quite frequently. I gave Karen the phone number and told her the hours she could call.

Chuck kept asking when I was coming back. I asked if he wanted me to send his class ring back as he made me keep it when I left. He said, "Not unless you plan on breaking up with me."

I didn't want to break up with him. I really liked the kind of guy he was, and I truly did miss being with him.

Mrs. Miller would joke with me about getting more mail than she ever did. All she got were bills. It was nice to see young people write to each other she told me. I told her a few were from my family.

Time was passing rapidly. When I went to the hospital, Bonnie said that once she was doing better Mom hardly ever came, knowing she would be heading home soon. Bonnie was not looking forward to being released from the hospital and going back to that house. She did not want to live in such an unsanitary environment. She asked Mom about staying with me.

Bonnie told me mom screamed at her, "Absolutely and positively not!" Mom called me a couple of her bad names saying I was an instigator and the cause of all their trouble.

Really, she was mad at me while being upset with Bonnie for even asking?
I asked Bonnie if she was ever going to ride Sandy again. I shared how I walked up to the fence when I went to see Barb, and Sandy ran right up to me. She remembered me. I petted her while she nuzzled into my arms for a few minutes. She was too thin and looked like no one was caring for her.

Bonnie told me she was afraid to ride anymore with the traffic on the road. I told her Sandy only threw her because someone frightened her. She needs to be fed better and rode more. Mom could care less about the horses. Bonnie said she wanted to sell them. She promised me when she got home she would fatten Sandy up. Bonnie told me the only thing she enjoyed at the house was working with the horses.

When all of us are gone, Mom will sell both the horses and keep the money we worked so hard for. She never gave us the money from the last two they sold without us knowing.

I told her it looks gloomy up there in that house so get outside a lot so you don't get depressed. I cannot understand how mom likes it. Bonnie replied, "She loves gloomy things," which is why the curtains were never allowed to be open.

I knew Dad and Mom still belonged to Search and Rescue, Dad loved the organization and I could understand that, as he always liked helping other people. He was a people pleaser and loved to do anything to help others in need, regardless of his situation. I told Bonnie when she was released from the hospital that she had my phone number and under no condition to let Mom see it! And don't lose it for heaven's sake. I asked if she was still beating on them and she said not since she got in trouble for beating us at the dance, except for a slap once in a while. They hadn't given her a ticket for what she did to us the night of the dance. They just warned her that they would have to remove all of the children if it ever happened again. So now she's reduced to screaming her head off at poor Barb and slapping her on occasion.

Name-calling was just as bad because my mother was loud as she swore to high heaven with her put-downs. I was suddenly depressed and had to leave.

School was about to start and I needed to find a new place to live closer to school and work. It was the weekend and I asked Mrs. Miller if she had any errands she had to do. I asked if I could borrow the car. I told her I would fill the tank but she said not to bother. I stopped at Eileen's Drive Inn to see if she had an opening for me. I asked if she had a job for me after school was out at 3:00.

She told me that when I received my schedule we would do business because I would always have a job with her. I explained to her that I would be leaving for college when the semester was over since I was graduating early.

I told Eileen that I had to go apartment hunting because

I had to move closer for school and my job ended when school started. She told me there would be some apartments on the second floor, over by the ice cream drive thru she had owned. It was right across from the train depot. It would be very handy for me.

The apartment had two bedrooms and the rent was ten dollars more a month then a one bedroom in the same building. It was two blocks from school and two blocks from Eileen's Drive Inn. It couldn't get any better than that. The man who owned the apartment knew my dad from Helena Sand and Gravel. When he saw my last name he asked if we were related. He said, "I could have the two bedroom furnished for sixty-five a month with all utilities instead of seventy-five because he liked my dad. The apartment was really cute. If I couldn't find a roommate to split the cost, I could still afford it and have a room for my sisters if they needed to stay with me. It would be better to have a roommate so I could save money for nursing school in January even though Grandma was going to pay the tuition for Cal State and for St. Bernadine's School of Nursing. I planned on paying every penny back when I found a good job.

I went to the hospital to see Bonnie and found that she had checked out that morning. I thought she wasn't supposed to go home until tomorrow. I called the house. Thank gosh, Barb answered the phone. I heard mom yelling in the background "Who the hell was it?"

Barb told her a friend of hers. "Tell her you will call her after your chores are done," mom yelled.

I reminded Barb, "Call me in a couple of hours when I am back at Mrs. Millers."

I called Georgia to let her know I was back, but she wasn't home. I told her mom I would call her back. She said that Jackie was there if I wanted to talk to her. Jackie told me she found out that I left Rocky Boy to go to California. We caught up a little bit; I told her about my sister and about moving into an apartment when my job was over the end of August.

204

I asked her if she knew of anyone who would be a good roommate and she told me Terrell, a friend of ours. Terrell's parents lived in Unionville. She was looking for an apartment. I asked her if she would talk to Terrell and ask her was she wanted to share one with me.

This was the weekend to go to Canyon Ferry with Barb and her friends. Barb kept the fact that I was going with them a secret from Mom. She called me Friday morning when Mom went out to get the mail and said they would pick me up at five. I was excited to do something with Barb and actually have time to visit with her. Barb and I sat in the back seat so we could visit. I told her the wonderful news, that I found an apartment and that I would be staying to finish school in December to graduate early.

I would make sure Barb and Bonnie we're safe before I went back to California for nursing school. I would send for Barb, or come back and get a place to be closer to her until she could leave my parent's house.

I didn't want to live in Helena because of the horrible memories from the orphanage and the Catholic school. The molestations and the guilt, each time I remembered, were still with me. The memories of the orphanage were horrendous and so were the memories of the despicable school. I could not forget what took place in the Cathedral with Father Gilmore. How could I ever feel at peace in a town where this all happened to me? I still had nightmares about what they did to my sisters and me. I saw the steeples every day that I was in town, and found myself sick to my stomach whenever they came into view.

I knew it wasn't just me that this happened to. It happened to my sister Bonnie as well because I knew she wanted away from these memories just like I did. I wasn't the only so called bad and rebellious child, as they loved to stereotype us. I was told over and over again by Father Gilmore and Father Callan, and there were others as well. They had several names for us. They called us the less fortunate, directionless, inconsiderate and reckless children, and made us feel that way.

It was kind of hard not to know what took place in the church and why I despised that place. Father Gilmore plagued me in my nightmares along with Father Callan and the other priests. I could not believe they hadn't been caught for what they did to children.

I tried to focus only on why I was in Helena. Poor Barb was only twelve and she had a long way to go, yet. She knew I would get in trouble if she stayed with me. Mom would have me put in jail as fast as I could say the word, *criminal*. Barb wouldn't even think of asking me. I did not want to deal with the problems with our mother.

Mom could never make me move home because of my emancipation. The same judge was still in office and the police told her she was lucky I didn't press charges. So I don't think my mother would ever bother me, although I did not trust her doing something to cause problems for me if she could. I still had another year before I was of age.

I was just happy to be with Barb. Rachel knew we couldn't be together at other times because of our mother. My sister told her that mom didn't allow me to have time alone with Barb for fear I would corrupt her. Barb told Rachel that I couldn't call the house for fear my mom would answer and hang up on me. I could not take the chance for Mom to find out Mrs. Miller's address or phone number. I was afraid she would repeat the incident, of having me let go when I was working for St. John's. Eileen could care less about what my mom would say or do because she could not stand my mother's attitude towards her children. Eileen would tell her to leave the premises.

Bill and Rachel's cabin overlooked Senior Beach where all the kids hung out. We used to come here when we were at Diane's house just to have fun and enjoy our friends.

Rachel and Barb fixed dinner. We had fried chicken that she had cooked before picking me up. Barb had helped her make macaroni salad, fruit salad and a chocolate filled cake. "Wow, I thought, so much food to eat!"

The cabin was great. It had logs on the outside and inside and two bedrooms and a sleeper porch with a roll away bed and a couch. Barb and I took the porch instead of the bedroom because it was really hot. The porch at night would be nice and cool. Furthermore, we wouldn't be disturbing anyone by talking. August was always hot in Montana. When dinner was over we headed down to the beach.

Rachel was kind enough to hand us beach towels. There were quite a few people at the beach but it turned out that we did not know anyone. I swam a little while Barb waded. Barb had a fear of water because of the nun's actions at the orphanage.

Barb and I talked a lot about what I had done in California and what she had done. She told me how horrible it was to move to Unionville. Barb had to do most of the packing, as Wesley wouldn't do anything but help Dad load up. Wesley told her at least she didn't get stuck carrying heavy boxes. That was because Dad told Wes to get his butt in gear and help him load up the truck. Maybe he could build up some muscle if he worked at it. One thing I said about my dad was he knew who the workers were in the family.

The sun was going down so we headed back up to the cabin not realizing the mosquitoes in the bushes along the dirt road were attacking us. The little buggers were eating us alive. When we got in the house, Rachel sprayed us so we wouldn't get bit in our sleep on the porch.

We played Rummy until it was dark out and getting late.

During the night, Barb woke me up and told me that I was having an awful nightmare and she couldn't understand all the words I was saying. She told me to try and go back to sleep, but I awoke again in tears and didn't remember any of it when she woke me up again. Grandma said I had nightmare after nightmare. I thought maybe she was exaggerating a bit, but others, who shared a room with me, always confirmed her story.

I knew they were not making it up. I didn't have them every night, thank goodness, some I remembered and others

I did not. All I could do was think that someday they would disappear. It would be awful to be married and have these nightmares.

Bill thought he heard us talking during the night. Barb said, "No that was my sister having nightmares." Bill asked what my nightmares were about.

I told him, "I couldn't remember," mostly because of the embarrassment of the content. I could never talk about them to anyone. So I simply said I don't remember what they were about.

Bill commented, "It was good that I didn't remember them."

I agreed and continued eating the great breakfast Bill had fixed for Rachel and us. When I eat food camping even in a log house, it seems to always taste better than indoor cooking. Barb and I went out to the tire swing while Bill and Rachel sat on the porch. It was wonderful to be this lazy and relaxed.

I asked Barb, "Do you think Bonnie knows I am here with you and feels badly that she couldn't be with us?"

Barb told me, "I didn't tell her so it wouldn't hurt her feelings about not getting to come."

Barb told me that Mom couldn't make her do anything because the doctor told her it was going to take a while to heal. Bonnie had bindings on her ribs and she changed her own bandages. If Bonnie ran out of bandages, Mom probably would not buy her more. I told Barb I would buy them for her. I didn't know if I could afford a phone in the apartment, unless I had a roommate, which hopefully would happen. Barb told me that Bonnie was having Jerry drive her to California the day she turned eighteen and was off probation.

It was starting to get pretty hot and we told Rachel and Bill we were going to head down to the beach. Rachel came down and took pictures of us standing in front of a huge willow tree and snapped a shot of us in the tire swing. We really enjoyed the time together. I told Bill and Rachel that I couldn't thank them enough for inviting me to weekend with them. It was the most fun I had since I'd come home. All I had done was work, go the hospital and worry about what was next. It was nice to have fun and not worry about anything.

There were a lot of people at the beach and we had just laid our towels down, when suddenly I heard, "Hey Wanda, come sit over here with us." It was my friends Georgia and Dina. I introduced them to Barb. They wanted to know whom we came to the lake with. I told them Barb's neighbors that were really nice people. I also said they had invited me to spend the weekend in their cabin, which we pointed out to them. We visited with them for a while and then Barb and I said our goodbyes. Georgia said to give her a call since she had the same number. We could keep in touch and do things together.

I could tell Barb was uncomfortable being with strangers, and I didn't want to spend what time we had left this weekend with them and not her. Barb knew she was more important than any of my friends could ever be. We enjoyed the rest of the day swinging in the tire, and then after supper of barbecued steak and potatoes we played Rummy. Finally, we dressed for bed and told Bill and Rachel that we were just going to go lay out on the porch and visit. They said good night and we told them we would keep it quiet. Bill said, "Not to worry that they were sound sleepers."

"Right," I said, "That is why he heard my nightmares. They heard you last night waking me up in my sleep," we both giggled like two silly little girls the way we used to. I asked Barb, how she was doing. I was worried about her. She told me the bus picked her up for school and she didn't have to walk in the cold. She also said that she had her own room now that there was only Wesley and her at home.

Mom made Barb and Bonnie sleep together knowing Bonnie was not all healed. I think Bonnie was just waiting for August to end so she could get out of there. I went to the school to see if they had my records from Marysville. The secretary handed me the two requirements I needed to graduate early from school. I would get my diploma on the 21st of December.

I saved every cent I made and spent probably five dollars max in the two and a half months I was at Mrs. Miller's. Barb came out to meet Mrs. Miller. Rachel wanted to buy iris and daffodil bulbs from her. Barb saw the room I was leaving and asked how I could give up such a nice place. I reminded her that I had school for a few months before I left for California.

Mrs. Miller gave me my final check and I couldn't believe she paid me an extra forty dollars telling me I earned it. I hugged her goodbye and thanked her for trusting me with her car, and for taking such good care of me and treating me like family instead of an employee.

She said, "Thank you for taking care of me, and for taking on the responsibility of the business and the house. I am going to miss you like the dickens."

I made a little over five hundred dollars for two and a half months of work. Now I had my safety net in the bank along with Grandpa's money he gave me. I had only spent sixty-five dollars of the three hundred and fifty from the money that I received from Grandpa. I called the phone company since I had plenty of money and had a phone installed. It was the last day of the month so I was able to move into the apartment.

Bonnie's boyfriend, Jerry helped me unload my boxes, since they gave me a ride from Mrs. Miller's to my new apartment. Bonnie told me her things were packed and hidden under the bed. She was leaving for California early the next morning. She just wanted to say goodbye. I told her I was getting a phone and to call Mrs. Miller and she would give her the number. I promised I would give the number to Mrs. Miller when I found out. Bonnie wanted to hug me but she still hurt. I wanted to know how she was going to make this trip.

She said, "I have a pillow behind my back on the bottom and top." Jerry had bought her a twin pack of pillows. He seemed like a nice guy.

He was paying for the trip because I asked Bonnie if she needed money. Jerry said, "No I already gave her some to get the heck out of here."

I was not going to ask too many questions, since Bonnie already had enough to deal with, trying to get away from our mother, and Helena. I found out that Bonnie had left for California from Barb. She left the day after Jerry helped me move. She had my phone number so I hoped I would hear from her. I wanted to leave too but I could not leave Barb stranded until I knew she really would be okay plus I was enrolled for school. I wanted my diploma as fast as I could get it.

My apartment overlooked the train station and the kitchen overlooked the street on the backside. Terrell came to look at the apartment. She loved it and said she would love to live there with me. She would give me the thirty dollars for the month. I told her next month would be the same since I paid for the phone bill.

We didn't have to pay for a television because I had antennas on the television I bought for twenty dollars from a neighbor who moved out when I was moving in. He also gave me some small appliances. I had to clean them only a little because they seemed to be almost new. I wanted to buy a rug for the kitchen but I thought I would watch for garage sales on the way home.

I finally had to buy a rug from a store. After that the apartment looked great. Mrs. Miller gave me a bedspread and matching pillows and sheets because she said she had plenty. They looked pretty new I thought. Terrell's Mom gave her things for her room. She was a year older than me so she was done with school. Terrell worked for Mountain Bell, which was the phone company in Montana.

I was busy studying for finals for the quarter and in two months and one week I would have my diploma and leave. Terrell said she would like to go to California, but not to Cal State. She was done with school. I was making fairly good money at Eileen's, counting my tips from the older crowd. The nice thing about Eileen's was we got to eat at work and it helped me save money. I was not buying groceries and feeding our friends that dropped in.

One night Terrell and I went to a party where some Carroll College guys lived. Of course, they were older than me by three and four years. I was a senior in high school and they were juniors and seniors at Carroll. I met the three roommates Rob, Dan, and Chuck. Chuck was shy at first but nice, and I liked him for making me feel comfortable. He knew I was underage. I wanted to leave but felt bad because my friends were enjoying themselves.

Chuck asked me if I ever drank and I told him not if I could help. I felt uncomfortable because I was the only one not drinking. Chuck asked me if I would like a coke, and I thanked him. We visited for a while and I told him I was going to go to California when I got my diploma on the twenty first of December.

He said that he was going on to get his law degree. I wished him well and he gave me a ride home since I didn't want to stay and party. He was a perfect gentleman and walked me up to the door and said maybe he would see me again, and left.

Terrell told me that Dan had asked her to come to their place this weekend and hang out. Chuck asked me to sit by him and patted the couch where he was sitting. Chuck was handsome, and I liked him immediately when I first met him, but I knew I was not staying long. He asked if I wanted a pop or a beer. I declined the beer. He said that's what he liked about me. He did not care if someone else was drinking as long as I was not. He put his arm around me but kept it on the couch not to be too forward. I liked him because he wasn't pushy and took it for granted that I did not want to be at the party. Everyone was talking about sports, school and graduation from college.

I let Terrell know I was leaving and would see her at the apartment. My friends called me a party pooper, but Chuck told them to leave me alone. He drove me home. When we arrived at my apartment, he walked me to the door and bent down and kissed me softly. I liked his soft kiss and he didn't linger and said he would see me again soon. I gave him my phone number before he left the apartment.

I was looking forward to my weekends off, but I knew Chuck and I were headed in different directions. I really respected the way he treated me. I couldn't help but like him. He was busy with school during the week, but there were a few times he came and got me and we just hung out. He knew how uncomfortable it made me feel to be around my friends when they were drinking.

I sent my boyfriend Chuck's ring back to him. He had been my boyfriend in California. Long distance relationships are tough enough as it is, but especially for teenagers. I knew when I left for California my Helena friend Chuck would graduate from Carroll and go on with his life. But for now, I enjoyed his company.

Time was quickly passing and my finals were coming up. All I did was study. I passed and earned three credits. I was very happy. I called Chuck and he told me to come on over. It was a Friday and I remember Terrell and Georgia telling me they were going over there for a party. When I showed up, I shocked him. The last time he had seen me I had my long hair. The day before, I had my hair cut above my shoulders in a bob, which looked really cute for my senior pictures. Everyone thought I looked like a very young Jacqueline Kennedy. I thought it was a wonderful compliment as I thought she was very beautiful. Chuck loved the haircut complimenting me by telling me it made me look very classy.

The fellows would be going home to their families for Christmas, so this was our last night together until they came back for spring classes in the later part of January. I told him I probably would not be here when he gets back for school. I told him I had to start school at Cal State the same time he did. He said we could hang out all weekend because he didn't have to head to his folks until just before Christmas.

We all ordered pizza and they all drank beer as usual, and I had my soda. I was tempted to try one, because everyone kept coxing me to celebrate now. As the night went by I told Chuck okay I would have one beer. If I didn't like it or felt woozy I would quit. I did not want to get sick. I did not know how I would react to drinking the beer, and I didn't want to make a fool of myself in front of him. I sipped on the beer and it started getting warm from holding it so long without drinking it. Then Chuck threw it away because I told him it tasted awful warm, and he got me a new one. It really didn't taste that bad I thought and it didn't make me feel different, so I drank with them.

As the night wore on, Terrell and I decided to head back to our apartment with them. They brought beer, which I would never allow before, but I had a little more beer in me and was feeling pretty tipsy myself. Since our neighbors were gone downstairs we put music on and danced.

Chuck and I danced slow dances in the kitchen off the living room. When the music was over, I could feel I was more than tipsy. We were making out like the others, when all of a sudden we toppled over and I hit the kitchen counter as Chuck tried to catch me. I hit my nose and eye. We did everything to get my nose to stop bleeding. I sure sobered up quickly because Chuck had me drink water as he held ice in a baggie on the bridge of my nose. He blamed himself because he had bent over to kiss me. I told him it was my fault for being a little drunk. We laughed about how I could not hold alcohol well.

Everyone wanted to go eat and I really didn't, but Chuck said if you eat you wouldn't have a headache in the morning. He also reminded me that I did not eat pizza when everyone else did at his apartment. He insisted that I go with them. I teased him and told him the other guys had pretty girls to go with, and he had a girl with a banged up face, and he still wanted to be seen with her? I told him I didn't think I would be drinking anytime soon if I got that tipsy from drinking a couple of beers.

I sure hated saying goodbye to him after we visited and looked at pictures. He gave me a ride back to Eileen's because I was going to help her close-up. Chuck still had to pack before he left for the Holidays. He dropped me off at Eileen's and gave me a nice goodbye kiss. I hoped I would get to see him again before I left for California. He thought he might come back a little sooner before his roommates were back, but he really didn't know for sure.

Barb called me when Mom and Dad were in town. I asked if they had a tree up and she said a small one. I asked if there was any way she could come to my apartment or meet me somewhere so I could give her myChristmas present. I hadn't seen Mom at all but I'd seen Dad drive by in one of the trucks from his job. I don't think he saw me.

Barb told me, Mom was being her usual bitchy self and yelled at Daddy and her constantly. She belittled our dad all the time. Barb asked me "Why does he put up with it?"

"I think he just spaces her out when she does that. She knows he tunes her out when he doesn't want to listen. She is always right and never, ever wrong. Heaven forbid, if she was!" I laughed.

I called the Roddy's and asked if they could stop by for it if they were in town. That way Mom will think my gift came from them. Barb told me that was the best way to do it. I couldn't go up to the house to give it to her because my mom and I were still on the outs. Rachel said they were coming in to buy a turkey and trimmings and a few other groceries, and they would be more than happy to pick up the gift, tomorrow.

I walked over to Osco where Terrell worked, to pick up a few extra gifts for Barb. It was pretty nice out even with the snow, but the cold wind was awful. I bought Barb some shampoo and quite a few feminine articles like lipstick and perfume that I knew Mom wouldn't buy for her. I knew she would appreciate them. While I was there I bought Terrell some hair spray and makeup for Christmas so she didn't have to use mine all the time. That was all the shopping I did for Christmas. That night I wrapped my gifts and went to bed early for a change.

Terrell went to her mom and stepdad's house for Christmas Eve and Christmas. The Roddy's stopped by at noon, I asked Rachel if she could please just hand Barb the package and not let on who it was from as Barb knew they were bringing it for her. Rachel understood as Barb told them how bad it was living there and that Mom wouldn't let her keep it if I bought it.

I thanked them for helping me. Rachel asked if I was going to be alone for Christmas. I fibbed and told her no, because I did not want her to know that I was. She told me to have a great Christmas and New Year and they were gone.

Terrell said her mother invited me to come to their house for Christmas but I told Terrell I was not going to impose on their family. Her brother and his family would be there too and they didn't need a stranger in the way. She told me that was outrageous and silly, but I just did not want to be an imposition to anyone, especially families.

We opened our gifts before her mom came to get her. She gave me some real nice slippers, and a robe. Terrell laughed when she saw the hairspray and the makeup kit. She loved the make-up kit I bought her that had everything she needed. It even had an eyelash curler.

Her mom sat out front honking the horn. "I hate when she does that. I can't believe she won't walk up the stairs," Terrell complained.

My mom would do the same thing if I ever spoke to her again," I replied. I was alone now. Everyone was gone and it was so quiet. I was glad we didn't put a tree up. It would really make me sad if we had decorations in the house. Barb couldn't call me, I didn't know where Bonnie was in California, or if she even made it. I was on the outs with my mom and so I couldn't see my dad. I had no one to share Christmas with. I cried into my pillow that night thinking I was alone for the holidays and had no one but myself to blame.

I called Grandma on Christmas, but it took me until late, because the operator always told me the lines were all tied up. I tried calling Aunt Maxine and Uncle Jim's house and couldn't get through to them, either. I knew Grandpa usually headed home not long after they ate dinner at my aunt and uncle's house. My Grandfather tired easily after big meals and he liked to take a nap at home.

I finally got through. Grandma asked if I had received her check for Christmas. She also said Aunt Maxine had sent a package a few days ago. Everything should have arrived on time for Christmas. I told her not to worry, as sometimes the mail was slow. The parcel still might be at the post office, but they usually leave a slip telling it has arrived. She asked me if my roommate was home for Christmas, and I told her that Terrell's mom had picked her up the day before and she was with her family.

Grandma wanted to know if I planned on anything for the day. I told her I was fixing myself a small dinner later in the evening. I told her I had two invites but I did not want to impose on families that were celebrating. She told me I should have accepted since they invited me for a reason. I should have gone but I told her I just didn't feel right accepting. The entire family missed me and wished I could be there with them. They had dinner at Uncle Jim's as usual and Aunt Maxine outdid herself again as she did every year.

I told her my friends and I celebrated at their place when I received my diploma. I didn't tell her I had been drinking beer, as I knew she would have been disappointed in me. I told her I would call her when I received the package and check.

I finally got through to Uncle Jim the next morning before he left for work since they were an hour behind us. I told him I tried to call all day Christmas into the late hours but the operators kept saying the lines were tied up. He asked if I received their parcel for Christmas, and I told him not yet and that it might be in today's mail. They said they all missed me and they hoped they'd get to see me on Spring Break once I was in school.

They asked if I had a nice Christmas, andI just said yes to avoid letting anyone know I was alone. It was sad when I couldn't be with family even more so because we lived in

217

the same town. My mom had not made any effort to apologize to me and I had a hard time being around her. Even when Bonnie was in the hospital, I had to leave the room just so there would be no tension around Bonnie. The thing that bothered me the most was how far back she sat in the room and didn't even hold my sister's hand or try to comfort her.

I could see she hadn't changed a bit. If she ever felt any remorse we never knew, whether it was stubbornness or meanness or a crumbling mind that kept her bitter we were left to our own painful imaginings. My mother continued in her justification always believing she was right and we were in the wrong.

I called the house after I got off work the next day. Wesley answered and I faked my voice and asked for Barb. When she came to the phone, I asked her if she received my present and could she keep the stuff I gave her. She pretended I was somebody else and told me she had received them and she liked them. She quietly said, Mom was in the other room and asked if I had a good Christmas. I told her yes, but I was alone. I was just checking to see if she was safe and let her know I was leaving for California soon.

"Watch for the mail when you could because I will write you," I promised her.

I heard mom in the background asking her what she was hiding in the other room for and to get the hell off the phone if she couldn't talk here in front of them. We said good-bye to each other and that was that. I didn't get to talk to Barb or see her before I left for California.

Terrell and I needed to decide when we were going to California or if she was going with me. My school started on January 21st. I needed to find an apartment and a job once I got there. I was thankful that Eileen was letting me work until I decided when I would be leaving. The Christmas Holidays were slow at the drive-in because people were gearing up for New Year's and planning their parties. Eileen was closed on New Year's Day.

Fortunately, The Foley Mill was right across the road so a lot of guys that work there came to Eileen's for lunch and they were tipping big for the New Year. I was thankful because it made up for my money I spent for Christmas.

Terrell had invited people over for New Year's Eve. I had to work until ten that night. When I got to the apartment, there were a few people I didn't know. I noticed one had two six packs of beer. Terrell told me they were just going to celebrate New Year's because everyone else was too. I was not too keen on Terrell's friends having beer in the apartment because it was in my name, however I told myself that Terrell paid rent too so it was her right to have friends up. I assured myself that most of them were of age.

Just before midnight, they went outside and watched the fireworks being shot off while Jackie and I watched from the kitchen window. After everyone came back in, there was a knock on the door. It was the police. A neighbor had called and said we were making too much noise. They started checking our identifications. I cringed when he asked for Jackie's and mine. We said officer we were only drinking Tang. He didn't believe us, so I put a little in a glass out of mine and asked him to taste or smell that there was no alcohol in Jackie's or mine. I told him we were just playing a game.

We did not even have music on because everyone was watching the game. The officer informed us that there were five minors and six adults at the party. Art was the one who brought the beer against my better judgment. He told us we were guilty by association and we all had to go to the police station and be ticketed for illegal possession of alcohol. I couldn't believe it. I had to pay a twenty-five dollar ticket because this jerk brought beer to my place. Art paid for our tickets, which he should have. We went home. I was so upset I couldn't even talk. I had the IP ticket on my record. I wouldn't let anyone come back to my place because I was upset that they were there to begin with.

Terrell kept apologizing and she too felt bad about what

happened. I told her that everyone should have left when they all knew how I was upset over the beer in the apartment. No one thought a neighbor would call the police. They were making noise outside when they were watching and shooting their fireworks. It had to be the noise outside that upset them. I had to stop thinking about it. It was over and done. The next day, we received an eviction notice on our door telling us we had to move in three days. I was sick to my stomach. We had three days to figure out what we were going to do.

Terrell had a friend she was dating off and on. He was headed to San Bernardino, California, and he would take us in his station wagon. If we helped pay for gas, we could leave in two weeks; he had to give notice where he was working. Terrell and I had to stay in a motel that wasn't too far from where we lived.

It was cheaper to rent by the week so we stayed for two weeks. We moved out of the apartment the day after they disconnected my phone so I knew it would be off. I was going to call Grandma and let her know I was heading to California for school in a couple of weeks and that I disconnected the phone so don't worry if you try to call me.

The motel was sixty a week and Terrell paid for the first week and my last check at Eileen's paid for the last week. It had a kitchenette, a television, and a big bathroom with a makeup counter. It had to do until we left Helena. Terrell looked at the bright side of this mess; we had maid service and free phone service as long as we made local calls. I informed her that it cost us a month's rent. The two weeks couldn't go pass fast enough for me. Chuck returned four days before we left. Terrell left a note on the boy's apartment door telling them where we were with the phone number. I spent the last few days before I left with Chuck.

On my last day of work, Eileen gave me a little bonus because I didn't miss any work, and I filled in for other people who quit without notice. She hated to see me go, she said. Then I stopped by Chuck's like he asked on my way to the motel to say goodbye and we kissed our last kiss. I figured he would find a new girlfriend. I was going to California and going to school. Who knew what was ahead for me?

Mom and Dad get married August 22, 1945

Mom and Bonnie at grandma's ranch 1946

Wanda age 9 months, Bonnie age 21 months

(Left to right) Bonnie, Wanda and Mom carrying Willard on our way back to Montana from Redding, California

(Left to right) Wanda, Willard, Bonnie, Wesleyand Mom holding Barb. Home in Helena, MT

At our home on West Main St. in Helena.
(Left to right) Mom holding Willard, Bonnie and Wanda

(Front row) Barb and Wesley
(Back row) Wanda and Bonnie

(Left to right) Wesley, Wanda, Barb and Bonnie

(Left to right) Wanda, Bonnie, Barb,
Mom, Wesley and Dad

(Left to right) Bonnie holding Spot our dog, Wanda, Barb,
Wesley and Dad on our car

The black bear dad killed up Rimini out of Helena.
This is the same bear that attacked us on our picnic.

Aunt Maxine and Uncle Jim

Grandma and Uncle Jim

Grandma and Grandpa Kroll and cousin Penny
in front of their house up Grizzly Gulch.

(Left to right) Bonnie, Barb, Wanda and Wesley
at our home on Waukesha St in Helena

(Left to right) Barb, Wesley, Wanda and Bonnie

(Left to right) Barb, Wesley, Willard, Wanda and Bonnie

Park Lake out of Clancy on family camping trip.
(Front row) Barb and Wesley
(Back row) Wanda in top body cast and Bonnie

CHAPTER TWENTY-FIVE

We packed up Bill's station wagon. He had a lot of room with the back seats folded down. The back of the station wagon was filled all the way to the brim with our belongings. All he had was one suitcase. Terrell and I sat in the front seat. I made sure to take a pillow since I was sitting by the door. We were driving all the way to Denver, then Salt Lake to Vegas, and on to San Bernardino. Then I would go on to Los Angeles to get to Fullerton. Or so I thought. The car was not in the best shape. Bill had to buy a new alternator somewhere before Salt Lake City.

Then as they were replacing the alternator, they discovered another problem. We had to get in a suite room in a motel. Bill had the small room and we shared a queen bed. We were there three days before we could continue on. Then we drove straight through except filling up for gas, getting something to eat, and taking turns driving.

When we arrived in Barstow his car was acting up again and smoke was bellowing out from under the hood. Bill thought we would make it to San Bernardino. We were by a police station and across the street it said apartments for rent. The guy at the service parts, on the corner where the gas station was, told Bill he needed a transmission and he doesn't know off hand where he would get one. Terrell saw the apartments for rent and they were furnished, Spanish style, for seventy-five dollars a month including all utilities for two bedrooms. "I am not doing this," I told her. Bill could take care of himself and go find his own place, since we were the ones who had paid for the gas coming here and for getting his car fixed too.

I had already missed the deadline for school. Terrell thought I should go to school here then go to Cal for the fall semester. I could get credits at the community college for

240

the first semester. I explained to her I wasn't going to do that, because first of all, my Grandmother paid for my classes and everything except my dorm. I would get signed up for the fall classes and tell them an emergency had come up. I felt like I was being punished for something with all this bad luck coming from somewhere, or someone.

I was paying for parts on a guy's car that I didn't even know. Now we had to pay for the rent from my money. But it turned out that Terrell found work before me, so it worked out where she had to pay for next month's rent. I had no idea where Bill went, who knew and who cared! I think he had money in his pocket to fix his car. He made us pay for everything until we pulled into San Bernardino. He sure had a good thing with us tagging along.

Terrell found a job at a movie theatre. I was so grateful when someone was fired and a job opened up. She told me to get down there that day. I got the job as an usher and sales girl. We actually liked working at the theater because we got to see free movies we wanted. It didn't cost us anything for our entertainment or our snacks.

We met some really nice young police officers because we lived across from the police station. Terrell met someone at the theater who she was dating. I met a really nice police officer named Woody. Woody invited Terrell and I to meet some of his buddies from the force at a get together they had on weekends. I thought this might be a nice way to meet people. At the get together there were deputies, police officers, and others professionals. They had a beautiful recreation room that they all used in the apartment complex, which consisted of eight 4-plex units. We had a terrific time with them and everybody kept introducing us to others saying "...these are the girls from Montana".

Gary asked me to dance a slow dance. He asked where we worked and where we lived. He asked how I liked living in San Bernardino and what brought me here. I amused him with our horrific trip. He sympathized with me over the trip. "It sounds like this guy got his car fixed for free," he

241

sighed.

I told him I was supposed to be in my first semester at Cal State and I had to wait until the next semester, which set me back a semester. Gary informed me, I could take night classes to make up the difference if I wanted to study day in and day out. At this point, I was willing to do that if it would get me into St. Bernadine's on time. Gary also told me the nursing program at St. Bernadine's was a good one.

Gary wanted to know if I would go out with him. I told him I had to find out what my schedule was and then I would let him know when I was off but right now we had no phone to call me ahead of time.

The worst part of living in San Bernardino was not having a phone, but I needed to hang onto every cent that was left over and not spend too much on extras. McDonald's was right by us and they had fifteen-cent hamburgers or hamburger and fries for 25 cents. I learned to drink a lot of water except at the theatre, where we were allowed to drink soda on our breaks and have popcorn. The only groceries Terrell and I bought was bread, lunchmeat, fruit that was cheap, lots of Mac 'n Cheese, milk and vegetables. Our groceries lasted us for a while since we ate at McDonald's quite a bit. Occasionally, we would go to the Denny's for breakfast after a date was over or go out for a cheap dinner.

I did not hear from Gary so I figured he thought I was too young or he wasn't interested since I had just graduated from high school. As luck would have it a few days later when Terrell and I were returning home from an evening walk to cool off Gary was driving around our complex in a white Avanti looking for me. He stopped us to ask if we knew where Wanda lived. He did not recognize me. I had my hair frosted and he was looking for a girl with dark brown hair.

San Bernardino was a nice city and we were beginning to like it. We went to the stock car races in the neighboring town of Rialto and Fontana. I met a new friend, Arden. I enjoyed being around her, as she was always positive and loved to joke around to make people laugh. She made me feel like I belonged with her. I mentioned to her that she would make a great stand-up comedian. After we met her she would always come and get me to go somewhere with her because she knew I didn't have a car. Terrell worked the noon shift on weekends and sometimes I got stuck with the night shift which anyone who worked at the theater hated because you had to count the till and close which made it late enough that I didn't like walking home in the dark alone.

Gary would often pick me up when he wasn't working. He thought it a bad idea for a pretty girl to be walking alone at night in any town and that if I had to walk I should try to always walk with someone. We had a "friendship" arrangement because I didn't want to get serious over anyone and he knew it. He wasn't the pushy type, and I always enjoyed being with him. He was twenty-six and I wasn't going to be eighteen until June fifth. I always liked guys older than me who were more mature and not goofy acting.

I also found a part time job at St. Bernadine's as a nurse's aide so I could get my foot in the door when I came back from school and wanted to get into the nursing program.

It was my birthday and I was invited down to the recreation room for a party. Everyone knew not to get me in trouble for serving me alcohol, so they made me virgin daiquiris. I really enjoyed the party and Arden and Terrell were having a blast too. I knew they were drinking because Terrell told me to take a drink of her Margarita and it tasted of alcohol.

The night wound down. I went home with a headache from the deafening music. Gary gave me a ride. He asked if I was okay. I told him I was, but it sucked that everyone else was older and drinking. I also found out he wasn't concerned about our age difference because he really thought I was older. He told me I didn't act eighteen and was very mature for my age. I told him I grew up too fast and that it was a long story. He kissed me goodnight, and I thought he was an amazing kisser. He had the softest lips I had ever kissed.

He told me he would see me soon, and happy birthday. I saw him again the next weekend since we both had the day off. He was a motorcycle police officer as was his roommate Dan. Terrell and I were enjoying the free movies as we got to bring a friend when we came to the movies. I asked Gary if he would like to go and he took me up on the offer. Arden or another friend joined us since she also was dating a nice guy from their complex.

Usually I only had to work weekdays at the hospital because they knew I had another job. I was up front with the hospital about working at the theatre and wanted this as a part-time job. I let them know I would be leaving for school soon. That way I wasn't working too many hours where I couldn't relax and be able to still save money. The money I made from St. Bernadine's was put aside in case of an emergency.

It was funny how much I remembered of the abuse. My life, as a child, was so chaotic and treacherous that I tried to forget some of it and couldn't. I seem to think that eventually I would forget the bad things that had happened to me, but I could not escape the nightmares.

They were to continue with me all my life. To live, I just had to get past the horrible details and it was easier said than done. So how could I ever have normal feelings for another person without feeling like I was a fake, a fraud, too fearful to get close? There was no way in the world I could share or trust anyone with what my life was like in my childhood. I still feel dirty today because of what took place with the Catholic priests. They knew what they did and it didn't matter at all to the priests or the nuns who themselves were cruel. Just a handful of clergy destroyed my childhood innocence.

I was not raised to love by my family because they didn't show me how to love. I had to learn that from my friends, grandparents and my relatives who cared so deeply for me. At least my grandparents and my aunt and uncle truly showed me, you could be loved and love back. So now all I had to do was keep learning that I could be loved for the right reasons. When a man could abuse me as a child, and tell me I was a very bad girl and God was going to punish me how could I ever understand love? If my mother didn't love me and God didn't love me, how would I know love at all?

That was why I think I had a hard time separating things in my head. I was smart so I hoped to figure the memories out on my own. Now, it was my time in life. I was working toward future goals, and I wanted to enjoy myself when I was not working to meet those goals. I could be selfish about the thoughts of others around me, and I tried desperately to please everyone in my life.

As soon as I started dating Gary, Woody the officer who introduced us was trying to go out with me. I told him not to ask me anymore as I was seeing Gary. I told Gary about Woody asking me out, and he told me that he would say something to Woody because it ticked him off that he was the one who introduced us. Gary was a huge part of my being happy. This was the first time I had distinguished the difference between what love must be and not just like. I was falling for him, hook, line and sinker. I knew he felt the same the way toward me, so very respectful asking his friends not to swear around me. He also made it quite clear to Woody we were an item.

We had a lot of great weekends and a few weekdays going out and enjoying each other's company. Gary told Terrell and me we could get a real nice apartment a few blocks up from where we lived with a swimming pool. They had other friends living there too. He said it was only five dollars more than what we were paying for the place we were in and it had no swimming pool or air conditioning. Arden helped us move. We had a bottom apartment right next to the swimming pool. Our living room looked right out at the pool. After moving in, we saw why we had this one a lot cheaper than other people paid.

All the noise from the pool and the big recreation room came into our apartment. Fortunately, they could not be used after ten. So, there were advantages and disadvantages.

Everyone had to be over eighteen to live in the apartments and thank god we got in thanks to Gary and Dan knowing the owner and giving us great references. They sure held a lot of parties at these apartments, though. Gary told me I did not have to participate, because a lot of them were just blowing off steam because of their tedious, grueling, and dangerous jobs. He would watch out for my safety.

There was a guy named Art who lived upstairs that liked Terrell, and I think she was starting to like him because she was spending all of her time with him when she wasn't working.

Gary was put on patrol car now and once in a while he would stop by to say hello if he was in the vicinity on his lunch break and have lunch with me. I would make him a sandwich and lemonade and we would sit by the pool at a table holding hands like teenagers. He asked me how I felt about him and I told him I cared for him deeply and we would see where it would take us. He asked me if I wanted to go out to dinner. He told me to dress up.

I borrowed one of Arden's real nice cocktail dresses. It was black and I wore the pearls my aunt gave me. He showed up in a gray suit and tie, and looked extremely handsome. Gary was well over six feet tall and I was five foot two inches. We sort of looked like Mutt and Jeff together. We went to a real nice restaurant and had a lovely dinner and afterwards we headed to his place for the party. He told me I was stunning and that was nice to hear. Before going into the party, he told me, he couldn't get enough of being with me.

Everyone wanted to know why we were so dressed up. Gary told them we had been out for a wonderful dinner. Several of his buddies from the department were very attentive to me when Gary excused himself to take a phone call. When he came back, he made the remark "Can't leave the wolves alone for just a moment can I." They burst into laughter and said he had only himself to blame "...leaving the lamb alone to fend for herself."

The party went past two in the morning, and I asked Gary if he would take me home, because I had to work at noon the next day. So we went back to the apartment and Terrell had gone to bed already and he didn't want to disturb her, so we kissed good night out in front of our door and made a time to meet after he got off work.

I was really starting to fall for this handsome young officer, but I was still cautious as I had plans. I really cared for him deeply as I had never cared seriously for anyone. He made my pulse go up and my heart beat fast whenever we embraced and kissed. It was a whole different experience with Gary. He would pick me up when he was off duty, and we would go to his place to listen to music or watch a little television. One night we sat all snuggled up and then Gary turned off the television and put on some music, one thing led to another and I told him I thought we had better cool it. He told me he was in love with me. I told him I had not been with a guy, and I truly was scared. He started kissing me again and again and soon we were making love as if it was okay because we cared and loved each other. I finally told him I did love him. We lay in each other's arms for a long time. Finally, I told him we better get going because I did not want Dan walking in. We had been dating for six months. I was in love with him, and I knew I wanted to be with him. He was such a soft, gentle man and once I spoke my love for him, I fell, like a stone into deep water. "I don't want you to leave," he said holding me in his arms.

When we had a few days off from our busy work schedules, we would take drives to Lake Arrowhead and Big Bear Lake for skiing, having our special time together. One time, we both had two days off. We decided to spend the entire time at Lake Arrowhead. Gary wanted to show me the shops they had there and how cool they looked at night. This was the first time I had seen snow since I had left Montana. They only had a couple of inches but it was cool to see it here in Arrowhead. He said in the winter months that people came up to ski. I asked if maybe sometime we could do that since we both skied. He loved to ski and skate too, but he was more into hockey skating where I figure skated. We had a wonderful day and evening at Lake Arrowhead. We ate a late dinner and did a lot of cuddling and making out. We stayed up late trying to use every minute we had left to be together. Leaving came too soon. I slept all the way back to San Bernardino and he woke me up when we arrived at my apartment.

He had to work the early shift and had to work off and on through the week spending what free time he had with me. He had me come over a few times to his and Dan's apartment to get away from the crowd over at our place and we just hung out by the pool or watched television with Dan. Then he had to get me back to my place so I could go to work at St. Bernadine's.

The following week we were both working a lot, but it seemed he was working more than me. He would stop by quickly in the police cruiser to say hello and have a coke with me. Personal use of a police car was against the rules so those times were brief as he was taking a chance with our little rendezvous. He told me he and three other guys were going to go to San Diego next weekend and that he would see me when he got back and we would go to Big Bear Lake again. We could take in a movie tonight and do something tomorrow after I got off shift he told me while holding me tightly in his arms.

We went out together with another couple to dinner and watched television at his place then he brought me home. He kissed me good-bye and said he would see me when he returned from his fishing trip on a charter boat off San Diego. I told him to bring back some good fish for me to cook. Gary said deep-sea fishing was a lot different than lake and river fishing in Montana. I told him about fishing with Dad as a little girl at Park Lake.

After Terrell and I got off work on Friday, we hung out at the pool with a few of our friends. We all made snacks for the evening and had music playing from the recreation room with the doors pulled open, everyone enjoyed themselves.

Then we saw a police cruiser pull up that late evening and thought we were going to be told the music was too loud. I saw it was Dan and thought he was stopping by to said hello and let me know if he had heard from Gary. He came over to me and told me I needed to sit down for a minute, he needed to talk to me alone. Terrell wanted to know what was going on. Dan asked everyone to let him talk to me alone, and we went inside the apartment. He told me there had been a horrible accident in San Diego and two guys were killed and two were hanging on for life, one was Gary.

I burst out crying and he held me tightly and told me he would be back when he got off shift because a lot of the deputies and everyone on the force knew about the accident now. His superiors let him come to notify me and another was on the way to his parent's house. He said Gary's family said I could come down and see him as Dan made them aware that I was seriously dating Gary. They knew about me because he talked about me and had been planning to introduce us as soon as he got back from his trip.

My friend Janet said she would take me to San Diego, but Dan said to wait until we received further word from his family at the hospital in San Diego. Dan said he didn't want to leave me at this point but he had to since he was on duty and they were busy notifying the whole department of the accident. He asked everyone there to keep an eye on me as he saw how upset I was.

Dan wanted me to find out from him and not someone else. He knew how Gary felt about me, and how fast word travels so he came immediately. I couldn't stop crying not knowing how badly hurt he was since Dan said both survivors were critical. The pain of not knowing was the worst a person could ever feel.

When Dan came back, he told me that they were in Jeff's Volkswagen and someone had T-boned the driver's door and turned them sideways on the freeway causing the Volkswagen with the four guys in it to flip over the overpass, and land on the Interstate below into the opposite lane. It had flipped upside down, ejecting two of them from the car, killing them instantly. Gary and his friend Ed had to be extracted with the "jaws of life," a hydraulic rescue tool, from the Volkswagen's back seat. It was a horrible mess the California Highway Patrol told the San Bernardino Police Department.

Dan and Janet took me to Gary's place where we waited to hear from Gary's parents. Terrell stayed at the apartment with everyone else and waited for news. Janet lived in the same complex as Gary and Dan. We were all hearing that Gary was in critical condition and might not make it. His parent's gave Janet the go ahead to bring me down to San Diego. I couldn't leave fast enough to get to him.

Janet rushed me to San Diego. When we got up to his room no one was with him, and the nurse told me to just go in since my name was on the list of family, thanks to his parents. Janet waited outside the room and told me take all the time I needed.

They had his eyes covered with cotton balls and taped as they do with coma patients. His poor body was covered with cuts and was black and blue and swollen. He was in a deep coma.I wanted to be strong for him, but when I saw his condition my heart just failed. I began to cry. Laying my head against him the tears flowed while I found myself repeating, "Don't leave me, Gary! Don't leave me." I begged. I pleaded, "You are the best thing that has ever happened in my life. Please stay with me. I need you."

The nurse handed me a box of Kleenex. I asked her if she thought he could hear me. She doubted he could with his vitals so weak, but not wanting to discourage me she said she frankly didn't know for certain. I bent down and begged, "Come back to me. I love you, and I want us to be happy forever. Please Gary, fight for your life!"

The nurse told me his parents had gone somewhere to find a hotel and didn't know when they would be back. I was surprised that no one was here with him. The nurse told me his dad had to get his mother to rest after being with him all night. The doctor gave her a sedative. I stayed for hours until the nurse said I had to leave, as she had to care for him. I bent down and kissed him goodbye and told him to "Please come back, fight Gary." The nurse told me she would tell his parents that I stayed for a few hours, and they couldn't let me stay longer. She explained to me that we normally only allow immediate family, but his parents insisted you were allowed to see him today.

Janet and I went back to San Bernardino and she told me to stay at her house with her, that I needed to call the theater and tell them what had happened. Dan had already taken care of St. Bernadine's. Janet assured me I was an emotional wreck and advised against working. Dan was given the day off and saw us when we returned. He asked about our trip to see Gary. I broke down and told him it's bad, real bad. I told him there was no sign of life except his soft breathing through the ventilator and that didn't sound strong at all. Dan said let's hope for the best Wanda. I told him I was going to my apartment if he should hear anything to please stop by and let me know. Dan said if he even heard one thing that he would come over and tell me right away. I mentioned that I was shocked no one was sitting with Gary. Dan didn't understand that at all because he knew his parents real well. I told him what the nurse told me, that they were there all night and needed to eat and rest. Two days went by. Dan had not heard any news yet and promised me he would come and tell me immediately if he did, but as far as he knew there were no changes in Gary's status.

Six days had passed since the awful accident and my nerves were shot, but I had to go to work. Dan had told me the Department called with the report that Gary was the same with no change. That day, I came home from work and spent some time by the pool. Around nine-thirty that night, Dan showed up in the cruiser and told me to come inside. I went inside warily knowing from the tears in his eyes what he was going to tell me. He sighed and choked, "Gary just passed away." I felt the wind get knocked out of me and collapsed into Dan. He held me like I was a rag doll and pulled me to the couch.

"Why has he been taken away?" In my shock, I felt the old traumas charge me from the gates of hell. What had I done to deserve this? "No, no, Gary, no-o-o," I sobbed.

Dan tried to comfort me by saying that at least Gary would not be in a vegetative state, like Ed was. His parents made the impossible decision to take him off life support when the doctors told them that their son would never recover.

Dan stayed with me until I could function then went back to work. I was grateful to Dan for his coming to me personally. I had a lot of respect for him.

At this point in time I really did believe I was being punished for my sins. Father Gilmore reminded me over and over that I was a bad child deserving everything that happened to me. I didn't want to believe him, but what could I do now but think why do so many bad things happen to me? When do bad things stop happening to me?

Gary's funeral was three days later, and they had patrol cars all the way from San Diego and Los Angeles and surrounding areas come for his funeral. It was nothing but two sides of patrol cars and motorcades for miles, going to Redlands where he was buried. It was such a long slow drive there from the church service. Janet drove us to the funeral. After, the funeral, she put the top down on her car, as it was pretty hot out that day on July 27th. I sat in the front seat by the passenger door unable to speak for the flooding of tears.

Dan was in the long procession of patrol cars and he asked Janet to take good care of me until we were back at the apartment. He had a few days off to help me through this awful loss. I just kept holding wet Kleenex under my eyes to catch my tears, while Janet, Arden and Terrell talked about how lovely the funeral was. I was so upset they finally shut up. Once at the graveyard I stood in the back because I couldn't stop sobbing. In my misery, I didn't want to disrupt the service.

After the memorial was over and each person had paid their respects, I came forward to place the roses I'd brought on the coffin. Janet waited in the car. She was such a true friend to me in this time of need. Terrell and Arden had left with others.

I was thankful for everyone when we went back to Janet's apartment. Dan had come over and it was clear he was struggling. He and Gary were best friends having been in the department since they were twenty-two and known each other since before they both went to the Academy. I wandered over to him and gave him a hug. I think it was more for him than for me. That's when Dan asked me why I didn't come forward to the graveside during the service. I felt isolated and afraid to be so vulnerable in front of Gary's parents. They didn't know me, and I didn't know them.I knew Gary was going to introduce me to them when he got back from his fishing trip but I just couldn't be in their presence in my state. All I could do was cry.

We talked about the fun times. How much he loved life and his job. How he also loved his beautiful white Avanti car. I was not feeling well and had a terrible headache from all the crying. Dan told me to go and lie down on Gary's bed;maybe I would feel close to him. I fell asleep and held his pillow in my arms as I slept. I was totally exhausted so Dan just let me sleep so people wouldn't bother me. Janet came down early to check on me. I was awake and decided to shower and figure out what I would do next.

When I saw Dan, he told me he had talked to Gary's parents. They wanted to meet and talk to me about Gary's and my relationship. There were some photos that Gary had taken on our trips to Arrowhead and a few snapshots of us going out on dates. They were curious to meet this girl who their son had fallen in love with. We went over to Gary's parent's house on Dan's motorcycle. Dan handed me Gary's helmet. I felt like I put him on as I snapped shut the strap and straddled the bike.

I had a case of the jitters anticipating meeting Gary's as I was graciously met. Gary's dad gave me a picture that was taken of Gary and me sitting on the hood of his car at his apartment on our first date. He had given it to them a few weeks before and said he was going to bring me out to meet them. All along I didn't think he even spoke of me to them.

After talking, I learned that Gary had a fiancé he was trying to let down easily after he met me. I felt a twinge of guilt, but since Gary chose not to tell me about her I figured I was blameless. His parents realized what was going on after he showed them the picture of us sitting on the hood of his car. They regretted that Gary hadn't brought me to meet them earlier.

I cried when I told them about our dates, how we met, and our last trip to Lake Arrowhead and the gifts he purchased for me there. I had all the wonderful memorabilia he bought for me to remember him by. I handed the picture of Gary and me back to his parents and told them I had our pictures from Lake Arrowhead. I told them to please keep this one of their handsome son in his suit. I had pictures of Gary in his uniform and several others I would give to his mother if she would like them.

I hugged Gary's parents when we said our goodbyes, and told them I was coming back to Nursing School here at St. Bernadine's after I finished my courses at Cal State. They asked me to have Dan bring me for a visit when I returned to San Bernardino.

When we arrived at Dan's apartment, I hugged him tightly and told him how much those three hours meant to me. Now, I need to take time and heal. Janet helped me do that for the next few days. I honestly will never forget this wonderful man that I deeply loved. This was the man I finally fell for, and I had given myself to him whole-heartedly several weeks before he was in the fatal accident that took his life.

I called Grandma and told her what happened and she told me Bonnie was in Norwalk and gave me her phone number. "You need to go and stay with her and get in school as planned. You have your sister to help you get through this ordeal," she stressed. Grandma knew I needed to be with family. I called Bonnie and told her what had happened. Bonnie told me to come to her place and get back in school so I could get back on track for nursing. Janet drove me to Norwalk, a suburb of Los Angeles.

CHAPTER TWENTY-SIX

Bonnie lived on Pioneer Boulevard, the main street of Norwalk. She answered the door. I introduced her to Janet. Grandma told her everything. Bonnie asked if we had eaten, and I told her not since breakfast, so she took us to a restaurant down the street from her place. After sitting down and ordering, Bonnie told me some shocking news. She had married a deputy sheriff. I certainly was not prepared for that!

Janet was concerned about me staying with Bonnie. Bonnie made it clear that I should live with her and her husband. They had a spare bedroom and the apartment was large. I did tell Bonnie that I would pay rent with the money that I had saved to live in the dorm.

Janet took my sister's phone number to keep in touch with me and would come visit when I got my own place. She then headed back to San Bernardino.

After Janet left, we talked about how she met Frank and how long she had been married, which was only five months. Grandma told her my boyfriend was also a police officer but had been killed in a car accident. I thought what a strange coincidence that we both ended with law enforcers. I told her my boyfriend lived in a complex full of policeman and deputies.

Bonnie told me Grandma was upset that I didn't arrive for the first semester and had put it off, but was relieved that I was in Norwalk. I explained to Bonnie about Bill and his car and the trip from Helena to California, and why we were late. I also explained that I had called the school about my tuition that Grandma paid. The college put it towards the next semester. School was going to start, and I needed a job.

I found a job for after school, working at Riverview

Nursing Home just down the road from Bonnie's place. I was a nurse's aide and I used St. John's as a reference. I made twice what I did in Montana. Wages were better in California, but the cost of living was higher. Bonnie wouldn't take rent money and neither would Frank. He was very quiet and bashful. I could tell Bonnie was the domineering partner. He would always say to her "Yes, dear, no, dear and is there anything you want, dear." He didn't seem like the type of guy she would be with, but I dismissed it immediately.

I asked her what happened to Jerry. Bonnie told me he was her ticket away from the hellhole and he had a girlfriend. Jerry was married and working in Long Beach now.

Bonnie had found a job right away as a go-go dancer, and made fabulous money at it. I asked her what the heck a go-go dancer was. Bonnie explained that she danced in a cage. If the men in the club liked one's dancing, they put money in the cage. The lounge had four cages. The girls wore outfits that looked like bikinis with fringe on them. She said tips were amazing. When I asked her what Frank thought, she said that was how she met him and they hit it off right away.

With school and my job, I was exhausted when I arrived home. I closed the door to my room and studied until late in the night. I never heard Bonnie come in at night because I was sound asleep from sheer exhaustion. Grandma called a lot to check on me, and most of the time I would have to call her back because I was either at school or Riverside Nursing Home. It was such a great experience for me, because I learned a lot about geriatrics. It also pleased Grandma that I was in school and working.

The head nurse loved my curiosity about the patients and the work. She appreciated that I wanted to be a nurse, so she taught me everything she could about working with geriatric patients. She had been working at the home for fifteen years.

Riverside was seventeen years old with an excellent reputation. Three doctors owned the facility and were known for hiring the best and most professional staff. Every patient was charted and cared for as if in a hospital setting. The facility was spic and span and spotless. A lot of nursing homes had bad reputations for not being up to standard health codes and getting fined or closed. I felt fortunate to find this job. I believed it was meant to be.

Frank let me drive Bonnie's car. He would drop Bonnie off at work and stay to watch her until she got off. I asked her if this bothered her and she said heck no, I feel safe when he was sitting there waiting for me. He sat way in the back so her boss didn't feel intimidated.

I had saved quite a bit of money. When I talked to Grandma, I told her I wanted to take night classes and get the credits I missed when I was in San Bernardino. I could then be ready for nursing school at St. Bernadine's.

My Grandmother asked me if I had enough money saved to do that. I told her I would have to calculate all the costs, but I wanted to finish school as planned. My grandmother told me, "You are biting off more than you can chew. I don't want you to burn out and quit all together."

I couldn't work and do night school at the same time my Grandmother told me. However, she was willing to pay for my tuition and books if I was willing to send her my grades to prove I was accomplishing what I set out to do. I had to get the fees and have them send the bill to my Grandmother since the night classes started in a couple of weeks. I gave my two week notice at Riverside and told them I could work in the summer but right now I had nothing but school on my mind. I told my supervisor I would work if someone doesn't show up or calls in sick. Staying busy helped me cope with the loss of Gary.

I did not tell Grandma that I had met a guy named Dan at work who was willing to tutor me. When I met him I commented to him unexpectedly sounding rude. "Not another Dan! I am so sorry," I explained, "My grandfather's name was Dan and three friends of mine were named Dan in the last two years. They were all great guys so I have nothing against the name Dan."

Dan was a student from UCLA that lived right across from the nursing home and volunteered there. He was from New York and he had the accent to go with it. Dan was very tall, lanky, and blonde with gorgeous blue eyes. We would talk about our schools when he came around to the patient's rooms to see if they needed anything like magazines or books or to go outside in the park behind the nursing home.

It was a beautiful garden with rock waterfalls. It was a very peaceful setting for the patients. Some even enjoyed asking if they could please take their meals out in the garden instead of their rooms. Dan would take them out and bring them back. He volunteered three days a week and he got university credit if it was fifteen hours a week.

I told him I usually didn't get home from my night classes until nine thirty or a quarter to ten at night. He told me, how crazy I was for doing it.

I was so thankful when Thanksgiving came. We had five days off and I was going to have all of my homework done in one day with Dan's help. He would eat Thanksgiving Dinner with us He would be flying home for Christmas Holidays. He stayed in Norwalk for Thanksgiving as his parents were in Europe. He was a 4.0 student that didn't have to work hard for his grades, and he belonged to a fraternity at UCLA.

I offered to pay for his gas money since he was tutoring me. Grandma told me to pay my tutor for helping me keep up with everything so I did not fall behind. Believe me when I said we studied, he would not let me give up if I was stumped on a problem. Chemistry was my downfall at the beginning, but Dan helped me get good grades.

Dan, from San Bernardino, told me he was going to try to come up sometime and maybe he could meet this tutor of mine. I let him know that Dan was my tutor and a new friend. I made it clear I wasn't interested in any relationship after Gary. He asked me if I was doing okay and I told him I kept my mind busy with school so I could still start the nursing program in San Bernardino as planned. I told him I would be back in August because the nursing program started the first part of September.

Dan informed me that everyone asked about me and wanted to make sure I was doing fine. He also told me that Janet had mentioned that I might try to go to San Bernardino on Christmas break. She wasn't supposed to mention it as I was going to surprise him and a few other friends. Bonnie told me I could use her car to drive up and spend a few days with Janet. Bonnie did not want me to stay very long because she didn't want Frank to be at her work place anymore when he got off work. I called Janet and told her not to tell anyone I was coming for a visit but let it be a surprise.

Bonnie and I fixed Thanksgiving dinner. It was so much fun cooking alongside her getting things ready. Frank and Dan watched football. They met when Dan came over to tutor me because some nights we were still working on my studies when Frank came home from work. Frank drank beer on his days off so Dan brought over a bottle of wine and beer for Frank. Dan liked wine. We had a wonderful Thanksgiving and Dan thanked us for a wonderful day.

Dan invited us to go to Disneyland on Saturday. Bonnie had to work, but I could go. We could hang out at the beach in Malibu if I would prefer he said. He could tell I wasn't real excited about Disneyland, and I would much rather go surfing at the beach since I haven't been lately with all the schoolwork. I suggested that going to Malibu sounded fun.

We had a perfect day at the beach, not too hot and not too cold, and the waves were just right for surfing and getting up on the board when we wanted to. He rented boards at the beach, so I made sure I used mine so he wouldn't be disappointed in paying for a board that wasn't used. He taught me how to do some things on the

260

surfboard that I would not have known how to do.

When I said Dan was a natural blonde, a lot of guys in California in the sixties dyed their hair or bleached it blonde. Why, I don't know, but I sure could pick the ones out that did. Dan was a cutie pie that I thought some girl should snap up and grab when they realized he was not only cute but also intelligent. I was sure he was from a wealthy family because he didn't work and had a very sporty BMW. Plus he belonged to a fraternity and took me to fancy places and tipped heavy. I enjoyed doing things with him because he never once took me for granted expecting me to date him and kiss him. Dan truly was like a brother to me.

It was back to my busy schedule. Dan was back at UCLA and back to his three days of volunteering. I was so glad Dan still had time to help me with my work. His tutoring had made such a difference. He wouldn't accept money from me so I thought for Christmas I would buy him a couple of nice sweaters. He would be leaving for New York to have Christmas with his family and would come back for the spring semester.

It was weird that neither of us spoke about our family except when Bonnie and I talked about wishing Barb could have been with us for Thanksgiving dinner. Dan asked where Barb was. We said she was home in Montana. I told him that we didn't get along with our mother and left it at that. Talking about the abuse didn't make it any better. I didn't want my friends to know about my family life when I was growing up. It was better just leaving certain things unsaid.

I worked my fanny off with getting fairly decent grades. I think I could have applied myself better, but a lot of time I let personal problems interfere with schoolwork. I had to keep telling myself to stay focused and be passionate to accomplishing my goals. It was a lot harder than I thought. Dan made it easier by helping me get over the hump, and I was forever grateful to him.

Bonnie and I went Christmas shopping two days before

Christmas. Grandma sent us each $25.00 for our presents, and here we were spending it for Christmas. I told Bonnie I wasn't going to spend a lot of money on presents because I had to quit my job for night school. I needed to keep my money in the bank for an apartment when I return for nursing school. Dan received the sweaters I gave him for Christmas. He wore them as promised, so I knew he was pleased with his gifts.

Christmas was a nice time, although Bonnie and I celebrated by us. Frank was really different and he actually kind of scared me. I never took a shower unless Bonnie was there.

My visit to San Bernardino was the best part of my Christmas break. Janet had everyone we hung out with at her apartment. Dan couldn't stop hugging me and finally said I looked great. I said I realized that I no longer had Gary in my life. I had to withstand the pain and make an appearance of being happy. I knew that my life must have gone on being young and living through a tragedy. I finally realized I needed to take it a day at a time.

The friends I had there made me feel very wanted. We partied and had a great time catching up. They knew I would be returning in September so I bid farewell until then and thanked everyone for getting together again.

The rest of the school year was studying and preparing my work to be finished on time. Attending school day and night put such a strain on my brain and I tired of it quickly. I finished and that was all that mattered. I owed Dan a great deal for helping me get through the year.

Dan was trying to decide if he was going for his law degree or med school or both. I asked him why be a lawyer and a doctor. He said he wanted to have both to fall back on. He was going to go to law school first, and then continue on to med school. That was why I thought he was from a wealthy family because he couldn't make up his mind or commit himself or better yet he just wanted to stay in school.

I knew one thing first hand. I would never go to night

classes and my regular classes ever again at the same time. All my electives, I had to pass with good grades to get in the nursing school. I received my acceptance to St. Bernadine's. I was so excited I had made it.

Things were going great and school was out and I finally was going to get to work again at Riverview. I asked for the seven to three shift, since Dan would be coming in on Monday, Wednesday and Friday from noon to three and then he said we could go to the beach after work and go surfing and swimming.

One weekend he invited Andrea and me to go sailing with friends of his. She didn't have to work that day, and Dan had two single friends he wanted her to meet. I was wishing he would like her. Andrea was very pretty and single with no boyfriend so she was excited about Redondo Beach. It was an absolutely gorgeous evening for sailing. There was a nice breeze so we could go out quite a ways. This was a first for me, as I had never been on a sailboat in my life. It had a nice cabin below for seven to eight people and a small kitchen.

Dan's fraternity brother from UCLA was kind of cocky. He was very rich and knew it. He flaunted what he had. He bragged a lot and his girlfriend was not any better. Dan's other friend Rob was a considerate individual and was nice like Dan.

We had gone out past the harbor and had a nice breeze. The guys had bottles of wine that they had brought up from below the deck. Andrea was getting very seasick and was leaning over the silver railings barfing relentlessly. Andrea was sicker as the sailboat hit the waves. I was so thankful that I was not seasick at all. I asked Andrea what I could do to help her.

The girlfriend of the guy who owned the sailboat said they had some Dramamine down below the deck in the cabinet. I went and got her some and found some ginger tablets that I knew were good for motion sickness. I gave Andrea the Dramamine and then ten to fifteen minutes later the ginger. She was getting better and her stomach settled down. She asked me how much longer we'd be on the boat.

It was getting pretty late, and I could barely see lights now. I asked Dan to ask his friend to turn around. The guy was drunk and making an ass out of himself and the party was just beginning. I didn't know the first thing about sailboats but I did know that we needed wind for it to go faster, and to move and not drift. The lights had disappeared. We were out there until after three in the morning with no wind. We went below deck and rested while the morons up above were partying. Then, the coast guard arrived to tow us in. They told the guy that they were notified of a missing boat when we hadn't returned to the docks. The guy who owned the boat got ticketed for operating a craft under the influence.

One of the other guys had to take over the craft since the driver was handcuffed until we returned to the dock. The police were called to the docks and he was taken to the police station for intoxication, resisting arrest and swearing at the Coast Guards personnel. Dan, Andrea and I couldn't thank the Coast Guard enough. Their jobs were tough enough without protecting drunks.

My sister and Frank were arguing. She had found a file in his cabinet full of child pornography and was so upset she told someone he worked with at the station. An investigation was launched and in time the newspapers and news stations picked up the story. Bonnie could not face the crisis.

I was at work when my sister tried to hang herself. Thank god the rope broke. I went to the hospital with her and tried to make sense of what she was doing. I begged her to confide in me. No amount of my assurance made her feel better. She was locked in a treacherous depression that emerged from her past. When I came home, the police had already removed his belongings confiscating everything he owned.

After Bonnie got out of the hospital she overdosed on pills. Her neighbor heard a loud thump on the floor

264

followed by moaning and cries for help. Her neighbor, but this being her second attempt, rescued my sister. She was ordered into treatment. She eventually recovered from the humiliation that Frank had put her through but not without the help of professionals.

Bonnie went back to work dancing after her annulment from Frank. She seemed to land on her feet but I still couldn't resist telling her sharply, "No man was worth committing suicide over. Take your self-respect from what you earn. You fought for your life when Sandy fell on you and you've survived Mom and the priests, don't forget that."

I started dating Daryl after he moved in next door. He asked me to go to a movie. He liked to play jokes and was a sophomore at Cerritos College in the fall. He and Bonnie got along great too. If I was down at their apartment then so was my sister. If he came up to our apartment then so did his roommate Tom.

In a month I would be going back to San Bernardino. I told Daryl I wasn't going to get into a serious relationship. I told him that Gary had passed away a little over a year ago, and I wasn't in any way ready. I was more conservative where he was outgoing and loved to party. Daryl was persistent and told me he'd come to San Bernardino to see me.

When I told Dan I was dating Daryl, he wasn't happy. He told me he wasn't my type, but what did he know? I thought hmmm, he's just jealous.

I told him I was moving soon so what difference did it make." I was glad to leave Los Angeles.

I returned to San Bernardino and lived with my friend Susan and her mom. I tried to pay but Susan's mother refused any money. Arden, Susan, Janet and I were good friends and it was great to be together. I had all of my books and registration taken care of and had nine days to enjoy time with them before school started.

Arden said Janet was expecting us over at her complex; it looked like no one was around as we walked by the recreation room. She opened the door and we were met with a resounding "SURPRISE!!" All of our friends from both complexes gathered to welcome me back. A lot of Gary's buddies were there. It made me feel good that Janet and Susan put this together for me. I hadn't felt this special since Gary died. Janet was afraid I would be upset but our old friend Dan said I'd be just fine. He was right I was fine and realized I was surviving.

Susan and Arden made all kinds of appetizers and barbecued ribs for our party, and of course there was wine and beer. Dan told me go ahead, have a glass of wine to settle down, "It'll make you feel better," he assured me. A lot of the guys from the force were there and no one was calling the cops on us, they wouldn't dare. We played music and danced into the night. I kept wondering if Gary was watching down over us the whole time. I missed him.

Dan thought I was pretty thin. I took immediate issue with his statement assuming he was judging me about my past choices of exhausting myself like I did going to school and working back then during my loss of Gary. I had no intention of repeating my mistakes.

Dan changed the subject by telling me that Gary's parents knew I was back in town and was hoping for a visit with me soon. I thought I would be fine, and seeing them would be nice. I wanted them to know I was thinking of them while I was away at school.

We went on Sunday. I met Dan at his place. He had not gotten a roommate yet, and I asked him why. He told me he wasn't ready for someone else to move in with him after losing Gary. It had been over a year since Gary died so I gently reminded him that "We both need to go on with our lives, Dan."

We arrived on Dan's motorcycle. Gary's parents welcomed us. His mom hugged me and told me I looked good but thin. They had set lunch up for us on the patio. Gary's dad was holding Gary's helmet and said to us as he caressed the helmet, "The days are still pretty rough for us, but God is helping us get through it."

I told them that God helped me through it too, even though I was angry that God had taken him from me.

Gary's mom had a surprise for me. Dan had gone through pictures in Gary's room and made copies for his parents and me. His mother made a little photo album for me of pictures Gary had of the two of us. I was overwhelmed with all the photos they had put together. His mother saw me tearing up and asked if I was okay, and I told her I was just elated that someone would be this thoughtful to make me happy!

I could tell they were both still grieving and heartbroken. Gary's sister had a son they named Gary and it helped his parents. It was like the good Lord gave them this child who resembled his uncle so well. The baby had mannerisms that were the same as Gary's. It turned out to be a wonderful few hours with them and they asked if I could stop in once in a while when I had free time.

I was still trying to understand why things happened like they did. I hoped I never had to endure a loss again. It was so very painful to lose a child let alone a boyfriend, or anyone I loved. I had almost lost my sister because of a jerk she had married who was a sick creep. But someone so young and handsome and very dear, like Gary, I couldn't understand.

When I left Norwalk, I called and let Grandma know I would send her my new phone number and that Bonnie was doing great now. I told her Susan's number and told her they wanted me to stay with them instead of in an apartment with Susan. Grandma wanted me to pay them rent regardless, so she would always send me extra money. I told her we were heading for Palm Springs to go to Arden's parents' house and there would be eight girls going in two cars. She told me to be safe and no drinking.

Grandma didn't say anything about drinking at the house, I thought to myself. I rather enjoyed feeling I could have a drink. It made me forget a lot of things that I would like to forget: the unwanted sexual assaults, mom's abuse and Gary's untimely death. I knew I had to restrain myself from making it a habit. I knew all about addictions. I had seen people who had overdosed on alcohol when I worked in the hospital. I actually studied about it in my classes.

Arden, Susan, Janet and I were going to Palm Springs for the next week. We were going to stay at Arden's parents' house with her sister and her sister's friends. There would be eight of us in a five-bedroom house with a huge pool. We were going to go water skiing at Sultan Sea and swimming and just relax around their pool.

Our first night there, we had a blast being tipsy and getting drunk. Linda, Arden's sister suggested we go get golf carts and have races. Their parent's house was on the golf course and we were not far from the clubhouse that was closed. No one was around to stop eight silly, drunk girls. We were really wild and having a blast when some of the girls started throwing-up; we knew it was time to call it quits.

On Wednesday, we joined the boys for a day of water skiing on the Salton Sea. It was a hundred and eleven degrees that day. We had been taking turns skiing when Arden suggested I had better cover up with a tee shirt because my skin was starting to get pretty pink and before I knew, it would be burned. I put on layers of suntan lotion hoping that would help but I was getting as red as the cherries on my swimsuit. I put on a pair of shorts trying to protect my legs. The water felt wonderful when I was water skiing. It cooled me down. My body was beginning to feel the sting of not using my common sense. The waves stung when other boats went speeding by. I knew I was in trouble and I knew tomorrow would be much worse than it felt right now. I needed to get out of the water as it was burning my legs.

We returned to the docks for lunch. The girls had enough sun for the day, as a lot of them were sunburned but not as bad as me. I was so thankful when it was suggested we go back to the house since I was really in a lot of pain. I used Solarcaine to stop the burning. We stayed in the house with air conditioning to keep me comfortable.

The next day, it was nice to just relax with a bunch of girls and enjoy the day and evening without drinking ourselves into oblivion.

We had to head back the next afternoon as some of the girls had to work the next day. Arden, Janet and I were the only ones with the day off. We drove with the top up. We stopped on the way to Arden's to pick up a gallon of vinegar, so I could bathe in it and relieve my sunburn.

We stayed at Arden's that night. Susan and I slept for a long period of time with the air conditioner going the entire time. Then we returned to her house and her parents couldn't believe how bad we looked when we came in. I had to get rid of this sunburn before I started back to nursing school next week!

Arden and Janet's parents paid for the rent on her apartment. Susan's house had a detached mother-in-law apartment, which was Susan's own private area. She didn't have to pay rent and refused mine. I honestly thought Susan's parents just wanted to keep her close and protect her. Susan told them how long I had been on my own and how I came from a very dysfunctional poor family.

CHAPTER TWENTY-SEVEN

I had put in for student work status at the school and hoped I would get it. I had lots of experience, but I knew the spaces were limited. There were lots of students requesting it. They might want to pick the girls that need the most experience, so who knew, I could only hope. We also worked on the floor when we were doing our labs for hands-on experience. Six girls and I were chosen which gave me real peace of mind. I learned we were chosen for our experience as nurse's aides and our knowledge would help train those who had no experience. We had to work in all areas of the hospital, OB, medical, surgical and ER plus the psychiatric and therapeutic areas. Once again I found myself on overload and soothed myself by the fact that I was getting credit and a stipend for my efforts.

The only thing I did not enjoy was the psychiatric floor. They taught us how to prepare a patient for electroconvulsive therapy, or shock treatment. It was being used from the 1930's on until it fell into disrepute in the 1970's. I found the therapy hard to support after getting patients prepared and taking care of them on their arrival back to their room after the treatment. It seemed so primitive.

I was to complete my Licensed Practical Nurse (LPN) degree two days before my birthday in early June, great timing for me. I also knew that I would not be going on for my Registered Nursing (RN) degree. I hoped that my grandmother would not be too disappointed.

Bonnie wanted me to come and visit her on Thanksgiving break. I didn't have a car, but was fortunate enough to find a ride with Sheila who was going home to the area for both Thanksgiving and Christmas.

Bonnie sounded really lonely and I worried about

hersince she tried to commit suicide, twice. I still couldn't understand her trying to hang herself, and failing, then taking an overdose because she failed at the first option. I hoped when she was depressed that she called for help and had someone to talk to who would understand and help her through tough times.

I thought that was why she wanted me to come for Thanksgiving, which I had decided was best for the both of us. I called Bonnie to let her know I would be coming. And it seemed to cheer her up quite a bit because she was very excited when I told her.

She was still dancing because she liked it too much to quit. Grandma did not know about Bonnie's dancing. If she found out Bonnie said Grandma would "...kill her and then she would have a heart attack." She wanted to know how long I would stay, and she would take time off of work so we could do things together.

I had five more weeks before Thanksgiving, so I had to buckle down and hit the books and work on the floor. It seemed like a never-ending process, but I actually liked working on the floor and was enjoying the girls I worked with.

We passed the weekends by going to a bar on Palm Avenue and it seemed to be everyone's favorite hangout, including mine. I was still underage, but I had the trust of a bouncer who let me stay and imbibe which was a downfall for me as I became accustomed to hard alcohol. Mixed drinks were cool however, I learned quickly about hangovers. In my drunken stupors, I was free of my nightmares which was a good thing in one way, but really bad another.

My life resumed in this fashion for a while then one weekend I was in for quite a shock as Bonnie had given Daryl my address without asking me first. He decided to pay me a surprise visit; at least I got a warning before he showed up. I wasn't happy about him ambushing me so Susan and I decided to play a trick on him. I pretended I had amnesia from an accident I was in. (Bonnie didn't know about the accident) Susan told Daryl that I would not recognize him. He believed the ruse and was about to leave after we acted it out. When he walked away he heard us laughing. He was super pissed as I tried to call him back to the house to apologize for the horrible joke we played on him, but I couldn't stop laughing.

Daryl was offended, naturally. After all he had ridden his motorcycle all the way from Norwalk to see me. I told him, I hadn't heard a word from him for the time I was gone so why would I welcome him and change plans for the weekend just because he decided to "surprise" me?

In my view, it just wasn't the way to impress me. He hopped on his cycle and whisked away. I went in the opposite direction.

Time was passing by rapidly with weekdays of work and weekends of partying and drinking. I think I was trying to fill a void. The drinking made things go away. I wasn't looking for a relationship with anybody, and I drank to wash away bad memories. It seemed to work. Drinking was the thing I did the most to relieve stress and the guilt from my past that made its home deep within me. The nightmares eventually broke through my alcohol-soaked psyche, visiting me in force once again.

Sheila and I were looking forward to the ten days we had off for Thanksgiving. I was looking forward to a little break and spending time with Bonnie who promised she only had to work one day, but threw in that she wasn't sure if she would get stuck with another shift. Sheila wanted us to come down to Long Beach and ride the roller coaster at "The Pike", a big permanent carnival. She added that there weren't any ugly Sailorsthere either (ha-ha). I also wanted to see Dan and visit Riverside. I was dreading seeing Daryl after the joke we played on him.

Once I was settled, I wanted to go to Riverside and see my friends and see if Dan was there. Bonnie had to get ready for work. She was dancing in a new place and making a lot more money.

She told me she was dancing at a new place and made

more money there. She asked me if I wanted to go see her dance, and I said, "Not really," I could tell I hurt her feelings, so I said, "All right, but I was not staying all night." Bonnie would drive to work and I would go window-shopping on Rodeo Drive, which was close to her club. Then I would go watch her dance.

But first, I headed over to Riverside, as soon as I walked in the door the receptionist Ann came around her desk and gave me a hug and said a lot of people upstairs were going to be surprised to see me. I worked on the second floor and didn't know too many on the first. My head nurse, Nina came rushing over holding her arms out and hugging me to death. I could tell she was about to say my name so I put my finger to my lips and said, "Shhhh" I wanted to surprise Dan. As I crept towards the door and peeked around the corner very carefully, Dan was just done feeding Jane, and was taking her bib off. When Jane recognized me, I had to hurry behind him before Jane could give away my surprise. I put my hands over Dan's eyes. I kept my hands on his eyes and said, "Guess who?" Jane began laughing now. As I let my hands down, and backed away, he turned and saw me. Jane was giddy from watching us hug! Dan had other plans Thanksgiving but asked me to go out with him Saturday night. I had promised to go and watch Bonnie dance for a while. Then I was going to go window-shopping on Rodeo Drive. Plus, I wanted to see the stars on The Walk of Fame. I wanted to take a picture of Clark Gable's, and Gary Cooper's stars since Gary Cooper was a favorite actor of mine and was from Helena.

"This wasn't Montana. It was a city full of crazy people with a bunch of big suburbs, and over five million people," Dan told me. Then he invited me to a movie and dinner and told me we could still window shop and see Bonnie dance.

Bonnie had to work the night before Thanksgiving. I could sleep in, so I decided to get the vegetables peeled and have everything ready so all we had to do was cook the turkey and food. I left a note for Bonnie to sleep in because everything was prepared.

On Thanksgiving, we were able to relax together and visit for the day until dinner was ready. It was so nice getting to have Thanksgiving dinner with my sister and not someone else that wasn't family. All we had to do was relax and catch up on all that we both had missed about each other. The one thing missing from the picture was our little sister Barb not being with us.

We never heard from our parents, and I was positive Grandma called our mom and asked her if she ever wondered where her daughters were and what they were doing. In fact, I knew Grandma mailed our addresses and phone numbers to her, so if she would ever have the urge to apologize to us for all that she put us through, she could do it. It never happened. We owed her nothing so we made no effort to call her. We took the abuse she handed out using us as her little punching bags. I think Mom blamed us for being tied down with so many children. Birth control, such as the pill hadn't been invented yet and women were left to fend for themselves with the rhythm method, the only accepted birth control allowed by the Catholic Church. I had never received a letter from my mother when I left home and neither did Bonnie.

We had a very long chat about what was going on with us. Bonnie was finally realizing that Frank, who she had just divorced, was the sick creep who had sex with children and kept child pornography in their home. She was glad he was going to prison. She felt guilty about him abusing children. The fact she married a pedophile turned her inside out. How could that happen since he knew nothing of her past?

Bonnie was dating someone new. I hoped she was on the right path with this new guy and that he was good to her. He was a sergeant with the Las Angeles Police Department (L.A.P.D).

I said, "What was it with you and me and cops?"

"I don't know," she said, "but I really like this guy and he is good to me.

On Friday, we went to Long Beach and met Sheila. We

spent the day down at the Pike. We wandered around watching the sailors with their girlfriends playing the carnival games. Sheila wanted me to ride the monster roller coaster but I was scared to do it. We ended up riding the other rides including the huge Ferris wheel. When we were done, we were famished so found a place for lunch. Sheila and Bonnie plied me with a few shots of peppermint Schnapps, to give me the courage for the roller coaster ride.

I knew I had a very nervous stomach that was about to tell my brain to get the hell off of this machine before it took off but it was too late as I heard the clanking and creaking as we began moving up the tracks. When we went down the first hill, it wasn't that bad and then we turned a sharp corner and started climbing up and climbing more, and more until we were so high up that we thrust down with such speed that when I went around the corners I felt like I was going to pee my pants. Then before I knew it, I almost felt like I was going to fall into the ocean as I was hanging on for dear life. It was the scariest ride I had been on, ever. After getting off, I was elated but very woozy, and then I threw up.

Later I called Dan and told him what we girls were up to earlier. "Oh you girls went bar hopping, huh?" "Why in the world would you go to the Pike, don't you know that's known for sailors picking up girls?"
Even though he may be right, I reacted huffily, "Thank you for thinking I would try to pick a guy up from a carnival, Dan." He apologized knowing I was angry.
I told him he sounded like a jealous boyfriend instead of a best friend. I felt so lucky to have someone like him, but only as a "big brother". I suppose he didn't see it like that.

On Saturday night, Dan took me to a fancy restaurant and then to an early movie. After, we went to watch Bonnie dance. As we were leaving, I saw out of the corner of my eye that Daryl was watching us. Daryl had never come to my apartment before. I felt it was his loss.

We arrived at the theater where Bonnie was performing. On the big Marquee in front of a theatre were three names.

The top name said, "Starring Tammy Montana." Bonnie left two tickets at the front window. Dan told me to look at the prices above the window. I couldn't believe someone had to pay twenty dollars to get into watch someone dance. Dan explained to me that these dancers were not go-go dancers, which was why it was so expensive. I would also learn why Bonnie made such big bucks for dancing.

There were a lot of people in the theatre to see what Dan called a burlesque show. "Tammy Montana" was the top entertainer and was about to come out. My sister made her appearance to the song "Tammy" wearing a long evening gown with a spectacular train. As she seductively walked across the stage she stopped mid-floor, timed her next move to heighten the excitement and began peeling her gloves off one at a time throwing each into the crowd. The bright feather boa she wore around her neck was sliding over one shoulder as she tugged it off and slung it into a row of excited men. The music suddenly changed into a raucous raunchy number and at that moment she tore off her dress.

I was in absolute shock! Dan could tell I was horrified. Bonnie was dancing around and had on a pink corset with stockings, she went over to a chair on the stage and took off her stockings one at a time and tossed them into the audience. Amidst the cheers, she removed her corset by pulling the Velcro apart which made it appeared it just popped off, just like the dress. Here was Bonnie dancing on the stage with tassels on her nipples and swinging her breasts around in circular motions and dancing unbelievably fast. The audience went crazy clapping and asking for more as she was finishing her performance.

Dan told me she wasn't doing anything wrong and she was great. I wanted to leave. He said, "Don't do that to your sister who had been there for you when you needed her. Wanda, she wasn't doing anything that bad. She is a dancer and loves to dance."

I responded, "But why like this, where she is taking her clothes off."

"Give me a break; look at some of the women and how they dress at the ocean. Some even have nipples showing. Hers were covered and she puts a robe back on when she is back stage." Dan made it clear that we had to go back stage like Bonnie had asked us to do. On our way back there, Dan told me to tell Bonnie how good she was. "Don't make a scene!"

I promised I would be good.

Bonnie had the big room with a gold star on it with "Tammy Montana". She also had numerous flowers in her room and I wondered who had sent them. I asked her why there were so many dancers as we passed their rooms. She told us the shows went until two in the morning and started at nine. She gave up go-go dancing because she made ten times the money being a burlesque dancer and only had to work four hours, and dance four times. "They love me here and that's why I do it."

Bonnie asked me out right if I was upset with her. I lied and said, "It is your life and what makes you happy makes me happy."

Bonnie asked us to stay for her next dance because the audience loved her second number. Dan piped in before I could answer that we would love to see it.

We watched all the girls hustling about backstage and plus the comedian getting ready for his act. I asked her why I didn't see burlesque on the marquee. It turned out, it was on the main side and we only saw the side with the three top performers. Bonnie was very proud that her name was first. They went by weird names that were not their own. Bonnie explained for anonymity, so no one could get their real name and make calls to their homes. They all had stage names so no one could ever call or hassle them. No one in the audience knew their real names. It was also the reason the dancers wore wigs and so much makeup.

I guess it all made sense, but it was hard for me to understand why Bonnie decided to be a stripper. She had to enjoy it or she wouldn't do it, I knew my sister. She had been through tough times like me, but she had married a creep, and I only knew what she went through in the orphanage and not the girl's reform school. Who knew what happened when she arrived in California?

While we were waiting, a police officer showed up at her door. I saw the stripes on his uniform and knew he was a sergeant. I figured this was the cop she was now dating. She introduced him to us as Walt, and they were seeing each other on his days off and obviously his days on since he was still on duty. We visited and he asked if I had a nice Thanksgiving with my sister. I told him we had a nice vacation together and that I would be leaving tomorrow to go back to school. He asked me if I liked nursing.

Then, he shook my hand and said, "I hope to see you again soon." Bonnie walked out into the hall with him. Bonnie then came back and said he had just gotten off shift. She said Walt was going home to change and that she had to get ready again for her next performance. She waved back to our seats;see me at home in the morning.

Dan and I thought meeting Walt was awkward. Dan said, "Your sister and Walt must be seeing quite a bit of each other because that kiss out by the door was a very long kiss."

I wanted to know what a policeman was doing coming backstage in a burlesque place in his uniform? Dan thought because he was getting off work since he worked three to eleven and it was well after eleven.

The place was packed for Bonnie's secondperformance. I had to admit she was great, but I still didn't like her doing it. I was ashamed for her even though it was clear she loved what she was doing, and did it so well. This time she entered in a maroon flared evening gown, which actually was elegant through the whole act until she got to the fast music with the tassel part. That was when I was embarrassed the most. I guess to each his own I thought, but that was my sister up there, and to me it was stripping, not burlesque. Dan and I had plenty to chat about on the way home. He was glad I didn't hurt Bonnie's feelings. I told him it was like watching her strip and why in the world would they call it burlesque when all the girls were doing was a strip tease. Dan explained that she was not naked at any time so it wasn't stripping it was burlesque.

Tomorrow was my last day and I planned to spend it with Bonnie until Sheila picked me up. I asked Dan to call me since he had my number at Susan's house. We said good night when we get to the apartment and he kissed my forehead and told me to keep out of trouble and keep in touch with him too. I thanked him for keeping me busy when my sister was working and for all he did for Bonnie and I.

The next morning there was a knock on the door. When I pulled it open, there stood Daryl. He wanted to know if I had given up on him and had come back to stay. It's too bad you didn't try coming by Daryl. I've been here for nine days. He was upset that he had seen me with Dan who he knew was my best friend.

Daryl was still ticked at the joke Susan and I had played on him. He liked to play jokes on people, but he did not like jokes being played on him. I reminded him of the joke he played on Bonnie when he hid me in his closet and Bonnie was looking for me and was worried sick because I wasn't anywhere to be found. Daryl thought that was real funny and she almost called the police for fear I'd been abducted. I could see Bonnie's face getting mad again over his joke. I told him quit pretending to be the victim of a joke that we had apologized for numerous times.

I gave him Susan's phone number and told him I would let him know if I had time to do anything. He asked if I would find time, and I told him I would try and that everything depended on what I had time for. He hugged me goodbye.

I told Bonnie let's get fixed up and go eat breakfast somewhere, but she wanted to stay at the house and visit without noise and people around. I was thinking she was going to ask about my thoughts on her dancing last night. Instead, she wanted to know what I thought about Walt. I told her all I care about was that he was kind to her and wasn't a pervert like the last one was. She said he was really respected on his job and he also went through a divorce and had no children. I told her he looked like he was in his thirties and she said he was thirty-three. I thought it was weird that he came to see her dance, and what did he think about it.

He said he loved watching me, Wanda. He always sends me flowers and takes me to nice restaurants and spends his days off with me. He didn't come over because he knew we needed to visit. But he knew you were coming to the theatre to see me dance. I told him I wanted him to meet you before you went back to San Bernardino.

We spent the afternoon after lunch getting my things packed up while I waited for Sheila. Bonnie and I went through some pictures she had. She told me I could keep the ones with Diane, Bonnie, Donna and me at the dance in Helena. Our friend Amy had taken the picture. Bonnie had met Amy after getting out of the Vocational School and Amy gave her some pictures she took of us that night. I asked her if she would give me the ones with my friends. Bonnie also had a few of our school pictures she had taken from mom and gave me a couple of her, and of me. Those were the only pictures we had of us at that time from home.

We talked about Barb. Bonnie wanted to know if I had talked to Barb at all. I told her mom won't let her answer the phone, and that she had a block on it so no one could dial out. "Poor Barb can't even make a phone call," she said gloomily.

Remember when she locked the cupboards, Bonnie reminded me. "She'll never change!" I told her she couldn't because she was mentally ill and didn't even realize it. We both agreed that we were in a much better place.

Bonnie gave me some money to put away in case I needed it. She really did make good money dancing burlesque but it's just something I could never see her doing. I did not even like speaking in front of a group of people as it made me very nervous. I hated standing in front of the classroom and reading poems or reading the stories we had to do for English and Literature classes. That was why I went out for cheerleading, to get better at being in front of a crowd. The only difference was all I had to do was yell cheers and tumble with gymnastics involved. No speaking to a crowd, just yelling.

I was a lot more reserved than Bonnie. I was grateful because she realized that trying to take her life wasn't the answer. If she was happy than I was happy, I just wanted the best for my sister who'd had it so bad. I made her promise to call me if she ever felt at a loss and needed help.

CHAPTER TWENTY-EIGHT

Susan was thrilled to see me when I got back to our apartment. However, it turned out she had bad news. Arden was moving to Taiwan in three days. Her dad had been transferred and her parents were insisting that she come for a year because it would be a once in a lifetime experience for her. She could come back the next year when she turned twenty-one. Susan gave her a necklace with a key on it telling her she would always be welcome at any place we were together. We were planning on getting a large apartment or house to share since there would be four of us to share the rent. I gave Arden the friendship ring saying that we would be lost without her and she told me she would always cherish the great times we had and promised to keep in touch.

After saying goodbye to our dear friend, we were back to our jobs and schoolwork. I had a wonderful Christmas with Susan and her family. Her sister and brother came home for the holidays, and I finally got to spend time with the rest of her family. Her mom and dad treated me as if I was one of their kids.

Christmas dinner, and spending time with Susan's family was more than I could ever ask for. Their generosity was so appreciated. I felt blessed by angels. Her parents wouldn't take rent from me, so I saved up and bought them a weekend at Lake Tahoe. They loved my gift. I asked Susan later if they really did like my gift and she said I was too generous and they didn't like me spending that much. I told her, I was in debt to them for letting me stay with them, having my own space, feeding me, paying for everything. Her parents were the ones who were too generous!

Susan and I went to a party at Dan's apartment

complex. I hadn't seen him for a little while so I was excited to go. I told Susan I really couldn't enjoy myself because I would think of Gary and how he wasn't there anymore to be with. How was I going to handle visiting Dan at his apartment if I felt this way? Next time I would have to tell him how I felt. I knew he would understand.

My nursing clinical went by real fast as I was working longer hours now and keeping up with the pace. Once in a while Susan and I would go out on the weekend. It was like in and out the door getting to see each other at bedtime with a quick check in.

Spring was here before I knew it. I didn't get to see much of my sister with school and work and her spending time with her new boyfriend. Janet was working a new job and worked nine to five. Susan was plugging away at the May Company, and I would be taking my finals soon.

Susan's parents came to my graduation with Susan and stayed for the capping and pinning ceremony. They knew I wasn't going to go into the RN program because I didn't have that kind of money. I had to pay for my state boards in six weeks. With an increase in pay I could afford an apartment. Susan let her parents know we were moving in with Janet, if I got my license. I was as nervous as a girl on a tightrope the next six weeks. After studying obsessively, I passed! Now I could officially wear a cap and work on the floor of the hospital.

Janet, Susan and I moved into an apartment complex close to the hospital. It sure was nice for us to have our own apartment and we had a blast getting things for it. It was furnished with Janet's furniture she had in storage and all we had to do was buy bedding and pillows. Susan's mom bought us a toaster, blender and silverware. Janet had all the dishes and pots and pans we needed. I only felt bad about one thing, Sheila needed a roommate after graduation and none of us were willing to share our bedroom and sleep with someone else.

Summer was nearly over, I hadn't heard from Bonnie in quite some time. I tried to call her and the number was disconnected. It was pretty sad that I wasn't able to get to talk to Barb or Bonnie now. Grandma called with the news that Bonnie was married to this cop named Walt. They had visited Grandma for a few days. Grandma told me they got married when they went to Las Vegas; it was one of those quickie arrangements. Grandpa and Grandma seemed to like him but she said they didn't really get to know him in only a few days they were there.

I asked why Bonnie didn't call to tell me, or even let me know she married Walt. I didn't dare tell Grandma what Bonnie did for a living or my Grandma would have had a heart attack for sure. It was her business to tell Grandma what her job was. I could not believe she didn't think enough about me to let me know she was married. Maybe, Walt told Bonnie I would find out in due time. I wasn't crazy about him when I first met him. I would wait until I get to know more about him before I formed any other opinion's against the man, especially a husband who would approve of his wife stripping.

Out of the blue though, my cousin Karen called me and asked me to come and live with her in Denver. I wanted to know why she was in Denver. She told me she wanted to be with her real father. I thought my Uncle Jim was her real dad, but it turned out that my aunt was married before. The marriage only lasted until after Karen was born. Uncle Jim didn't deserve this I thought to myself. He adopted her and gave her his name, but what did I know?

Karen begged and pleaded with me and said we could get an apartment together once I was there. She was working for Blue Cross Blue Shield by Cherry Creek in Denver and her supervisor Carol said she would have a great job for me processing claims. I would make more than I would being a nurse. Karen and I were very close when I lived with them. I told her to make sure I had a job before I moved, as I had to give a two-week notice and let Sheila know she could move in with Susan and Janet. They knew I wanted to get away from San Bernardino because of the memories of Gary and his death. I called my cousin and told her I had some money saved up but I would come by bus, so I still had plenty of money for setting up an apartment with her. I called Dan and told him I was leaving for Denver. I just had to get away and this was a great opportunity.

My friends were sad to see me leave as all good friends are, but I needed a change and was young enough to want a new adventure.They threw a bon voyage get-together at our apartment sending me off in good fashion. I would miss all of the great friends I had gotten to know. I called my cousin and let her know what time I would be arriving.

CHAPTER TWENTY-NINE

It was such a long bus trip from California to Colorado. I swore I would never get on a Greyhound ever again for a long trip. From now on any traveling I would do would be by air. Karen and her dad Buck picked me up at the station. She said she found us an apartment. I had to go in for my job interview first thing in the morning. Karen went to work, and I went to the interview. We planned on checking the apartment afterwards.

When I was done with my interview, Carol asked me when I could start. I told her right away. She said, "There was no better time than the present, my dear." I thought she was joking. I needed rest, but she had me start that day since I had dressed nicely for the job interview and met their qualifications.

Karen worked in a different department. Carol let me go over and tell her I would be working on the next floor in processing. Carol took me upstairs and showed me to my desk and then took me to the claims room to see where I would get more claims when I finished processing the claims I had on my desk. The codes for procedures were placed in front of me while I worked so I could memorize them.

The time went by really fast for me, and I found I liked the work. I had no trouble making friends, which made it feel like home. The climate was similar to Montana so that made me feel at home too. Loving winter sports such as skating and skiing helped.

We found an apartment in an old Victorian building. The dining room was in a round area; the living room and kitchen were large and the bedrooms were medium sized, which I was used to. The floors were all hardwood so we needed to buy a couple of rugs for the living room and the dining room otherwise the apartment was furnished and cost only sixty-five dollars a month, including utilities. We were within walking distance from work. Buck let us use his second car until I was able to afford one myself. He said it was for emergencies.

Some weekends we would go out and have dinner with Buck and his wife. Karen not only gained new parents but new half-siblings, Leon and David and a sister, Susan. Her dad was a real character. He loved to joke around, and he reminded me of my Uncle Jim, Karen's other dad. It was very strange that she now had this family and they were just as kind and generous as my aunt and uncle. Buck's wife Jean would always cook us up a fabulous meal, as she knew we didn't fix big meals ourselves. I was happy I made this choice to come to Denver.

I was getting to be really close friends with my boss Carol. She said she had a nephew she would like me to meet. I told her I would think about it and let her know if I wanted to meet him. I shared with her my loss of Gary and that it was taking time to feel like I could date again. I gave in finally and agreed to meet her nephew Bob who assured me I would like very much.

Carol asked me to have dinner with them and Bob was invited. He and I hit it off right away. After dinner we began to talk and found we liked to do the same things and had a lot in common, plus he was a handsome guy to boot. He asked if I would like to go on a motorcycle ride the next day. I was very hesitant because I was not that crazy about getting on a motorcycle with someone unless I knew they were safe drivers.

I told him I wasn't ready for any serious relationships and we could just date and see where it goes from there. We had fun times together. Karen finally met a guy she liked as well. His name was Steve, who I really liked when I first met him. But as time went by I was changing my opinion. Bob didn't care for him either, but this was Karen's choice for a boyfriend so we had to respect who she chose at this point. If we were going to double date with them we would have to give the guy a chance, like it or not. We both agreed.

What bothered me about Steve was his constant hanging around our house while we were working. He helped himself to the food I bought and paid for with no hesitation. He did not have a job to pay his way. I informed Karen he had no business in our home while we were not there. I loved my cousin, and I didn't want to have a tiff over a guy, but if this kept up with him thinking he could stay nights we would have a problem. I asked Karen what he did for a living and she said he was looking for a job right now. I continued to bug her by asking why she let him stay with us all the time. After all, I was the one who paid for the deposit and the first month's rent. I didn't hold back telling her that Steve should not be staying in our house and eating the food I buy if he doesn't pay rent or help with the food bill. I thought that was bad character. I was fervent about this and told Karen he should leave or I was going to look for my own place to live.

I told Bob what was going on when he picked me up from work complaining that I had to go and look for another apartment. I was upset with Karen and Steve but especially with Steve. I absolutely would not support a dead beat taking advantage of women who paid their own way. When I got home from work the next day, I told Karen that she and Steve could have the apartment to themselves. I was moving out that afternoon. I took the things I paid for including the pots and pans, the rugs and the bedding on the bed. They were pissed at me. I felt bad for Karen and told her I was sorry, but I couldn't live with Steve living off of her and eating the food I bought.

I luckily found a studio apartment the next street over. It was an enormous room with a bed, a television set, kitchenette that had a half partition to separate the sleeping area, and a bathroom. It was only forty dollars a month rent and they paid all the utilities. It was very clean and had hardwood floors like the other apartment.

I hoped that Karen could see my point, but when I went to work the next day, she wouldn't speak to me.

Bob and I had been dating for a few months. He wanted to know if I was serious about him. I told him I adored him but I wasn't in love and it wasn't his fault, the blame was mine. I wasn't ready for a serious relationship. Bob was very much a gentleman saying he would wait for me to love him.

I missed Karen. We were so close when I lived with Granny and spent all my free time at their house. Karen and I would do everything together, especially after I moved to Denver. We were like two sisters. Now I was living alone, and it was so lonely at night. She and I spent many a night staying up late laughing and having a great time before she met Steve. Now, I thought our relationship was a disaster because of a deadbeat who did not want to work.

I found out through the grapevine at work that Karen had to move back in with her Dad because she couldn't afford the rent after I moved out and Steve didn't have a job to help her. Buck and Jean told me not to feel bad. Karen would eventually come around.

I called Grandma when all this took place and she agreed with Buck and Jean that Karen just had to find her way and it wasn't with Steve. I could always tell my Grandmother anything and she would always make me feel better about it.

CHAPTER THIRTY

An emergency call had come in to the main desk at work. I needed to call my sister Barb in Montana as soon as possible. I was really freaked out because she would never call me at work unless it was serious. Carol authorized me to call Barb from my desk.

Barbara was crying, telling me I needed to come home right away. Wesley had been shot in a hunting accident and the sheriff's office was trying to get him out of the mountains near Townsend. They had to carry him out of rugged terrain and get him to Broadwater Hospital in Townsend before he was transported to Helena. It sounded bad!

Carol arranged a direct flight to Helena. Then she called Bob to take me to my apartment to give me a ride to the airport. I called Barb back and told her when I would arrive and if someone could pick me up. I let Carol know I had no idea how long I'd be gone, but I would keep her updated. I asked Bob if he and Carol could please pack up my personal things in boxes just in case I couldn't get back. He gave me a hug and a kiss and I disappeared down the jetway.

I was a nervous wreck. I had no idea what the heck was happening. I didn't even know if my brother was alive or dead in the mountains. My imagination worked overtime. The trip from Denver to Helena was quick, thank God. When I arrived I called Barb from the airport because no one was there to meet me. Wesley was still at the Broadwater Hospital in Townsend. The doctors were trying to get him stabilized before transporting him. She thought they had just left Townsend but she wasn't sure. I ended up taking a taxi to meet them at the hospital.

When Barb and I finally spoke, she told me that Wesley had lain on the ground for a few hours before help arrived. Mother found him first and used her belt as a tourniquet to stop the bleeding from the wound. If she hadn't he would have bled to death. Her first aide training from Search and Rescue saved Wesley in the mountains. When I arrived at St. Peter's, I told the front desk nurse who I was and why I was there. She told me they were stabilizing him at the hospital in Townsend before they ambulanced him to Helena. They were preparing for his arrival.

Just as the nurse told me Wesley was in route and would arrive at the hospital in twenty minutes, my cousin Penny walked by. I asked her to call someone to go get Barb at the house and bring her to the hospital. We waited for him in the emergency room.

When Wesley arrived, he was as white as a sheet from all the blood loss. The holdup had been trying to get some of the blood loss replaced with transfusions. He was on his second one. Wesley had been shot in the groin and the top of the femur was shattered. The deputy told me he had run in front of my mother just as she had fired the gun with a scope at a buck. Because of the scope, she couldn't see him in front of her as she pulled the trigger.

My mom and dad were not here yet. They had signed papers for surgery in Townsend, but not yet for St. Peter's. The ambulancearrived before my parents got there and Wesley was rushed into surgery without a signature.

When they finally arrived, they saw me standing there. My mom came over and for the first time in my life that I could remember, hugged me and thanked me for making the trip so quickly. I hugged Daddy and he began to cry, which made my mother totally break down. I had never seen him cry like this.

I could tell mom was in a bad way. "I just didn't see him. It's all my fault; it's all my fault," she wailed. Dad tried to soothe my mother, but as soon as something was mentioned she was at it again. The nurse finally gave her a Valium to quiet her down. It was going to be quite some time before Wesley would be out of surgery. The doctors had to cut some bones and fix the shattered ones and torn ligaments he received from the compound fracture.

After a couple of hours of waiting, I told dad I had to make a couple of phone calls, "I'd be right back".

I called my old landlord, Hank, who had been so good to me, to see if he didn't happen to have an apartment available. Miraculously, he did! He'd just evicted the tenants for partying and the apartment was a mess, but if I moved in before he finished cleaning he would give me a month's free rent if I finished the job for him. I agreed and he brought the keys to the hospital and dropped off my suitcases to the apartment for me. He charged me fifty dollars a month, including utilities because he knew what a good tenant I was. I gave him fifty dollars, which covered two months' rent. He was happy that he could help me out.

Dad asked me if I was going to stay for a while now. I told him yes, that was why I had rented an apartment. He wanted to know why I wasn't staying with them. I told him mom and I bump heads too much and she wants to control everything. I just couldn't deal with the stress and the same abuse all over again. I hope you and mom will let Barb come on weekends and keep me company since I haven't seen or been with her in a long time. I told him I missed him more than he would ever know. I knew deep down my father understood how I felt.

Wesley was still in surgery when we got back. Mom was asleep in the chair in the waiting room. Finally, the doctor came into the waiting room and told us Wesley was in recovery, and he would need more surgery. They could not do all of the repairs because of the blood loss. The doctor had to cut bone to mend the femur and Wesley's left leg would be two inches shorter when all was said and done. They also had to wait for the swelling to go down. He had a long recovery ahead of him. His groin area had to be stitched up and he would have a morphine drip for the pain. He would be in and out of consciousness for several days, on a constant watch for infection. We could expect him tobe hospitalized for several months with more surgery to come.

The hospital made a special room for him that at one time had been the sunroom. Wesley would be in the hospital for a good eight to ten months. The first two weeks were going to be the roughest for him. He would have twenty-four hour care. I volunteered to help but the doctor would not allow it since I was not an employee and did not have a Montana license. I could be there to help the family but not do the nursing duties. It was to protect me if anything went wrong. He did tell me to let the nurses know if something wasn't right.

When they brought Wesley up to us in his room I could tell it was going to be a long haul. He was so pale it was no wonder he was getting blood transfusions. I hadn't seen him in three years. Here he was lying in a hospital bed fighting to live. If only he'd been found earlier and not exposed to hours lying on the frozen ground, I agonized. He was only fifteen years old. It was hard looking at my little brother lying there between life and death. My regrets of not being more thoughtful of him growing up even if he was Mother's favorite, lingers upon my mind.

I had the most dysfunctional family one could possibly ever imagine. I promised Barb I would come back to her but I knew deep down I could not stay in Helena. The memories of the past would go on overload when I was here. Eventually, I would like to find some kind of peace in my life, but I did not know when that would happen. The Cathedral and school were just blocks away from the hospital and the abuse was still too fresh in my mind. It seemed like something always came along and changed the dynamics of what I wanted to accomplish in my life. Now I had to once again prepare to be in this town that had robbed me of my childhood.

I was tired and wanted to shower so I asked my cousin Penny if she wouldn't mind running me to the store so I could buy some towels and wash clothes and pick a few things up that I needed for the apartment.

I called Bob from a pay phone and had him ship the boxes he'd taped up. I let him know that I would not be back to Denver because my brother would be "touch and go" for a couple of weeks and then would need care for eight to ten months. He was really bummed out.

I then called Carol to let her know I needed to quit. She let Karen know that Wesley was shot in a hunting accident. Carol also said she had sent a letter to Blue Cross Blue Shield to let them know I was a terrific claims processor and how speedy and thorough I was. I thanked her for the referral letter and told her I missed them all.

It took a couple of hours scrubbing walls and cleaning the kitchen, spotless. Hank wasn't joking about the walls and floors being filthy. I put everything away and unpacked my suitcases and finally took a shower. I bought a blanket to cover up with on the couch and a nice pillow. I would have to sleep there until all of the bedding arrived. The couch smelled like it had been cleaned.

After a few hours of naptime, I walked up to the hospital. My apartment was only a few blocks away from the hospital and downtown and the stores I needed to go to within walking range. When I arrived to the hospital mom was sound asleep in the recliner and they brought one in for dad to sleep in as well. I told Dad he and Mom could use my apartment to rest in. With the doctor standing there, I pressed that they were no good to him without rest, and the doctor agreed with me. I would call them if there were any changes at all through the night. The doctor said, "Listen to your daughter and go get rest. I think Wesley was going to be just fine with you going home to rest and sleep." Dad said they would head home shortly. I would call them if there wasa change. This is going to be a long haul I thought to myself.

The biggest danger for Wesley was his blood pressure, which dipped very low at times. The nurse had to take it every five minutes. He was restless during the night but I was sure it was from pain. Sitting in the room reminded me of Gary. Only my brother's outcome looked much brighter than Gary's. I knew Gary was in a deep coma and wasn't coming back, Wesley was. He was sleeping heavy and would until they let up on his meds. They were keeping him comfortable and watching for any sign of infection.

Mom and Dad arrived in the morning. Dad's boss was giving him a medical leave with pay. They asked me how his night was and I mentioned he stirred about a couple of times and went right back to sleep. He was going to be like that for a bit until he was well enough for them to do more surgery.

Mom was against any more surgery until the doctor asked her if she wanted her son to be crippled or worse. I just needed to be forceful sometimes with mom and take control away from her. I told her I was really tired and was going to go home and rest and would be back later this afternoon. Dad ran me home. That's when I asked him if I could see Barb. He said she would be at the hospital this evening while they went and ate dinner. I could visit with her then.

My phone was installed just after I got home. I called Grandma and reported all the news from Montana. She asked how mom was treating me. I told her right now she was worried about Wesley and wasn't too concerned with me. I think my mother realized I was my own person and had to be careful dealing with me. I let her know Wesley was in pretty bad shape with his blood pressure bottoming out. I felt he was restless during the night because of the drugs.

My Grandmother was also a nurse. She was an LVN for forty years, she told me how much Grandpa and everyone missed me. Grandpa had me send you more money because you don't have a job yet; we know you are sitting with your brother at the hospital. I told her when he was better I would get a job at Blue Cross Insurance in Helena since Carol had sent a letter of recommendation for them to interview me at the Helena office. She said she was glad I had something to fall back on until I could take the Montana State Boards. I told her I really wanted to come back to California. Grandma didn't think that was in the cards for me at the moment. I knew what she meant with recovery time for this type of gunshot wound.

I hoped Barb would be at the hospital when I returned but she wasn't. Mom was asleep in the recliner and I didn't disturb her. I went over to Wesley's bed and saw they had moved him a bit and put pillows under his side to keep him from getting bed sores. While I stood over his bed, I studied him. I saw this lonely boy growing up with nothing but sisters, and now I saw a teenage boy who was fighting for his life.

It had been three days and he had not made a sound, which actually was bothering me. I put my hand on his forehead; he was burning up with fever. I charged to the nurse's station and told them my brother had a fever and someone needed to check it.

The nurse told me there was a thermometer in his drawer. I stormed off and took his temperature.

Mom was awake when I came back and asked what was wrong. I told her the doctor was going to hear about this problem! I had to take his temperature under his armpit, as I was not allowed to do it rectally or orally. One cannot put a thermometer in someone's mouth in a coma. I took the reading and stormed back to the station. The doctor was just arriving as I handed her the thermometer. It read 104.8. I said, "My brother is running a high fever and you are sitting down here talking and visiting. You told me where the thermometer was without batting an eye implying what, that I should take his temperature? That's your job, not mine!"

The doctor overheard me and asked what the commotion was about and I said, "My brother was running a high fever and not one person has come to his room while I was there. He looked awful so I felt his forehead. That's when I hurried to the nurse's station for help. She just looked at me and told me where the thermometer was, and you wonder why I am upset."

The doctor walked very quickly to my brother's room and took his temp again and it was 104.6 this time and told them to fetch ice packs and take a sample of his urine and blood to the lab immediately. When the labs came back they had to started antibiotics immediately. He had a bladder and wound infection because someone had not cleaned and changed his bandages properly. The doctor saw green and yellow puss oozing from the wound. I'll bet somebody caught hell for that one.

My sister Barb showed up. She asked what was going on, and of course mom had to tell her about the nurse's not doing their job, which was fine. I was thrilled to see my little sister. I asked dad and mom if I could walk her to the restroom because I had to go. Once we got to the bathroom, I gave Barb the biggest hug. I told her I would be here for some time to help with Wes. I gave her my new phone number and asked her to come by and see me when she could.

She said, "Are you kidding? I'm stuck in Unionville unless I can come and live with you?"

"Do you really think Mom is going to permit that?" I looked at her knowing how Mom felt towards me.

I told her that she was only fourteen years old and could not be emancipated.

"Maybe, they will let you come and spend weekends with me once in a while." I felt horrible that she was stuck in that awful house.

"It would be a cold day in hell before she would let me do that," Barb growled angrily. "I have to do everything in that house! You know what it's like to be her slave."

Mom came in and said the doctor wanted to see me. Oh boy I thought, he was going to chew me out for telling that nurse off, but to my surprise he did the opposite. He told me she had been written up and if she was rude in any way to let him know. He thanked me for watching my brother a little closer than the nurses had. The nurse came down to my brother's room and apologized to me telling me she was inconsiderate and thoughtless about his needs.

I asked Mom if Barb could come over to the apartment for a while after school. She snapped at me loudly"No, Barb had her chores and plenty to do at the house." I asked about this weekend then for one overnight. Mom said if she got her chores done and everything seemed okay it would be fine with her. I told Barb to think positive and maybe she would let her come.

The weekend arrived and I asked mom if I could please have Barb for the weekend. I told her we would only be at the hospital and my apartment resting. Dad chimed in and said he could feed the horses and take care of a few chores so he didn't see any reason why not. Mom gave in. I was so thankful Dad spoke up on Barb's behalf. He knew she was cooped up in the house with nothing to do.

I stayed at the hospital until Barb got out of school on Friday. Wesley's fever was finally normalizing. When Barb came in he opened his eyes for a few minutes. It was clear that he was in horrible pain; the nurse called for the doctor. When he came in the room he examined Wesley asking him if he was having pain. Wesley winced and moaned struggling to nod slightly. The doctor ordered morphine. He prepared us to expect Wesley to have more pain as he was gaining consciousness. "We need to stay ahead of his pain, otherwise his healing process will take longer. As long as he stays calm and comfortable he will rest and heal faster. The nurse tried to get him to sip some juice but he wouldn't wake up to eat or drink. Mom was concerned that Wesley wasn't eating yet and the doctor told her that was the least of their worries right now as he was getting plenty of fluids intravenously.

As the days went by, Wesley remained pretty much the same while we were hoping he would get rid of the infections he had going on. The sooner he recovered from them, the sooner he could get better.

I asked dad, if he could give us a ride to the house because it was below zero. Neither Barb, nor I wanted to walk. I did not feel like freezing my butt off. Dad ran Barb and me back to the apartment so we could spend the weekend together. I told him that I would pick up a turkey and fix food for them to take home since it looked like everyone would be at the hospital for Thanksgiving. He said Mom wasn't going to have Thanksgiving. I told him that was why I was going to cook some food for them to take home after they visited with Wesley. Barb would stay with me through Sunday afternoon.

Thanksgiving was Thursday and Barb doesn't have school so I was hoping she could come to my apartment for a few days. Mom and dad would be at the hospital with Wesley, and Barb didn't want to sit at the house by herself. I'll just carefully bring it into a conversation I explained to Barb and we could take it from there.

Barb told me mom would never change. She still sits on her butt and barks the orders at me for what has to be done. She still slaps the hell out of me if I say one wrong word. I took off to the Roddy's after she hit me last time. It will be much worse, because when Wesley comes home. I will have to do everything, plus take care of his needs. Mom still treats him like he was her baby. It will be much worse now that this had happened and that she blames herself. Barb continued to pour her heart out. I understood where she was coming from because Wesley always was mom's favorite child, like it or not. He never had a spanking in his life that I knew of except when he wouldn't listen to dad a few times.

I gave Barb some things that she didn't have at home. I told her that anytime she was in town, and could sneak to my place, do. I had a key made just in case anything happened where she had to use it. We had a great visit and watched television and relaxed. When it was time to walk to the hospital, we dreaded every step we took, it was so damn cold and worst of all, and our visit was over.

Wesley was stirring about and looked like he was finally starting to feel a bit on the mend. "When did you get in?" he asked me with a soft and scratchy voice.

Dad explained to Wesley that I had beaten the ambulance here when I left Denver. He told him how it took several hours for the rescue team to come in with the stretcher to get him out of the mountains, and how he rushed to Townsend to get help. He told him how his mom had saved his life by using her belt for a tourniquet to help slow the bleeding down.

Mom said he ate a little soup and took a few sips of orange juice, which was his first taste of food since the accident. The doctor came in a couple hours later and looked at his wounds after removing the bandages. Wesley's blood pressure was back to normal and his infections had subsided. The doctor was hoping he could get him into surgery probably the day after Thanksgiving.

I told Mom I was going to have Barb help me cook Thanksgiving dinner so we could bring them prepared dinner plates. Then they would have left over turkey for sandwiches. She seemed okay with that since she didn't have time to cook.

"You get those horses fed plenty and get the housework done before you go anywhere," she warned Barb. "I don't want you out running around either."

I told Mom it was too cold for us to go anywhere and that she would be at my house and the hospital, the same as she had this weekend. Mom made it clear that Barb could only stay three days. We were happy to get those three days.

I went over to Blue Cross Blue Shield. Pat who did my interview told me I had come highly recommended as a claims processor. She explained she needed somebody immediately as they were under staffed. I told her I could start today. I would have Thanksgiving and Friday off. I explained about my brother's condition because during the interview she asked why I left the Denver Office. If I started today it would help them get caught up. "Thank you."

She showed me where my desk was and told me they usually go to the *Parrott* for lunch. I was welcome to join them and meet a couple of the girls from the office.

Dad and Barb arrived at the hospital just before me. He was picking up mom and dropping Barb off. Mom had been there the entire day with Wesley. I told him about going to work immediately with Blue Cross. I told him my boss was very impressed with my work. My parents had their medical insurance through them and dad laughed and said what if you do our claims. I told dad that there were other claims processors and the odds were pretty high that someone else would get them in their pile. He laughed, and I could see why he was in a good mood. Wesley looked better than any day since he was injured.

I asked Wesley how he was feeling and he told me rough because of the pain. Mom said he hadn't had anything for pain recently and asked me to check if he was due. Once he had his medication the pain subsided. I was surprised the doctor hadn't told him about scheduling another surgery after Thanksgiving. I suppose he'll know soon enough, poor Wesley.

Barb and I bought all the fixings for Thanksgiving dinner. We stopped at Eileen's to eat and she was so happy to see me. She bought our food as usual. She asked if I needed a job and I told her I was working at Blue Cross. I told Eileen I would have to get a nursing job but I would need to take my State Boards. They were seven weeks away.

My boxes from Denver arrived! Barb helped me unpack them and washed my pots and pans and dishes for me. I called Bob to thank him for shipping everything. He asked how Wesley was doing. I explained to him the doctor was waiting for my brother to get better before he could repair the femur and put in a rod to keep the bone from breaking again. I also told him today was the first time he actually took a few sips and ate a tiny bit of soup. "It's going to be a long haul, Bob. It might take longer than I thought." I did not want him to get his hopes up that I would be back. I thanked him and told him to thank Carol and to have a happy Thanksgiving.

After I got off the phone Barb noticed I hadn't told him I loved him or that I missed him. She wondered how serious our relationship was. I told her I thought the world of him and appreciated everything about him, but he was not the guy I could get serious and fall in love with. I enjoyed his company, and I wanted to leave it at that.

The mailman arrived with a nice surprise for me on Friday. My Grandmother had sent three hundred dollars to hold me over until I had a job. I immediately called and thanked her and Grandpa for always helping me out.

"We were your guardians and always will be young lady," Grandma insisted. "I am sorry you are in this predicament with your brother. It is interfering with your dreams, but you hang in there honey."

The hospital knew I lived close by and if anything came up, mom and dad knew that I would get there as soon as possible. I was excited to go to work. It was great to be doing something other than sitting in a hospital all day and night. My apartment was in order and looked great and was clean.

When I got to the hospital with Barb on Thanksgiving, Wesley told me the doctor had told him he would have surgery the next day. He said the doctor had explained what would happen, but Wes really didn't understand it.

When my parents arrived, I told them I would put their food on plastic plates they could keep and the turkey legs and white meat on another platter covered in foil. I asked dad if he could come pick us up. They were thankful for all the work Barb and I put into making their dinner. We were very proud.

I made Wesley a fruit basket with fresh fruits if he felt like eating anything. He could not eat after midnight to prepare for surgery in the morning.

On Friday, Wesley had his surgery. They had a late start and he wasn't back in his room yet. The nurse called recovery and he had only been in there for a short period and wasn't ready to come back to his room. When mom and dad arrived, I told them he was still in recovery and what had taken so long. Wesley was not fully awake. They had to make sure he didn't have any side effects from the anesthesia and his blood pressure had to be stable.

The doctor found us with his report of how the surgery went. His vitals all looked good. He would always walk with a bad limp once he had healed. His upper groin area will be caved in somewhat but he shouldn't have any other problems that will interfere with the healing process. He would be in the hospital several months until he was released for rehabilitation.

The doctor let the nurses know he wanted him to drink lots of milk and have lots of dairy products to get fortify him with Calcium. He should be drinking milk by the quarts. I told the doctor that won't be a problem with my brother, as he loved milk and it won't be powdered milk. My mother scowled at me for making the comment. The doctor explained to mom that powdered milk was not the best milk to give a child, as it didn't have the calcium that whole milk did. I was positive I hit a sour note with my mother about the powdered milk comment because that was all we were ever allowed to have as kids. She was very cold to me after that for a while.

The nurse only wanted one or two people in the room so no one was in their way of doing their job. Barb and I walked home so we could have dinner. I told her how much I loved my new job, but I missed being with my friends in California and Denver.

Barb knew that Mom and Dad would only be visiting Wes in the evening hours and she would not get to spend as much time with me after this weekend. "I can't wait to get away from that house," she said to me. As time went by I saw less and less of Barb just like she predicted because mom wouldn't let her get that close to me. It really bothered mom that I was the one who stood up to the cruelty and pain she inflicted upon us. When I would call for Barb, mom would tell me she was out doing her chores and she wasn't coming to town. She told me I should not bother to ask dad.

One or two times, Barb snuck over to my house on her lunch break. She had her key to get in and left me notes when I was at work. I didn't care about the notes; I just wanted to spend time with her like we had in the past when she got to spend those few weekends with me. I told her to ask dad in one of the notes I left for her.

Mom was a difficult person to understand why she did the things she did. We never knew what would set her off. I thought she might not let Barb come to my house because maybe she was afraid Barb would run away. I would bet Barb would try to get emancipated after she turned fifteen in December. Barb would have to prove mom was unfit like I did. I knew mom would not let that happen again, since she almost went to jail over the incident. I told Barb she had to have pictures and proof and a legal guardian. I couldn't be her guardian until I turned twenty-one in June.

I didn't get invited for Christmas at my own parent's house. It goes to show how much my mom resented me for having Barb at my apartment and the powdered milk incident. It showed her lack of appreciation for my returning home and being here for my brother. Once they said he was on the road to recovery, she kicked me aside and had nothing to say to me.

While Barb was on Christmas vacation I did get to talk to her on the phone. She called me from the Roddy's house. They told her they would bring her in to visit me for a few hours when they had some shopping to do. Barb came Saturday morning. I gave her the three Christmas presents I had bought for her. As she opened her gifts, she asked what I had done for Christmas. I told her I stayed home and watched Christmas shows on television. I asked her if mom or dad had even wondered what I had done and she said my name wasn't even brought up.

It upsets me that dad didn't stand up to mom when she had this crazy attitude towards her kids. He just let her get away with it. It seemed for real that Wesley was the only one she cared about. It was not his fault that she was that way. He was truly an innocent bystander but it aggravated us that she favored him. Barb loved her gifts and said mom would think they were from Bill and Rachel. When the Roddy's showed up, Barb hugged me goodbye, and said she didn't want to leave. I told her, "Hang in there and wait it out, that is the best you can do until we can do something for you."

After she left, I checked my mailbox in front of the apartment. I had three letters. One was from Bonnie; the other from Grandma and the final one was my phone bill. Grandma told me Bonnie wanted my address. She also gave Bonnie my phone number. Grandma was happy that I loved my job, but kept reminding me to take my State Boards, which I had already set up to do in a couple more weeks. I didn't tell her that I was staying with this job because they paid me well, and I loved working there. The other letter from Bonnie was telling me she wished that I would come and stay with her and Walt. They were really happy. I was glad for her but I was not about to quit a job I enjoyed and I had no intentions of living with them at all.

~~~

Bonnie wrote me that Daryl had asked for my address so he could write. I thought it would be nice to hear from him. I did like Daryl a lot and had fun with him. We were like two teenagers when we were together and that was what attracted me. It was funny that I was more attracted to older guys. Daryl did start writing me and it was nice to hear from him.

Pat invited me to a dinner at her home. I met her sister's family and their son John. He and I visited with each other since we were the youngest ones; we found we had a lot in common. He lived with his parent's in the basement since he was just getting out of the service.

I was nervous as my State Boards were less than twenty-four hours away. I had to polish up so I was studying with my books and going through all of my clinical notes. Pat gave me time off the morning of the test.

I would get a letter telling me if I had passed in a few days or if I had to retake the tests. Grandma nagged me to take the test so I promised her I would, just for her. I was glad I came back to work instead of taking the rest of the day off because it settled my nerves down after being so stressed out.

John picked me up from work and we went to his parent's house for dinner. Elizabeth was an amazing cook. John and I went down to his apartment. He showed me some of his ideas for a business to fly chartered and cargo flights. He told me his parents wanted him to put his business degree to work. I agreed with his parents that he better find some kind of employment. He was in Vietnam as a helicopter pilot and thought about working with something with transportation of some kind since he loved flying.

When I got home, I had a card from Daryl saying he missed seeing me and wished we were together again. I wrote him back and told him I missed him too. I didn't want Daryl to think I found someone else because deep down I cared more than I wanted to admit.

I also received a letter telling me I had passed my Boards! I would have to take them again in three years if I was not working as a nurse. I called my Grandma to let her know; she was very pleased for me.

Wesley was recovering and things were going great for him at the hospital. He would have to lie in that bed for another four to five months and have physical therapy. He was getting so much bigger from all that milk he drank and the food he received. He never complained of hospital food because they fed him well.

John went up with me a couple of times to see him. He didn't say much except to complain about this or that. His pet complaint was the nurses didn't come down as much as they had. I told Wesley they had other patients to take care of beside him. John just laughed at me for chewing Wesley out for wanting all the attention from the nurses. He said to me "So would I if I was in his place. Leave the poor guy alone," he sympathized.

I was happy for John a few months later when he finally got a job offer, flying parcels with a cargo plane company out of California, but his parents were very disappointed that he didn't want to start his own business.

Work was the same every day. I hadn't seen Barb in quite some time. She had called but most of the time I was at work or seeing John.

I had been getting lots of letters from Daryl asking me to come to Fort Sam Houston where he was stationed as a green beret in the Special Forces. I was shocked that he joined the service and didn't bother to tell me. He probably thought I wouldn't approve because of the Vietnam War and he was right. I had lost several friends in the war and everyone was against it, including me. The draft put a large percentage of the guys in harm's way and people had turned their backs on our Vietnam Vets when they came home.

I wrote back to him and told him I was worried about him having to go to Vietnam. He told me it wouldn't happen anytime soon. I think he was saying that just to pacify me.

CHAPTER THIRTY-ONE

Daryl told me he loved me now in his letters and said he fell for me when he met me at my sister's apartment. It was love at first sight and he was sorry for not keeping in touch with me when I was in San Bernardino after the joke episode Susan and I had played on him. He said he was stubborn as hell and he surely was not joking.

I wrote back and told him he never told me he had those feelings for me before this letter and I didn't know if I could believe him. I finally gave him my phone number in the next letter and wrote to him telling him not to call late at night or he would get hung up on.

I knew he wouldn't call while I was working because he worked all day too plus more hours than me. Finally one night around seven or eight, he did call saying how great it was to hear my voice. He asked about my job and about my family. When he and I were dating I told him I was from a very poor family and it was a dysfunctional one. He knew all the details pretty much about my life except the assaults on me as a child from the school and orphanage.

I let him know my mom wasn't letting my little sister come to visit and about what had happened to my brother. He told me Bonnie had told him about Wesley's accident. He also told me Bonnie and Walt had moved out of the apartment and they had moved into a house in Burbank.

He begged me to please come to Fort Sam Houston and see if we could make a go of it. "I am madly in love with you and I can't stop thinking about you! I know you care about me or you wouldn't have written back."

I flatly said that I didn't think I was capable of love. He argued that he would do all in his power to make me happy and love him. Just wait and see, he said, trust me.

I told him he was going too fast that I was not ready for marriage. He told me to think about it. I kept thinking how lonely I was. All I did was work and come home, had no car to go anywhere. All my friends had moved away. My loneliness grew worse each day until finally I made up my mind and announced to Pat that I was going to move to San Antonio, Texas. I was giving her my two-week notice from work so I could be with an old college sweetheart from California.

Obviously, I followed my heart and not my head. Deep inside, I knew I truly wanted to be loved again and couldn't find it in Helena which held such awful memories. The evil still lived in Helena, and I was aware of it every single day. Any convincing opportunity presented to me was reason enough for me to follow it.

Daryl found a mother-in-law house behind a very nice lady's home. The rent was reasonable. He had to stay at the base at night until his training was finished but he would be able to come and get me when he got off work. We could do things on the base for a while until he brought me back home at night.

When I went to work on Monday the week before leaving, Pat said she would store my things in her garage until I came back and got them. She was very kind and wise in her offer to hire me back if things didn't work out. At the end of the workday the girls gave me a nice going away party the last hour of work.

I called Barb and hoped she answered the phone, but of course mom did. I asked mom if I could talk to Barb for a minute. She told Barb to make it quick as she handed her the phone. I hated telling Barb I was going to San Antonio to be with Daryl. "I will write you from there so be sure to check the mail all the time this summer." I told her she needed to beat mom to the mailbox.

That evening Daryl called. I told him they were going to shut my phone off. He seemed so happy, "Everything is set up for you babe". His favorite thing was calling me "babe" at the time.

I told him I was very nervous about leaving. He said the nervousness would wear off once I got there. Pat gave me a ride to the airport. I would never forget the butterflies I had in my stomach all the way to San Antonio. Once I arrived, I settled down and my nervousness did disappear just like he'd said it would.

He introduced me to our landlady. She asked if we had set a date yet for our wedding. It made me feel weird.

The place was clean and meticulous and had a full size bed off of the living room with a little kitchen and a bathroom. It was a large studio apartment and would accommodate one person just fine. I asked him how often I was going to get to see him. He told me most days except when they were training and gone for jumping.

Daryl had to get back to the base. Mrs. Benson came over and asked me if I would like to join her for a bite to eat. She had fixed a very nice little dinner for the two of us. Mrs. Benson was an Italian lady who had married an Englishman.

I always loved her beautiful house and asked her how the house in the back came about. She told me it had been built for her mother-in-law when she came to live with them years back.

I heard a knock at the door. It was Mrs. Benson who parked in front of our house and asked if I could help her with some things in the car. I thought she meant for me to help her with her shopping into her house, but she assured me these bags go into my house. She had gone out and bought me things for the apartment. There was a brand new bedspread in one bag, and in another were toss pillows for the large sofa, another, brand new bath towels, hand towels and washcloths. She'd even bought some plants to cozy up the place. I told her I had money to help furnish my apartment. It was unbelievable what this woman had spent money on to fix up our place. What a woman was Mrs. Benson!

I learned that the Benson's had a son, but lost him in the Korean conflict (she called it the Korean War). I think it was hard for her to talk about him. She looked away when she added, "...and now we have the Vietnam conflict."

Daryl wanted to help me buy Mrs. Benson a thank you gift for all she'd done. She always had fresh flowers on her dining room table, so we decided to buy her two-dozen red roses at the base commissary. I told Daryl he couldn't have found a nicer lady to rent from. In the morning, I took the roses over to Mrs. Benson, and she loved how gorgeous they were and remarked the same about the crystal vase we bought to put them in. She told me that we kids shouldn't be spending our hard-earned money on gifts like this. I told her she had done so much for us that we didn't know how to thank her.

Once I got settled, Daryl wanted me to meet the members of his team, so the next night we went to a delicious dinner and then to their favorite hangout on the base. One of them wanted to know where Daryl had found such a gorgeous chick. Daryl told them first of all I was not a chick and second of all because he was one lucky guy. It made me feel like a million for Daryl to set them straight. His buddy Vince said "Amen to that brother." The guys proceeded to tell me I was all they had heard about since they had met Daryl. They thought I was a figment of his imagination even though he had the pictures to prove it.

I laughed at that one because I remember Daryl begging me to send pictures, especially my graduation picture from nursing school and my senior picture from high school days. A lot of the other pictures had guys in them so that's why he didn't want those.

The guys apologized and said they didn't know how to act around a lady because they were not around them enough. I felt bad and said they had a lady sitting right next to them, referring to the IC whose name was Audrey. One of them made the remark she was one of us and I said she was STILL a lady.

"I think we'll keep Wanda around for a long time," Audrey commented. "This was the first time I had seen these guys act like gentlemen since you walked in with Daryl," Audrey commented.

When Daryl and two other guys went to get more beers, she thanked me for doing that. I told her I hate when guys do that to any woman and the other guys that were still sitting with us said, "Hear, hear!" I felt more at ease now and they were nice guys.

Daryl asked me to dance. He told me the guy's danced with the IC's that don't have their wives or girlfriends with them so that included his platoon. I am glad you are here; I have you and won't be a wallflower anymore. He kissed me and held my hand the whole time we were sitting there, and it was nice.

On Saturday, I cooked a delicious dinner. Daryl had the weekend free and did not have to return to the base until mid-night. After dinner, he told me to stay seated. He pulled a little box out of the bag and handed it to me. "Well open it!" he said.

It was a beautiful engagement ring. Daryl proposed and wanted to set a date, immediately. He wanted to get married in San Antonio. It felt rushed all of a sudden, but evidently his platoon found out they were to leave for Fort Gordon, Georgia, the first part of January. On our way to the base to meet our friends, he asked me if December 2nd would be good. I asked him how he came up with that date and he said all of his friends would still be here until then. It really was fine with me, I was just nervous that we were getting married so soon.

He also had a surprise for me besides the ring and getting married; he had a weekend of leave so we could spend it together, a whole weekend! I hugged him so tight thinking it would be nice not having to wake up alone and having the guy I loved to cuddle me. I told Daryl I was sorry for not saying I loved him sooner, but I did love him.

We had a great time after that. Daryl asked me if I would go watch him jump when Vince's girlfriend came to visit. Vince said I could drive his car to the jump site if I knew how to get there. That wasn't the problem. I just couldn't drive a stick-shift. Vince thought I was kidding because I was a girl from Montana, whatever that meant. The guys told Daryl he should buy me an automatic shift so I could get around. I agreed because I didn't want to depend on anyone to get me to and from.

Daryl promised we would go car shopping the following weekend he had off. Vince would be happy to chauffer us around. I'd heard that Daryl first wanted to surprise me with a car when I first showed up, but his buddies warned him that I should have a part in the decision too. I offered to help pay for it, but Daryl told me his Uncle was covering the cost for us.

On the way home, I felt very anxious because we had never slept in the same bed or had really cuddled except on a couch. When we arrived home, I felt calmed and very relaxed. It must have been the alcohol in the daiquiris I thought to myself. Daryl felt my tension. I told him I was just tired after all the dancing and the drinks. He hugged me reassuringly and said, "Relax honey we are only going to cuddle, and sleep, so we can get the car tomorrow." I grabbed my nightgown and went into the bathroom to brush my teeth and get out of my clothes. I was a very modest person and like my privacy.

Vince had family in San Antonio and his uncle had checked the best places to get a good deal on a fairly new car for us. We test drove car after car and it seemed hopeless finding one that was at least two or three years old that we liked. His uncle told us not to buy a brand new one because they lose value not long after they are driven off the lot. We also had to make sure it was a one-owner car with highway miles on it, and we'd need to get it checked out by a mechanic whom Vince knew. We found a 1965 Chevrolet Impala and it had 9,000 miles on it. It was spotless without a scratch and was bronze colored. The mechanic said it was a great car. It was well maintained and had the records in the glove compartment. Daryl talked the salesman down to a lower price. He told him he was a serviceman at Fort Sam Houston. The salesman gave us a better break than we thought he would. Daryl had me drive back home. He gave me directions while I was driving. I loved the car and so did he.

We went to dinner at Vince's aunt and uncle's house and met their wonderful large family of three sons and five daughters. They wanted to know about the wedding plans. I told them I had not started on the wedding plans yet. His aunt asked if our parents were coming. I told them mine couldn't afford to travel as my dad was in construction and my mom didn't work. Daryl's dad passed away when he was younger and his mom couldn't make the trip from Alaska so none of our family will be there.

Daryl asked me how I felt about having to move to Fort Gordon when his training was done. I asked him if we were going to have a honeymoon. He said after we were married we would go to Las Vegas and visit his Grandma before heading to Fort Gordon. We would be in Vegas for a week. It was a lot for me to take in so I didn't think about it.

I enjoyed being held and loved after being lonely for so long. We talked about when Daryl was done with the service and about our going back to Alaska and raising a family. I told him we were getting ahead of ourselves. We had to wait and see what the service had in store for him. He kept reassuring me we would be fine.

I told myself, I had to get over this phobia of being hurt again and that nothing was going to happen to Daryl. I was here, he loved me, and we would stay together. Nothing was going to happen to him.

We were always invited to Vince's aunt and uncle's for dinner. I was becoming good friends with the girls. They were going to be my bridesmaids and maid of honor in my wedding. Yvonne, who was the oldest of the girls and same age as me, twenty was my maid of honor, her sisters were going to be my bridesmaids. I told Daryl I had all of my girls picked for our wedding so he had to get his four groomsmen picked. I knew Vince was his best man.

We talked about the cake with his aunt and her friend and they volunteered to make it five-tiered with the bride and groom on top. I just had to get my bridal trousseau together. I had my money to use for that. I was finally becoming comfortable with the idea of getting married. We were going to have a military wedding. Daryl would be wearing his dress uniform.

The only sad part of this wedding was, not one member of my family would be attending. I would have given anything for Barb to be my maid of honor but that wasn't going to happen. Daryl knew how bad I felt over neither of us having family at our wedding.

Mrs. Benson wanted us to have the reception at her house instead of renting a place. We would only have about seventy people attending and they were Vince's family, our friends, Mrs. Benson and all the guys and gals from Daryl's platoon.

Mrs. Benson wanted to help me shop for my wedding dress. I was thrilled because I liked her and valued her opinion. It would be nice to have input from someone else about the dress besides me. I hated sales people who were pushy, so I was always guarded. The first bridal shop dresses we looked at were beautiful but very pricey. I told the clerk my price range and she brought out dresses that were the worst I had ever seen. The woman was very rude after I told her I couldn't afford to spend thousands of dollars, and that I was looking for something in the five-hundred dollar range. Mrs. Benson and I both agreed this wasn't the shop for us.

At the next shop on the list, I tried on several dresses and found a couple that I approved of and Mrs. Benson truly liked. She preferred the one that had long sleeves and showed my figure somewhat and had lace throughout the entire dress with satin underneath. The price tag was six hundred and fifty dollars. I told Mrs. Benson, I had to put it back as it was over my limit for spending.

She hugged me and said, "Don't worry honey, we will find you the right dress." Mrs. Benson treated me to lunch

315

before we started looking, again, but we never found one I liked. The one dress I liked was too pricey and out of my reach; it was one hundred and fifty dollars over my limit. I also looked at some veils. The ones I liked were very expensive so I put them back. My favorite cost one hundred and eighty-nine dollars.

That night at dinner, I told Daryl about our unsuccessful shopping trip. I told him, I was not used to spending that kind of money nor would I put us in the poor house for a wedding. "Why don't we just elope? It would be a lot cheaper."

Daryl replied firmly, "You know you want a wedding and you are getting one."

When we returned home there was a large box sitting on our front porch. Daryl brought it in the house and set it on the table. He carefully pulled the tape back from both sides and inside was a lot of white tissue. Daryl lifted out a bridal dress in a clear plastic bag that turned out to be the very dress I had loved in the first shop. Lying under the dress was the beautiful crowned long tulle veil.

I told Daryl there was no way we could accept these expensive gifts. Daryl pulled out the card that was with the box. It was a gift for a bridal suite with champagne and dinner for the day after the wedding.

The card read,

"Daryl and Wanda, I am a lady of means and I cannot imagine you, my dear sweet child not having what you deserve. I give this gift to both of you as a wedding gift from my heart. I love and treasure the two of you very much, Hilda."

I sat on the couch and cried. Never in my life did anyone do something this kind and extravagant except my Grandmother and Aunt Maxine. Mrs. Benson was like a mother to us, especially me, when Daryl wasn't there. I was fortunate enough to get this kind of love from Granny and Aunt Maxine. They truly made me feel loved. I could return that kindness and love to this beautiful lady Mrs. Benson.

Two weeks went by so fast with all the planning. In the midst of all the work, I enjoyed going with the other wives and women to watch our men jump from a plane and parachute to a certain designated spot on the ground. Daryl was spot on as were many others in his platoon. He explained to me why they had to keep doing this. Their training was different from other men in the army. He was a part of "special forces" or better yet, *The Green Berets.*

Barb turned sixteen on December fifteenth and I wasn't there to celebrate with her. I bought her a birthday card to let her know somebody loved her enough to think of her sweet sixteenth. I could not send her cash for fear mom would open her card and remove it. Daryl suggested I buy her a money order in her name. That way mom could not touch the money.

The two days before the wedding were crazy. I was anxious and was trying to relax and enjoy the preparations. I told Daryl I was not happy about leaving and did not want to leave Mrs. Benson. Starting over was just too hard. She had become the mother I never had. Mrs. Benson was sad that we would be leaving and made me promise to write her faithfully.

We were getting married on base and having a military wedding. Mrs. Benson insisted on having the reception at her house. She also made it clear that we were to call her Hilda.

Hilda arranged someone to come to her house the morning of the wedding for decorating and putting together the flowers. Both of our houses would be decorated so guests could go between. She would be my mother-of-the-bride. I had to order the flowers, which were soft pink roses and white and pink mums that matched the bridesmaid dresses. Daryl arranged and paid for the catering.

Vince's Aunt, Yvonne, her sisters and some girls from the base were putting together a shower while Daryl was going out on a bachelor party with his friends from his platoon. Hilda was invited as the mother-of-the-bride. She had never been to a bridal shower before which was hard to believe, and I told her this was a first for me too. The house was decorated with bells and doves with pink and white crepe paper. We had wonderful food and played games with bridal shower themes. Hilda won a nice set of Swarovski crystal napkin holders. The gifts were exactly what any young bride and groom to begin their marriage.

I mentioned to Daryl that my grandparents wished they could come for our wedding, but my Grandpa had health issues and couldn't fly. He told me, I know that they love you as much as I do. Hopefully we will get to visit them after I am done with the Army. They sound like good people whom my future wife adores.

At the church, Hilda helped me get into the beautiful dress she had purchased for me. I grabbed a few tiny branches of babies-breath from my bouquet and placed them in Hilda's French roll as well as in mine. She helped me put on the crown of the veil and spread the tulle over my shoulders. I was looking in the mirror when the rest of the wedding party showed up. I told the girls that someone special was walking me down the aisle and they asked me who. I grabbed Hilda's hand and said, "My best friend and someone who is truly like a mom to me. I adore you Hilda!"

I walked down the aisle to the wedding march with Hilda holding my arm gently and before I knew it we had said our vows and walked out of the church under crossed swords and into our limo to the wedding reception with Hilda by our side.

The reception was a great success and the only alcohol was a case of champagne that Hilda had purchased. Thank goodness, I didn't have any drunken soldiers to embarrass me. Daryl whispered that we had another wedding reception at the hotel where we were staying. Dinner was being served at the hotel. He and Hilda had planned it out.

Daryl and most of the guys paid for the second reception. It was like I was a princess!

After leaving Hilda's house we took the limousine to the hotel. As we walked in everyone threw rice all over us. When we entered the reception room the guys were whooping it up and clapping. I saw nothing but a sea of green uniforms including the IC's with whom I made friends. I asked Daryl if we were going to be in debt over this reception. He said it was our wedding gift from the guys plus they had given us an envelope with a thousand dollars in cash for our honeymoon.

We danced the first dance and then the floor was open. I was so happy when a few of the guys asked Hilda to dance. I sat with her numerous times to take breathers and two of Vince's aunts were sitting with us. It was a wonderful reception. The party and dancing continued into the night. Daryl told me quite a few of the guys in his platoon had rooms at the hotel so no one would get in trouble for drinking and driving. I was relieved when it was over. I was absolutely exhausted by the end of the day. We said our goodbyes to everyone and had a wonderful night together.

The next day, one of the guys came by the room and told Daryl he had some tragic news. Just after the reception, a car while crossing the highway to get to his car hit Daryl's friend Rob and his date. Rob's date was killed instantly, and Rob was critically injured. I was in shock and could not believe something this horrific happened on our wedding night. I was filled with dread that it was my fault. I said to myself, if only this didn't happen, or that didn't happen. Daryl asked the guys to keep us posted of what was going on when they got back to the base.

If only we had stayed at Hilda's house this probably would never have happened, but the guys wanted to make a big party out of it including my new husband. It was late evening by now and Daryl's buddies hadn't called. Daryl was calm and collected but he was upset that it happened after our wedding reception. I felt we were to blame because they had been drinking at our reception. Daryl told me, "How can we be to blame? It happened after they left the reception." Finally, Daryl's sergeant called and told us that Rob was in critical condition.

He apologized to Daryl saying he was sorry this had to ruin the wedding. I begged Daryl, that when we woke up in the morning, we needed to go back to the house and try to recuperate. He tried to reassure me that we would work this out together.

When we got home, Hilda came out and asked why we were back so soon. Daryl told her that we were on our way over to tell her. He grabbed a beer and a box of Kleenex. I began crying again and said I would never get over a girl being killed leaving my wedding reception. I couldn't get rid of the picture of the car slamming into Rob and his girlfriend, leaving her dead and him fighting for his life. Shaking my head, I kept saying over and over, "Why? Why? Why, God? How could God let this happen?"

Hilda told me she hoped I wasn't thinking it was my fault. She used her soothing voice trying to ward off my shock that was quickly growing into anger. "Many things happen that we can't understand Wanda. Getting mad at God is how you are reacting right now. It's normal." Hilda tried to settle me down and told me to quit blaming Daryl and myself for this awful tragedy.

Hilda, as sweet and well-meaning as she was could never know what my abuser priests set in my mind those many years ago. Every time I was abused I was told God would punish me in more ways than the punishment I got from them. I couldn't help believe I was bad and somehow deserved terrible things to happen to me and to anybody who was around me. I was living behind a wall of silent suffering. No one knew what I'd been through as a child. I lived an untruth, always protecting myself from judgment, condemnation, and shame, never wanting to reveal who I was under the facade. The secret kept getting heavier as I matured and grew into a young woman, but I was fraught to let it out. I just couldn't, not even to my new husband, or to Hilda.

Hilda made sure that my time was filled while Daryl was gone for a few days on training. She took me to the San Antonio Zoo and Park and then we drove to visit her sister in Houston for overnight.

We spent our day shopping with Hilda's sister. I was never as spoiled as I was on this trip. Hilda would not take no for an answer when she saw something for me. She bought it behind my back without me knowing. She gave me a dress at her sister's, but when we got home she handed me three bags that I naturally thought were hers. Inside were perfumes, a makeup case filled with makeup, and several tops and dresses. My mom never thought once about buying me anything like this. My aunt did and so did my Grandmother but not like Hilda. It made me feel cared for and loved. Hilda taught me a valuable lesson about giving and receiving. She loved to give, and I found that giving was the better of the two. I had an idea how I could do that for Hilda.

I wanted to make Daryl his favorite meal for his homecoming. When he walked through the door I was there to give him a nice long kiss. He quickly said in his tantalizing voice, "I smell something delicious and fishy" he laughed.

After we were done with dinner he complimented me on how tender and delicious the halibut was and the hollandaise sauce on the asparagus, and how good of a cook I was. I had to learn to cook at six years old so I had better be fairly good. I did feel proud of my cooking. I smiled and quipped, "It's all for you sweetheart."

After dinner, I showed Daryl the package that had come for Hilda. I wanted to give it to her right away, "Let's go over and surprise Hilda now, okay?"

We knocked on the door and Hilda said to come in as she saw us at the back door. Daryl came in with the wrapped gift. "What do we have here?" We told her this gift was our love to her for all that she'd done for us.

321

Hilda opened the gift and suddenly with she cried, "Oh My, you kids shouldn't have done this for me!"

It was a photo we had taken on our wedding day. Hilda and I were sitting on a whitebackless loveseat while Daryl stood behind us in the middle, a hand on each of our shoulders. The picture was large, sixteen by twenty inches in a gold frame. It was stunning.

Hilda asked Daryl to grab her handkerchief for her tears of joy. She told us it was the best gift anyone could ever give her. She asked him to hang the picture for her above the fireplace. Daryl put it up for her. We all stood back and looked at the photo feeling filled with deep satisfaction. "Every time you look at our picture think of us Hilda and know that we love you!" I must've said it at least twice that we'd always be with her no matter what!"

It was packing day. Our car was packed high with just enough room to see out the back window. We had nine boxes to send to the new address. We left them with Hilda, in her garage, and gave her a check to pay the postman when he came for pickup. Thank goodness the Impala had a big trunk because we stuffed it full of four large duffle bags filled with our clothes and numerous other loose objects. The apartment got a more than thorough cleaning (a Wanda cleaning) and was in better shape than when we got it. I struggled saying goodbye to Hilda, giving her unneeded advice about her always checking the new renter's references. She just smiled and hugged me tightly.

CHAPTER THIRTY-TWO

It was not the greatest trip at first because Daryl was going the speed limit but hit ice on a bridge about five hours out of San Antonio and we slid like crazy spinning around a few times. No one was in the other lane, thank God! We were spared a terrible accident. I asked Daryl to take our time and slow down until we were in warmer weather. It was a long trip to Las Vegas but he drove straight through going through New Mexico, Arizona to Nevada. We only stopped to grab food and use rest rooms when we gassed up. We took turns driving once we got into Arizona because I had slept quite a bit, and we were away from the icy roads. It was a long haul, too long without stopping for sleep and rest at a motel.I made it clear to him that we were NOT driving straight through to Georgia!

I was so exhausted when we finally reached Las Vegas all I wanted to do was shower, brush my teeth and take a long nap. We surprised Daryl's grandmother by arriving a day early, which worked out well for me in order to acclimate. She had plans to play Bingo in the evening leaving us to ourselves to settle in. She lived in a large house, with three guest rooms and a great room with a pool just outside.

Hi grandmother bought us tickets for three different nights of entertainment and said we should enjoy the city while we were here.

We had a great time in Vegas. She showed us a good time, and lent us her car so we could go on our own and enjoy the shows. We did a lot of pool time and just relaxed when we wanted to be alone and have fun by ourselves. Daryl was enjoying the sun tanning idea with his pale white skin. Grandma was a big Bingo player and we only saw her at breakfast and twice for dinner, most of the time we ate out. All in all, it was a great honeymoon!

We were leaving the next day. I asked how long it would take to get to Georgia. Daryl pulled out the map and told me to guess how many states we had to go through? "Five," I answered. Daryl told me, "Eight" and showed me the orange line he penned in on the route that we would be taking. Daryl changed the oil and made sure we had fluid for window-wipers if we hit rain or bad weather. We had all-season tires on the car so we were ready to break for the road about five in the morning. He promised we'd get a motel later in the evening.

Daryl's Grandma heard us up and came to fix breakfast for us. Daryl told her we could go until lunch. She said, "I don't think so kiddo, she has to eat something and so do you." She cooked up eggs, toast and orange juice and sent us on our way and we thanked her for the great time we had. As we were driving, I told Daryl we didn't get to really spend a lot of time with her. He thought she made herself scarce so we could enjoy each other's company. I agreed and added that it was nice to relax more than it was to go and try to gamble and waste money. I was not a gambler or a big drinker.

It was late the first night when we stopped in a little motel in Oklahoma. The motel wasn't the greatest probably less than one star. It was dirty and the bed sheets looked like they hadn't been changed after the last customers. I had two pillows and gave Daryl one so we slept on top of the bed and used our own blanket.

We hit the road around six and decided to get a better motel. We drove all day and we ended up going through Memphis about six, then we were in Birmingham, Alabama hours later. Daryl said he wasn't tired so we drove on into the night arriving at a nice motel in Oxford, Alabama around one o'clock in the morning.

After good sleep and breakfast, we only had a four to five hour drive to Fort Gordon. At least we were more relaxed now and did not have a real long drive ahead of us. To this day, I don't like long drives I'd rather fly.

The base was about thirty miles out of Atlanta, which put us in a newer trailer along the road to the base. Since Daryl worked on base during the day until late at night. I felt completely isolated and I came to hate that we weren't living on the base. I felt utterly alone. He told me he would do what he could to get us a place on the base.

I was depressed and hoped things would change soon. Daryl did begin coming home after a few weeks earlier at night. We spent a little more time together and that's why I found myself throwing up in the mornings. I thought maybe I had the flu because I was throwing up in the evening too. It finally dawned on me that I might be pregnant. We had been married for a little over two and a half months. He asked me if I really thought that I was pregnant, and I told him I was a nurse and I knew the symptoms. He made an appointment for me to see the doctor. I was very upset when he dropped me off and did not come with me.

"Well, what's the news?" He asked when he picked me up.

"I'm six weeks pregnant." I was not pleased that my own husband couldn't go to the doctor's appointment with me, and he was the one who was bragging to everyone about wanting a dozen kids.

"I am not ready for a family," he replied. He told me, he was happy about the baby and he was sorry for not going in with me. I asked him what was more important than going to an appointment with your wife to see if she was pregnant.

I was very upset with Daryl and his buddies. I had been putting up with them coming to our house, getting drunk and putting their cigarette butts out in my flower pots. They were loud and obnoxious showing no regard for me in my condition. Daryl wouldn't ask his buddies to quiet down so I could rest. The parties continued and Daryl became more arrogant and cocky to me. He just quite caring and didn't give a damn about me anymore.

I was starting to have a negative attitude about my marriage. I was certain by Daryl's lack of concern that he had pulled away from me. Regardless of his lack of support, I was happy to be having a baby that I could love.

I became more and more convinced that I did not want to go through life not being loved. The old language of the priests kept hammering in my head that I was damaged goods and not deserving of love. It didn't matter that I had never confided in Daryl about my past, but it was obvious to me he must intuit it by the way he treats me now, his pregnant wife. It was beginning to tear at me.

He constantly had parties at our house with the guys who were his best buddies, being that they were now the Green Berets, Special Forces. They were so full of themselves there wasn't room for a housebound pregnant wife to get in their way. I was so angry I told him he needed to find another party house. He would have no part of it because our house was the perfect place to drink and get rowdy without getting caught on base.

The partying continued until April when I confronted him again. I was talking to a hard head and no matter how I protested he wouldn't budge. I was four months pregnant and he showed no compassion whatsoever. I felt so alone because Daryl was about Daryl. He eventually stopped talking to me about his orders or any other part of his life.

The last few weeks, Daryl was making me feel hopeless and not knowing why he didn't care was the last straw. I had it by mid-April. I decided I was going back to Montana. I would get my own place and take care of myself.

Daryl told me that going home wasn't an option; I wasn't taking the car and to get the idea out of my head. I told him I could easily find my way home. He didn't believe me. My friend, Lydia who lived in the trailer court, said she would give me a ride into Atlanta when her husband left for work so I could fly back to Montana. She helped me pack my things. I could only take three suitcases and a carry on.

Lydia said to me, "I hear how he talks to you and it disgusts me. He is obnoxious when he is drunk. I don't blame you for leaving the way he treats you. Who does that to a pregnant woman, and expects her to entertain his drunken friends? We hear them at night, Wanda, when your windows are open. We have no air conditioning so we have to leave them open and we hear his parties."

I called my Dad and he said he would pick me up at the airport. I had to do the unthinkable and stay with them until my landlord would have an apartment available again.

I took money out of the checking account, which I knew Daryl would be pissed about for the plane ticket. Since, I was married to him it was just as much mine as it was his. I was so glad I still had most of my money left in my savings and haven't transferred it from Montana, so I old have those funds when I got home.

I was very emotional and confused with a husband who seemed to have withdrawn since learning of the pregnancy. I wondered if I had a marriage worth saving. When I left for Montana, I left a letter on the table telling Daryl that he had "...broken my heart with all the changes he had made in himself. Now he was an arrogant and irresponsible man. It is very sad when a pregnancy can spoil a relationship and a marriage. Good-bye Daryl."

CHAPTER THIRTY-THREE

I arrived in Helena after a late snowstorm that blew in during the night. I was in sandals and a pair of shorts with a summer top. Dad ran to the car and got a musty blanket out of the trunk that always kept there. It was better than nothing.

Mom was sitting in the car with Barb. Barb jumped out and helped with the suitcases. I told her I was not looking forward to this visit at all. She was excited and said that she was just happy to have someone to be with.

Mom said hello to me, asking if I was okay as I got into the car. I said hello back asking how she was feeling. I hated small talk, but when I had to come back to my humble beginnings with my tail between my legs, I felt like the world had just crumbled to pieces. What could I do? What I could do was hold Barb's hand in the back seat and whisper to her that I would tell her everything when we got home. Her room had been made up neatly for us. We could lie on the bed together. She was a good listener, and she knew I needed one.

My parents were going to fix dinner. I told Mom, I could not eat anything with my upset stomach; she told me I was going to need my strength for the baby. I gave in and said okay when dinner was ready.

I asked Barb, how she could live in this house. It was so old and ugly and the toilet did not flush, even though they had running water. I was so squeamish!

I needed to buy a car. Barb told me she would ask Bill Roddy to find one for me. I needed it to look for an apartment. I was tired of people taking care of me badly.

I cried when I told Barb about being married to Daryl who had become such a jerk once we moved to Georgia. I want to take care of myself and not ever rely on any man or any person whatsoever!

Barb wanted to know what caused everything to fall apart after the wedding. I shared all of the details about his egotistical behavior thinking he was top notch and I was suddenly nobody. I couldn't believe his friends seemed more important to him than me, after I told him I was pregnant. We were going to have a baby and he didn't even care. I could not believe he could change so quickly into such an ass. I told her, "If he crawled on his hands and knees I could not forgive him and his behavior."

I woke up in the morning and ran to the bathroom vomiting. Dad told me since I had an army ID I could go out to Fort Harrison and get something to help me with the nausea. I knew Dr. Whitesitt who was an Ob-Gyn, and I called his office for an appointment. I did not want to deal with all the paperwork with the government to get a medication. Dr. Whitsitt's office informed me they would bill the U.S. Army, as Fort Harrison was not set up for OB checkups. It was nice to hear that, because I would prefer the care from a local physician that I knew. The doctor gave me Compazine, which took care of the nausea.

After my appointment, my mom then gave me a ride to look at an apartment that was in the paper. It was a block from my old apartment. I let the landlord know I had left my husband and was pregnant. I explained to him that my husband was in the service so he wouldn't be trying to visit and that furthermore, I didn't smoke and kept a very clean house.

It was a one-bedroom apartment upstairs and in a wonderful location. The apartment was not available until May fifteenth, three weeks away. I honestly did not think I could hold on that long, but I would if I want this reasonable and furnished apartment.

I would give Pat a call to collect my things now that I was back, but needed to know I had the apartment for sure before I did. I was not sure what I would do if things did not work out for me. I certainly did not want to call my

Grandmother, and have her upset over the news of leaving Daryl. She was very old fashioned, thinking a woman had to put up with just about anything in a marriage. Then again Grandma was married four times. She lost two husbands and divorced the other. She and Grandpa Dan's marriage lasted forty years, so I guess she might understand.

Barb and I spent quite a bit of time taking the horses out and walking them until we knew we were far enough from the house to be out of listening distance. When we returned home one morning, mom had a phone number for me to call. I noticed the name right away. Mom had been surprisingly nice through this entire ordeal. Barb saw the smile on my face and told me don't get over excited. It was good news. I had an apartment!Now I needed help getting my boxes from Pat's. I didn't want her or her husband to go out of their way for me. She'd already been so kind to me.

A visitor showed up at our house the next day. My mom had heard a knock on the door and when she opened it she had no idea that it was Daryl. He asked if I was home and my mom asked him who he was.   "I'm Daryl, Wanda's husband," he said.

Mom yelled to tell me I had a visitor, but she did not let him in. When I met him on the front stoop, I asked him what he was doing here. He wanted to know why I wasn't asking him in. I told him I was sorry but I was shocked that he was standing there without as much a call from him. After introducing him to Barb and my mom, I again asked him why he was in Montana. He said he wanted me to please come back to Georgia to try and work things out.

I was furious. I raged, "Daryl, you were a living hell to me the last month I was there. I am still in shock about what took place down there. You were not the man I married when you stood before God and swore to love and cherish me forever and always. You treated me with disrespect in front of your so called friends knowing I was pregnant and didn't care."

Daryl said he had to go to Fort Bragg, North Carolina for his special training before being shipped to Vietnam.

"I knew it, you told me you would most likely not go and now you're telling me you will go. The thing that bothers me the most Daryl was I truly loved you. I was afraid to love someone again. Then I told the man I love, that I was pregnant and you told me with your behavior that I was on my own, because you didn't sign up to be a parent. Now you want me to come back and trust you again?"

Daryl had driven a long distance, I decided to hear him out, but I was not going to promise him anything. Dad and mom told me he was still my husband and to let him try to convince me how much he truly loved me. I told dad honestly, I was not sure there was anything to save after what happened to me. You owe him and yourself that chance, daddy said.

Barb slept in the living room and let Daryl and I have her bed that night and the next if need be. He tried to have sex with me. I asked him just what did he think I was. I knew that he did not care for my innermost feelings and my pregnancy. He asked if we could drive to town tomorrow and talk away from my family since he was uncomfortable with the condition of the old house.

"Do you really think you could live here in these conditions?" he asked me.

I asked him what he meant. The toilet has to be flushed with a bucket of water for God's sake. The house is over a hundred years old and your mom and dad cook on a wood stove.

"I told you how poor my family was Daryl so don't even go there. I am not happy having to live in this house but it sure beats what was going on in that trailer. Neither way is acceptable to me. I have found a place to live. I am not living in a State where I have no one or no family while you are in a war in Vietnam. Information that you were going to Vietnam you never bothered to share with me, your wife. Do you honestly think I could live where you left me alone to fend for myself, while you and your buddies were out partying? I have never felt so let down by a person, Daryl. And you ask me if I had another chance to give you. Now you bring up how poor my family lives and you were told long before we actually started dating and we were only good friends at that time, how dirt poor my family really was."

I was furious that my husband was stereotyping my family and how I grew up. I told him I needed to rest and mull over what really happened to our marriage, if I had a part in it, or if it was really all his doing. Either way, I did not want to continue a loveless marriage. I was beginning to think it was all about sex and never about love. A man who truly loves his wife doesn't give a crap where she came from.

I would live up to my part and try to make amends if need be. I really did not feel like I was the responsible party. I was too tired to think about it and wanted to get some rest. I wanted to stop squabbling about who was right and who was wrong. I also had a child to think about in the near future. I was not raising the child alone or with two parents who could not live together and fought continuously. We would discuss more tomorrow after I could sleep.

Daryl made reservations on a flight going out the next day because I told him that there was absolutely no way that I was going back with him regardless of what we decided. I was not going to be left alone in Fort Bragg, North Carolina without any family, not knowing anyone there at all. I will never be abandoned again. Daryl did agree that I should stay in Helena. I promised him I would think about what we talked about and see what happened after he left. He knew that I wasn't a run around woman, and would not jeopardize our marriage if I wanted it to survive. I told him I did not know if I could forgive a man if I was unsure I could trust him.

He left the car with me so I could get around to appointments and shopping. I did not have the money to purchase a decent car. I still felt there was an ulterior motive like I was being bribed. I felt Deep down, Daryl was not the man I married. My biggest wish was that Daryl would tell me he was sorry. I never heard those words.

I kept asking myself why these awful things were happening to me and were they indeed my fault. Why did I have to go through these ordeals? Only God knew. As a child who was continuously abused over and over and told she was a bad person and the devil was doing his work. It caused me to think I was this bad person. I tried so desperately to work at being a good person but then I found myself trying to please everyone but myself.

I took Daryl to the airport and told him to keep me updated on what was happening and if he wanted to really save our marriage. I could not believe I received two cards and one letter from him and then nothing at all for weeks. Without any support from Daryl, I needed to find work once again. I wanted to work until I had the baby. Pat gave me my old job back just like she promised.

I was elated to move out of dad and mom's house and into my new apartment. My life seemed more normal again. I knew dad was not happy about my moving into the apartment and living alone while I was pregnant. But, I made it clear to him that I could not live in that house any longer, and I was going to take care of myself regardless of the situation I was in. Mom was kind while I was there and I gave her credit for trying hard to make amends.

I knew I was going to have to quit my job quite soon, after getting back to work for only a few months. One day at the office, Pat's supervisor told her, I could not work after my eight and a half month of pregnancy, because of the risk of something happening to me on the job. I was okay with that. I had saved enough money to help me get through everything and to buy a crib and bedding for the baby.

My girlfriends from the office and other friends I went to school with held a fabulous baby shower where I received so many things for the baby. Then my girlfriends, Donna and Pat held a second baby shower once again with personal friends of ours from our group. I had enough baby things to last for quite a spell, and nice little clothes with gift receipts in case I had a little boy instead of a little girl. I would not run out of diapers, either.

I had not heard one word from Daryl except that he had filed for an annulment and told his uncle who was filing for him in Butte that I was not pregnant and had lied to him. My Dad's friend Leo Kotas was my attorney. He told me Daryl would be shipped off to Vietnam soon. I told Leo I would gladly do a paternity test because Daryl knew the baby was his when he dropped me off at the doctors. He also knew I was never with anyone but him. He was trying to get out of his responsibility of supporting his own child. I told my attorney if he was that desperate to get out of paying for child support I would support this child myself. Daryl was ordered to pay fifty dollars a month and never once paid a dime for his child. As so many women do, I never forced the issue. Daryl's uncles had some guy from the bank come and pick the car up. He told him I wasn't pregnant and Daryl needed to get his car back.

I didn't think he deserved to see the baby and be around her if he should ever try. I knew I had a good reason for not wanting to get back with Daryl after what took place in Georgia. It worked out in the long run, but I was so thankful that my heart told me that he was not the man he said he was. As soon as he heard the word pregnant that changed his whole outlook of our marriage. I was happy I'd made the decision to leave for my child and for me.

CHAPTER THIRTY-FOUR

Carol, Ria, and my Mom, stayed with me at the hospital through my thirty-six hour labor. Holding my baby girl was the most exciting experience I had ever had. I could not take my eyes off of this gorgeous baby. She was so tiny. I felt comforted holding this precious girl in my arms. I was so fortunate to have been given this tiny life to care for.

I had to force Daryl and the government to pay for the medical bills with my attorneys help. The doctor told me I would not be able to go back to work for at least six weeks, which was fine with me because I did not want to rush having to find someone to care for my baby girl. My friend Janet came by with a gift and told me in no uncertain terms, that she would like to take care of my baby when I had to return to work. I told her I would go back to nursing at the Cooney Convalescent Hospital, once Mr. Roddy found me a car.

Bobby, her boyfriend, knew someone who would sell me a 1965 Chevrolet station wagon for almost nothing. He sold the car to me and brought it over to my apartment telling me I could pay him once I was on my feet. He signed the title over to me. The car was a pain in the guy's neck, because it was being ticketed for sitting on the street too many times. I guess I did him a favor.

I had to go back to work to pay my bills. Janet volunteered to watch Dee as long as I took the three to eleven shift at the hospital. She and Bobby lived together and she didn't have to work. He made good money playing for the local Tracy's Lounge in Helena. Charley Pride played there a few times before he became a big Country star.

I started at Cooney Convalescent and got the hours I asked for, but I still needed to find a part-time job during

335

the day and that would pay for my monthly bills. There was a part-time secretarial position at the Social Security office. It was three blocks from my apartment and would be perfect. When I asked Janet's mom Jean if she could watch Dee for me, she jumped at the chance. I had to bring Dee to Jean's house. The charge would be forty a month. I told her that was hardly fair on her part to be paid such a ridiculously low charge. She told me she had been a single parent once. She understood what my ex–husband had done to me leaving me without a dime.

Dee was six months old and my girlfriends Pat and Donna wanted to pick me up from work and go out with them. I agreed to meet them downtown as soon as I was off work at the convalescent home. They wanted me to meet a friend of theirs. I think this was all planned out. It seemed fishy to me because Janet was in on it and was pushing me to go. I was still in my whites from just getting off work and told them I was only having a couple and then I was going home.

There were a group of guys playing pool next to us. One asked Donna to dance the other named Jim asked me to dance. I danced with him, which I enjoyed. The next thing I knew, Jim came over to the table and asked me if I was seeing anyone. I told him no and he asked if I would consider a movie and if I would let him call me. Donna informed me he was a good guy who had gone through a divorce and had two children. I gave him my number and warned him ahead of time, I was a single mother of a six-month-old baby girl. He told me that was no problem to him, if it wasn't a problem to me. I liked his personality, and his manners. I wanted to date again and this guy was a lot like Gary. I was lonely for companionship and Jim had what I liked.

I was tired of dating immature guys, like my ex Daryl. When I dated older guys I seemed to be happier and I noted that they didn't make everything up about themselves. Gary was eight years older than me when I met him. Jim was older than I was; I just didn't know how much older.

We went on our movie date and we enjoyed each other so much we started seeing each other daily. He was a bartender and construction worker. We dated for a few months and then before I knew it, he moved in with me and helped with the bills. He loved my baby girl who he held constantly and taught her to walk. I quit the Cooney job a couple of months after Jim moved in and kept the Social Security job.

One day, Barb called me. She was terrified and said she had to get away from Mom. Mom was beating her and slapping her around again. I told her she could stay with Jim and me, but she needed to go to school and follow the rules. I did not want the police at my doorstep because of Mom.

Barb packed her things up and snuck out. I told Jim I was letting Barb move in because my mother was beating her again. He understood how I felt and said it was my place and he was fine with it. We needed to look for a bigger place because Barb needed her own room. Barb brought the rest of her belongings to my house and moved in. I had a lot of her things here to begin with because we had planned this from the start when I got the apartment.

Mom had crossed over the aggression boundary again and Barb needed a safe place. When she didn't come home from school, my parents figured it out that she had left. Mom called the police and Barb found out. She hid behind the curtains and saw my parent's car out across the street in front of my place. When the police showed up, they told Barb that she needed to go home. She would need to see the judge and get his permission for me to be her legal guardian. We loaded the baby up and went straight to the police station and to the judge's chambers.

The judge asked what the problem was. I told him what I had gone through with my mother. I told him the last judge had granted me emancipation from my mom because of all the abuse I had endured. I thought the decree was on file. The judge asked me if I was willing to take the responsibility for Barb until she was eighteen years of age and make her attend school. I agreed.

I made it clear to Barb that she had to stay out of trouble and come straight home from school and get her schoolwork done. She offered to help me with Dee. I loved my little sister; I was going to make sure she was taken care of. She also helped me with the care of my daughter when I needed her to babysit for me.

Mom was furious when the police would do nothing. She wanted me arrested for harboring my own sister. The police told her, "Helen give it up, the judge had the last say and he gave your daughter permission to live with her sister. So be it."

Barb did great living with Jim and me. Jim loved how Barb stepped up to the plate when we needed her to give us a helping hand with Dee. Jim had two wonderful children, Diana and Jay from his previous marriage. Their mother was not that fond of my relationship with Jim. They were divorced and in the eyes of the Catholic Church they were not divorced even though a piece of paper had said they were at the time. His ex-wife and I had a few unpleasant incidents. I did not know how I would have reacted in her place losing a man she still loved and cared for even though she was the one who filed for the divorce. Life seemed to be a lot easier once she realized we were going to remain together and be married.

O'Toole's offered me a job as a bartender and cocktail waitress, where I would make good tips and quite a bit more money than I was making at the Social Security office. I found it to be easy work and not as demanding. Another place called Tracey's Lounge, asked me to cocktail for them at night once the owner saw how I could take drink orders without having to write them down for the large booths. With the two jobs, I could actually save money I desperately needed to take care of my little girl and help Barb get through school.

Barb had to stay in school and try to keep good grades at the same time so she wouldn't be taken away from my care. She had a tougher time with school. She had a hard time paying attention. She also did a lot of acting out because of what happened to us as children. I knew she had gone through the same abuse at the orphanage because of her behavior. It had affected me the same way except the drinking part of it. I found out the easy way to forget things was to drink, but the drinking only helped me forget, until the next day.

Barb was starting to party a lot her senior year with kids from school on the weekends. Jim and I were both working and I was beginning to worry about her partying. It appeared that she would go in the same direction I chose to forget the past abuses, by drinking and denying feelings that I would never be good enough.

I worked at O'Toole's the day shift and Jim worked the night shift. I then worked at Tracy's Lounge for my second job. One particular night when I had the night shift off and our babysitter was watching Dee at our house Barb decided to go to a party. At the party, she was so smashed that one of her friends drove her to where Jim worked because Barb had forgotten her key to the house. She knew I was there to give Jim a helping hand that night. Friday nights were crazy downtown and O'Toole's at that time was the place for the young crowd.

Barb's friend carried her into the basement of O'Toole's. In the basement were small studio apartments where a couple of renters shared a group living room. A friend of ours laid Barb on the couch downstairs. She reported Barb had passed out. Jim went down and checked on her while I watched the bar. He was unsympathetic when he woke her up and packed over his shoulder and carried her up to our apartment. He opened the shower door and laid her down, cold water running. She was screaming like the daylights, as he kept the shower door closed to prevent a wet mess. I stripped her clothes off in the shower, got her dried and put her into bed. Jim asked her if she had learned her lesson. Barb told him she would never pull that stunt again as long as she lived with us, and she stuck to her word.

When Barb woke the next morning with the worst hangover, we were not sympathetic. She could've gotten alcohol poisoning and ended up in the hospital, or worse. I reminded her she was lucky that no one called the police or she would have been back at Mom and Dad's. Barbara knew our mother would have put her in the Vocational Girl's School that she had placed Bonnie in. Barb assured us that she never wanted to be that sick again.

Our boss Bill installed a poker room in the back since it was legal to gamble. Bill taught me how to deal cards and I would get to take a percentage off the chips for the house. I was allowed to drink while I worked, and the customers at the poker table could buy me drinks. That was all fine and good, but I was beginning to have the same symptoms I had when I was pregnant with Dee. I found that I was pregnant. Jim and I were going to have a baby! I was dealing cards instead of cocktailing and making more tips in chips, which I cashed in at the end of my shift. It was a part of my job that I enjoyed. I decided I wanted to work as long as I could. We loved working for Bill who treated us very well. He protected me by not allowing smoking at the gaming tables so I could continue dealing while I was pregnant. More than often he gave me a bonus if I had a great night.

Jim and I would get off shift early sometimes and head home so we could have time to ourselves. He was excited about the baby at first but worried about how we would manage. I told him I could work as long as I was comfortable. I would save our tips instead of going out to dinner. We made such good money that we would go out for steak and lobster often.

I quit working when I was eight months along.

I enjoyed spending quality time on camping trips with Jim, Louie and Ria out at Canyon Ferry. Jim had adopted Dee at eighteen months. On her second birthday we took our last summer camping trip. While camping, Jim said he was taking a job with a construction outfit out of town for extra money. He would be building power plants which was great money and lots of extra overtime.

It was good news but it also meant I would be spending less time with him, shades of my parents. He assured me it was only until I had the baby in January and go back to work when it was old enough. Ria told me she would be happy to watch the children after I had the baby since Barb would be moving out after she graduated in the spring. On January 30, 1971, I had Jamie. She was a beautiful little girl with coal black hair.

Jim and I found a much bigger apartment. The rent was only ten dollars more a month and included all utilities. It had a huge fenced backyard. The apartment was near a Laundromat and a grocery store, and within walking distance of downtown. We moved into the new apartment when Jamie was three weeks old. I was so grateful for friends who helped move us. I couldn't do any lifting and Jim couldn't get off work to help. Once I was settled in and everything put in its place, I felt comfortable knowing the girls would have a yard to play in. I had three more weeks with my girls before I had to go to work.

Dee loved having a fenced back yard so she could swim in her wading pool and play outside. I went back to work. I enjoyed working the lunch hour at O'Toole's and at Mr. Lucky's at night. The rest of the time I spent with my little girl and her baby sister who was now six months old.

One morning while I was giving Jamie her bath, I smelled smoke in the house. It must have scared Dee because she came running to me and said her macaroni was burning. She had pulled the stepping stool over to the stove and turned on the gas burner and put a pan with a packet of noodles and cheese but she did not add water. She stood at the stove stirring it.

The fire department was called because there were flames and smoke coming from the pot. The man from the upstairs apartment ran in our apartment and grabbed the pot off the stove and threw it out the back door. I stood outside with other tenants. The trucks pulled up in front and were pulling their hoses out when I told them it was just smoke. I let them know what my neighbor had done and the fire was out.

Dee stood there in horror, frightened and scared out of her wits. She was crying, "I just wanted to cook you some lunch mama and for baby sister." The fireman was great. He explained to Dee that the only time she could cook for her mommy was when Mommy would be helping her.

Ria babysat during the day and Barb relieved her after school. I had the entire morning with my children, since I did not have to work until 11:30. Bill always had a busy lunch hour since he and Joyce were known for their corn beef sandwiches and Joyce's homemade chili. The place was always packed at lunch. The tips were great, and I enjoyed getting to eat after the lunch crowd died down. I also went back to work for Sandy, my boss from Tracey's.

Sandy was a partner in a new place called Mr. Lucky's, which was a supper club and lounge. After the supper club closed at nine o'clock, the band started and I worked as a cocktail waitress until 2:00 in the morning. I finally bought a small red station wagon so I could get myself to work. Jim also bought a "cherry"1950 Chevrolet, which he fixed on the weekends when he was home. The tips were fabulous since they paid for my gas and the many extras we needed. We were back on track with me working and not having to live on such a tight budget. I really enjoyed the people I worked for and was making a lot of new friends. We had regular customers on Friday and Saturday nights. We were always jam packed with people waiting to come in.

CHAPTER THIRTY-FIVE

Jim was offered a job as an apprentice boilermaker in Green River, Wyoming. His friend, Dick, told him this was a great opportunity. The money would be beyond belief because they would be working seven days a week and fourteen hour shifts with over time and double time on Saturday and Sundays. The job would last for a few months and then they would head to Colstrip.

Colstrip was out in the middle of nowhere in Montana. It was freezing cold in the winters and the wind blew like crazy because there were no mountains to protect the land. Eastern Montana was in the flatlands with wheat fields, farming communities and plenty of cattle ranchers. When the temperatures dropped to below zero with a wind-chill of twenty below one was house bound.

Jim told me he thought we should have a house and not an apartment. I told him I dreaded moving, and I did not want to do that. If you go to Colstrip for a long period of time, I am not staying here while you drive home every weekend. The job in Green River might last longer than they predicted. "I will be home before you know it," Jim repeated several times in our phone conversations.

I missed him terribly and so did Dee. She kept asking how come Daddy wasn't coming home from work. I showed her on a map where her Dad was working and how far it was from our home. "Can we send Daddy cookies" she asked? I told her we would send him a package with goodies, which her Dad would appreciate when he opened our package.

Summer was over. Dee was four now and in pre-school. Ria watched Jamie who was fourteen months old and getting into everything. I was still working more hours for Bill. Bill asked if I would start his poker games up again but I told him I was still working at Mr. Lucky's making good money, adding that my tips were phenomenal.

Jim sent me money to pay rent and groceries. He had me buy diapers and clothes for the kids with my money with the rest going into savings. In his line of work we needed to have good padding in the bank just in case he got laid off.

The owner of the apartment complex notified us that he was selling. The new owner was remodeling the apartments and all tenants had to find other places to live. I told Jim and he said to rent the apartment on Broadway we knew was empty. I told him it was filthy. It took me three days just to scrub floors and walls with bleach. The neighbor next door helped me haul out the garbage the last renters had left behind. It had a large living room, huge kitchen, dining room, bath and two bedrooms plus we would use the backyard for barbeques. The landlord gave us the first month's rent free, for cleaning and scrubbing the place down. Barbshared a bedroom with Dee. Barb loved that the bedroom was huge enough for the girls to have room to play. Jim and I had a sizeable bedroom with a huge closet for the two of us; it was perfect. We were still close to the Laundromat and the grocery store. We now owned our own furniture and I would finally get to buy a dining room table!

Jim made it home for Christmas. I asked him if he would please come to our Christmas Party at Mr. Lucky's. It was a formal occasion. He even bought a nice suit jacket to go with one of his nice shirts and ties. Barb shared in on the homecoming and decided to spend the night with her friend so we could have alone time. The girls couldn't get enough of their dad. They were in his lap most of the day until he asked them to give poor old dad a break. He was amazed at how fast Jamie had started walking and sad that he had missed out on her first steps. He said the girls would have a nice Christmas. I was thrilled he felt that way. I didn't have a good Christmas growing up and I wanted our kids to enjoy family time. Jim and I attended my Christmas party at work and did quite a bit of celebrating. I was so glad that Sandy, my boss, lived the next block over from us and gave Jim and me a ride home after the night of partying. The next day the girls and Barb got to open their Christmas gifts.

The next two weeks we enjoyed each other's company and did family outings like taking the girls sledding and Dee ice-skating for the first time. We took them up Grizzly Gulch sledding above my grandfather's old house. We built a campfire. Jay, my stepson, went on some of the outings with us. He loved listening to the girls scream with delight as he rode the sled with them.

We knew time was closing in on us for Jim to leave. I hated having to tell our little girls that Daddy had to go back to work and we wouldn't see him for a couple of weeks or more. I did not want our children to go through being alone without both parents, but this job would help us buy our own home and give us a foot up.

Jim often called and told me it was nothing but trailer city in Colstrip where the plant was being built. He had to live in the men's barracks until he could find something for us to purchase. It meant that we would have to live in a trailer if he could find one available and from the sounds of it, it wasn't very promising. Jim and I saw each other every other weekend, which we endured.

We didn't get to spend much of the winter together except when the weather was nice, which wasn't often. We had one of the worst winters in years with too much snow and bitter, windy, freezing, below zero weather. Jim didn't do much traveling because of the roads.

Meanwhile, Barb ended up with tonsillitis. She had to return to our parents because I did not have insurance to cover her surgery for a tonsillectomy. She was very sick and needed to be hospitalized. Dad told her if she moved back home that she would be covered by his insurance. So she made an arrangement with dad to go back for at least a little while. Rose took over babysitting for Barb. I told Barb that when she was ready to move back she could. She knew that option was always open for her. Dad told her that she had to stay with them if she came back. She had to help mom once she was healed. She agreed. I told her if things went bad to just call me. I felt that mom was only helping her so mom could be lazy once again and use Barb for her purposes. We stayed in touch whenever she had the time or was free to do so. She was a teenager and found a boyfriend after she recovered.   She wasn't home much after that except to go to school and back home on the bus and then to disappear with the boyfriend. Rose informed me she was going steady and would need to give notice so I had time to find a babysitter.

Don, one of Jim's friends who lived across the street from us, had a terrific family with two teenage daughters and a young son. The daughters were looking for babysitting jobs. Kathy and Cherry were the two daughters and they both asked if they could babysit for me. It couldn't have worked out better for Jim and me to have the girls watching our children. Their parents lived right across the street, and I knew the girls were in safe hands. I explained that I could only afford one at a time. They worked out their schedules and split the money. If I had a good night in tips, I would give the girls extra money. They kept the house as clean as I left it. They were my best babysitters besides Barbara and Rose.

Winter went by very fast and it was early spring, I told Jim that when he came home I had some special news. He wanted me to tell him what it was over the phone. I told him, "No, because I wanted us to share the news together."

He asked, "Is something to celebrate, if it is something for us to celebrate I will take you out to the Nite Owl and you can tell me the news."

At the Nite Owl, Jim pulled my stool from the bar and sat down beside me. He turned to me and said he was ready for the good news.

"I will tell you when we go into the dining room and after we order our food." I was nervous. What if Jim wasn't as happy as I was I thought to myself?   As the hostess poured Jim's wine, I looked at the hostess and then glanced at him letting him know to wait until she left our table.

"I went to the doctor the other day and he informed me that we were going to be parents once again," I blurted out.

Jim was thrilled. I told him the baby was due in early July. "I hope we can find a place before the baby is born, but it doesn't look very promising."

He was happy about the news but was stressed because we had to continue staying in Helena until they put more trailers in Colstrip. He said the roads were not even paved. We would have to live across the street from the noisy plant. I told him I didn't care as long as we were with him. I knew it was going to be awhile before he would get us moved there.

This meant I would pretty much be going through this pregnancy by myself. He said we couldn't afford to lose the job in Colstrip. He might not be home for the winter with a few exceptions. The plant would not have family housing until the fall of 1973.

I had to work as long as the middle of my eighth month. Bill said if I felt up to it I could keep working. I told him I had to get things ready for the baby. I had to start buying diapers and clothes. My friends gave me two different baby showers. Summer had arrived and it was hot as Hades. I was so miserable being pregnant in the middle of summer. I was glad my friends came and got us to go out to the lake to cool off.

Dr. Whitesitt said I was a ten-month mother, and I think he was absolutely right, because once again I was overdue. When I finally went into labor, I was rushed to the hospital by ambulance. Jim was out of town and my neighbor came over to help. She called Kathy, my babysitter, and my mom. I was surprised when Ria showed up, but what surprised me even more was my mother sitting in a chair by my bed when I came out of the bathroom. She wanted to be with me because Jim was gone and she didn't know if anyone would be there to help me. She remained through the entire time I was in labor and visited with Ria while I was in the delivery room. I was in labor thirty-eight hours with another baby girl.

My beautiful baby girl with black hair was as strong as she could be kicking and screaming and throwing her arms about. I heard Mother say how tiny she was and she seemed worried about her size. My tiny girl weighed five pounds at birth and had gone down to four pounds eight ounces when I took her home. She was only seventeen inches long and could fit in a boot box. I actually saw my mom tear up when we went to look at the babies in the nursery window.

Jim made it home. I was still in the hospital. He rushed in to see another beautiful girl. "She was so tiny and so precious," Jim declared. Our Tanya was a day old and her daddy and her brother Jay finally got to see her in the nursery. Jay was betting she would be a boy and now he had another beautiful little sister. He joked about having an all-girls softball team, as he held this tiny little creature, softly touching her fingers. Jay was afraid to hold her at first and so was his Dad because she looked quite fragile to them.

The girls were thrilled at how tiny their new baby was. I had the girls sit on the couch so they could each have a turn holding her. I made sure that since she was so tiny that Mommy would let them hold her but they could not take her out of the bassinet without me there to assist them.

Dee was ready to start kindergarten. She wanted a puppy for her fifth birthday, but we told her she couldn't have one until we moved into our own place. We promised we would get her one then. She was happy and settled for craft items to add to her collection. She loved to paint and draw pictures.

I needed to go back to work. I had accepted Gary and Jim's offer to work as a card dealer at the Capri Lounge. I told my boss that I would need to have every other weekend off to spend with my husband when he came home from Colstrip. They agreed that they would do that for us. It was a good job and I made fantastic tips on Thursday and Friday nights.

On the weekends when I dealt cards, I made even more in tips than my wages. When people win at the table they tip big for each hand they win. I did not have to work two jobs anymore. I got to spend all day with Jamie and the baby. Dee had morning kindergarten so I saw her all afternoon until I left for work.

Jim came home on the weekends. We hung out and watched television and played board games with the girls, or took them sledding up Davis Gulch with Jay. He was teaching Dee to ice skate. The winter months were more entertaining with my own children. I would reflect on my own childhood wishing it could have been like this. As an adult, it didn't seem to matter because I loved hearing the squeals of excitement from my own children and the fun they had with their dad.

We had a great Christmas and enjoyed the outdoors with Dee and Jamie. I bundled them up for the cold. We bought a pair of double-bladed ice skates to entice Jamie to learn how to ice-skate.

I kept hoping that Diana, Jim's oldest girl would eventually come around and like me and get to know her sisters. It is hard for teenagers to accept a stepmother or someone else intruding on their dad's territory. I didn't see my parents go through a divorce like her parents did. I did try to understand her feelings.

It was easier for Jay because he was a tad bit younger when his dad and I married. He loved doing things with us. I don't think he told his mother about going with us on family and friend outings for fear of upsetting her.

We were getting ready to go out to dinner with friends for the evening before Jim heads back to work the next day. I heard a knock on the door, there stood Vern, Jim's brother-in-law from Spokane. I had only met him once before and that was with Jim's brother Art, who worked with the Foreign Relations Committee in Washington D.C.

Vern told Jim his mother was sitting out in the car and wanted him to come out and talk to her. I asked Vern what was going on and he said they would be right back and for me to hang tough. Jim's mother did not approve of our marriage because she was a strict Catholic.

Vern came in with his sister's Lucy and Francie. Jim was still talking to their mother. She did not want to meet me or see her granddaughters. Jim's sisters wanted to see the new baby they had heard so much about. I brought Tanya out and they fell in love with all three of the girls.

Lucy told me not to worry about their mother. She still felt like Jim should amend his marriage to his ex-wife. I said that was terrible, as we had our own family and that his ex-wife was the one who asked for the divorce when they filed years ago. "He was divorced when I met him," I said quite bitterly. "I am his wife now and she knows it."

They explained to me that their mother was very stubborn, but she would come around because of the children. They asked me to please write to them and let them know how everyone was doing. Lucy and Francie both gave me their addresses and I promised I would keep in touch with them. They promised they would keep in touch faithfully and they were sorry they didn't sooner.

I met all of Jim's brothers when I started dating him. We were very close to Pius (Pi) and his brother Rich, who owned a bar in Bozeman. I met Art twice when he came to town working with the Foreign Relations Committee. Jim and I were from Catholic families. He had three brothers and two sisters, where I had three sisters and two brothers, just the opposite of his. My husband was an altar boy at the Cathedral in the forties when I was a toddler in St. Joseph's Orphanage.

After they left we went to dinner with our friends as planned. They were amazed that my mother-in-law would not come in the house. During their conversation, she told him to go back to his first family. He told his mother that wasn't ever going to happen. We were happy and he would not do that to us and to please get used to this family being around for a long time. I was stunned and hurt that his mother felt that way about me. She never met or knew me. I told them that my sisters-in-law loved the girls and hated to leave them. Our friends thought it was nice that I had given Lucy and Francie each a picture of the girls holding their new baby sister at the hospital and one for their mother.

It was a very rough winter, and I couldn't be happier for spring to be around the corner. Jim missed out on several family events because the weather was too dangerous to travel in. So I took pictures and sent them to him and he tacked a couple on the wall above his bed along with other photos. Louie said the guys teased him about having a photo album on the wall and that he should just make a collage so the pictures didn't take up so much room.

Jim finally found a trailer right across from the main gate. Some guy was going to a job in Portland and he was selling his. It was 12 feet by 66 feet long and had a kitchen in the front with a good size living room, one medium size bedroom, bathroom and a master bedroom. I told him I wanted the house completely empty and clean, so I wasn't scrubbing as hard as I did in this place. We would need to buy a refrigerator, stove and freezer. They had put new linoleum down in the kitchen and the bathroom. It was going to be very hard to get used to a small space after having this big apartment, but at least we would all be together.

Once I arrived in Colstrip, I was mortified at how tiny the town was. I would have to do my shopping in Forsythe, which was thirty-seven miles from Colstrip. They didn't have a grocery store or any store for that matter. Colstrip had a post office, school, park, and a Town Pump gas station. There were about 300 townspeople not counting all the new people moving in bringing their families with them. Jim was thrilled that we found a trailer right next to the plant.

We returned to Helena and loaded a U-Haul and headed back to Colstrip. I tried calling Barb to tell her goodbye, but Dad said she was out with a guy named Dave. I asked him to tell her goodbye for me and that I would call whenever I could. He asked how long we would be gone, and I told him a couple of years. I told him I loved him.

When we returned to Colstrip, everyone came over and introduced themselvesand volunteered to help me. I knew I was going to like this little group of people. They told me I would get to like it in Colstrip since everyone here was one big family and most were welders, or boilermakers with an exception of pipefitter's, plumbers, and electricians.

It did not take long for the lots to fill up. Jim said Bechtel was putting in new lots behind the Colstrip Café, which was also in a doublewide trailer. The community called Colstrip a trailer city. I could see why. I was getting used to the noise of the power plant. When the whistle blew at 8:00am, noon and 4:30pm it took a little getting used to since we were right across the street. The barracks where the men live was quite a ways back away from the trailer court and the whistle was meant for them to hear it.

Jim always came home for lunch since we were next to the gate. He asked me if I would mind if Louie and Jim Noble come to have lunch with him during the week and they would pay me for making their lunch. I told him it was silly to charge them to eat a few bites, and I would be more than glad to do it. Louie was the girls' godfather for heaven's sake.

We had a birthday party for Dee and all the little friends from the trailer court came for her party. I remembered the promise we had made to her about getting a puppy when we had our own place. So, Dee's birthday present was a Dachshund puppy.

Vicki was my friend who lived two rows over from our house. She was also the girl's babysitter. We spent a lot of time visiting. She would bring her new baby over. When we put the kids down for a nap, she and I would sit in the living room visiting and knitting Mary Maxim sweaters that I sold to the guys at the plant who worked with Jim. Word spread about the heavy wool sweaters and before I knew it I was making them for a lot of people. The men loved the ones with a big elk on the back and a smaller version on one of the pockets. They sold for two hundred and fifty dollars. The children's sweaters were ninety-five dollars.

The Holidays were upon us. I received a letter from Jim's mother saying how sorry she was for not getting to see the girls. She apologized about being very stubborn about Jim and me. She knew she had missed her opportunity to see the kids. She wanted to make the trip to Helena when we moved back to meet her grandchildren.

She realized we were a family and would treat us as one. She started writing very frequently sometimes two or three times a week. Her letters were very refreshing and always asked for pictures of the family. We sent her numerous pictures and letters and finally the ice was broken. She accepted me as her daughter-in-law and called the girls by their given names. She told us how thankful she was for me writing back to her as Jim would always write a little note to her at the bottom of the letters. He wasn't good at letter writing and now she heard from him because of my letters to her.

Jim's sisters wanted us to come to Spokane for Christmas vacation but it was impossible. It would take us a day to get there and a day to come home, as it was eleven hours one way. I would have loved to visit and get to know my sisters-in-law because they were very kind in their letters to us. The visit they made to Helena before we left, opened their eyes when they saw how happy we were as a family.

It was a wonderful Christmas for everyone. The day was filled with laughter and excitement since the girls believed in Santa. Those were the memories that would stay with me forever.

The town was growing with all the new people transferring here. Louie and Ria finally found a trailer with a lot behind the Colstrip Café. Louie's son Duke was moving with them. Jim found Jay a job as an apprentice. He would be moving in with us after Christmas.

Jay would sleep on the couch. He was happy to have a job that paid high wages. The girls were so happy that their brother was coming to live with us and spend time with them when he was off work. I was also excited that one of my dearest friends would be moving here, and I would get to see her every day.

I would read a book to the girls before they went to sleep every night. One night, Jay told me he would like to do it. The girls absolutely adored him. I kept thinking about his sister Diana who was now in Florida. We enjoyed spending some time with her when she came to see us before she left for Florida. She was pregnant with her baby girl Mariah who we didn't get to see for a few years. Jim and I both worried about Diana's well-being so far away from home.

CHAPTER THIRTY-SIX

I woke up one morning throwing up like crazy and I had missed a period. I thought I probably had caught the flu because I didn't notice any other changes in my body. I kept vomiting and knew something was wrong so I made an appointment to go into Forsythe and see the doctor. He ran some tests and came back into the room and told me I was once again pregnant. I hoped Jim would be happy.

The girls jumped up and down with joy. I might get a baby brother yet," Jay beamed. "I know we can make room," Jay was giddy with laughter.

Jim replied, "The more the merrier!"

I was so glad that they saw the bright side of everything. I just hoped it didn't put a strain on us, living in such a small space. Jim made me remember this was temporary and eventually we would get our own house. We were not poor like a lot of people and were saving money to put away for a house and land.

Jim's brother Art came to Colstrip to visit us since he was in Billings on business for some bill they were trying to pass in D.C. We went to lunch with him and his friend Pat Williams who was a congressman from Butte. They were also checking out the power plant while they were there. Art was very distinguished. We took pictures of him and Jim together and then Art, Jim and the girls, and then our neighbor took pictures of all of us together. We didn't get to see Art that much as he was busy with the Foreign Relations Committee and was often out of the country? It was nice to at least spend the day with him before he had to head back to Billings. Jim told him the good news about another baby on the way. He told us to send him a card and let him know when the baby arrived, if it was a boy or yet, another lovely little girl.

That Easter we took the girls to the company Easter egg hunt. At some point, we remembered we left the dog in the backyard, not so awful, but she was in heat. All Dee could think about was getting home and checking on her puppy. A little male dog that looked like a miniature Doberman was mating with our female who was just a little over a year old. I wouldn't be the only one pregnant in the family!

Barb and her husband, Dave, had stopped in Colstrip to pay us a visit on their way home from Lubbock, Texas. Barb was moving back to Helena and I couldn't wait to spend time with her again. I finally got to see my niece and nephew. I was with Barb when she delivered Carrie but I was meeting my nephew for the first time. She told me the marriage was not working out and to keep in touch. She knew what I had gone through with Daryl. How I had rushed to get away from Helena and thinking I was in love once again when all along it truly was loneliness and not love. I now know what love was when I look at my husband and my beautiful children.

I promised I would. I had begged her to spend the night because she looked stressed and very frail. I was more than concerned for her wellbeing. I knew she had married Dave because Dad told me. I asked her why she didn't tell me she had gotten married. She said it was a long story and she would tell me when we had more time together.

In the meantime, Jay bought himself a Camaro so he could go home on weekends and be with his girlfriend Jolene whom we had already met along with her family who lived Helena.

In my sixth month I started having severe pains and they wouldn't go away my friend Vicki thought I was going to lose the baby, so she called for an ambulance. I was rushed into Miles City, which was eighty miles from Colstrip to the hospital. The doctor admitted me in order to stop early labor. I was told I would have to be on bed rest for a while to get things settled down.

Jim saw an ambulance over our direction. Vickie explained what had happened and that she would pick Dee up from school and keep all three of the girls.

Jim took off as fast as he could drive. He was there a little after they had taken me to a room. The doctor came and spoke with him to let Jim know I could not be doing any heavy lifting since the baby had dropped a bit. He said if everything went well through the night, I could return home the next afternoon after another exam.

I felt sorry for my hubby sleeping in the recliner they had in the room but at least they had a television for him to watch. The next morning I felt much better, but they wanted me to wait a few more hours before they would check me out of the hospital.

I was up and moving before I knew it thanks to my dear friends. We took them out to dinner to show our appreciation for all that they had done for us while I was recuperating. I was very fearful of losing my child at the onset of my pains. I felt confident that God was with me regardless of what those priests told me back in those awful days.

CHAPTER THIRTY-SEVEN

Living in Colstrip presented some interesting past times, like watching coal being dumped into trucks as big as houses. The girl's eyes bulged like giant marbles while the watched in amazement the monster trucks move tons of coal. It was better than the movies. I was living out my pregnancy taking care of the kids and taking it easy.

I was able to "hold" the baby to full term. When my due date wasn't far off, I called Doctor Whitesitt in Helena to let him know I needed an appointment the first week of September, which my doctor in Colstrip agreed to. We made arrangements with Cliff and Jeanette in Colstrip to care for the children while I was in the hospital. Jim and I stayed with Louie and Ria. Louie was laid off for six weeks so they had gone home. They had fixed their guest room up for us.

The letters continued from my mother-in-law. She was so kind and thoughtful to me now. She asked if we would consider the name Michael Anthony if it were a boy and Mary Grace if it was a girl. I wrote back and told her they were beautiful names. I would name him what she requested because Michael Anthony was close to Marc Anthony, my choice for a boy. I suspect she wanted Michael for the Archangel who watches over us and Mary for the mother of Jesus. I felt both names were strong and promised to use them because she finally accepted us as her family. She was overjoyed.

The baby was two weeks late. Dr. Whitesitt reminded me about being a 10-month mother. I called my dad to let him know I was in Helena waiting for the baby to come. He told me my mom wanted to come to the hospital and sit with me when it was time. I told him that would be okay. Ria would give her a call. Jim and I patiently waited. I wanted to rest and do nothing else for fear of being in the wrong place at the wrong time. We were all getting restless; I suggested that Jim and Louie go get a beer, that Ria and I would be fine.

Strange how the minute one gives into impatience whatever you were waiting for happens. Not long after the boys went to the bar, I started having contractions. During one my water broke, time to get to the hospital! Ria tried calling the bar in vain for whatever reasons no one picked up. She then called Mom to let her know we were heading to the hospital. I prayed that my baby was healthy, regardless of its sex.

Dad thanked me for letting my mom come and sit with me. I knew it was her way of making amends which I was open to. I'd been glad she was with me through Tanya's long labor as it seemed to help. I had grappled with the fact that if I knew my mother was mentally unbalanced, then how could I go on hating her? I chose not to.

I had to forgive to move on and that was what I was working out with Mom. I could forgive her, but her trust had to be proven. I could not find it in my heart to forgive the priests and nuns for what they did to me. I supposed that one day I might forgive them, if I wanted peace in my life, but I would never forget.

Dad still wasn't aware of the awful things Mom had done, like making us lie so he wouldn't know of her abuses; she used horrible threats of bodily harm to keep us from telling Dad anything. One day it would come to light.

I could never erase the cruelty of the priest's actions toward children as young as we were. I carried this heavy burden deep in my heart, and I sensed some time in my life I would have to let it go. No one could understand the effect the abuse had on me unless they had gone through the same thing. A three-year-old is delicate, fresh innocence, so is unspoiled and pure. Every year for the next eight years that three-year old was polluted by the vilest of crimes, and told that she was to blame. Eleven years of believing that these things happened because she was bad and needed punishment hung on like lava on human skin. Every time the possibility of loss, like losing Gary or a baby, opened up the old pathways to terror and sin.

At the hospital, Dad and Ria had a terrible time trying to get ahold of Jim at O'Toole's. Dad finally went to find him. "What is taking them so long" I whined? Eventually, they came in. Dad thought he was helping by telling me to hold on another two hours so the baby would be born on his grandpa's birthday. I wasn't finding that amusing at all.

Ria and Mom took turns rubbing my back. This was the first time I had severe back pain with my labor and it was quite intense, so maybe, just maybe I was thinking, I will have a boy.

When I heard the doctor say, "Head, shoulders, BOY," I started to cry. Michael Anthony arrived nine minutes after the midnight hour to join his grandfather on his birthday.

Dr. Whitesitt teased, "You finally did it young lady. You now have yourself a screaming little boy who is going to get spoiled by all of those big sisters!" And he was healthy and beautiful!

After the delivery and I was back in my room, everyone said their goodbyes and congratulated me. Dad was very proud and had tears when he gave me a kiss and told me he loved me and thanked me for his grandson.

"Jay looks as proud as a peacock having a baby brother," Louie said smiling at Jay. Jay closed the door and kissed me on my forehead and said how excited he was that we finally had a baby boy. Jim was just like dad, emotional and choked up.

"I was positive this was going to be a baby boy and Grandma Kuhl told me to call her when it happened," Jay said.

"Don't call her this late," I said quickly. "You will give her a heart attack calling at this time of night. Be sure to let her know his name is Michael Anthony like she had requested."

We called the girls, and I could hear their screams of happiness and also anxiety in Dee's voice for us to hurry home. Jim needed to call them when he got to Louie's so he could tell them the baby was a boy and his name was Michael Anthony.

Jim wanted to stay two extra days after I had the baby, but I told him I wanted to go home the next day after I get out. The girls were anxious, and frankly so was I. It had been too long away. Jim told me he was worried that the trip would wear me out or that it would cause me to bleed more. I told him I was just fine and that he was trying to find an excuse to stay longer.

It was such a long drive to Forsythe. When we got out of the car and the girls came running out to greet us, I couldn't stop hugging all three of them. They clung to my neck like gum.

When Jay came back Sunday night he told the girls it was his turn to hold the little guy. He told his Dad that he couldn't believe he finally had a baby brother and boy was he going to get spoiled. I told him, if he did that he would get to deal with the tantrums, or I want this or that syndrome. His Dad laughed his ass off because he knew Jay was going to do it because this was like a dream come true. Jay kept talking, "Just think he could get a motorcycle like mine and we could go biking together..."

"I said whoa there, buddy. Not on my watch, Jay. We worried about you on your bike and still do even though we know you're a careful and smart driver. I don't want to think about him and a motorcycle right at the present. He is a tiny baby and you are planning his future already."

I was thrilled that Jay loved this tiny little boy so much, and he never left the girls out of the picture making sure he showed them he cared for them too. He always brought them their favorite treats or something that he just happened to pick up. They felt loved by Jay.

We had a great group in Colstrip. Everyone was so thoughtful about the needs of everyone else. It was like a brotherhood of guys looking out for one another's families if something happened or if they needed help someone was there to take care of matters for that particular family.

Dee's dog had her puppies finally and what a sight to behold. We had five black and white spotted dachshund puppies that did not seem to belong to our sweet natural brown dog. All of our friends thought it were hilarious that these were mutt dachshunds, but they were as cute as could be. We certainly didn't have any trouble giving them away as they were spoken for within a week.

It wasn't long before we were into winter again. The Farmer's Almanac predicted a bad winter. The light of day was becoming shorter and shorter and it was dark around six o'clock.

It was so nice having Jolene here to help me with Michael. Christmas was right around the corner and we were snowed in. I told Jay that he and Jolene were probably not going to be able to travel to Helena until the weather clears up. Jay and Duke decided to go out and cut down a tree so we could at least get our tree up before Christmas. We had a wonderful time putting the tree up together. I was grateful that Jay helped me with the lights because he'd cut down a much bigger tree than I could've managed. This one took a lot of tinsel, and decorations, but it was beautiful in the end. The kids couldn't take their eyes off of it and Michael would lie there and stare at the lights laughing with delight.

We had a wonderful white Christmas as it snowed the entire day. Nobody was going anywhere that lived here because of the bitter cold. The Company gave the guys five days off for the holidays, and also because of the weather conditions. If it was unsuitable for work, the guys still had to show up for two hours and then they would get paid for the day. The girls wanted to go out and make a snowman. They were disappointed when I told them no, not with it below zero!

I could never find kinder and giving people then my neighbors in Colstrip. Construction workers families do stick together and no one knows that better than me. I was forever grateful for the people who taught me love and support.

CHAPTER THIRTY-EIGHT

Jim was notified at work that his mother had passed away in March. He deeply loved his Mother. She had the flu and had gotten up during the night. She was so weak that she fell in the hallway of their home. Francie, who was a nurse, tried to resuscitate her, but couldn't. Jim had to leave right away to meet his sisters and brothers in Helena to help make funeral arrangements. I stayed to find a baby sitter the day before the funeral and rode to Helena with Louie and Ria.

Lucy told me her mother looked forward to receiving my letters. She was excited about finally spending time with the kids at Christmas as we planned to spend a week with them over the holidays. It was such a blow to know that Jim's mother was gone. I knew that she was thrilled about our choosing the name she wanted for her grandson, but now, she would never meet him. It was all so hard.

The next June Jim's job ended so we decided we would move back to Helena. We landed in Clancy in a trailer just south of Helena. After we settled in, Jim began drinking. He was working at the smelter in East Helena and partying with the guys after work instead of coming directly home. He didn't seem the same after the death of his mother. I began to worry.

We began to have fights and argue in front of the children. After they went to sleep I would lie down in my bed crying myself to sleep. Jim decided I couldn't live like this and thought replacing the trailer with a modular home would make a difference in our disputes. We paid a large down payment and they took our trailer as part of the payment.

When we changed our living circumstances Jim settled down and life resumed normally. We took the kids camping and socialized with friends at our house. He built a horseshoe pit and always invited the guys and their wives out with their children so our kids would have friends as well. Dee and Jamie both made new friends with the neighbor kids and would soon be going to school. Jim began partying once again with the guys he worked with. I was beginning to think he was going through a midlife crisis.

One night he came home very intoxicated at two in the morning. He got meat out of the freezer and demanded that I cook it. I refused and told him to quiet down because he was waking up the kids and scaring them. I told him his drinking was out of hand, and I couldn't take it anymore. He slept on the couch that night. I went back to my bed and cried myself to sleep. I couldn't believe my husband had changed so dramatically. He was a very loving individual when sober. If things did not start changing, I was going to have to decide what to do. I could not continue along this route. I put a lot of the blame on myself for all our problems.

With the money I had saved because Jim's checks always got us by with bills and extras, I decided to take Wesley's suggestion and buy his red sport Mustang. It was a 1968 cherry red and in great shape. I needed a car since I had nothing to drive. Jim knew I was stuck at home, with no job and no way of getting around. He always took our only car when he went to work and went out partying.

When Jim came home and saw the car in the driveway, he asked me what the hell I was doing now, spending my money on a car.

I told him I was tired of him leaving me stranded with four children and nothing for us to do. I had no car to depend upon if an emergency came up or to even go to a grocery store.

"You're paying for the damn thing because I'm not!" he said to me.

I took a job at a nursing home down the road from our house and saved every cent I earned. I threatened Jim with leaving if things didn't change. He knew I meant it because he began to get better. I had saved quite a bit of money and paid off my car. It seemed that Jim was back to acting like a family man. We spent time together on the weekends on several outings and camping during the summer.

I had been working at the nursing home for four months when Jim said we would go on a family picnic with Ron and Judy up to Park Lake for Labor Day weekend on the following Sunday. Judy and I were excited that they finally planned to do something with us as families for Labor Day weekend. Her husband Ron ran with Jim when they partied. I asked Jim not to bring any hard alcohol to our outing.

We drove to meet Ron and Judy at their home and would go to Park Lake from their house for a picnic. The guys said they would run and get beer. Judy was just finishing up the deviled eggs and wasn't quite done packing them and the sandwiches. I made three salads and had chips and dip. I helped Judy finish up so we would be ready when they got back. We sat and waited and waited with the kids wanting to know when we were going. I called O'Toole's to see if they had left. Rosie was working and told us they followed a bunch of people up to Park Lake for a keg party.

I was so upset I was shaking. Judy and I put the kids in the backseat of my car and headed up to Park Lake to find out what the story was with them leaving us behind without a word.

It took us forty-five minutes to get there, and indeed there was a huge party. I asked Judy if she would stay with the kids while I went to find Jim or Ron. I went through the crowd looking and found Jim getting on top of a human pyramid they were building. He was close to the top when I went over and shoved one of the bottom people and they all crashed down. I laughed my ass off trying to cool down from anger. Everyone bitched and bellyached over what I had done.

I was so angry with him I asked, "What the hell was the reason for leaving us sitting at Ron and Judy's house and taking off with other people." I added, "You don't give a damn about your children being affected by your stupidity and selfishness."

Jim yelled at me to, "Go home and cool the hell off."

I told him, "Don't bother coming home because I am leaving you. Your friends are more important than your family. I have called my brother to get a U-Haul and you can have the house to yourself and your drunken friends."

Jim walked away from me and grabbed a beer from a cooler then ignored me. I left for the car. Judy and Ron were arguing close by. I told her I was leaving that it was not worth the fighting. She said she wasn't leaving without her husband, so she had her daughter get out of the car. They continued fighting in front of that poor girl with everyone looking on and laughing. I said to her, "Judy let's get the kids out of here. They don't need to see this." I was not waiting to have a beer poured over my head as Ron had just done to Judy. She wouldn't get in the car so I left. Dee asked where her Dad was, and I told her the truth, what her Dad had said to me, that he and his friends were partying and he told me to go home so we were.

CHAPTER THIRTY-NINE

I called my sister Barb who was now living in Washington and asked her if she would start calling around and find me an apartment. I told her everything that had been going on, and that I had the money for the move and an apartment, but I would need to find a job right away. I then called my brother Wes who got the U-Haul for me, which he would drive to Olympia and then fly back.

My brother Wesley brought the truck out to load along with some of his buddies. It did not take me long to pack. My brother took the kids bunk beds apart and included a television since we had two. Then the third day Jim decides to show up with a buddy and told me I wasn't going anywhere. I called the police and they sent a deputy. We told the deputy that we were almost done and would be out of there so the deputy could leave. He warned Jim that I had a legal right, to remove belongings for the children and I. I did not want to create a scene.

Barb gave us directions to her house so when we arrived we wouldn't have trouble getting there. Before we left I called her to see if she had found a place, and she did a townhouse in Lacey. The landlords were Christians and after explaining my circumstances they offered to let me pay the deposit later.

I was so grateful to Barb. I went and picked up my pay from work, and had seventeen hundred dollars saved up counting this paycheck. My car was paid in full. Wesley figured gas would run about one hundred and fifty dollars to get there. His airline ticket was paid for to return to Helena so I embarked on my journey without Jim.

He was angry with my decision. I was scared to death to do this on my own, but I was not living in a situation where his friends came before his family. I wanted to get out of there as the girls were upset and Michael had no idea what was going on. I had never felt so horrible, mostly for our children's sake, but I deeply loved my husband and he was lost to the partying and the drinking. I missed everything that was good the last nine years in our married life. I prayed that he would realize the mistake he made once we were out of state and out of his reach.

We arrived in Olympia after one long drive; the kids had been incredible on the trip. The only stops we had to make were for food and the bathroom. Barb told me that the lady didn't expect us until the next day. We spent the night with Barb. She got a babysitter for the kids so we could catch up after not seeing each other for a few years.

I hoped I would find some work the next day. It felt surreal to be in an unfamiliar place. I legitimately was frightened for our future. I hoped the new day would bring us good home and new beginnings without regrets. I just could not put the kids through all the fighting and bickering that were going on between their dad and me. Right or wrong, the decision had been long in coming. I promised them they would get to talk to their dad on the phone once we were settled and that made them feel a little better but it wasn't the same as having their dad hold them and hug them. The sad thing was he wasn't home much to hug them in the last two months. The kids would ask, "Why isn't daddy home?" or "How come you and daddy were fighting last night?" I felt it was no environment for children to be in, so I acted. My radical response no doubt had to do with how I felt as a child living in the midst of hostility and fear.

Dee and Jamie came with Barb and me to look at the townhouse. They loved it, and they loved the lady who would be our landlady. It was perfect for us and the girls loved the large bedrooms and the idea that mommy would sleep upstairs with them. The townhouse was brand new. They were going to sell it, but after listening to my sister's pleas they decided to rent to me.

The Jacobs were incredible people and Christians who truly believed in helping others. I was a Christian and no

369

longer followed the Catholic religion after the abuse that took place in my life. She asked me what I could afford with four children and I asked her what she wanted to charge. She said I could have the place for three hundred and fifty a month with utilities included except for television cable. I paid for two months in advance. I didn't have to pay a deposit, because my sister told her I was OCD and would keep things spotless. I couldn't believe Barb had told her that, but if it helped me get the place, I was grateful. I couldn't have asked for more amazing people than the Jacobs to rent from.

Barb and her new husband John with some of his friends helped me get the U-Haul unloaded and the beds put together. I had to go and find furniture for my living room, as Jim wouldn't let me have ours. I took our king-size bed though since I bought it with my own money and the dressers and end tables. I would worry about that later. Once I had everything put away and things organized I had to go job hunting.

Mrs. Jacobs told me the hospital was on Martin Way, and that I wouldn't have a problem getting a job there. After receiving my references, the personnel manager said I would be hired for the day shift 7:00am to 3:00p.m. They would have to wait for my references to be cleared.

Barb babysat the kids so I could go and check on another job. I accidently missed my turn-off for the next job and saw a restaurant with a sign in the window that said: Help Wanted. I thought anything right now, even if it was waitressing.

I went in and talked to the owner, which was a Rumanian woman who owned the restaurant. She said the job was for a bartender for the night shift from 6:00pm to 2:00a, five days a week. I would have to work every other weekend switching with the other night bartender. I would get my pay plus tips and would have to bring in meals from the restaurant to the lounge for customers who had their dinner in the lounge. They had a lot of business people that wanted a cocktail with their meal. A motel was across the street where many businessmen had conferences.

They didn't serve cocktails in the restaurant because of Washington laws, which I needed to be aware of. I told her I had been a bartender and a cocktail waitress in Montana as a second job, my primary job was nursing. I gave her my references, which she called right away and came back to the table and told me I was hired. She needed someone to start immediately as they were shorthanded. I told her I could start anytime she wanted me to that all I needed to do was find a babysitter.

I went back home and told Barb I found a job right away at a place she knew about called Lee's. I told her I had to find a babysitter though. She had anticipated this and already checkedwith Mrs. Jacob's who supplied her with three possible babysitter's names. All the names on the list were from her church, and she knew them personally. The first lady I called on the list was married and had no children but went to church with the Jacobs. Sandy and Dean both came over together to meet me.

Sandy brought several references from people from their church. The kids loved her instantly, and I hired her on the spot. She loved my four children just from the first visit. I was so lucky that Barb had called on this house for me to rent. Good things were finally happening.

The hospital called me in for an interview. I had to take the state boards in order to work there and they were two months away, so they would hire me as a medical clerk on the floor until I could take the Boards. The pay wasn't as good but it got my foot in the door. I would be working 8:00am to 4:00pm, which was not a problem for me. The supervisor gave me a book to study for the Washington exams. WOW!!! I thought to myself. I had to work two jobs, and study! What had I gotten myself into? I was mad at Jim for putting this on my shoulders. I was lucky I had Barb to help or I would have been in a world of hurt.

I went shopping and got my furniture for the living room, and kitchen. There was already an expensive dining set in the townhouse. My furniture would be paid off completely if I saved all my tips in the next couple of months. The thing about having two jobs was I didn't get to spend much time with the kids. I was with them in the morning to help get them off to school and spending a couple hours with them after school before I would leave for work once again. It wasn't the best of circumstances.

The weekends were kinder to us. We made a point of always finding something to do and going over and visiting their Aunt Barb. Carrie and Jo was both a couple of years younger than Dee and Jamie, but were in between Jamie and Tanya so our kids loved spending time together as much as my sister and I did.

Any free time we had we spent together as a family doing something with our kids. John was a drinker. I never left my kids with him, but he was never there much to begin with since he spent most of his time in bars. When she was working, John would plop himself on a barstool and drink up her tips. I never liked him from the moment I met him.

I knew their marriage wasn't going to survive because my sister would only put up with so much before she booted him right out the front door. She was a very, headstrong girl that wouldn't take his guff. John was a policeman on the Indian Reservation in Shelton and a boozer on top of it. I only had hoped she would get rid of him sooner than later, because I certainly was not at all impressed with him. He was rude and obnoxious, and treated Barb like a slave. She deserved much better than John. After all we went through growing up we didn't deserve men to treat us poorly too.

I loved my jobs and the kids got to talk to their Dad on the phone when he decided to call. We loved where we lived. The only thing I wish I had, was a fenced yard for the kids to play in.

The Jacobs told me they had a 2400 sq. ft. house that would be available in eight weeks and it came with a huge cyclone fenced in grass yard so the kids would be able to go out and play in a yard without me worrying about them chasing a ball out in the street. The rent was Five hundred dollars a month because it was a huge house. With the good tips, I was making and with both paychecks I was doing very well. I had paid off my furniture and had money saved up from my tips.

Everything was going very well except my nightmares were on the increase again. I felt as though stress or life changing situations make them return. They seem to come and go, and I couldn't get good rest the nights that I had to deal with them. It had to be from all the stress I experienced as a child because every day was an uncertainty. I never knew when to duck.

Some of the nightmares pertain to the "hole" in the orphanage. I could not get out of the hole and kept trying to get away from the priests who were chasing me. I kept wondering why these nightmares continued and didn't let up even when I moved away from Helena, and the Church. I had to try and forget the past if I could. This disturbance continued for years on end.

I thought maybe Jim might want his freedom, and I wouldn't hold him back if that was the case. I held back on certain sexual activities that I did not approve of. It made me wonder if that was my problem with Jim. It was impossible for me to tell him what I was forced to do as a child and why I detested those sexual activities now.

I checked on the kids at night when I got home. I hated the fact that I did not get to spend time with them let alone quality. I kissed them goodnight when I came home, but they were deep in sleep, unaware of their kisses from mommy. It would be nice to have just one job and have my evenings and bedtime with my children. Michael was growing quickly and his dad was missing out on all the cute baby stages. Jim was drawing unemployment and hadn't sent any money to help with the kids.

He had to make the payment on the trailer and keep the booze coming. I kept hoping he would see the light and realize what he was missing.

While bartending I met a guy who was buddies with Jim years ago. Jack McDonald told me all about going to high school with Jim and how they had all ran in the same group. When he heard someone call me Mrs. Kuhl he asked where I was from. When he found out I was married to one of his childhood best friends he always would ask if Jim was coming to see his children.

On a particular day when Jim called to talk to the kids, I mentioned to him his buddy Jack said to say hello. He told me he guessed he would have to see him when he comes to see the kids and me.

"When do you plan on doing this," I asked him since this was all news to me. Evidently, he already told the girl's he would come.

I told Jim that wouldn't work for me. I'd already told his sisters that I would come to Spokane at Christmas on the bus. "You just can't come whenever you want to show up, and certainly you go through me first. We'll need to plan. I made arrangements with my jobs to take four days off so the kids could go see their dad. When I came back I would get to work on the floor at the hospital since I passed the State Boards.

The kids and I were on the way to Spokane early in the morning and their Jim and his sister Lucy picked us up from the station. When the kids got off the bus they went running into their dad's arms with tears in their eyes. They hugged one by one; Jim asked to hug me and I let him.

I was still so angry with him for putting us in this predicament. I was working my ass off to support our four children.

The girls went shopping for Christmas presents with Lucy and Francie so they could buy gifts for everyone. I gave them each fifty dollars to spend. I kept Michael at home with us. Jim begged me to give him another chance. I told him, I couldn't trust him yet. I did not want to lie to our kids to cover his drinking habits with his buddies. I would never go back to him if we lived in Helena.

Our time together opened up discussion about any future we might have together, but I stood my ground where his behavior was concerned. I would never be without a car for the rest of my life. "I will never depend on a man's trust. You have to earn that back." I said fervently.

"I made it clear to the kids that you and I were disagreeing and fighting way too much. Then I couldn't believe you left me stranded without a car to get around. When you finally decide we are more important than your partying and drinking, I will consider coming back to you. Until then, things will stay the same and I will stay in Olympia."

His sister Francie told me that she wanted us to work things out for the sake of the children. I told her I had already talked to Jim about what he had to do to get us to come back to him. She didn't know the circumstances until I told her what happened. She then told Jim if you want your family you will have to fight for them. He would be starting a job in Wheatland, Wyoming in May, which was still five months away. He wanted us to move back to Helena before he started the job

I told him I had some thinking to do and I wasn't ready to commit to a relationship with my husband until I knew the children and I were the most important part of his life.

We had a very nice Christmas. I finally got to know my sisters-in-law and found out that they were a close-knit family. Jim's brothers showed up the second day we were there. Rich and Art came together and Pi drove over from Helena. I finally felt like I fit in somewhere with this family.

The girls had a blast down in the recreation room visiting and dancing with their uncles and cousins. It was wonderful to finally do something with members of Jim's family and help Lucy and Francie with Christmas dinner. The kids and I absolutely enjoyed ourselves and we hated saying goodbye to everyone. We would come back next year regardless of what our situation turned out to be.

When we were on the bus going back home the kids were unhappy leaving their dad. I was too and didn't want to admit it to myself. I had wished Jim would have tried harder, but I honestly didn't think he was ready to give it his all and make an honest commitment to us.

It was now May and I finally received the call from Jim that he was coming for a visit and wanted to stay two weeks before he would be taking the job in Wheatland. Jack his buddy that lived on Federal Way in Seattle would pick him up at SeaTac.

I had to work while Jim was here. Jack brought him to Lee's after his plane came in at midnight. I was still working. I had gotten to know Jack from his visits to the lounge. He told me about his family. His wife left him because of his drinking. He could identify with our problems. When Jim showed up he was dressed neatly and looked like he had taken better care of himself. He told the girls we were going to be a family again and wouldn't let anything get in the way of it ever again. He promised he would think of his family first and that we would start over again, and mend what was taken apart.

The entire two weeks Jim's visit was a healing process for our marriage. My employer at Lee's was understanding and told me to take the time off while Jim was here. She was hoping for the sake of the children that we would get our family back on track and repair the damage that had taken place. She had Barb fill in for me while I took the time off. She trained Barb for my position if I should leave. On my days off on Sundays, she would ask me to bring the kids in for lunch and treated them with whatever they wanted on the menu. She adored my children and said how well behaved they were when they came to eat with their Daddy. She thought that he wanted to fight for the right to be with his family again.

She told Jim I was one of her best employees, and was like family to her. She hoped things would work out for him. You have to win her back and on her terms since you are the one who messed up. Jim thanked her for taking such good care of me, and the kids.

I gave her notice; I would be leaving in a week. Barb would take my place. I also let Barb and the hospital know I was going back to Montana with Jim. Jim went back to Helena and got an apartment for us until we could find a house. Our friends helped once again to load the U-Haul. Wesley and his wife Vicki came to the rescue and drove us back to Helena since Jim left for work in Wyoming.

Jim would be working in Wyoming until the job was done. He wouldn't be able to come home for weekends, as it was too long of a drive. They said absence makes the heart grow fonder but this was ridiculously true for the kids and me.

Bill asked me to work for him again. He made me an offer I couldn't refuse since I wanted to have days with my kids for the summer months. I would be working nights. My car broke down, so I sold it and put the money I saved, and bought a Thunderbird, which was a very nice car and safe for the girls and Michael. I was making good money with the card room and putting money aside for a deposit and rent on a four bedroom house that would be available the first of December. I was hoping Jim would be off work to help. My hoping helped, but in a bad way.

The men in Wyoming went on a strike and the Montana guys followed suit. They had to back up the boilermakers from Wyoming; it was a Wildcat Strike. No unemployment benefits for the guys who walk off the job; boilermakers support one another so everyone left the job. Jim came home and the kids were thrilled to death. They finally would get to spend time with their dad. Once again we would be moving.

I was thrilled Jim had all the guys to help us move because the weather was below freezing. It was a miserable move. I showed our appreciation by having everyone over for a big dinner after I was unpacked.

The house was next to my childhood friend Diane's house. It brought back a lot of memories that were good

377

and bad. Now I had my family and it didn't seem to matter to me.

Jim finally started getting his unemployment until work became available. Colstrip wasn't hiring yet for Unit Three. We heard they were putting in a new high school and new paved streets because there were so many Montana Power employees. They finally had Units One and Two going. In the meantime there wasn't any work because of winter.

It was nice having Jim home and we had been really bonding as a family and in love with one another again. I had never stopped loving my husband but I had lost respect for him when he picked friends over family. He admitted that he could never say "Sorry" enough.

He watched the kids during the night when I had to work and was home with them all day long. Jay and Diana came out to the house visiting together. It was wonderful that she had accepted our marriage. I couldn't be more grateful. Diane was so beautiful and resembled her sisters. Our girls were quite a bit younger than Diane but they looked up to her. They always adored Jay because he lived with us and shared our lives when we lived in Colstrip. Jay always had time for the kids when he came home from work, taking them skating and sledding and finding time to entertain them.

Things were going so smoothly. It was the end of February. Lucy called Jim. I handed him the phone and within seconds Jim broke down in tears. He couldn't talk for a few moments. When he regained his composure, I asked what was wrong. His brother Art had a heart attack on the Capitol steps in Washington D.C. He had walked to work in a blizzard, and was going up the steps when suddenly he fell, grabbing his chest. He was in cardiac arrest. The guards at the Capitol applied CPR while waiting for the ambulance. The ambulance didn't get Art to the hospital in time because of the blizzard. He died in route to the hospital.

Art was Assistant Secretary to the United States Senate when he passed away in 1979 under President Carter's Administration. He was an attorney, who worked with the Committee of Foreign Relations before being appointed to his new position as Assistant Secretary. Art was fifty-four years old when he passed away on February 19, 1979. He gave thirty years of his life working in Washington D.C. The Government honored him in many ways. He was given a funeral in Washington D. C. then was brought home to Helena for another funeral in the Cathedral. (It was the first time I had been back in the church since my abuse.) Many dignitaries from all over the country including people he worked with in the nation's Capital, Mike Mansfield and Lee Metcalf, Montana's U.S. Senators, Governor Tom Judge, and many Montana legislators. Art was not only very successful with his work. But, his immediate family loved him dearly.

After the burial service, we hosted the dignitaries and friends in our home. Once the house began to thin out somewhat, Dorie, Jim's ex-wife stopped by our home. She was very upset. She had just lost her father, Sam who was Jay and Diana's grandfather. He had passed away from a heart attack the same day we buried Art. Diana and Jay suffered yet another loss and my heart went out to my husband's ex-wife and to my stepchildren. It was a horrible month for our families.

CHAPTER FORTY

On Memorial Day weekend, Jim and I decided to invite our friends to the house for a spring get together and a barbeque. While Jim and Skip had the barbeque going, the children were in the back yard playing. Unbeknownst to us, the older girls had dared Tanya to walk on a rope that was off of the ground on our cement patio in the back yard. The next thing I knew my little girl was screaming as she tried climbing the brick stairs. I saw Tanya with her arm dangling down crying. She knew she had a broken arm and her shoulder could have been too.

I asked Jim to call the hospital so they knew we were on our way. They met us at the door of the emergency room and carefully placed her on a gurney as she was crying in pain. They gave her pain medication since they knew she had a break or more. They took her to X-ray, not only did she break her Humorous bone in her arm she had also cracked her scapula. She would be in her cast for the summer and had to play carefully.

We had received monies from Art's insurance. Jim had made a promise to me that when we could afford to, we would put a down payment on the house. Jim and I decided to purchase an 18' by 80' modular home with wood siding and move from Helena to Missoula. We had gone to the plant in Belgrade where they were built, and ordered ours custom made, since we would have to live in it for quite some time until Jim quit the construction business.

We bought brand new furniture for the entire house keeping a few of our old things. The company notified us that the house would be set up and on blocks before we arrived in Missoula. It was a beautiful home for us. No more tiny trailers for us. We lived on Big Flat Road in a large court with amazing neighbors who I still stay in touch with today.

Jim was working a turnaround in Frenchtown for six weeks. Then he and Louie would be leaving for Columbia Falls, to work at the aluminum plant for a few months.

We were so fortunate that Jay came and visited us on his days off from the railroad. When the job had finished up in Colstrip, he took a job with Great Northern as a switchman and a brakeman. He loved that job and he was earning retirement. Diana was back in Florida and we haven't heard much from her except on birthdays and Christmas cards. I was working part time at St. Patrick's, bowling on a bowling league, and having a wonderful summer with the kids.

Our camping trips were always fun for the kids and the adults alike. It was work for me, but it was the kind of work I didn't mind because I did get to enjoy myself after getting the camp cleaned up. Jay and Jolene camped with us a couple of nights and gave the kids rides on Jay's motorcycle.

Once we were back in Missoula Jim had to pack and say his goodbyes. He and Louie left for Columbia Falls to start the job at the aluminum plant. They would be working six days and twelve hour shifts. Jim loved this job, as it brought in good earnings and money to put away for savings. When one worked construction jobs, and had large families, they needed to make sure and save for a rainy day, in case there wasn't work for a while.

He would be in Columbia Falls until the middle of November, and then would not have work until the January he'd return to Colstrip to finish work on Unit Two. When the company starts Units three and four, we would be moving back to Colstrip.

We had my parents and Jay over for Thanksgiving dinner. Jay told us he would have to have Christmas with his mother in Helena. His Mother was having Thanksgiving with her mother and sisters. He told her he wanted to have a holiday with his dad and his family. Dorie agreed since he would be with them for Christmas. She understood that Jay was very close to his dad. We had a wonderful Thanksgiving. This was the first time my parents had seen our new house in Missoula.

The worst day of our lives took place on December 14, 1982. We were on an eight party phone line and someone had taken their phone off the hook and left the rest of us without a phone. At seven in the morning when the kids were getting ready for school, we heard a knock on the door. There was a highway patrolman who asked to speak to Jim. I went to the bedroom and told Jim. He quickly dressed and came out to talk to the officer. The patrolman told us Jay was dead. My husband and I collapsed together to the floor. The officer explained to us that family tried to call us in the early morning hours.

At 3:30 in the morning, Jay was shot dead in his bed by a police officer. An investigation was going on as the patrolman spoke with us. We had to call Dorie to get the details. Her family was with her at the time we called and told us Dorie was in shock. They asked if we could come over right away to help. Judy, my friend and neighbor stepped in to take care of the kids for us. I would drive to Helena since Jim was in such a bad way. I told Judy I would come back to Missoula tomorrow after getting Jim over to Helena. She told me to stay with Jim until after the funeral, she and her daughter Sherry would take care of the kids.

The shooting made the front page of the newspaper because of the officer using force on a young man sleeping in his bed with three other officers there. We would have to go back to Helena in a few weeks after Jay's funeral. There would be a coroner's inquest and all the legal technicalities that would take place because of it.

The ballistics showed that Jay was shot in the neck and 12 inches away in the shoulder. The officer was found guilty of negligence to his duties and was given a ten-day suspension. It was an outrage! We were angry and devastated to lose our twenty-two year old son Jay.

Our lives were never the same because of the event that took place that horrible day. My husband was forced to live with the loss of his son. Jim had also lost his brother. Diana had lost her brother and grandfather within months of each other. Jim was still getting over the loss of his mother three years earlier. Diana suffered immensely since she and Jay were very close. Dee, Jamie and Tanya understood they would never get to have their brother around anymore. Michael on the other hand was too young to understand what had happened and why daddy cried a lot. Knowing that Jay was in heaven, the girls were able to deal with his loss.

We did not feel like celebrating Christmas that year, but we had to for the little ones sake. I did not cook a Christmas dinner because it was not a year for celebrating. We lost three wonderful people this year. My heart ached for the first time ever for my husband's ex-wife. It took a couple of weeks for Jim to get up and go on.

Jim would be working in Colstrip and Missoula the next two years. Then he would be working another job in Wisconsin in between both of these jobs on a turnaround that lasted several weeks. When he came back from Wisconsin, he brought back a huge pumpkin that took up a large part in the back of the truck. Our neighbor Bill came out to help get in onto our steps by the house. I told him the kids won't be able to cut the tough skin on this pumpkin and he told them he would get it started for them. Jim finally realized he was stuck carving it himself. Flocks of people took pictures of this monstrosity of a pumpkin on Halloween night. We shared the information that it had come from Wisconsin and weighed fifty-eight pounds.

Jim would get two weeks off before he started the job in Missoula. He would be working at Stone Container as the company changed the name from Champion Industries. The kids loved when Dad had some time off between jobs because it meant more quality time for them with their dad home.

Meanwhile, I was having migraines three and four times a month and had to go on medications to help control them. Often, they couldn't be controlled so I would take stimulates and narcotics for the pain. Sometimes it was so bad I almost wanted to die to make it go away.

I was never suicidal like my sisters had become. I told the doctor about my stress and my nightmares that I had since childhood. He suggested I talk to a therapist to help with these issues. I couldn't bring myself to talk about that horrible embarrassing part of my life. The awful smell of the priests that won't dissipate and lingers, left such a distinctive memory in my mind that I could not erase it. Sometimes I felt useless, ineffectual and dulled because of the nightmares.

I found out I was once again pregnant and told Jim we were going to have another baby. We were hoping we would have another baby boy. My headaches were still happening through the first trimester of the pregnancy, but I wasn't able to take medications now.

Jim was at work and his friend Tom, who was staying with our family, took me to the emergency room because I was vomiting violently and couldn't stop. In the ER they gave me Compazine and Demerol for the pain. Finally, things were going smoothly until we met my parents in Seeley Lake to go on a family camping trip a few months later. My sister Barb and her family, my parents, Jim and I and our family were meeting for a mini-reunion. I was six months pregnant and looking forward to sharing our news. It was pouring rain the first night we arrived. The second night I was not feeling well. Jim told me to lie in the tent and see if I would feel better. I could not get comfortable laying on the blown-up mattress and sleeping bag. Early in the morning I began to bleed. She called Medical Center in Seeley Lake and they said they would call for an ambulance. We were fifty miles from Missoula. Jim told them I would bleed to death by then. Jim did not wait for an ambulance and headed out at a high rate of speed.

By the time we arrived at the hospital, I was covered in blood and had bled so profusely they started transfusions and took me to surgery. I was there for three hours. When I awoke I asked about my baby and they told me I had lost my child.

I went into depression for a few weeks blaming myself and did not want to talk to anyone. I thought it was my fault and I was once again being punished. That was when my doctor stepped in and said I had to talk to a professional about issues I had with myself. I didn't want to share my childhood with anybody especially the sexual abuse that had happened at the orphanage. I felt the sexual content would damage my character. I couldn't say what happened at the school and the abuse from home because of the sheer embarrassment. I felt they could do nothing to help me and I wasn't on board to share this kind of information with anyone, including a professional. I knew I was having problems. I would go on shopping sprees, try to hide things I bought and most of all I would outright lie to my husband about my spending habits.

Jim would always ask me why I felt the need to have so much of one item or why I had to keep our cupboards full with food when some of it was expired. I bought things I knew I wouldn't use and would just sit on the shelf. I always felt I had to give stuff away then turn around and buy something new to replace it. I couldn't understand why I felt the need and the urge to do the things I did.

Eventually it would get much worse. That was why I should have listened to my doctor, and got the help I needed. I brought a lot of my stress into my life by hiding the things that happened to me as a child and blaming myself for the abuses. I would convince myself that I was being punished because I was a bad little girl. I didn't know if I acted it out because I was deprived of these things as a child. I felt I wasn't wanted or needed as a child by my own mother.

I was still trying to figure it out. I was not a hoarder, as I had to have everything in its place, neat and tidy. That

385

was another issue that drove my family crazy and sometimes myself. My Obsessive Compulsory Disorder I would have to figure out on my own. I prayed the headaches go away for now. I had faced the reality that we did not have the money for me to be spending. I wanted my dead baby, but that wasn't going to happen.

The doctor told Jim he would have to get a vasectomy so I wouldn't go through another pregnancy. I felt guilty about him doing it.

We were ready to move to Colstrip and hopefully to better situations than we had gone through these last few years. The move to Colstrip alleviated some stress issues. Hopefully, my spirits would pick up after losing the baby, everyone was hopeful.

It had only been six weeks and I was still having headaches and my stress level had increased tremendously because of the move. My great grandmother had passed away and I had to drive to Helena and back, in the same day. She was such a lovely and special grandmother and did so much for us when we were little and in our preteens. She lived just shy of one hundred years by eight days. My dad was glad I made the trip knowing I was in the middle of a move. I told him there was no way I would not come to granny's funeral. She would be missed by all of us.

We had the summer months to get everything done and we would take plenty of time for camping on weekends, barbeques with neighbors. I found a job substituting in the school system. I could not believe how big Colstrip had grown with all the paved roads, grocery store, Pizza Hut, bowling alley, fast food and they were in the beginning of a new phase for a new high school not far from our house.

We had a lot of our friends here and we would be socializing together on weekends once again. Jim had hoped this would bring me out of my seclusion and depression over the loss of our child. The boilermakers always enjoyed throwing social events including a softball team that Jim loved playing for. He played the first summer we were back. The kids enjoyed watching their dad. On some weekends, we would hold pinochle parties and take turns hosting the parties. I was the only nondrinker at this time.

I stayed home and started teaching macramé classes and ordered supplies. Jim and Louie built three stands that would hold five hangers each for the students to work on. I put a sign in the grocery store and filled up with students immediately. I taught them how to make tables and plant hangers. It was very fruitful and paid very well. I had fourteen students and our living room was large enough to hold them. Jim had to build me two more stands to accompany the students.

The first part of August, I received a call from the school to come in for an interview for substitute teaching and was hired a week later. I told my students that I would be teaching the macramé classes twice a week at the high school for adult educational classes in the evenings now since I was teaching during the day. I was called for substituting quite often with the four schools. Substitutes were paid a flat fee, which was more than the teachers were getting. It suited me just fine. I would be called at least three or four times a week and then I had the adult classes twice a week, enough to keep me busy and not get bored. My headaches had subsided somewhat and that was due to less stress in my life.

I took a flagging position for a construction company for the summer months. The company was widening the Colstrip road to Forsythe. It paid very well, but you were on your feet for the entire day (except lunch) and in the heat. We had two-way radios for stopping traffic and then letting them resume. It was a tedious job, but when you get your paycheck it was well worth it. They let us wear short sleeves and I would get a great tan on my arms, we wore bright orange vests and sometimes had to watch people who drove recklessly and did not follow our signs and directions.

Jim and I decided we would drive to Spokane for Christmas and he would take two weeks off for the holidays. Lucy was thrilled we would be there for a week withthe entire family. This year was going to be hard since it was the first Christmas without Art or Jay. I was not a good traveler with long distances and especially winter months. I was praying that we would have decent weather conditions for driving.

We would be going over four passes traveling to Spokane and that was my worst fear. It was snowing, and we had a Chrysler Cordoba with snow tires. I wasn't concerned about the highways because we did have the snow tires, I was concerned about the passes and my fears were validated when we started sliding going up Bozeman Pass and then Pipestone into Butte. We followed the sanding truck on Pipestone Pass. Several cars were off the road. As we came into Butte there was an awful accident. When we hit Deer Lodge, the roads seemed to clear up somewhat and we hoped that it would stay that way. We hit snow at Lookout Pass. Jim had to slow down because of the truckers. Coming off of Lookout and going into Wallace, Jim hit a patch of ice and we slid so bad going across a bridge that I thought we were going to end up in a ditch, but Jim pulled us away from that disaster. We drove over the 4th of July Pass without any incidents and arrived in Spokane several hours late. I told Lucy, I knew God truly was watching over us through the entire trip. The brothers, Rich, Dick and Pi were arriving the next day; Laura and her family were already at their hotel and had to drive in bad weather from Missoula. We had driven seven hundred miles in thirteen hours with bad roads to boot.

Lucy said how hard it was going to be without Art and Jay this Christmas. I told her that Jim couldn't even talk about Jay without crying. I asked her if she could tell the others not to mention Jay unless Jim did. The next morning the house was filled with kids chattering and laughter in their Aunt Lucy's kitchen. Lucy loved the sound of children and she was at their beckon call. She made them her famous light pancakes, sausage, bacon, eggs and toast. It was nice to sit at the table with my hubby's family listening to them exchange memories of their youth. They always made you feel so comfortable in their home. We pulled two tables together so the kids could be included with the adults for dinner and it was a very happy occasion for the family to be together once again for the holidays. The kids were excited; it was Christmas Eve and that Santa.

We always started the festivities early afternoon with snacking on goodies and watching the kids with all of their new gifts. We always had wonderful Christmas memories with my in-laws and actually hated the thought of leaving for home when it was all over.

The drive back to Colstrip wasn't any better than when we came over to Spokane. The roads were icy except for the passes. They had those sanded and were still sanding them as we came over. We were thankful we made it back home safely and the kids would have a couple days to rest before they would return to school. Life would return back to normal.

I told Lucy I quit drinking any kind of alcohol years ago because of my migraines. I couldn't share my nightmares that had returned in force. I tried my usual technique of dealing with them, which was to pretend like they weren't happening at all. I continued to live in my own silent hell.

My Mother never made the effort to get close enough to my children where my dad put forth the effort hugging them and smiling with pride of who they were and would engage with conversation. My mother wouldn't sit and hold a conversation with them at all. That was why I was relieved that my in-laws showed our children how much they were loved and was why I felt it was so important for us to travel that far for our holidays.

My grandmother in California called and told us grandpa had died. I told her I would come to be with her and that I would catch a flight out of Billings. She told me she was not having a service for grandpa per his request and that she was fine and for me to remain home with my family. She was at my Uncle Jim's house and she did not need anyone to take care of her. My grandmother was a very headstrong person and what she said, she meant. I told her if she needed anything to please call me and I would be right there since the kids were older and Jim was home shortly after they came home from school. I was heartbroken that my wonderful grandpa was no longer with us, and I would never see him again. He had a heart attack and was gone quickly. It was hard to bear.

Jim was playing softball again that summer and we spent quite a bit of time at the baseball field on weekends. I was still teaching macramé during the week. The kids were out doing their thing. It was almost like a ritual each and every day during the weeks of summer that the guys had a few beers before dinner. There really wasn't much for kids to do in Colstrip during the summer months except go to the park and swim at the pool.

CHAPTER FORTY-ONE

Our summer came to an abrupt halt. I received a phone call from Combustion Engineering that my husband had just been taken by ambulance to the clinic and they were preparing to take him to Billings. There had been a terrible accident at work. I asked them what had happened and his reply was it was a serious accident from a fall. His reply to me was my husband wanted me to come to Billings where they were transporting him by ambulance. I called the clinic to check on Jim's condition. They were getting him stabilized and he was just leaving to be transported to Billings. She told me I would have to find out more in Billings.

I called Vicki to ask her if she could come over and watch the kids. I explained the situation to her telling her they said it was serious. I got Tanya and Michael home. Vicki would tell Dee and Jamie why I had to go to Billings. I would let everyone know what was happening, once I was there.

I drove ninety miles per hour trying to catch up with the ambulance, which I knew was ridiculous, but I did not know the severity of my husband's injuries, and I was sick to my stomach trying to find the ambulance. I finally caught up with it twelve miles out of Billings. I followed the ambulance right through the red lights and kept up with them, because I didn't know which hospital they were taking him to. He was taken to St. Vincent's Hospital and as they opened the ambulance doors, my husbands shattered shoulder and arm were completely black and swollen terribly. He had a swollen neck and bruising, and was in horrible pain.

The surgeon was standing by and they rushed him into surgery. He was in surgery for three hours.

The date of his injury was August, Friday the 13th and he was injured at 4:20 with only ten minutes before the whistle blew for the job to be over. All of these thoughts had been running through my head. I couldn't sit still as I thought how bad he looked when I saw him coming out of the ambulance. The nurses told me to try and relax as he was stable and would be down in an hour or more. Jim was having a hard time coming out of the anesthetic. The doctor told me Jim had a shattered shoulder, which was stapled up, and broken a humorous(they had to place a rod in to repair the bone), and a fractured scapula. His injuries would require several months of healing and would need the bandages from the surgery changed and cleaned twice a day to prevent infection. He would have to stay in the hospital for a short period and will have a tough go for the ride home. They would medicate him for that. I should have someone there at our home to help him into the house that could handle his weight in case he was dizzy.

I called the kids to let them know their dad had an accident and they had to do surgery and he would be home in a few days. Vicki and Bonnie would take care of the children. I asked Bonnie if she would get Skip and Louie to help Jim from the car to his bed when we did get home. I would call and let them know when we were leaving the hospital so they could be prepared. I thanked them for being such good friends and being there for us.

Everyone was concerned because some of the guys saw him fall and hit the railroad track from the top of the semi-truck. A come-along had snapped and broken when he was on top of the truck helping unload cement sections for the stacks to the power plants. What was really a strange coincidence, was our daughter Tanya broke the same bone and cracked her scapula when she had her accident.

Jim was home in bed. The recovery was slow. I would be taking care of him for several months. I had to let the school know that Jim had an accident, and I would be caring for him. Jim would have to go through therapy sometime in November or December. They did have a physical therapist at the clinic in Colstrip, so we didn't have to drive to Billings.

His doctor told him he would be out of commission for quite a while in terms of work. He would be on worker's compensation until he could return to work. The months dragged for me; I was taking care of Jim and getting kids off to school so I had plenty to keep me busy. Jim did have guys coming to visit with him, which lifted his spirits.

We tried to make our Christmas as cheery as possible considering we were living on a budget so we wouldn't touch our savings unless we needed to. The kids understood because their dad wasn't able to work, and Mom had to take care of him. After Christmas, Jim had to have surgery to remove his rod. He began his physical therapy soon after that. After he had his staples removed he had arthritis set in his shoulder. Jim's therapy had gone slowly and the doctors would not release him for work. We decided that we would like to take the kids camping at Lodge Grass just to get away from the house and Colstrip for a week.

Jim wanted to teach Michael to fish and the girls already love fishing from previous camping outings. They were very excited about the trip, which was, a couple hours away. As soon as we arrived the tent went up, and the kids were already finding things to do. Dee found a huge spider with babies on her back in her white sac and decided to put a fork between the spider and the sac not knowing there were babies attached. She screamed as hundreds of tiny spiders were all over the place including the tent. I told Dee that wasn't too smart right next to the tent and now she had to sleep with the spiders. That night, we had field mice running everywhere including towards the tent, so between mice and spiders we were off to a bad start. It was nice to see the kids had so much freedom up here as we were the only campers in sight and right next to the reservoir. We did catch fish and ate them for dinner and sat in chairs around the campfire Jim had built. We roasted marshmallows and the kids made their S'more's. When it was time to get into the tent, I of course took a flashlight making sure we didn't have any visitors waiting for us in the tent. I told the kids the coast was clear and they made me shine the light all over the tent so they could see for themselves. I don't think they realized how tiny the spiders were they couldn't see them. I think everyone was ready to go home after a week of camping. The kids were bored and missed their friends and jobs.

CHAPTER FORTY-TWO

It was the end of June and Jim's buddies wanted him to take a fishing trip up to Lolo and stay at the Lumberjack with our friends Tom and Patty. I told Jim to go ahead and go with them and we would stay home because I had a dental appointment and a doctor's checkup in Billings on Friday and wanted to take the kids school shopping for a few things while we were there. He would only be gone for ten days and that would also give me a break having him around all the time.

Jim and Louie left on a Wednesday and I had my appointment on Friday. I got the kids up early for breakfast and we left by 7:00 to make my appointment in Billings on time. After my appointments we ate lunch and headed for the mall to shop. We had to take our dog Ziggy with us because our neighbors were gone. We could take him for several walks to get him out of the car. At the mall I would stay out and walk the dog as long as the girls promised to stay together. The girls were old enough to shop for what they wanted, and they had their own money. When Dee and Jamie were done they would stay with Ziggy, and I would take Tanya and Michael shopping. It was a win, win situation with the dog, and the girls were happy they didn't have to listen to my choices for clothing. We had a delightful afternoon with everyone buying what they wanted and each of them happy with their choices.

I was very tired and excited that we were close to home when I saw the two tall stacks from the power plants from a distance away. As we drove down to our house something strange was in our front yard with tarps covering them. I didn't even get in our driveway when I realized it was furniture from our living room. I thought we were being robbed. I jumped out of the car not knowing what in the world was going on at our house. The kids were yelling at me not to go in the house for fear of robbers. I ran up the front steps and the kids were yelling no Mom don't go in there. I stopped in my tracks at the front door, because there was a huge note on the door. My neighbor Vicki who had just returned home, "Wanda, don't go in there yet, wait for me." From the outside of the house, it looked fine, but when she opened the door I screamed and fell to my knees.

The entire interior of the house was burned from front to the back. The few pieces of furniture in the front yard were all the firemen could save. When I finally calmed down, Vicki gave me the number the firemen had left for me to call when I arrived home. They said it was not safe for me to walk through the house and don't go through or touch anything until the Fire Marshall comes first thing in the morning to find out what started the fire and to make it safe enough to see what can be saved.

I had no way of calling Jim. They didn't have phone service at the Lumberjack. After calling the fire department for me, Vicki said Missoula County would send a deputy up to the Lumberjack to let my husband know what was going on and he was needed at home immediately. He needed to call first and was given Vicki's phone number. The deputy found them fishing up Lolo Creek. Once he heard the news he called Vicki's house to let me know he and Louie were coming back immediately.

Vicki's husband had a twenty-six foot travel trailer. He pulled it in front of their house for us to stay in until we could figure out what to do. I was a total mess. Our kids were upset over losing their home as much as I was. They were so thankful we didn't leave Ziggy home. We couldn't have left him alone for twelve hours anyway. That would have been cruel and he would have torn the house up.

The Fire Marshall showed up first thing in the morning to start his investigation. He asked me if anything had ever been a problem in our house. I told him it was only three years old and all the appliances were new. I never had problems with anything. He told me he would come back to the camper trailer after his investigation was over.

Jim showed up about ten, a couple of hours after the Marshall started his work. He could tell the kids and I had been crying a lot because of all the red eyes. He told me to be thankful that we were not in the house sleeping when the fire started. Jim said they could always pinpoint the fire and about what time it started. About four in the afternoon the Fire Marshall came over to take Jim and I to the house to show us what had started the fire.

It was our toaster. The wiring to the toaster had shorted out and he showed us how badly burned the plug cover was and the wiring to the toaster was fried black. It was faulty wiring to the toaster and it started in the morning because the fire department had the call at 8:50am. He figured it started after eight. He was thankful we were not at home.

There really wasn't much to save except a few things from the kid's bedrooms and a few things in ours. Everything else was destroyed. Jim and I only had the clothes on our backs. The kids were lucky to have bought themselves some new clothes to change into.

On Tuesday after the guys got off work two of them from Jim's company came to talk to us. They had brought over two thousand dollars that all of the guys pitched in for donations to help us get food and clothing. They knew we had to wait at least two weeks before our insurance company was going to cover us. We couldn't believe the generosity that was shown to us by everyone.

Three days later we received a phone call from Hal and Cathy who were very good friends from Billings. Hal was working in Boston for three months on a job. Their house in Colstrip was vacant at the time, and Hal told Jim he heard what had happened to our house from Skip and Louie. To our surprise they offered us to live in their house in Colstrip.

They thought the house was better off with someone to take care of it. Jim thanked Hal and told him we would only need to stay in Colstrip two more weeks until the insurance was taken care. Then, we planned to move to Lolo since his next job would be in Frenchtown just out of Missoula.

With the insurance taken care of, I cleaned and dusted the house and locked everything up, and we were on our way. The sad thing was leaving all of our dear friends behind, and knowing we were homeless until we would find a house in Lolo, our chosen area in Missoula.

CHAPTER FORTY-THREE

We would stay with Tom and Patty in their log house at the *Lumberjack*. We had a camper on the back of our truck where Jim and I slept. The girls and Mike would sleep in the house with Patty's two kids. Jim told me to think of it like camping.

The first thing I did was go house hunting. I found a few houses to look at the first day. The first house on the list was the home I wanted. It was on a little over an acre and overlooked the Bitterroot Valley. It was up a steep hill that I was a little concerned about for winter driving for Montana winters, but I was told it was well sanded.

I was excited for this double story house built into the mountain. It had an open floor plan. There were fireplaces upstairs and downstairs. The kids knew this meant we would be making trips into the woods for firewood and they enjoyed doing that except for Dee and Jamie since they were older and had better things to do.

I was excited to tell Jim I had found the perfect home for us. I made an appointment for us to see the house together the next day and Jim loved the house as much as I did. This was going to be a lot of upkeep he told me plus who was going to do all of the landscaping in the back yard and finish off the two bedrooms in the back that were partially finished.

We told the realtor we would like to buy it but we had to come in at full price because there was another offer on it. We would not be able to move in for thirty days until closing and that meant another month of camping in the truck. We didn't realize that insurance companies were responsible for our housing up to hundred percent until everything was settled. We found out after the fact.

We could have stayed at a motel but the kids loved staying at Tom and Patty's. To be sure we weren't a burden, Jim did some projects for them, and I bartended in return for all that they did for us. Our kids became very close friends and would end up going to high school with them when they were older.

We were so happy when closing day came. I'd heard of people removing things from a house after a walk through but never thought it would happen to us. The seller stripped the house. He removed the garage door opener, the mirrors attached to the bathroom walls and any fixtures he could. We had to dump more money in the house than we bargained for. We had already bought and signed the papers. Apparently, he was going through a nasty divorce and was angry with his ex-wife making him sell the home. Now I understood why she divorced the man.

I went to furniture stores and bought new furnishings and let the girls pick out their bedroom sets. It was overwhelming; I had to start from scratch. I lost everything including all of my children's baby pictures and sentimental things I had collected over the years. We learned to have a firebox for birth certificates and important documents. We did not have one, and lost all of our important papers.

I wanted to find a job so I would have extra income since Jim was still not allowed to go back to work. The doctor's would not release him until his shoulder was strong enough for the type of work he did. At least he still was on worker's comp.

I found a job with Hospice and enjoyed the work. I was a traveling nurse and did medications and checked the patient's progress. The job in due time became tedious with long hours since they were understaffed. I was paid mileage and a good salary. Jim was home still recovering. The kids had to depend on their dad until I came home. Dee was a great cook and helped her dad out with meals.

I was extremely lucky to have such a good daughter that helped me out when it came to babysitting and helping keep the house up and stay on the honor roll. I really appreciate all that my daughter went through, and in my lifetime I will never be able to thank her enough for helping me with the kids and other responsibilities that was laid upon her. It was unfair how much responsibility was put on the oldest child in many households when there were several children, but my Dee, went above and beyond in our eyes.

We were enjoying Pi, Jim's brother visiting us. He would drive over from Helena just to spend the day with us. Living in Lolo put us close enough to visit friends in Helena. We were also close enough to Jim's family in Spokane that we made more frequent trips to spend time with Lucy and Vern during summer vacations and Christmas holidays.

One Christmas, my sisters-in-law wanted me to go to Christmas Mass with them. They knew I had grown up Catholic but didn't know I was a Christian attending a Christian church. I politely made it clear I do not practice Catholicism.

Going to a Catholic mass made all the ugliness in my life come back and made me think of how it affected the things I did. I wasn't proud of the bad choices I made in my life. I avoided a funeral of a very special friend of mine from my school days who passed away. The funeral was in the Cathedral. I could only send his wife a sympathy card when in reality I should have attended his service. I just couldn't bring myself to that again after the trauma I endured from Art's funeral with the nightmares returning more frequently. I will never walk in that Cathedral again without remembering the evil Father Gilmore and his assaults upon me.

Jim was finally able to return to work and work turnarounds in Frenchtown repairing boilers. It was nice to have both of us with stable incomes. The turnaround only lasted a couple of months but we found out that worker's comp wanted to settle his claim from his injury.

Dee was now a senior in high school and Jamie a freshman. Tanya and Mike were still in Lolo School. Jim's settlement came right after Dee graduated from where she was on the honor roll the entire time. We were so proud of her achievement and her grades. She was going to University of Montana in Missoula and would live in the dorms her freshman year.

We made a trip to Spokane because Vern told Jim there was a Laundromat for sale and he thought it would be a great investment with the money from Jim's settlement. After seeing the business and liking it, we decided to buy it and move to Spokane. The kids were heartbroken having to leave their friends. We told them we wanted to try buying the business to see where it took us.

I wasn't real excited about the move either but Vern seemed to think it would be a good investment for us. We were trying to work out a deal with the Laundromat. By the grace of God, we saw a new one being built with a gas station one block away from the one we were going to purchase. We backed out of buying the Laundromat and decided to save the money until we knew what to do.

In the meantime, we had our house rented out to a doctor and his wife, who also owned her own business. I kept asking them to send money for the deposit they still owed on and was getting no response from them. They sent the rent each month but never included the deposit. We also reminded them no pets. Neighbors let me know they had seen two large dogs there.

I told Jim I would be making a trip to Missoula, so I could get the fifteen hundred dollar deposit we were owed and the rent of one thousand two hundred dollars. When I pulled up to our house, I was very upset over what I saw. They had a camper shell on the lawn. There was dog pooh all over our lawn front and back. The lawn was dying from not being watered and under his camper shell it was already dead.

I knocked and nobody answered the door. I left and returned when they were due home from work. Sitting on the front porch were two very large Labradors. They barked and ran up to me when I was getting out of my car. My renter called them in and she asked what I wanted.

I informed her I wanted to see the inside of the house; reminded her about the no dog's policy, and ask for the deposit and rent for the month. She wrote me a check for five hundred dollars, which bounced. The dogs had damaged the walls and floors. We could not believe the condition of our house. They had plugged up the plumbing in the upstairs large bath and it smelled of sewage. The plumber said it had been plugged up for some time and somebody bathed dogs in the shower and the tub. Our carpets had to be vacuumed and steam cleaned by professionals before we could unload our furniture from the trucks. We also had to paint trimmings and polish our oak cupboards from grease stains, scrub walls, and fix sheetrock and paint where they damaged the walls from moving their furniture out. They had forty eight hundred dollars in damages from having dogs chewing on our beams in the downstairs and a cracked sliding glass door and torn window screens. The dogs did quite a bit of damage to our house along with the renters. We took pictures so we could have an attorney get the damage costs taken care of. It wasn't hard to do with both of them having their own business. With the money they were forced to pay along with attorney's fees we recuperated the loss. The house was filthy. I told her I wanted them out of our house and gave them a thirty-day eviction notice,

Jim and I decided it just wasn't working out for us living in Spokane and using our money for rent and with no work for Jim. The kids were thrilled that we were moving back home as soon as we evicted the renters.

It was extremely exciting to be back in our house once we had taken care of all the repairs. I was planning on opening a family daycare and preschool once the kids were back in school. I planned ahead and bought items I would need for the children and eventually I wanted to hire a preschool teacher for children three to five years old. I prepared myself taking the required classes. I was the only daycare that took newborn infants for mothers who were forced to return to work shortly after their child was born.

The mothers felt very secure with my nursing background in case of emergency. I decided I would never join the work force and would be self-employed until retirement. I had my fill of moving, and I think the kids had too.

Pi called us and asked if we would come and spend the weekend and visit. He did not sound well on the phone, which concerned me. I was so bothered that I insisted we take a trip to Helena to check on him. When I saw him, he seemed lethargic and had raspy breathing. I listened to his chest told him he needed to let me take him to Fort Harrison Hospital because I knew he had pneumonia. I suspected congestive heart failure as well but only a doctor could tell him that. He was very thin and pale with severe wheezing. He wouldn't go that night in spite of all the pleading from me. He promised that if I picked him up first thing in the morning, he would go to Fort Harrison.

I told Jim he should go there immediately because he seemed to me to be in critical condition. Jim felt it was his choice and we should follow his wishes. Pi could not be forced to do something he doesn't want to do.

When I arrived the next morning, Pi did not answer the door. He must be sleeping I thought, so I went to his bedroom window and knocked on it. Therewas no answer. I panicked. I checked to see if the front door was open and it was locked. I couldn't see through any of the windows except the kitchen where I saw nothing. He always kept the kitchen door locked, but I tried and for some strange reason it was unlocked. Pi never left this door unlocked. I stepped into the kitchen. There was a terrible odor in the house. I ran down the hallway to his bedroom and he wasn't there. As I walked past the bedroom to the bathroom, I saw Pi slumped on the floor next to the toilet with his pants halfway up. I quickly ran to him. I could tell he was gone and had died sometime during the night.

I quickly called 911 and told them we needed the coroner at Pi's address and then called Jim. Jim could not believe he was dead, felt terrible that I had found him. I told Jim he needed to come quickly because the coroner and police were on the way, and I thought he should be also. The motel brought Jim right over after he told them he would need a ride because of a family emergency.

After the ambulance, the coroner and the deputy left, I had to settle my husband down and let him know we had to call Lucy and ask her to call the others. Pi was fifty-five years old. His death was caused by congestive heart failure and pneumonia. We called home to Jamie and told her the news and let her know that Aunt Lucy and Francie would pick them up on the way to Helena.

After the funeral was over, my sisters-in-law thanked me over and over for going to the house and finding their brother. Pi lived like a hermit and very seldom went out except to pay bills and get groceries. He had a very large check on his kitchen table that he didn't even deposit. It was his first Social Security settlement check, of all things.

Jim had a very difficult time getting back to normal after all that had happened. His first brother Art passed away at fifty-four, then Pi passes away at fifty-five, and their father passed away at fifty-six from pancreatic cancer, not a good track record for the Kuhl men. I prayed fiercely that my husband would have a longer life!

It was now September and the Montana Power Company was building another power plant in Colstrip and it looked like Jim was going to be working for some time. The project had just taken off and he would once again come home every other weekend or when they had three days off.

I was having awful nightmares again and was extremely exhausted from them. I knew deep down who the culprits were in my nightmares as their faces began to appear once again from my childhood. I just did not want to explain to anyone about them. I was visited by them off and on for the last thirty years, but now they were increasing, causing me to lose sleep. I was waking up in tears and cold sweats. I thought the dreams had stopped, but here they were again. Sometimes I felt like I couldn't breathe when I awakened from these horrible dreams. I'd be gasping for air as I struggled with being chased and caught, my mouth muffled so no one could hear my cries for help. The dreams occurred more when Jim was away when I had no one beside me to help me get through it.

My doctor thought therapy was the only way to deal with the nightmares. However, he didn't think it would cure them, but told me it certainly would help.

Jim was not coming home as often as he was during the summer months. It seemed that my weeks were going by very quickly since my daycare and the kids kept me quite busy. Being busy helped alleviate my loneliness in Jim's absence.

Christmas was nice because we had Jim home for the holidays with us. He wasn't home for Thanksgiving due to the weather and the road conditions, and for Christmas he was only able to spend four days with us, not enough time to go to Spokane for our yearly trek to Lucy's. In spite of the little time we had together, it was a really nice Christmas.

I brought the New Year in without Jim, which didn't bother me, as I didn't go to parties, and rarely drank unless it was a tiny sip of wine. I watched the fireworks from the deck with the kids. Things went back to normal after the holidays were over.

CHAPTER FORTY-FOUR

The next fall, I got a phone call from my dad telling me he needed a hip replacement. I suggested a second opinion from Dr. Jacobson in Missoula. If he needed surgery it had to be in Missoula because I would need to take care of him. He told me that a lump was found in my mother's breast so both of them would come to Missoula and schedule his hip replacement and my mother's biopsy the same day. Unfortunately, Mom's biopsy was cancerous so they did a mastectomy after the biopsy.

When Mom came out of recovery she was understandingly upset about losing her breast. The doctor spoke to her telling her that he was sorry, but she had cancer and it was best to do the surgery then and there. She refused chemotherapy so was put on oral Tamoxifen. Mother was an emotional wreck and would cry at the smallest thing. I had to tell my dad about the cancer, and the surgery. I was caring for both of them, running back and forth to the hospital so we could take mom to visit dad in rehab. It also allowed me to check on his recovery process. I would be taking care of dad and mom at my house for six weeks.

I wanted to confront my mother about the abuse that happened to me as a child, so I could see if those damn nightmares would let up. It wasn't the time however. I was still angry. It was wonderful having my dad around for so long because his grandchildren got to see more of him and mom. My real beef with mom at that time was that she did not interact with her own grandchildren.

My mom sat and read all the time when she wasn't crying. I never wished ill for my mother because of our relationship and the things she had done to me growing up. I could never please the woman for all that I did for her.

Icontinued to wait on her hand and foot while she recuperated from her surgery.

Jamie was the only child she seemed to take interest in and talk to, and the other kids were left out. Whereas my dad loved to talk and interact with all of my kids, telling them about his experiences and jobs he worked on. He even told them the story of D-day. I was very fortunate to have a dad who worked hard all his life to give us what he could and still be a proud of a man. It was not easy, having to support a family of six when times were tough in the forties and fifties.

When my parents were both pretty well healed and on the road to a full recovery, it was time for them to head back home. Dad was walking without a walker and using a cane to help him get seated.

Jamie graduated from high school. Life was going smoothly. Two weeks later, my Grandmother came and paid us a two-week visit. She adored the kids and had a wonderful time visiting with the family. She didn't want me to call anybody to come over and visit including my parents. I was positive my grandmother was afraid of a dispute between my mother and herself, and she wanted to avoid it at all costs. She wanted only to spend time with us, which I didn't complain about.

Grandma asked me if I still had my awful nightmares, and I nodded and told her they seem to get worse and more detailed. She tried to persuade me to get professional help. I had never been able to discuss them with anyone and I doubt that I ever would because of the shame they caused me. I told her maybe one day I would be able to ask for help and would get it if the nightmares continued to get worse. "Don't wait too long she said to me as they could get the best of you," she would tell me. Grandmother was worried they were about mom's abusive behavior. I knew my grandmother knew about some of the episodes.

My life seemed to be one thing after another happening to us. I kept blaming myself for the incidents because of what I was told as a child. Father Callan and Father

408

Gilmore both told me that bad things happen to sinners and I was a terrible sinner. The sexual abuse was my punishment for being that sinner, and I was told over and over that God punished people like my sisters and me for our bad deeds. I grew up thinking that I was this terrible person and I did not deserve the good things for myself that other people had. I knew this was untrue. Their teachings were lies and wrong, because God had blessed me with a beautiful family. I felt I was truly loved by God to bless me in this way.

So who were the evil persons? The priests were. They took from my sisters and I what we could never get back, our childhood and innocence. But at the same time, they tried to brain wash us into believing we were bad people.

~~~

Jim was injured in another accident at work and would be brought back to Billings for surgery on his right and left knees. A Tugger operator was not paying attention to another's signals and had hit my husband's knees with a beam while he was rigging on the new power plant.

Once Jim had recovered from surgery, he would be home in Missoula. He would have to have another surgery. Dr. Burton told us that he doubted that even after the second surgery that Jim would ever be able to return to his profession. This was not good news for a man who loved his work and was now fifty-five.

After his surgery there would be rehabilitation and therapy. Once again, my Jim would be home all the time. After, he was healed he could help me out with the daycare. Jim didn't seem to mind knowing it would save us money. He could help with the cooking and driving kids to and from school. I had four children who we took and picked up from school. It took him three months to heal from his surgery and his therapy.

The accidents continued to overshadow my life and made me wonder sometimes if that was more punishment from Our Lord.

School had just started when Aunt Maxine from California called me. Two months after visiting us, my grandmother was in the hospital and was not expected to survive a massive stroke. They had called and informed my mom and would. Uncle Jim and Aunt Maxine would like Barb and me to drive my mother to California, so she could see her one last time. I kept asking myself why everyone I loved was passing away. Was it a form of my punishment?

I had to let all of my daycare parents know the circumstances. I explained to them I didn't know how long I was going to be gone. I also explained they said she was critical and dying. We made it to California; Uncle Jim took us straight to the hospital to say our goodbyes. Grandmother was in a coma and incoherent and we didn't know if she knew we were there. I still talked to her and I was sure she knew we had arrived. Her blood pressure went down somewhat. The doctor came in the room and told us she could be like this for days or pass away anytime. She would not recover.

We knew it was just a waiting process. We hated each day, watching our grandmother deteriorate before our eyes and unable to do anything for her. I would softly rub her arms. Her eyes were halfway open; I hoped she understood how much I hated to see her lie there. I deeply loved this woman and my aunt. They were the ones who taught me what love really was about. Grandma was stern. She wanted me to succeed in whatever I did. When I would walk in the door coming home from school, I was greeted with a kiss and asked how my day went in school. Then Grandpa would do the same once I was in the house.

On the tenth day, my grandmother passed away. Nobody would ever understand what this incredible woman did for me in giving me a new chance at a loving life. Grandma and Aunt Maxine were my life givers. I never knew loving someone truly meant giving to his or her

410

needs. I was taught to love others, as I would want to be loved by these passionate and instrumental women.

Aunt Maxine reminded us; grandmother was no longer suffering and she was finally at peace. Her wishes were to have family only at her service. She did not believe in cremation. Two days later, the service for the family was held. Grandmother was buried next to grandpa at Hill Cemetery.

We left the following day so Barb and I could get back to our families, and Barb would have to drive mom home and listen to her ramblings. I could imagine what the trip was going to be like. Mom was trying to tell us how to drive or tell us we did something wrong while driving. Uncle Jim wanted me to take grandma's station wagon home with me for one of the kids to drive. I was not thrilled about mom getting in the car with me, and Barb smirking and conniving her way out of driving her to Montana.

We were almost to Redding, California when all of a sudden I smelled smoke. I pulled over to lift the hood. We waited a few minutes and started the car up again. The air conditioner had burned out and we were without cool air. I told Mom we would have to drive with the windows down. I couldn't hear with the windows open and mom knew she couldn't tell me how to drive like she did Barb. It was a godsend from Grandma. I asked Barb to stay behind us in case something else would happen. The station wagon had sat in grandmother's driveway for five years. I should have had Uncle Jim check everything out before we left. He put new tires on it and didn't drive as far as he should have to figure out if it was okay to drive.

When we stopped to get something to eat and drink, I asked Barb how long she wanted to drive. "Drive until you know you can't go any further," she told me, and I agreed with her.

Almost one hundred miles from home over the Lolo pass into Idaho and it was two in the morning. I couldn't go any further as my eyes kept burning and I was extremely exhausted from the heat. I pulled into a turnoff and told

Barb I could not drive up the pass this late in the night. My eyes were bothering me terribly and I needed to sleep for a while. She agreed even though we were close to home. The highway was windy and had several sharp curves on both sides of the Pass. Plus, there were also deer and moose using the highway. I wasn't taking any chances as tired as I was. Barb got in the car with us and locked the doors, telling me how tired she was and thankful that I had pulled over. She planned on continuing to Helena once we arrived at my house.

We slept until seven in the morning when a knock on the window from a highway patrolman woke us. He asked if we were okay and we told him we had left California yesterday and were too tired to continue. He asked for my driver's license and insurance. After he was done checking the station wagon's insurance papers, he let us leave since we were awake.

Jim was shocked when I walked in the door a little after eight in the morning and asked if we drove all the way. I explained what had happened and told him I did not want to keep the car. We sold it immediately for $350.00 and put it towards a car for the kids.

Jim said he seen in the paper how hot the weather was in Sacramento which was sixty miles from Yuba City. I told him it never get out of the 100's the entire time we were there and missed our Montana weather. It never rained and I never saw any clouds to shade us. It was not a pleasure trip, except Barb and I were swimming quite a bit to cool off.

CHAPTER FORTY-FIVE

The next two years ran very smoothly. I was keeping busy with the daycare and having a great time doing so. I wanted to expand soon and hire a girl to work with me once again. It was really nice to have babies in my care and now that the others were older. I would love to get licensed for a group home but that would have to wait until I was ready to hire someone to work with me, and I was not ready for that.

On the days that I was not working, my girlfriend Wanda and I would go shopping. She had the same taste as I did in clothing and furnishings our shopping trips were so often that the clerks knew us by our first names.

Does that not spell shopaholic or what, I thought to myself. I knew I should have been saving the money I was making. When I shopped it seemed to alleviate or replace an emptiness I felt. As soon as I arrived home with all of my new possessions, the empty feeling came back. I was never much for material things when the kids were growing up. The shopping addictions were a new habit I was not proud of. The trouble was I let my spending habits get out of control and didn't realize how bad it was until I ran up several credit cards. I always had buyer's remorse when I returned home. I would actually feel guilty for the whole day and yet I would still continue shopping even though I knew I didn't need to do. I always knew what I was doing but couldn't stop my actions. I felt like I didn't have enough. It certainly wasn't me trying to keep up with the Jones. This horrible empty feeling did not disappear. I could not find any peace of mind, and it was always an emptiness and loneliness I would feel. I had wonderful children and a loving husband. My friends would tell me, it was growing up and going without that made me feel this way. I knew that wasn't it.

413

My nightmares had continued and I had no one to talk to about the ugliness that was within my soul as I sat crying and trying to convince myself it would all go away, eventually. I had been told that we couldn't live in our pasts, and need to move forward into the present.

I ask myself what I did at such an early age in my life, to have brought on the awful things that were done to me. At three years old, was I really a bad child that needed to be punished, and had to go through this sexual ungodliness through my childhood? I was told at three and four years old, I was a rebellious and sinful child and this continued until I was eleven. What would provoke a man of God to put a child through the terror of a holy hell? How could a three or four year old child conceive this idea of being sinful? Why was I a sinful child? Would those terrible things had happened if I weren't rebellious?

The nuns and priests made it quite clear I was not a good person. My mother also made it quite clear I wasn't a good person. This was why I had the emptiness in my heart for so many years. I tried so hard to please everyone in my life. I still think I could never do enough to be a good person. Father Gilmore told me I would pay for my sins throughout my life. When bad things happened I felt I was being punished and bringing the punishment on myself.

I hoped that in due time God would forgive me and forgive those who used my body for their pleasure. Father Gilmore and Father Callan were the responsible parties for making me feel this emptiness and loneliness. I felt they had taken so much away from me.

As a victim I could not find peace in my mind or in my life. I had been robbed. I could only forgive those who sinned against me. That was why my nightmares continued never to be forgotten.

Thankfully some days, I could not remember the dreams when I awakened. On other nights, I woke up to nightmares, I was once again crying in the middle of the night. I prayed that eventually I could find some peace through God. I could not put into words some of the atrocious sexual assaults that were done to me while I was trying to escape; and then, to be tossed in a room with nothing to lie on but a hard little cot and told to say the rosary all night and beg for my forgiveness before being released.

I knew of prisons that treated adults better than the priests and nuns treated some of the children of St. Joseph's and the Cathedral of St. Helena. It was hard to put this into perspective, but believe me this was not what any child should have to go through. My sisters also went through this holy hell.

CHAPTER FORTY-SIX

A Mother always hates to see her children leave the nest and then go off to college or get married. Then they will be starting families of their own. I only saw my girls if they went camping with us or if drove out to see us. I had separation anxiety each time one of them left.

The winter months were miserable once again, but I was excited that our children would be home for the holidays. We had a wonderful Christmas. Mom and dad came over for Christmas Eve and Christmas Day. They left the next day because it was starting to snow again and they wanted to get on the road. The house was very empty after all the laughter and all the excitement of everyone being home.

It was December 27th and around 3:30 in the morning the smoke alarm went off in our upstairs. Jim had fallen asleep in the recliner in the living room watching television and I was asleep in our bedroom with a short nightshirt. He was yelling at me to get a move on in the dark. He had looked downstairs to see what was going on and saw black smoke billowing up the stairwell. Jim yelled at me to grab the dog to go to the neighbors and call 911.There was a huge fire in the basement and it had filled the house with smoke. I was coughing with soot forming on my face, as Jim continued to yell at me to get out of the house now and go to the neighbors. Fritz our little dachshund was scurrying as fast as his little legs could carry him behind me. I ran to the neighbors in nothing but a T-shirt nightie and underwear, and I and barefoot in a foot of snow. Jim grabbed the car keys by our kitchen wall, to pull the car out of the garage.

All three of us were out of the house when we an explosion. It was our glass sliding doors blowing out downstairs and breaking. Mt neighbor Carol grabbed a robe for me, and some slippers to put on my feet. We stood there in horror waiting for fire trucks to arrive. With the doors blown out the fire blew-up causing the house to be consumed, flames were billowing out the windows with more explosions taking place. I heard the sirens down below our house leaving the station but it seemed like forever before they arrived at our house. The house was in flames by the time the fire department arrived.

We couldn't save anything, as it was already filled with fire and smoke. This was a nightmare and I couldn't stop screaming, because once again we lost everything that mattered to us. We stood there in shock until the firemen had my neighbor Judy takes Jim and I to her house and keep us there. My neighbor made me stay at her house to try to keep me away from what was going on, as there were more explosions when our propane tank from our barbeque on the deck had exploded.

I thanked God that our son had spent the night with BJ his buddy who lived just down the street from us. He wasn't aware our house was burning down as he slept through the night. The boys took turns spending the night on weekends and it was BJ's turn. All of my kids' pictures and every belonging we had burned. We never saved a thing from the smallest to the largest of items. I had over forty antique reproduction dolls I had made in the last seven years. I had taken up the hobby in the evenings to keep busy.

The fire lasted until 10:30 in the morning. They had two fire trucks from Missoula, two from Lolo and one from Florence trying to put it out. We had a very large double story house that had been built into the mountain. We had no fire hydrant except down the street and at the park below us. Their hoses were stretched everywhere trying to save what they could of our house or to keep hot embers from falling on homes nearby. Two firemen barely escaped injury when our sunken living room dropped to the lower level of the house. I would never have recovered if someone had lost his life due to a fire in my home.

While the fire was still smoldering, we looked at nothing but some burned walls that were still standing. I didn't even have clothes. Jim was dressed in sweats and a tee shirt with no shoes on his feet. Leo, a neighbor gave Jim a pair of slippers after he had the car pulled out into the street. While we were waiting for the firemen to let us see what we could salvage, my friend Wanda came running down their driveway, which was above our house, asking me if we were okay. They didn't realize what had happened during the night until they awoke to all the fire trucks and smoke.

They didn't hear the sirens or hear fire trucks, nor hear the explosions at all that night. Wanda and Dave took us up to their house until the Fire Marshall arrived. They offered us breakfast but neither of us could eat. Wanda took me up to her bedroom to get some clothes. She found some pants that were too small for her and a shirt. We both wore the same size shoe.

I had to call BJ's parents and asked them to tell Michael he could not come home. They told me he had just left. Wanda and I ran down to catch him. I heard him standing there screaming. I ran down the hill and hugged him while we both cried. He thought we were in the house and the firemen didn't see him when he approached the house. He was so grateful his father and I were safe. Nobody would ever want to live through that nightmare. I was in total shock. I did not realize we were homeless.

The Fire Marshall put yellow tape around our house and no one could go in because of the dangerous situation of floors caving in. He also told us the fireplace downstairs started the fire with the fireplace insert overheating and catching the ill on fire and the wood in the firewood holder was the accelerator that made it take off as fast as it did. The builder should have had a firewall behind the insert. We were so very lucky that we get out of the house safely he told us. I was thankful we made it out okay but we were still homeless and had no clothing. Our insurance was never increased over the years, which our insurance man should had told us to do. It would be our loss. We ended up borrowing money to rebuild. We were put up in a hotel for six weeks until we could find an apartment to live in.

I didn't have to tell my daycare parents what had happened as they saw it on the news Saturday morning and evening, and in Sunday's Missoulian paper. Wanda's little girls were in my daycare, and I had other parents that needed to still be notified. Wanda took care of that. She told me after we were settled all of the parents wanted me to still watch their children. Wanda asked me to run the daycare out of her house until we would be able to move back into ours once it was rebuilt. I thought she was joking when she came up with this idea, but she hated to look for someone else to care for her children. She would rather have the kids at her house, since she saw how well they behaved in my home. "You would be able to save up the money the parents pay you and still had something positive in your life," she convinced me.

We had two rooms side by side at the hotel so Jim and I would have one and Michael and Jamie could have the other room. It was nice getting up early and heading to Wanda's house to care for the kids. It was also traumatic each and every day watching them demolish my house below her home.

I bought food and the necessary items to prepare meals for the day care kids and while they napped I would clean Wanda's house. She said I didn't have to do that. Working out of Wanda's home was working out for both of us.

We finally get moved into an apartment, but there was no way I would have room for a daycare. Our living room was average and three small bedrooms and a small kitchen and dining room. The apartments were new. We knew it was temporary.

The house nightmare continued once the demolishing was over. I had written checks to the contractor for materials to begin building since the foundation was saved.

It took him weeks to get started after I complained about the materials sitting out there in the elements of the weather. I told him I could see the site and no carpenters were there working. The contract promised it would be done by July. I finally informed the contractor that there would be no more checks until the materials on the site were up and ready for the next phase of building. There would be days that no one would show up for work and it would be a perfectly fine day. I let the contractor know I was not paying for days his carpenter's didn't show up for work and I wanted our house done by his deadline. The contractor stalled. He wanted more money. I had to have a separate contractor with a painter since the walls had to be textured for the inside of the house. When I walked in after work one day, the painter's secretary was trying to paint a room. Paint was dripping all over the place, I asked her to leave and told her boss he was fired.

We fired the contractor and had to take the man to court. We won the lawsuit for $38,000. He filed for bankruptcy protection. I paid the painter and the carpet layers. I had to paint all of our trimming and window frames. We finally were able to move into the house. I finished all of the touch-ups and the landscaping.

I hoped I would never go through this disaster again. It was a hellish nightmare to deal with a contractor who I was not happy with, let alone living through a second fire, and having to live in a hotel and apartment. On top of all of that we had gone through, our contractor ripped us off.

I had the upstairs a new floor plan for upstairs of the new house. Jim knew I was still planning on continuing daycare since I enjoyed it so much. I had a huge room with three windows with shades built inside, with the daycare in mind. The bathroom had a regular size toilet and a tiny toilet that matched, and the double sinks were child size so they could brush their teeth and wash their hands without standing on a stepstool. It had built in shelves for children's toys and books. I had ordered from a Little Tykes company a complete order full of children's toys and play center with three slides and objects for climbing. We had six inches of bark put down so if anyone fell they were safe.

CHAPTER FORTY-SEVEN

The following spring of the next year, my mom and dad were coming over for my dad to have his hip checked once again. He could hardly walk on it without severe pain. Dad was not the type to complain of pain, so I know that something was terribly wrong. He was eighty-nine years old and I was surprised when his doctor said he would run him through tests to make sure he could survive yet another hip replacement. His hip had been replaced once already. Dad was a real trooper. He passed every test they ran on him. His surgery was scheduled. I asked the doctor if he truly thought dad could survive the surgery and he said to me that my father was as strong as an ox and had quite a few more years to go. My father had no dementia, no blood pressure problems or other health issues; other than a hip that was making him miserable.

My dad surprised them all how fast he was on his feet and on his road to recovery once again and they knew him well there from his previous surgeries. Dad recovered quickly at our home since Mom took care of his needs during the day until the daycare children went home. After three weeks of care Dad was walking with his cane and said he was ready for home.

The next eight years, were good to us. The daycare thrived. I had taken care and raised over one hundred children. Jim enjoyed the daycare as well, taking and picking children up to and from school.

During that time, Vern, Lucy's husband, called us with sad news. Lucy had been diagnosed with lung cancer. She was in an advanced stage and only lived six weeks after the diagnosis. We were devastated by her loss. She had been so good to us with her kindness and thoughtfulness over the years. I could not have asked the Lord to give me a better sister-in-law. I dearly loved this gentle woman.

After fourteen years of childcare, I had to retire to take care of my own growing health issues. I had not been feeling well and I was having muscle and joint pain. I finally broke down and went to a rheumatologist. The tests revealed I had rheumatoid arthritis. I had other issues as well. The stress of running a daycare and preschool was not helping me. My health had deteriorated for a few months and after a prescription for arthritis and pain medication, I was back on the road to recovery.

I was a lot like my dad; I bounced back quickly after an illness. My doctor hoped the arthritis would go into remission but she doubted it would at my age and the fact that it was a later stage diagnoses. It was also found that I had degenerative disease in my bones and my back, as well. The remedy and control was exercise. I was a faithful exerciser so that was not a problem. I did not feel well if I didn't exercise. So first thing in the morning, I did at least fifteen to forty-five minutes of exercise. Then I was good for the day. Some days, my joints flared up so severely that it took me awhile to get out of bed, other days I had no problems. Cold weather was my enemy, which caused the flare-ups. I learned to live with my setbacks and continued to exercise.

Dad was having problems with his hip again, and needed to have it checked. The hip replacement he had seemed to be giving him severe pain. He was walking with a horrible limp. The doctor told my dad, who was ninety-eight, that he would have to have it replaced once again. It was the only way he could walk and not be in pain. The doctor told dad that they had new replacement hips that were so much better than the old ones. He knew that dad was very healthy. He thought dad would be around for a few more years, and he didn't want to see him to be confined to a wheelchair. Dad agreed to the surgery. I made it clear to my father that he could possibly not make it through and he said he was at peace with that. He did not want to live a life where he could not walk and always remained in pain. Mother was pushing him to get it done. I agreed I would care for my father.

Dad survived the surgery, but did end up in ICU once again with his blood pressure bottoming out. Within four days, he snapped out of it and started to be his old self. He was in the Rehab Center for a few weeks and then I took him to my home for some extended care.

I needed to go pick up his prescriptions after we brought him home. My mother told me in an angry voice, "Your dad doesn't need those damn pills and we can't afford them so don't bother getting them!" That voice ground into me like gravel just like it used to. I was instantly angry and snapped, "The hell he doesn't! I will pay for dad's medications and you will do nothing about it!" Now you want to abuse dad by denying him medications for him to get well. "Not on my watch mother, not on my watch!"

Once I opened up in defiance to my mother the deep waters of decades of pain and suffering drained out of me like a flash flood. I was so angry that I could not stop the words that rushed out of me. I began to systematically recount every evil thing she'd ever done, in front of my dad. I turned on her.

You need to stop! How could you? After all the lies you've told Dad? You lied about our bruises, our injuries that put us in the hospital! It was because of your beatings that we were removed from the house, not from the lie you told Dad that the school ordered it, but because the neighbors reported you to the Department of Family Services. That's why we were placed in St. Joseph's Orphanage! There were no falls from fencesMother! You lied to cover up everything. I was like a train out of control. *You forced Bonnie and I to lie to our own father about what really happened! You left us time and time again at the orphanagewhere we were assaulted and harassed by the nuns who punished us because they said we were rebellious and defiant children! For God's sake Mother, your own little girls were molested and raped daily by the priests. We were thrown into a hole in a dark cold room scared to death after being violated. Our cries were ignored once the door was locked! Remember Mom! We tried to tell you, butyou wouldn't believe your own children instead you slapped the hell out of your five and six year old daughters. You called us little whores and liars, and that we were not to ever repeat our story to anyone including daddy or you would give us something to cry about!*

The air in the room hung like ice. I felt so bad for my dad when I saw the tears well up in his eyes as he began to cry. My mother started crying too, but I wasn't finished. There was so much more to tell.

I am so sorry I have to tell you Dad, but you needed to know why we ran away from home.We couldn't stay. It was not possible. We were in danger ALL THE TIME. Mom was so violent that we girls ended up in the hospital because of her beatings, except for Wes of course. He could do no wrong. We had to fend for ourselves to find safety and to survive. Poor Bonnie ended up in reform school until she was eighteen! She ran away to California, just to get away from Mom, like I did.

When Bonnie and I were five and six, Mom sat and gave orders. She threatened us to wash the clothes. She had no concern that ringer washing machine's were dangerous! We were forced to clean the house and cook, at five and six years old, Dad! She sat and read. She made us do everything! If we did it wrong she'd beat us!

Mom has to stop hurting people, including you. I was so tired of her telling you to shut up and calling you a knucklehead and demanding you use your brain. She was always putting you down in front of your friends and people you worked with.

Mom has to learn that she has hurt all of the kids in this family except for Wesley except when she accidently shot him. Look at poor Willard who wanted to be loved. She couldn't love him or even try to show affection to any of us. She can't even love her grandchildren except for Wesley's kids because he was her baby. His two kids get the love that should have been given to all of the grandchildren. My kids cannot stand her because of what she has done. Jamie is the only child of mine that has feelings for her and why I don't know.

I was shaking so bad from all the anger and truth telling that I could barely stand up. I was just so sorry for the timing of my outburst, especially since Dad had had just been released to come home.

Dad turned to my mom and toldher she needed to go home. I agreed, I could not deal with her treatment towards my father any longer, and I no longer wanted her in my house.

I called Rick and Suzanne, who were Mom and Dad's friends, and asked them if they could please come and get my mom and take her home. I explained the situation to Rick saying that my mother and I had a disagreement and thought the best thing for her was to leave while Dad was on the mend. Dad needed this time to be alone with me since he was upset over the revelation of mom's lies. I asked Jim to go and pick up Dad's medications because I did not want to leave him alone with her, because I knew she would try to manipulate him into leaving with her.

Mom manipulated every move my father had made from the day they met. I knew how much my dad loved my mom or he wouldn't have been married to her for fifty-nine years. I knew in my heart he would forgive her as I would too, eventually.

My father was a wonderful father, and I never blamed him for not knowing. His work kept him from home as his family grew too quickly. He had their first child ten months after they were married and then I was born eleven months later. Mom and Dad had five kids in seven years, and were very poor. It was a rough life for dad to support a family of seven, working two jobs and having hardly any time for him. He had no idea what was happening in his household. My mother gave him a mitigated version to suit her own purposes. Now he truly knew what had taken place. He said to me and mother that he would talk to Mom when it was time for him to go home.In my emptied state, I altered the course of my heart. I told him I wanted it all in the past. I directed my gaze to mother and said, "Be kind, you are both old now."

After mom left, I apologized to my dad for my outburst. He said, still in shock, "I always wondered why and how his daughters were so difficult. I told him that he did not know all we had gone through. Mom would be the first person I would put on a list for anger management. "Daddy, she treats you badly in front of people, and I was hurt when I heard her call you names and make you out to be dumb and told you to use your brain and calling you a

427

numbskull in front of people. That was cruel, and I would not have her treat you like that anymore, that was why I wanted her to go home. You still have to recuperate a couple more weeks and this will give her time to think about what she put us through years ago. I only pray she takes my advice and lay off.

I took my dad home two weeks later. Mom seemed to be just fine and acted like nothing had happened. I suspected she was thinking about all the things that Daddy was going to be asking her since he now knew the truth. I gave them both a hug when I left.

Two months later, my mother slipped on ice and fell hitting her head, but did get up, saying to dad that she was just fine. She and dad drove to a few garage sales, her favorite past-time. As she was driving by Carroll College in Helena, she had a massive stroke and slumped over the wheel putting her and dad in a ditch while almost hitting a semi tractor-trailer. Mom was taken to the hospital in critical condition.

I had to leave for Helena immediately as I thought I had provoked this stroke and felt guilty about it blaming myself through the two-hour drive. She was in ICU for two weeks and was not doing well.Once they stabilized her, she was moved to a regular room. The stroke affected her speech and her mobility on both sides of her body. After a month, it was decided that she needed to be in a nursing home because she was not going to recover from the stroke. I returned home and made trips once or twice a month because Dad was staying in the room with her so she wouldn't be alone and he could watch her care. My brother would not let dad stay alone in the house, and I agreed. He had his ninety-ninth birthday in the nursing home. Mom had her seventy-eighth birthday the following month.

I received a phone call that Mom was not doing well on March 11, 2003 and that I should get there as soon as possible. My sister-in-law informed me that they didn't think she would make it through the day. When I walked into the room,poor dad was beside himself. I went over to mom's bed and began to rub her arm gently, "I forgive you Mother."As I continued caressing her arm she came out of her coma and very slowly tilted her head toward me. Her lips parted and she spoke very weakly, but I heard her. "I am so very sorry."

Tears welled up in my eyes when my mother spoke these words for the first time ever. I told her I had forgiven her. "Go Mom peacefully to The Lord." As quickly as my words were spoken, my mother was comatose once again. My mother, Helen (middle name Grace,passed away the next day in the early morning. I felt the truth had set her free, just like it says in the Bible. She had been purged of her sins and was now free.

Now I was in a battle with my brother to have my father released from the nursing home. Dad had begged me to please get an attorney and get him out of that place. My brother did not have my dad's best interest at heart. I hired an attorney after speaking with my father. He told me to sign my father out of the nursing home and take him camping for ten days in our motorhome so he could get the paperwork finished. It was Memorial Day weekend. We checked dad out for the ten days and took him Placid Lake. He stayed there until the lawyer called us to come back and sign the papers a week later. In the meantime, my dad was in seventh heaven at Placid Lake knowing my brother's plan had backfired. It would turn out to be the place he always wanted to go when we went camping for the summers he remained with us.

I took dad to Helena to get the papers releasing him from the nursing home. Dad finally had his wish to live with Jim and I. He signed a power of attorney for me to care for his affairs without any interference from Wesley.

CHAPTER FORTY-EIGHT

I was teaching doll classes and was enjoying the company of my friends. I had seven friends and students learning to make dolls. I had the classes twice a week and we enjoyed each other's company. The girls in my class love to listen to my dad's laughter and stories. He in turn loved the ladies visiting with him when they were here. When I was not doing the classes, I made and sold dolls on the Internet and had a little income coming in besides Jim's retirement and social security. With both of us retired, we still did yard work, went camping and had our ups and downs with my spending habits. I wished I had a wand and I could make myself stop my compulsive shopping habits but I couldn't. I did not know what made buy the things I did.

Then a tragedy struck Dorothy, one of my dearest friends. She was murdered in her beauty shop she owned in Lolo along with two other women. I went through another trial in my life that I could not understand. Dorothy and I had a lot in common. She and her husband had their ups and downs like Jim and I. She too had spending habits that would get out of control. She told me, I needed to ask myself each time I shopped, did I really need this item and why do I need it. Or could I just put it back on the shelf and walk away. Her advice did work to some extent, but my compulsive habit was hard to break.

It was so hard to understand the crimes that people have to live through. This was a terrible crime that still lingered and I was often reminded of it. The building that held the beauty shop where the murders occurred was torn down and replaced with a new building. When I drove by the new building, I was still reminded of the incident. I missed Dorothy's friendship. Jim missed her husband who decided to move out of state.

Jim and I realized how short life could be when Dorothy's was snuffed out so quickly. We had been through tough and rough roads and had survived them. We truly realized how much we still loved one another. I couldn't feel more satisfied with our lives and happy for our children's beautiful families.

Dad lived with us and enjoyed the pleasures of doing what he pleased. He went for strolls with his walker and visited with neighbors. He had a real nice scooter so he could go up and down our road, which was a long block and we lived at the end of the cul-de-sac.

Dad celebrated his 100th birthday at the fairgrounds in Helena. Search and Rescue brought their newest mobile command vehicle. They thought Dad's birthday was the best time to commemorate their oldest and longest living member. He was tickled to death with the turnout of family and friends there to celebrate his life of giving and volunteering to his community.

Dad and I went on a cruise to celebrate his 100th birthday to Hawaii and Tahiti. I never thought I would see my father in a tuxedo, let alone three different kinds. He never lived this kind of life and he was enjoying all of the passengers giving him special attention. He deserved it after all the years of his hard work. The ship's company gave him a birthday party in the formal dining. Everyone stood up waving their napkins as stewards came in carrying Baked Alaskan flaming cakes. It was a beautiful sight with people singing Happy Birthday to dad. When we arrived home, all my dad could do was talk about his great trip and the fun he had shared with me.

The following year his 101st birthday, I took him on an Alaskan Cruise with my dearest and best friend Maryann and her family. For his 102nd and 103rd birthdays, everybody, including my sister Barb and her kids, my brothers and their wives, all of my children, grandchildren and dad's great-grandchildren came to celebrate his long life. Dad lived the last four years of his life to the fullest. We lost my dad who passed away a week after having a stroke and fighting pneumonia October 30, 2006. I miss his laughter, and truly I will miss him forever. Rest In Peace Daddy.

CHAPTER FORTY-NINE

After dad's passing I finally decided to seek the help I needed. I had promised my father I would get help. I had shared my horrible habits, my awful nightmares and things I wasn't proud of with dad. He said it was time for me to heal and a therapist was what I needed. My therapist helped me understand that much of what had taken place in my childhood was not my fault. I no longer blamed myself for the abuse that was inflicted on me by evil and sick men and a mentally ill mother. I was taking life one day at a time.

On May 8, 2017 I lost my beloved husband James to a massive stroke. He was one of the kindest and giving husband's a woman could ever want or imagine. I thank you for that Jim. I love you and miss you.

AFTERWORD

It wasn't until 2011 that Wanda Kuhl began to write notes for a book about her experience of sexual abuse by priests in the Catholic Church. It was in 2012 that she read a newspaper advertisement looking for victims/claimants for a lawsuit against the Roman Catholic Diocese of Helena, Montana for sexual abuse. She filed a "Future Proof of Claim" with Blaine L. Tamaki of Tamaki Law Offices in Yakima, Washington in March of 2012.

After joining the Does lawsuit, her lawyer, who knew Mrs. Kuhl was writing a book, told her that she would not be allowed to release it until after the trial. The lawsuit was won in August of 2015 and Mrs. Kuhl finished her book and self-published it on Amazon.com.In2015. The title of the book *Jane Doe 46* was chosen for her identifying name and number given her in the lawsuit. The book is now in its second revision (edition).

Once her personal perpetrators were listed on The Roman Catholic Diocese of Helena web site www.diocesehelena.org, she was able to bring her book forward. When reading the list, one will find both of the named clergy in the book are listed in a sub-topic that states, "Diocese cannot verify the following individuals in claims as priest." Both the last names of Callan and Gilmore are listed but are documented (first name unknown). We know them in the book as Father Francis Callan and Father Joseph M. Gilmore (later to become Bishop Gilmore). This may create doubt in some minds of the readers by giving less credibility to the author's story. However, there are still many more victims to emerge and their stories will support Jane Doe 46.

Whether provable, personal stories can be evaluated qualitatively and as more stories are written or told, they give power toward a concluding outcome.

Additionally, Mrs. Kuhl's youngest sister Barbara has written a testimonial that is featured at the back of the book. It is simply called "Barbara's Story."

Wanda Kuhl—Author

Katherine Sterling—Editor

BARBARA'S STORY

I was born in Helena, Montana at The County Hospital on December 15, 1951. I was the youngest of five siblings: a half-sister, (whom I had never met) two sisters and two brothers. One of my brother's was institutionalized before I was born because of a serious head injury. He had fallen out of a high chair at twenty-two months. It had left him mentally impaired. The only time I saw him was when the family would take trips to Boulder to visit him. When I turned two, my Father gave me my first puppy who I named Duke. He was a black Cocker Spaniel who lived to be nineteen years old.

My childhood was not a happy one to remember, as my Mother was a very cruel woman, who loved to beat on us, especially my two older sisters who she seemed to target the most. If they did not do something the way she wanted it done, she would beat them with belts, hairbrushes, or whatever she could get her hands on. The cupboards were locked, so if we were hungry it didn't matter. We had very little food to eat and all our clothes were hand me downs or from garage sales. I was a little luckier than my two older sisters, because I had a cousin in Peoria, Illinois who was an only child who had expensive clothing. When Rita out grew her clothing, Aunt Margarite would send them to me, and Mom would only let me wear them on special occasions.

My sisters and I shared a bedroom. They had a full size bed and I had a twin bed on the other side of the room. Our brother had his own bedroom, which was a good size compared to ours, with the bathroom separating us. With a family of six, we had a very small house, until Dad built an addition for him and Mom to have their own bedroom.

They used to sleep in a sleeper sofa in the living room before he built their huge bedroom.

Our Christmas's were not anything special to look forward to since we only received one gift each, which came from the Salvation Army along with a turkey and some other food. I turned three just before Christmas. We never had birthday parties. Dad would take us for ice cream at a drive-up to celebrate our birthdays.

When I was three years old we were taken away from my parents and placed in St. Joseph's orphanage. It was a terrible place where evil happened. The nuns were mean and did terrible things to me. I wet the bed and Sister Margaret grabbed me and pulled me to the bathroom and placed my face in the toilet as she continuously flushed it. The next thing I knew my sister Wanda tried to stop her, and she hit my sister so hard that she hit the wall.

My sister pulled at her habit and grabbed her rosary on her dress and broke Sister Margaret's rosary. While doing this, my sister was screaming at her to leave me alone, and to quit dunking my face in the toilet. Wanda had caused quite a commotion in the dorms and the nuns were very angry with her. The other nun had taken Wanda away and they put me in a bath of very ice-cold water. I didn't know what they did with Wanda because she wasn't anywhere to be found. I was frightened and didn't understand why I was being treated so badly for an accident in my bed.

My sisters and brother all went to school except for me. I would cry when the bus pulled away with them in it. I had no one to protect me when they were gone. I would scream and cry when they left, and my punishment would be, back to the cold water. Sister Margaret and the other nun would run my face under very cold water. Some days, the nuns would take me to Father Callan because I wouldn't stop crying. My punishment was Father Callan would remove my underwear and place me on his lap with his pants opened and rub him against me until he was hard. He would then put his fingers in my vagina. It was painful and I would cry harder and then he would place his hand over

437

my mouth so I couldn't scream any longer. He would then make me suck on his penis, and when he was done he would take me to a dark room, which had nothing in it, the whole time carrying me with his hand over my mouth. Once he was gone I hovered in a corner and stayed like that until they came to get me out.

We were in the orphanage for six months, until they returned us back to our parents. Mom picked us up as usual because Daddy was working. The second time we were placed in the orphanage, it was worse. Father Callan was more brazen now and continued his abuse of me. This time he would play with my privates and take me in a little bedroom with only a bed with a cross above it and a nightstand. He would force me to have intercourse and the pain was so bad I screamed with his hand covering me while he was hurting me and I was bleeding. We were in and out of the orphanage four times that I remember.

When I was five years old I ended up getting a terrible virus that paralyzed me. I could not get out of bed and had wet myself. I screamed for my sister Wanda to please come and help me get up. A neighbor came over to our house and told my Mom that I needed to go to the hospital, but she just waited to see if I would get better, which I didn't. Finally the neighbor took me to St. John's Hospital.

Mom never let my sisters visit me while I was in there. When I finally returned home Wanda took care of me, reading to me after she returned from school. She taught me how to write. I'm not sure how long I was in the hospital but when I was first put in there it was so scary because the first person I saw before the doctor came in, was a nun.

They were much kinder than the ones in the orphanage. One morning they brought me a, soft-boiled egg, which I had never eaten before, and when I broke it open I get yolk everywhere. I hid it because I was afraid I would get a beating for making a mess like in the orphanage. In the orphanage if you dropped your silverware you were beaten and sent to Father Callan. This nun was nice and changed the sheets and gave me a bed bath.

I didn't get to start school until I was 7 years old. My birthday was past the deadline so I had to wait a year. I went to Broadwater School for the 1st and 2nd grades. Then I went to Central School for the 3rd and 4th grades. Then they built a school not far from our house, which was C.R. Anderson where I would attend the 5th grade. I didn't like this school because the other kids made fun of my clothes and how poor we were, and I didn't do well in school because of this.

One day when I had returned home from school my sister's had gotten a really bad beating from our Mom and they had decided to run away. I begged my sister to take me with her so I wouldn't be left all alone with them gone. I told my Mom I was going to tell Dad what she had done to my sisters and then I get a beating for saying that.

Wanda decided to take me with her. We left that night after our parents were sound asleep. Bonnie went her way because some guy had picked her up and Wanda and I walked to one of her friend's house. He was her tutor who had helped her with her homework. He wasn't home so we slept in the hall by his door and huddled together with my head in her lap. In the morning, a milkman, who couldn't see us up the stairwell, awakened us.

Wanda stole two bottles of milk and we left so we could have something to drink while we were walking. We decided to go to our aunt's house but we ended up getting caught by the police. They took my sis and another officer took me home. I get a very bad beating and sent to my room and locked in. I never got to see my sister Wanda again for years.

Mom wouldn't let me go see her. I was sick, I missed Wanda so much, she was the only one who took care of me and protected me and now she was gone. I don't remember much more about my childhood, maybe because there were not many good times to remember. On Saturdays and Sundays, I do remember Mom and Dad dropping us off at the Marlowe Theatre for matinee movies so they could go do what they want and be away from us. We also went on several trips camping at Park Lake. So many times they dumped us off at Memorial Park and Wanda and Bonnie had to care for us.

I was eleven years old and my parents decided to sell our house in Helena and move to Unionville, which was six miles from town. It was south of Helena and up in the mountains. It was a small town with a community center and that was about it. There were about twenty-two homes in this tiny town. The area was beautiful with lots of room to roam around and to ride our horses. The only problem was the house was built in the 1800's and had no bathroom so I had to use an outhouse. There was no running water or a toilet in the house and I had to go outside to pump water from a well. I might as well been living in the 1800's. The house had one bedroom, which my Dad made into two bedrooms.

My parents slept in the living room in a queen size bed, and Dad had made the large one bedroom into two bedrooms by putting up a wall to separate Wesley and me. We both would have a small bedroom. Dad finally built another edition on to the front of the house to make a large living room. The kitchen had an old wood stove that one had to shove wood into, to cook or bake. The addition for the new living room was the only source of heat with yet another wood stove for the whole house. The bedrooms never received heat, because they were in the far back of the house, so needless to say my brother and I went without heat and had cold bedrooms, especially mine way in the back of the house. I spent as little time in that house as possible.

I rode the bus to Central School and attended the sixth grade the year that we moved. It was Montana's Centennial Year with several celebrations taking place in the city of Helena. I remember being in a play that year in school and when the play took place, no one from my family came to see me perform. Bonnie and Wanda were both in California.

I finally met new neighbors and a lot of friends who were close to my age for me to do things with. Most of my friends who lived in Unionville had horses and we would ride every day during the summer after I finished my chores. I did anything to get away from being in the house. Then once a week I would have to go into Helena and do the laundry with my mother at the Laundromat. The only entertainment I had in this tiny little town was the privilege of riding my horses. There wasn't anything else to do because; they didn't even have a store to purchase things.

I was being bussed to Helena Junior High School for the seventh through ninth grades. I became good friends with an older couple Rachel and Bill who had took me under their wings since their children were now grown up and gone. They live down the street from us. They came to our house and asked my parents if I could please come down to their house and give Rachel a hand with some chores. They were very kind to me and treated me as their own. They would invite me to come to their cabin on weekends with them during the summers. They were also kind enough to let me come and bathe at their house so I would not have to do the sponge baths anymore.

After my bath, they would feed me well since they knew I was undernourished and not eating well at home. They had a cabin at Canyon Ferry on the west side of the lake, which had an apple orchard on it. The cabin setting was on the side of a sloping hill. They had a very large tree close to the house that had a tire swing on it for their kids when they were small and it was still there for me to swing in. I was so thankful that they had talked my dad into letting me go the lake with them on the weekends even though mom would had to do the chores alone. It was so peaceful with them and they treated me like I was very special, letting me bring a friend along with me.

One of my friends who lived close by me had a thirteenth birthday party at the old school house. (It is no longer a school and is still there today.) At this party, she had a band that consisted of boys our age. We became very good friends with the boys who would then drive up and get us and then we would go out in the woods and make out. I had started smoking and drinking with these boys.

The boys would sneak alcohol out of their parent's houses and off into the woods we would go. We had built an underground fort by the old school house and hung out there after school when the chores were all done. It was a good hiding place if one of us would ever get in trouble, and didn't want to be found.

One of the boys had made one of our neighbors mad, and in return he came up and caved our fort in with us in it. We all got out safely but now our fort was ruined and we had no place to go when we wanted to get away. There was an old abandoned house in the woods close to a pond that we started hanging out and which was much cooler than the old fort. In the winter we would ice skate on the pond and have a small bon fire.

One day in the spring, I was out feeding my horses and a man named Jim came and asked me if I had seen a buckskin horse. I told him I had seen it on the backside of our land and didn't know whom it belonged to. He caught her and asked if I could please ride her home for him. I rode the horse home for the man and learned her name was Taffy. He thanked me for bringing her home for him and said if you would like you could ride her anytime. He couldn't ride her anymore, and she needed to be ridden.

Jim and I became good friends, and then he introduced me to his wife. I really enjoyed visiting with them when I would come to their house to ride Taffy. Sometimes all of us in the area would take our horses and go to town or up in the mountains. Sometimes we would ride on the other side of the mountain up Grizzly Gulch to see a friend who lived over there above my grandfather's old house. Mom and dad sold my horses and kept one, Coaly. He was okay to ride but was small and not as fast as Taffy was. Coaly also had kind of a mean streak in him if you didn't know the horse.

When I was in the eighth grade my brother was in a hunting accident. He was a ninth grader at that time. My mother shot my brother in the groin and he would be laid up for almost a year in the hospital. Mom and dad were not around much when that happened. I was ignored as usual, which was fine with me. Wanda had come home to help take care of Wesley when it first happened but I wasn't allowed to see her. She wasn't allowed to call and talk to me. I spent a lot of time in Helena with one of my girlfriends.

In the tenth grade, I was invited to a party and had decided to get very drunk. At this party I met a guy named Hal and had started dating him. Mom was not happy about it but my dad liked Hal and let him come around.

My mother started in once again with her name-calling. She called me a whore and a heifer and started slapping me around. One day a friend of mine came up to my house to pick me up and I wasn't quite ready, so she came in to wait for me. She had seen the chain around the refrigerator with a lock on it and asked why in the world do your parents have that on your refrigerator. I told her I wasn't allowed to get in the refrigerator for any reason, whatsoever. Then before I knew it, I was staying at her house a lot instead of my own.

Jim and his wife had company from Seattle and his niece was my age. He asked me if I would hang out with her for the month that she was to be here. We became good friends. When she left, we kept in touch writing to one another. Jim and Dot were going out to Seattle for Christmas and took me along with them. It was a lot of fun as we took the train. I had never been on a train so the excitement was overwhelming. We spent a week in Seattle. I had never enjoyed myself this much. We went to the mall to the Round Cinemax Theatre and saw 2001 Space Odyssey.

When I returned home I discovered my boyfriend, had started dating one of my girlfriends. So, I lost a friend and a boyfriend all at once. I started hanging out with boys from the Vo-Tech, which was across from Helena High School. I would skip school and go over to the Vo-Tech. I would borrow one of the boy's cars, and go hang out with my friends who were not in school anymore. I was dating a few different guys now but none of them too seriously. While skipping school one day my mother caught me and I received another beating from her. I hated her so much. I was no longer allowed to go anywhere.

My sister Wanda had left her husband and was pregnant and needed to move home and stay with us until she found an apartment in town. It didn't take her long to find one and she couldn't wait to get out of this awful house and the conditions we had to live under.

When she moved out, she removed some of my belongings so I could come and live with her. My sister had her baby girl and once she was able she would move the rest of my things. Dee was two months old and my sister was picking up the last of her things. On her last trip, she took everything of mine. After school, I went to her apartment instead of going home.

When I didn't come home from school mom and dad came looking for me. They knew all of my belongings were gone and where I had gone. Mom and dad came to Wanda's apartment on Ewing and sat out in front of the house as if they were waiting for somebody. I was so scared because I knew they had called the police. The police had showed up. Wanda told them what had happened. They told her to go see the judge in the morning and help me become an emancipated teen. They told my parents to go home because Wanda was going to assume guardianship first thing in the morning. She did and now I was free to live with her as long as I remained in school and kept my grades up. Wanda met a really nice guy named Jim. After several weeks of dating, they were living together and happy. Jim treated me like a kid sister should be treated.

I was sneaking drinking, smoking and partying without Wanda knowing since she was working. One night I got drunk and was sick. I lost my house key and a shoe. I had to

444

walk downtown to O'Toole's where I thought Wanda and Jim would be. The bartender in O'Toole's took me downstairs to the apartment in the basement and placed me on a bed and said he was going back upstairs to call my sister. Jim and Wanda came to get me, and boy did I get in trouble. Jim put me over his shoulder and carried me out to the car chewing me out all the way home. He packed me upstairs to our apartment and then put me in the shower, clothes and all. I learned a valuable lesson that day. If I screwed up again, Wanda would lose custody of me, so I never drank again and cleaned up my act.

Wanda and Jim decide we need to move to a bigger place since there were now four of us. We moved to an apartment on Broadway. She had to clean it before we could move in because some hippies had lived there before and it was bad. Now that it was all cleaned and ready to move in, Wanda had new furniture put in. It was a much larger apartment for us.

My friend and I help her with babysitting while she and Jim were at work. I had my own bedroom right off of Dee's with a bathroom separating us. It was nice not being yelled at and told to do things.

While we were living there, one of my friends and I were at the house with some boys when some other boys showed up. There ended up being a big fight out in front of my sister's apartment. Then before I knew it there were police all over the place. My friend accidently hit one of the officers and ended up in jail. We had to go and get her out the next day. I was so thankful my sister never found out about it until later years when we shared information.

I was a senior in high school now and ended up getting really sick. I needed to have my tonsils taken out and my sister had no insurance to cover me. The only way to have the insurance was for me to move back to my parent's house because mom would not sign for the surgery unless I moved back home. I was sick for six weeks. I had to take medication before I could actually have the surgery done. After the surgery was done my friends could come and

445

visit. Wanda could not visit me because my mother accused her of harboring me. My mom got legal custody back because of the surgery.

My friends from the Vo-Tech and my girlfriend were allowed to visit me in Unionville since I couldn't go to school and would have to make it up. Summer came and we all hung out at Hill Park which was across from the police station, back then the police didn't bother us unless there was trouble or fights on the park grounds. That was when I met Dave and we started dating, until I once again became ill. I had a miscarriage and ended up missing a lot of school. I quit school because I wasn't going to get enough credits to graduate and would just have to go the following year. Instead, I went back for the second half and went to night school to get enough credits to graduate.

I get married to Dave a month after I graduated just so I could get away from home. My marriage was a disaster from the start, as all we did was fight. I was only nineteen when we had a horrible fight and I ended up having a nervous breakdown and was in the hospital for a week. We moved to Anaconda for a year and that didn't work out so we ended up moving back to Helena. I had a job cocktailing at a nightclub and the marriage was only getting worse, so I left him. He was supposed to be getting the divorce, when I met a guy named Conrad and we started dating. I ended up getting pregnant, and when I told him, he was with one of my friends, who had been dating one of his friends. Twice now I lost boyfriends to so called friends.

I was lost and didn't know what to do so I ended up alone and got a little apartment until my daughter was born. Wanda was there for me once again and stayed with me while I had my baby girl. She was tiny and only weighed five pounds, but had lost two pounds and had to stay in the hospital for another 10 days until she had regained her weight. Dave talked me into going back to him. When she was three weeks old, we moved to Houston where he took a job. We were there for three months and then we moved again to Lubbock, Texas. Then I ended up pregnant once again and had a baby boy in February. Once again things went bad with the marriage to Dave. He was cheating on me and saying he wasn't the father to my son, which he knew darn well he was. I never knew anybody to have an affair with; so that wasn't flying with me because he was the guilty one who was having an affair.

I left Dave and moved back home and filed for a divorce. I then moved to Missoula where Wanda lived and stayed with her while bartending close to her house. I had a place of my own with my two children. I met my next soon to be husband John. We were dating when he talked me into moving to Washington. I moved to Olympia and got a job and moved into a trailer court. Things didn't go very good because he lived with his sister who hated me. So I left and moved back to Helena where I ended up back in Unionville with my parents.

My mom let me know what a failure I had become, alone with two small children and no man. I ended up taking a bottle of sleeping pills. My mom called my ex who had moved back to Helena, and he took me to the hospital. What mother does that? Once they pumped my stomach and knew I was safe, they kept me in a secured area for a week to see a psychologist. I could not deal staying with my ex or going back to my parent's house in Unionville, so I went and stayed in Colstrip with Wanda and her family. After getting better and on my feet and feeling more confident, I got an apartment and got my life together.

John once again showed up and asked me to go back to Washington with him and get married. In 1979, I had another daughter and a year and a half later I had another son. Life was going great all this time, and then John started drinking. It seemed as if we did nothing but move. We moved from Washington to Oregon, then back to Washington, then on to Idaho. The drinking was really bad and John became violent. I decided to get divorced once again, and move back to Montana. I was thirty-three years old and alone with four children to care for and support. I moved close to my sister who lived in Lolo, eight miles out of Missoula. Id moved into a trailer park called Blue Mountain Park.

It was right between Missoula and Lolo close to my sister and her family so I could be near her again. It was nice that we had each other in our lives and being there for one another. If she needed someone to care for her kids I was there, if I needed someone to care for mine she was there. I met a 19 year old and was dating him for a while until I get real sick and had to have a hysterectomy. I tried to get the state to help me with supporting my kids and helping with their care. Wanda cared for my youngest child who was three. My five year old was in Head Start. My kind neighbor took her to school because she was a friend of her daughter, and the two oldest stayed at home since they were old enough to care for them selves. My neighbor and my sister checked in on the children quite frequently. When I came home from the hospital, my sister who was a nurse at that time showed me how to cough into a pillow and she was there to change my dressings. While I was home recuperating from surgery, the pipes froze in our trailer and I couldn't get the landlord to get them thawed, so we moved out and I moved in with a friend up Donovan Creek out of Missoula.

I was bartending at the Turah Pines. One day, an old boyfriend from high school came in and we started to see each other. He asked me to move up to Lincoln where he lived at the time so he wouldn't have to come so far for us to see each other and be with one another. I moved up there with my four children and he and I were married. He treated my children as his own and they to this day call him Dad. On weekends we still did a lot of partying, which didn't help this marriage.

We both worked during the week and partied hard on weekends. In the middle of December of 1989, I was going to Missoula to meet my sister to go Christmas shopping together. When I decided to go earlier, I called my husband to tell him I was leaving earlier. He took it wrong and came

448

home and told me if I left the only way I could come back was to get down on my knees and beg like a dog.

Without calling Wanda to let her know what was going on, I ended up taking a bottle of Valium, and tried to commit suicide once again. I was taken by ambulance to Helena and stayed in the hospital for a few days under lock down for fear I would try again. I talked with a psychiatrist and they decided I was fine and let me go home. When I left Lincoln, I started seeing a psychiatrist at Mental Health Services, and my regular doctor who was great with me. I was put on Prozac and Lithium and was diagnosed to be Bi-Polar and also diagnosed with ADHA.

Things did not get any better; all John and I did was fight and argue. My oldest daughter was off to college. I had had enough of the negativity in our lives, so I decided to move back to Helena. I stayed with a friend until I got a job and an apartment. She was the best and always had been there for me when Wanda was gone and living in Lolo. Then she introduced me to a guy who I dated for quite a while. Eventually, Tom and I married. With all of my problems in the past, I was sure I had brought them into this marriage. Tom and I had our ups and downs and would eventually end up in divorce. After quite a while, I was doing much better and the doctors took me off of the pills.

My life was so much better now with my four children grown, with eleven grandchildren and four step-grandchildren all of whom I love dearly. I thank God every day for how well they have turned out. Both of my daughters had wonderful men in their lives now and have great careers. My sons are doing great and have families of their own. I have learned to control my bi-polar episodes and have had a great job for the last eighteen years.

I, like my sister, wanted to try and put the evilness that we endured behind us. We had done things in our lifetime that we were ashamed of and wished we could turn around, but we couldn't. If only we had a mom, who would have loved and nourished us. Who would have listened when my sisters tried telling her what was being done to them. If she had only listened to the claims my sisters were making instead of beating them and calling them whores. I probably wouldn't have endured the shame we lived with and how badly our lives had turned on us. All because of the sexual abuse and the mental and physical abuse from people we thought we were supposed to trust. Nobody will ever know what pain I had as a toddler when this priest, a grown man, penetrated me and then pushed my face over his penis and forced me to have oral sex.

Like my sister, I want this story to reach as many as possible to tell them not to be ashamed anymore and come forward so they can help others and heal themselves at the same time. This is the only way we can stop priests and nuns from hurting other children. I was a survivor of the heinousness, stomach churning, crimes that were forced on me against my will. The humiliation is theirs, and is no longer mine.

BIBLIOGRAPHY

ANNOTATED PRIMARY SOURCES

Berry, J (1992). *Lead us not into temptation: Catholic priests and the sexual abuse*
    of children. New York: Doubleday.

> Between 1984 and 1992, Jason Berry's even
> handed reporting has turned up more than
> 400 priests and brothers in North American
> who have molested youngsters. With a
> novelist's touch that has won him two
> religious press awards, Berry defines the
> enormity of the problem with scholarship,
> compassion, and the poet's ability to find a
> balance.
>
> A Review

Boston Globe Staff. (2002). *Betrayal: The crisis in the Catholic Church*
    New York: Little Brown.

> A fine source for the millions struggling to
> understand the history of the scandal, the
> irreparable damage of the cover-up, and the
> steps the Church must take if it is to
> survive."
>
> ~*American Catholic*

Burkett, E., & Bruni, F. (1993). *A gospel of shame: Children, sexual abuse, and the Catholic Church.* New York: Viking.

This study by two Pulitzer Prize nominated journalists addresses the issues of trust, sacredness, and corruption within the Catholic Church. It chronicles the extent of sexual abuse by Catholic priests, who are protected by the secretive hierarchical nature of the Catholic Church.

Cahill, L. (2002, March 6). Crisis of clergy, not of faith.*New York Times.*

I am a lifelong liberal, unshakable Catholic, educated by nuns from age two through high school, and a proud feminist. I keep asking how archbishops, cardinals and even our pope can justify protecting pedophiles. Apologies and money to victims will never be enough. Where are the apologies and justification to all Catholics for disgracing our religion and shaking our faith? I will never be ashamed for my faith, but I sure am ashamed for and embarrassed by these enablers running my church.
Wendy Cole

Dokecki, Paul R. (2004). *The Clergy Sexual Abuse Crisis: Reform and Renewal in The Catholic Community.*Washington, D.C.: Georgetown University Press.

Dokecki chronicles the devastating delinquencies of the priest-pedophilia crisis and he maps necessary steps the Church must take toward credibility and integrity. He takes his readers from the shadowy secrets of the chancery to a church illumined by the wisdom of God's people. Anyone looking for solutions to the pedophilia crisis ought to read this book.

Edward Vacek, SJ., professor of moral theology,
Weston Jesuit School of Theology and author of
Love, Human and Divine: The Heart of Christian Ethics

Moffatt, Gregory K. (2003). *Wounded Innocents and Fallen Angels: Child Abuse andChild Aggression.* Westport, Connecticut and London: Praeger Publishers.

This book presents a thorough discussion of the causes, the symptoms, and the treatment of these children. The writing style is easily read and understood by the professional and by those interested in violent children or child victims. The book's broad appeal should prove to be a valuable resource for social workers, law enforcement, school counselors, child therapists, and others who work with child victims and violent children.

Karla D. Carmichael
University of Alabama

Plant, Thomas G., Editor (2004).*Sin Against The Innocents: Sexual Abuse by Priests and the Role of the Catholic Church.* Westport, Connecticut and London: Praeger Publishers.

Thomas Plante has edited the most comprehensive and penetrating analysis of the clergy sexual abuse scandal to date. The authors make an important contribution to our understanding of the causes, dynamics, and clerical systems that both spawned and sustained this "Sin against the innocents."

Donald Cozzens
Visiting Professor of Religious Studies,
John Carroll University;
author of *Sacred Silence: Denial and the Crisis in the Church*

Robinson, Geoffrey, Bishop Emeritus (2013). *For Christ's Sake: End Sexual Abuse in the Catholic Church...for Good. Mulgrave, Vic., Austrailia: Garratt Publishing.*

> This is the book designed to move the Church back into the hands of the millions of shocked and bewildered Catholics throughout the world who are saying: enough is enough.

SECONDARY SOURCES FROM NEWSPAPERS, PERIODICALS AND ORGANIZATIONS, WITH NOTES

Against Abuse. 8 October 2002. *Boston Globe.* Retrieved from www.boston.com/globe/.

Appleby, R. S. July 14, 2002. *'Betrayal':* Covering the church crisis. New York Times. Retrieved from www.nytimes.com.

Canadian Conference of Bishops. 1992. From pain to hope. Retrieved from www.usccb.org.

Day, S. 24 April 2002. Cardinals to recommend removal of serial abusers.*New York Times. Retrieved from www.nytimes.com.*

*Deedy, Alexander. April 29, 2015. Diocese names priests, sisters, staff accused of sexual abuse. *Independent Record Helena, Montana.* Retrieved from http://www.helenair.com

John Jay Report. 2004. *2002 Nature and Scope of Sexual Abuse of Minors by Catholic Priests and Deacons in the United States.* A research study conducted by the John Jay College of Criminal Justice, the City University of New

York, February 2004 for the United States Conference of Catholic Bishops (2004), Washington D.C. Retrieved from www.philvaz.com/apologetics/PriestAbuseScandal.htm

**Moore, Michael. September 5, 2010. St. Ignatius woman tells of abuse at orphanage.
Missoulian. www.missoulian.com/news

O'Brien, D. 20 November 2002. To reform the church, laity must take action. *Boston
Globe.* Retrieved from www.boston.com/globe/

Pope John Paul's address on pedophilia. 23 April 2002. Reuters. Retrieved from
www.nytimes.com

Stille, Alexander. January 14, 2016. *What Pope Benedict Knew About Abuse in the
Catholic Church.* The New Yorker. Retrieved from www.newyorker.com/news-desk/what-pope-benedict-knew-about-abuse-in-the-catholic-church

* Note: On this list, you will find the names of Gilmore and Callan under "Diocese cannot verify the following individuals in claims as priest." Both Gilmore and Callan are listed but are documented (first name unknown). We know them in the book as Father Joseph M. Gilmore (later to become Bishop Gilmore of the Helena Diocese) and Father Francis Callan, a priest at St. Joseph's Orphanage.

** Note: More than 60 years after she endured physical and sexual abuse at the St. Joseph's Home Catholic orphanage in Helena, Mary Lou Veal, 70, is coming forward with her story. "I want the church to take responsibility, to own up to what they did," says Veal.

IMPORTANT WEB SITES

All Shall Be Well: One Woman Survivor's Story of Clergy Abuse.
www.thehopeofsurvivors.com/stories/all_shall_be_well.ph
p

Database of Publicly Accused Priests in the United States.www.BishopAccountability.org

SNAP (Survivors Network of those Abused by Priests).
www.snapnetwork.org

The Final Call. Retrieved from
www.finalcall.com/artman/publish/National_News

Made in the USA
Columbia, SC
14 May 2017